D0434907

The Limits of U.S. Military Capability

Lessons from Vietnam and Iraq

James H. Lebovic

The Johns Hopkins University Press

Baltimore

© 2010 The Johns Hopkins University Press
All rights reserved. Published 2010
Printed in the United States of America on acid-free paper
9 8 7 6 5 4 3 2 1

The Johns Hopkins University Press
2715 North Charles Street
Baltimore, Maryland 21218-4363
www.press.jhu.edu

Library of Congress Cataloging-in-Publication Data
Lebovic, James H.
    The limits of U.S. military capability : lessons from Vietnam and Iraq /
James H. Lebovic.
       p. cm.
    Includes bibliographical references and index.
    ISBN-13: 978-0-8018-9472-5 (hardcover : alk. paper)
    ISBN-10: 0-8018-9472-7 (hardcover : alk. paper)
    1. United States—Military policy.   2. United States—Armed
Forces—Operational readiness.   3. United States—Armed Forces—
Combat sustainability.   4. Vietnam War, 1961–1975.   5. Iraq War,
2003–   6. Military readiness—United States—Case studies.   7. Military
planning—United States—Case studies.   8. Asymmetric warfare—Case
studies.   I. Title.
    UA23.L447 2010
    355'.033273—dc22

                                                                2009033017

A catalog record for this book is available from the British Library.

*Special discounts are available for bulk purchases of this book. For more
information, please contact Special Sales at 410-516-6936 or specialsales@
press.jhu.edu.*

The Johns Hopkins University Press uses environmentally friendly book
materials, including recycled text paper that is composed of at least 30 percent
post-consumer waste, whenever possible. All of our book papers are acid-free,
and our jackets and covers are printed on paper with recycled content.

Library
University of Texas
at San Antonio

*To my mother, uncles,
and grandparents, and the
other Baghdadis of Rangoon*

Contents

Acknowledgments

This is a very personal book, though not in style, substance, or approach. It is personal in the sense that the subject is immediate for anyone who came of age in the United States during the turbulent 1960s. This book would probably not have been written, however, but for a fumbled toast in August 2006 in a poor Vietnamese village in Quang Ngai province. There, the "American Professor and his wife" were guests of honor at a party thrown by the parents of a young man we had befriended in the city of Hoi An. Our friend hosted the party to thank us for a long-delayed ride back to his home village and to introduce the village—once part of the strong Vietcong support base in the province—to actual "Westerners."

The party of forty people took place in a single room of a farmhouse. In an inner circle, over a dozen men, my wife Holly, and I sat on the floor around dishes of food; in an outer circle, women and children sat in chairs or stood to discuss our apparently amusing behavior. The mood turned somber when our host spoke of our trip earlier the same day to My Lai, where we talked to a woman cutting grass for her ox. She was working near the very same irrigation ditch in which she had lain wounded in 1968, one of the few survivors of the notorious massacre by US troops. Our host broke the awkward silence by raising a glass of rice whiskey to his guests, but the toast was halted when an older man interjected. "First," he told the host, he wanted to know "what the American had to say to him knowing that he was Vietcong." The question echoed defiantly when an older woman stood to offer an emphatic, "Me VC too." I knew now that this was an important occasion, and I regretted that I was not better suited for such situations. I also wished, for the moment, that I could think in black-and-white terms—about valiant struggles, "good guys" and "bad guys," and all the rest. The best I could do was pronounce, after a long pause, that the "war was over"—more silence—before discovering, to my relief, that a slight rephrasing would approximate a toast. "To the end of the war" did the trick—maybe because I conveyed that the war was not good for anyone but more likely because, when I downed my drink, it was clear that that was all I had.

The unremarkable toast triggered a long series of jovial toasts. But, for me, the moment lingered. "What I should have said" prompted much thinking and reading and eventually this book on lessons from Vietnam and Iraq. As the reader is sure to agree, none of the book's "lessons" work very well as a toast.

If, however, these lessons contribute to our general understanding of the challenges of military operations, some of the credit belongs to a number of people who commented on portions or all of my book manuscript. For their useful remarks, I thank Deborah Avant, Nathan Brown, Joseph Clark, Eugene Gholz, Nathan Jones, Marc Lynch, Medlir Mema, Jonathan Monten, Patrick Morgan, Elizabeth Saunders, Holger Schmidt, and the various participants in panels at the annual meetings of the International Studies Association in San Francisco and New York (where I presented material from chapter 1 and an early version of chapter 4) and the RIGS Seminar, International Studies Program, at the University of California, Irvine (where I presented chapter 5). Shannon Powers deserves substantial recognition for her skilled—and, I might add, relentless—assistance in tracking down valuable research materials for this book. I also thank Henry Tom of the Johns Hopkins University Press for recognizing the potential contribution of the manuscript and pushing me, then, to complete and revise it *on schedule,* Martin Schneider for his meticulous copy editing, and the anonymous reviewer for the Press who provided valuable suggestions to improve the quality of the work. I owe special thanks to Elizabeth Saunders, the only other member of the Political Science Department's "Vietnam-study group." For what it's worth, *I* benefited enormously from its meetings in the doorway of her office, late each Friday afternoon, when she probably wished she was working on her own manuscript rather than talking about mine.

I must extend appreciation to Barry Steiner, my undergraduate mentor, for nurturing my early interest in US foreign and national security policy. I look back at the Vietnam War era with enormous gratitude to him, disbelief over the years and events that have since passed, and astonishment at how black and white so quickly fades into gray. I would be remiss, then, if I did not thank Lee Sigelman, my colleague now for almost twenty years, for teaching me by example. He is what I want to be when I grow up, and I owe him more than I can say.

Finally, I reserve my greatest thoughts of appreciation for Holly. As always, she insists that she would rather not be thanked. Too little, too late—again—I suspect. This time, I won't try to make up for my mental absences by promising her an increase in my scholarly production.

The Limits of U.S. Military Capability

CHAPTER ONE

Introduction

Few who achieve popular renown for a phrase are quoted (and misquoted) as often as George Santayana, who observed over a century ago that "those who cannot remember the past are condemned to repeat it." The "present" for this book—and principal focus—is the half-dozen years of US military involvement in Iraq that commenced with a US aerial attack on Baghdad in March 2003 and culminated in the pullback of US combat troops from Iraqi cities on June 30, 2009 (in advance of a total US troop withdrawal from the country scheduled for the end of 2011). The "past" is the US effort in Vietnam that ended with the calamitous fall of Saigon to North Vietnamese forces in 1975, after nearly a decade of active US combat (1965–73) and the transfer of duty to the South Vietnamese army. It is a past that is easily remembered by an aging generation of American leaders who served (or chose not to serve) in that war, witnessed its fallout in social turbulence and political protest, and coped with a profusion of contradictory post-hoc "lessons" that the war supposedly offered.

One legacy of the Vietnam War is that it is still fought by policy analysts and former US government officials who disagree over whether the United States could have succeeded given US military (and moral) disadvantages in combating a people's war, would have succeeded but for perfidious congressional intervention, or might have succeeded had the United States adopted an alternative military strategy. Into the 1990s, negative lessons of Vietnam inspired a backhanded acknowledgment of the limits to US military capability in the principles (of the so-called Weinberger-Powell Doctrine) that the United States must choose its battles, set winnable and publicly supportable goals, and intervene militarily abroad only with overwhelming force. The specter of Vietnam hangs over policymakers who explicitly reject the application of the Vietnam analogy, including President George H. W. Bush who declared after the Desert Storm victory over Iraq in 1991 that "we've kicked the Vietnam syndrome once and for all."[1] Why else exuberantly pronounce the syndrome's demise—based, for that matter, on results of an engagement that bore no resemblance politically nor militarily to the Southeast Asian conflict?

The Vietnam War as past stands in uneasy juxtaposition to successive US combat operations—foremost among them the 2003 Iraq War, which consumed the attention and political capital (both at home and abroad) of the George W. Bush administration in subsequent years. Whereas some critics of the US (post-invasion) war strategy in Iraq saw clear parallels with Vietnam, administration officials resisted the comparison.[2] An obvious question follows: How relevant were the lessons of Vietnam to fighting (and peacemaking) in the sectarian-driven conflict in Iraq? Some answers are found in examining what it means for a policymaker to "remember history." Historical "lessons" do not stand tall for all to see. Nor are they imposed uncritically upon the present by policymakers who surrender their personal judgment, ideological perspectives, and political interests.[3] As this book demonstrates, the relevance of lessons depends on the assumptions and reference points that policymakers, policy analysts, and social scientists employ when struggling to make sense of the past and the present.

In applying insights from the Vietnam War to the Iraq conflict, this book argues that US military capabilities are fundamentally limited and that US costs rise and benefits diminish appreciably in wars in which the US stakes are low and its goals broad and ambitious. Specifically, it establishes that challenges are pronounced for the United States when reaching its goals depends on the choices of adversary leaders, their foreign allies, indigenous societal leaders, groups, and populations, and the American public such that a military operation essentially becomes a "leverage problem." As the United States seeks to overcome adversary resistance, gain the acceptance of a local population, secure the participation of a host government, avoid antagonizing outside parties to a conflict, build national institutions to achieve or sustain progress in combat, and keep the US public on board, US influence is limited when other parties capitalize on political, psychological, or sociological conditions to offset US military and economic strengths. Viewing outcomes as products of such "asymmetries of conflict" redirects the focus of strategy and analysis usefully from the military capabilities of the combatants to the assorted capabilities, strategies, and relative influence of the various parties to the conflict.[4]

This book argues that the Vietnam and Iraq conflicts presented an especially difficult challenge for the United States insofar as the host governments lacked effective institutions to support the US effort and consistently undermined it. From the US experience in these conflicts, it asserts that success goes to the party that pursues realistic goals and exploits available military capabilities, existing political resources, and prevailing perceptions. It also argues, however, that the United States is disadvantaged in these contests given quantitative and qualitative limits on US capability, potential US aversions and concerns, and strong resistance to US goals from local adversaries *and allies*. Put simply, it asserts that the size, strength, flexibility, and adaptability of the US military do not ensure victory in asymmetric conflicts: US influence—and success—depend on conditions that the United States cannot easily manipulate.

The book assumes that useful lessons emerge from these two conflicts by weighing judgments critically against the evidence and generalizing with care, knowing that these conflicts are compelling subjects precisely because they are exceptional. The discernment of lessons is aided, however, by two critical characteristics of these conflicts.

First, both conflicts generated positive outcomes over time once the United States changed its strategy to cope with evolving conditions and the failings of prior US approaches. The longitudinal evidence speaks, then, to the effectiveness of US policy instruments when adjusted for performance even in a harsh environment. With US assistance and support, the Saigon government did eventually field a large and well-equipped military and obtain control of much of the country, and the Baghdad government did assume responsibility for national security and presided over a period of national calm. Indeed, it is these positive outcomes over time that impressed policymakers and analysts as they attempted to remake the US military to fight future wars and address challenges in Afghanistan.

Second, both conflicts generated similar negative outcomes despite the differences between and within the conflicts in operative conditions and approach. In Vietnam and Iraq, the United States exerted tremendous effort over a long period but eventually had to accept the limits of US power—on the battlefield, at the negotiating table, and in the offices of host-government officials.[5] Overall, the evidence from Vietnam and Iraq suggests that the United States, despite its best efforts, is vulnerable to unfavorable conflict asymmetries that produce leverage problems.

That this general lesson was underappreciated by US policymakers, when acting in Vietnam and Iraq, owes in part to their reasoning, by analogy, that the United States had no choice but to use force. This assumption was bolstered before the Iraq War by an unwarranted faith in US military capability.

Lessons about Lessons: Vietnam as Appropriate Analogy?

Neither the Bush administration nor its critics were quick to grasp the Vietnam War's lessons on the challenges of exerting leverage and the limits of US military capability. Indeed, civilian and military officials tried hard to distance US action in Iraq from the failed policies of the Vietnam era. President Bush avoided discussions and situations that might suggest a connection between the two.[6] For its part, the US military sought to erase Vietnam-era symbols when conveying information on Iraq, for instance, by eschewing the reporting of enemy "body counts," considered key measures of progress in Vietnam, and by withholding photographic images of flag-draped coffins arriving at Dover Air Force base, which, decades earlier, had driven home the painful realities of the war in far-off Southeast Asia.[7] But policy failings are not attributable simply to the burying or neglecting of history. As much as administration officials seemed determined to disconnect Iraq from the prior war experience, policy critics exaggerated the parallels between the US military operations in Vietnam and Iraq.

Critics of the Bush administration's prewar and wartime conduct were perhaps too quick to see a repeat of Vietnam in Iraq based on circumstantial similarities between the two wars. These similarities include congressional deference to the president with a seemingly open-ended endorsement for war based on faulty intelligence (pertaining to North Vietnam's actions in the Gulf of Tonkin and Iraq's alleged possession of weapons of mass destruction) and with strong suspicions later that the intelligence had been used as a pretext for intervention. The similarities also include a false promise of an easy victory. In Vietnam, the Lyndon Johnson administration tried initially to signal to Hanoi that the United States hoped not to deepen its involvement in the country—but would, if necessary.[8] In Iraq, the Bush administration signaled infamously, after the first weeks of fighting, that the war was in its final stages—a "Mission Accomplished" sign was perched behind the president as he pronounced the end of major hostilities from the deck of the USS *Abraham Lincoln*—only to regret the implication in the face of a growing insurgency. With unexpected enemy resistance, both administrations urged perseverance and warned repeatedly of severe global consequences of a US defeat.

In linking Iraq to Vietnam, the messenger was no less compelling than the message. It was hard for policy critics to resist the striking resemblance between the main protagonists—Secretary of Defense Donald Rumsfeld and his Vietnam-era counterpart, Robert McNamara, in their physical appearance and deportment (brash self-confidence, controlling and peripatetic management style, zealous challenge to prevailing military culture). As much as Vietnam came to be seen as "McNamara's War," the Iraq War was soon viewed as "Rumsfeld's Folly" (Korb 2003). By the time of Rumsfeld's dismissal, "Vietnam"—long synonymous with failure, quagmire, hubris, deceit, incompetence, and worse (Elliott 2007, 17–44)—had become a crude brush used by critics to blacken the entire Iraqi venture. The defense secretary was impugned, among others, in a tangle of pointed fingers, as high-level officials left the administration, one after another, to write books that implicated opponents, rival agencies, and those higher up the chain of command for the failings of Iraq policy (for example, Bremer 2006; Feith 2008; McClellan 2008; Tenet 2007).[9]

The fact is, however, that the two wars differed in critical respects. Albert Wohlstetter's gloomy prediction about the Vietnam War—"of all of the disasters of Vietnam, the worst may be the 'lessons' that we'll draw from it" (Wohlstetter 1968)—today appears prescient. Important and numerous characteristics impugn the validity of the Vietnam analogy with respect to Iraq.[10]

First, the Iraq War started as a conventional war and became a battle against a growing insurgency. Conversely, the Vietnam conflict started as a guerrilla war and became a conventional war. In the 1968 Tet Offensive, Hanoi mobilized Vietcong irregulars in an all-out push to take control of South Vietnamese cities. In the aftermath of the costly offensive, Hanoi relied upon its regular forces to carry much of the burden of warfare in the South.

Second, the Vietnam War was conducted on a massive scale, with millions of personnel under arms, civilian and military fatalities ranging into the millions, and a US strategy that relied heavily upon mobility, firepower, and aerial bombing. The United States eventually fielded over half a million troops in South Vietnam and suffered troop deaths at an average of 100 per week throughout the period of active US combat, and a soaring death toll with the Tet Offensive. Almost 4,000 US soldiers were killed, alone, in the eight weeks following President Johnson's announcement, as a peace gesture, of a US bombing halt on North Vietnam (Spector 1993, 25). In Iraq, by contrast, US troop levels rose to one third the peak levels of Vietnam, military deaths per week only occasionally reached the average daily death rates of Vietnam, and injuries and fatalities resulted primarily from planted explosive devices rather than firefights with the enemy.

Third, the Vietnam War pitted the United States and Saigon governments against nationalist forces, united in pursuit of an overarching political objective (rooted in Marxist ideology and forged through colonial opposition) under the control of a central (Hanoi) government, with considerable economic and military backing from abroad (especially China and Russia). In Iraq, by comparison, the United States became a party to sectarian fighting among fluid coalitions of groups that were not beholden to any external party. These groups varied in organization structure and religious, ethnic, and nationalistic emphasis given the various grievances and interests of the membership. The United States worked, then, with, around, and against changing sets of parties.

Fourth, the United States had to contend with successive South Vietnamese rulers who were engaged in *personal* power struggles with key intra-governmental opponents. In Iraq, the central government was a critical battleground among warring *societal* elements—between Shiites and Kurds that were repressed ruthlessly and Sunnis that benefited disproportionately under Saddam Hussein, between Shiites deferent to Moqtada al-Sadr and Shiite loyalists of the major political party in Iraq, and between Kurds and Arab Sunnis in the north of the country. These sometimes mutually reinforcing conflicts strained the US relationship with Iraqi governing coalitions and left the United States with less-than-perfect alliance partners. Paradoxically, the United States maintained (a) its support for the central government even as the government cultivated a friendly relationship with an external state (Iran) that the United States identified as a primary regional (if not global) threat; (b) an awkward (but not unremittingly hostile) relationship with the group (the Mahdi army faction of Moqtada al-Sadr) that pushed vociferously for a US military withdrawal from Iraq; and (c) the strongest relationship with the portion of the Iraqi population (the Kurds) that was distinct culturally, ethnically, and linguistically, and most keen to establish its independence from the Iraqi state that the United States sought to build.

Fifth, in Vietnam, the United States championed the status quo. It was engaged primarily in the military defense of a government that was under attack from a coherent, fierce, and determined opposition. US nation-building in Vietnam, to the extent that it occurred, was meant to support the main military effort. In Iraq, the United States sought to transform Iraqi governance and society in opposition to a mix of groups that presented a relatively modest military but substantial political threat. The opposition flexed its muscle, then, by vetoing progress in government and national stabilization, which would increase the costs, difficulty, and longevity of the US military and institution-building effort.

The evidence for distinguishing the Iraq War from the Vietnam War is hardly conclusive, as the many important differences mask significant similarities between these conflicts. In Iraq, the United States once again found itself battling irregular forces (Shiite militia groups and a Sunni insurgency), struggling with local leaders and institutions, managing relations with reluctant allies, trying to influence conditions in a war-afflicted country from outside its borders, and redefining, expanding, and contracting US goals and definitions of success. In consequence, the Iraq War—much like the Vietnam War before it—offers a large variety of lessons on the hazards of playing to US comparative disadvantages, the challenges of counterinsurgency, the liabilities of escalation, the perfidy of host governments, and the battle against accumulating costs over time, as we shall see.

The Bush administration was slow to appreciate these parallels, as it drew inspiration, both implicitly and explicitly, from another analogy—Munich in 1938, when British Prime Minister Neville Chamberlain ceded part of Czechoslovakia to Adolph Hitler for a false promise of peace. The cataclysmic war that followed inspired the image—countries falling like "dominos"—that came to dominate Cold War thinking about the consequences of capitulation.[11] For Cold War–era policymakers, the lessons of Munich and the Korean conflict, separated by the Second World War, dovetailed in a compelling message: "In 1950, the United States met North Korea early and head-on. In the 1930s no one met Mussolini and Hitler early and head-on; that only postponed the reckoning until later and under tougher circumstances" (Khong 1992, 101). For these policymakers—and the Bush administration to follow—the message was simply that failing to act in the face of threat only emboldens and strengthens the adversary.

Missing from the historical lesson is an awareness that the "right" course of action—in 1938 as in 2003—was a legitimate matter of contention. As Jeffrey Record (2005) concludes, sources of strategic and moral ambiguity in the prelude to the Second World War included widespread beliefs that a war with Germany would bring disaster, once again, to Europe and might end inconclusively or unfavorably, that Germany had legitimate grievances and could be placated (as recent history had shown), that the artificial states of Eastern Europe need not be defended at all cost, that shifting attention to Europe would abet the rise of Japan in Asia, and that a winning alliance against Germany must include a communist "evil" in the form of the Soviet state. Indeed, the perversity of the view that leaders failed to do the right thing when all moral arrows pointed in that direction is no clearer than when Cold War–era leaders spoke in terms of good and evil to argue, later, against compromise with the Soviet Union. After all, it had been an ally of convenience—due presumably to a necessary *compromise*—in the prior period.

Any lesson drawn from Munich must also concede the atypical character of that case—the historical rarity of leaders who pursue their goals ruthlessly at all cost (Record 2005). A potential result of exaggerating these leaders' historical prominence is to justify the offsetting use of force when it imposes a prohibitive price. Policymakers can reduce a nation's security by acting on "worst-case" assumptions that create a self-fulfilling prophesy (Jervis 1978, 182) or leave no reasonable alternatives (Garthoff 1978, 23).[12] Indeed, even the Munich events suggest that positive consequences ensue from waiting, watching, and preparing. Yes, the world might have been better served had countries rallied forcefully to oppose the Munich demands and, certainly, had states mobilized earlier to defy Hitler. The consequences of Nazi occupation and the drawn-out war that followed were absolutely catastrophic and conceivably avoidable had states risen quickly to the challenge. Yet positive results of the Munich concessions were a substantial military buildup and public preparation to oppose the Nazis and sustain a successful war effort. Although Munich "came to symbolize naïveté, failed diplomacy, and the politics of cowardice," the documentary evidence suggests that the British government was hardly sanguine about the prospects of placating Hitler and sought instead to delay a confrontation "as a means of buying time for rearmament" so that Britain could confront Germany from a position of strength (Ripsman and Levy 2008, 149, 151).

Despite the overreading of its messages, Munich became a fashionable reference point when, on September 11, 2001, al-Qaeda operatives used hijacked aircraft to attack the World Trade Center in New York and the Pentagon near Washington, D.C., to inflict the highest death toll ever in a foreign attack on US soil. With the shock of the deadly attacks, the Bush administration was loath to distinguish between any of a host of new US foreign enemies—Islamic terrorist groups and state adversaries—supposedly desiring to impose maximum destruction upon the United States at any cost. To wit, the administration repeatedly labeled Iraq (under Saddam Hussein), Iran, and North Korea "rogue states" and suggested that they were acting in conspiracy (the "axis of evil"). It even claimed proof of cooperation between Iraq's former leadership and the al-Qaeda terrorist network to suggest that Saddam Hussein was behind the World Trade Center attack. In the administration's view, the events of September 11 were encouraged by a feeble US response to terror strikes in the years leading up to the World Trade Center attack. As Vice President Richard Cheney put it, "Time and time again . . . the terrorists hit America and America did not hit back hard enough."[13] The United States did not respond directly to the attacks on the US military barracks in Lebanon in 1983 (despite the death of hundreds of Marines), the Khobar Towers in Saudi Arabia in 1996, and the USS *Cole* in 2000. Through its inaction, the United States supposedly communicated that terrorists would not be held accountable for their actions and was now living with the consequences. To compensate, a broad-based and unyielding US response was now necessary.

In cautioning against "self-deterrence," the Munich analogy echoed a popular critique of US war strategy in Vietnam, that meek, meddlesome, and politically self-interested civilian officials had asked US troops to fight "with one hand tied behind their back."[14] The Bush administration seemed to embrace this view when it belatedly alluded to the Southeast Asian conflict to imply that the bloodletting and oppression that followed was a consequence of shunning a security commitment. As Bush observed, "One unmistakable legacy of Vietnam is that the price of America's withdrawal was paid by millions of innocent citizens, whose agonies would add to our vocabulary new terms like 'boat people,' 're-education camps' and 'killing fields.'" In his view, the withdrawal betrayed humanitarian principles and posed a direct threat to US security. In Bush's words, again, "There's another price to our withdrawal from Vietnam, and we can hear it in the words of the enemy we face in today's struggle—those who came to our soil and killed thousands of citizens on September the 11th, 2001."[15]

From this perspective, the United States had no choice but to attack Iraq (in a preventative strike) before Saddam Hussein could unleash his (purported) arsenal of weapons of mass destruction—which he would most surely do, as soon as he was able. Nor did the United States have any choice but to confront al-Qaeda in Iraq, once it joined the insurgency. Thus, at various stages of the Iraq War, US policy was placed in service of the Munich analogy and its admonition against equivocating with evil. This was surely the implication in President Bush's 2008 speech before the Israeli Knesset, which employed the image of Nazi tanks rolling into Poland in 1939 to argue against negotiating with "radicals" (in this case,

Iran's leaders) and "terrorists."[16] Indeed, Henry Kissinger, who served as an informal advisor to the Bush administration on Iraq and as a principal architect of the Vietnam War (as national security advisor and then secretary of state in the Richard Nixon administration), was no less reluctant to read the lessons of Munich into Iraq than Vietnam. If anything, he believed the stakes were higher now than in prior decades. As Kissinger observed,

> Because of the long reach of the Islamist challenge, the outcome in Iraq will have an even deeper significance than that in Vietnam. If a Taliban-type government or a fundamentalist radical state were to emerge in Baghdad or any part of Iraq, shock waves would ripple through the Islamic world. Radical forces in Islamic countries or Islamic minorities in non-Islamic states would be emboldened in their attacks on existing governments. The safety and internal stability of all societies within reach of militant Islam would be imperiled.[17]

It is unsurprising, then, that the administration first viewed the persisting conflict in Iraq as rooted in evil-doers from the newly defunct Baathist regime ("dead-enders," in Rumsfeld's terminology) and "outside agitation" (terrorists with external links), not tensions within Iraqi society that could undermine US objectives. It is also unsurprising that the administration adopted harsh military tactics to disarm and dismantle the violent opposition. From the administration's perspective, the strategy of taking the war to Sunni insurgents and Shiite militia was not the problem but the solution to the problem. Was not another message of Munich that the "good guys" win, if they commit and persevere?

The administration appeared confident that it understood the situation in Iraq. Like its Vietnam-era counterpart, it stayed "on message" with positive interpretations of events. With an upswing in hostilities, the administration still had a favorable end in sight, claiming publicly that Iraqi insurgents were escalating attacks in last-ditch efforts first to forestall the handover of power to the provisional Iraqi government, then to disrupt the election of an Iraqi legislature, then to counter the blow that had been inflicted on the insurgency by the capture of Saddam Hussein, then to prevent the finalization of an Iraqi constitution and to disrupt a referendum on the constitution and elections scheduled for later in 2005. With a dramatic escalation in terror attacks on civilians, government officials, and police officers in the summer of that year, the evidence was still being read for signs of progress. The top US military leader in Iraq interpreted *increased* enemy activity to indicate that the insurgency was in decline: "Insurgencies need progress to survive, and this insurgency is not progressing . . . the level of attacks they've been able to generate has not *increased substantially* [emphasis added] over what we've seen over the past year."[18] Not up for discussion was that these tactics could serve enemy purposes by promoting national and regional instability, fueling discontent, fostering ethnic and religious divisions, and provoking US military responses that could play into the hands of insurgents.

That the Bush administration struggled to make sense of the Iraqi conflict is understandable. The administration had the unenviable task of managing an increasingly frustrating operation that could produce any number of undesirable futures—a safe haven for terrorists, a fractured country that served Iran's interests and threatened Turkey, and so forth—while keeping the American public on board with promises that US policies were succeeding and warnings about the consequences of defeat. To its credit, the administration did change its tune and offered an increasingly somber appraisal of conditions in Iraq. By the late summer of 2005—with thousands of civilians dead from violence in Baghdad in the preceding four months, US forces under growing attack from roadside bombs, the majority of the Iraqi workforce unemployed, electricity supplies sporadic, oil production below expectations, and constitutional wrangling exposing major tensions in Iraqi society—the administration conceded, at least privately, that progress in Iraq would fall well short of what was initially envisioned.[19] These sentiments were increasingly expressed publicly too. A US military official injected a dose of realism about where things would stand in Iraq even after the 2005 elections: "You're still going to have an insurgency, you're still going to have a dilapidated infrastructure, you're still going to have decades of developmental problems both on the economic and the political side."[20]

Thus, the administration *did* finally modify its goals. For example, it appeared to be resigned to an accommodation (short of a reconciliation) among warring factions; deferred increasingly to local traditions, practices, and biases; placed a larger share of the blame on the Iraqi central government for political impasses and administrative failures; forged alliances with Sunni insurgent groups in opposition to al-Qaeda; tolerated the leadership of a Shiite faction (Moqtada al-Sadr and his Mahdi Army) that the United States had violently opposed; and pressed the Shiite majority to bring former US adversaries (disenfranchised Sunni groups) into the Iraqi government.

These adjustments in US policy—no less than its failings—speak to the leverage challenges in asymmetric conflict that are central to this book. These challenges must inform all attempts to link Iraq to Vietnam and any number of other recent conflicts. It is then that the limits of US military capability become clearly apparent. As Kilcullen (2009, 152) concludes, "we might say that operations in Iraq are like trying to defeat the Viet Cong (insurgency) while simultaneously rebuilding Germany (nation-building following war and dictatorship), keeping peace in the Balkans (communal and sectarian conflict), and defeating the IRA (domestic terrorism)," and doing so when all aspects of these operations are interdependent and mutually contingent.

The Limits of US Military Capability

The leverage challenges US policymakers in Vietnam and Iraq appreciated so belatedly were hardly more central to the thinking of US military analysts. Actually, neither the Vietnam War nor the post-2003 US experience in Iraq provoked a fundamental reevaluation in the academic and policy communities of the extent and, more to the point, the limits of global US military capability. Given the attention to US preponderance in the prelude to the Iraq War, this is a striking deficiency.

Much has been written, in fact, about the extraordinary depth, breadth, and reach of contemporary US military power with the dissolution of the Soviet Union and the alleged transition to a "unipolar" global system. The United States—more powerful than any other state or likely coalition—can presumably exert its prerogatives and intervene militarily as necessary to promote US interests around the world. This view of unlimited US military power is perpetuated by US critics abroad who seek to vilify the United States for its grandiose and aggressive designs, as when Russia's President Vladimir Putin admonished "those who would like to build a unipolar world, who would themselves like to rule all of humanity."[21] Certainly, the widespread judgment that the United States stands as a "lonely superpower" (Huntington 1999) has provoked debate over the extent and permanence of the capability gap between the United States and potential contenders. Some analysts argue that the pronounced global shift in relative power protects the United States from any possible challenge (Wohlforth 1999). Others insist that overwhelming ("unbalanced") US power fuels an irresistible demand for offsetting military capabilities that any number of contenders, acting alone or in concert, can satisfy (Layne 1993, 2006; Waltz 1993). Yet, by presupposing US military preeminence, analysts miss a crucial point: military unipolarity is an insufficient characterization of the current international system in large part because the United States must inevitably cope with *limits* on military capability. As Daalder and O'Hanlon (2000, 225) conclude, "The United States is no hegemon or hyperpower; it is a superpower more prone to underachievement than to imperial ambition." These capability limitations are appreciated by assessing aggregate measures that are typically employed to convey the *enormous scope and magnitude* of US military capability.

By aggregate measures, it seems obvious that the contemporary global system is unipolar. After all, the United States now possesses exceptional relative capabilities even by the historical standard set under British, Dutch, Spanish, and Portuguese hegemony. Like its hegemonic predecessors, the United States has the lead economy and extraordinary military reach; unlike its predecessors, the United States is strong on land, in the air, and at sea (Thompson 2006). Whereas uncontested sea power was a primary attribute of the dominant state, the global reach of prior maritime powers was actually predicated on maintaining a stable power balance in Europe.

The extent and expanse of US power is compellingly conveyed by statistical evidence. Ikenberry (2003) observes, for instance, that the United States "spends as much on defense as the next fourteen countries combined. It has bases in forty countries. Eighty percent of world military R&D takes place in the United States. What the 1990s wrought is a unipolar America that is more powerful than any other great state in history." US predominance is more impressive because it stems from a strong economic base. Unlike the former Soviet Union, the United States need not strain to remain competitive militarily when its economy falters. Not only does the United States enjoy "a much larger margin of superiority over the next most powerful state or, indeed, all other great powers combined than any leading state in the last two centuries," the United States "is the first leading state in modern international history with decisive preponderance in *all* the underlying components of power: economic, military, technological, and geopolitical" (Wohlforth 1999, 7).

Notwithstanding the statistical evidence, scholars invite controversy when assuming that global shares of power are measured meaningfully with broad aggregates. The effect is to exaggerate the capabilities of ostensibly strong states and depreciate "weaker-state" capabilities that can prove decisive in war, depending on where and how they are fought.[22] Thus, the power concentration associated even with today's reputedly unipolar system provokes the age-old question, "power to do what?" (Wagner 1993, 103). The question applies whether state capabilities are measured by raw aggregates (population, energy consumption, gross domestic product, land area) or by gross military capabilities (military spending, troop levels, size and diversity of national arsenals). There is a difference between having lots of measurable capability and being able to produce desirable policy outcomes. True, the big military budget of a major power is likely one that is optimized for power projection—for the United States, by land, air, and sea. Yet, a preponderant power might lack actionable intelligence, a quick-response capability, or an ability to sustain and replenish equipment and personnel in specific contingencies. The paradox of size in military budgets is that small budgetary items (body armor) promise great returns while large budget items (a B-2 stealth bomber costing billions of dollars) might provide little usable capability—ironically, because they are too expensive to risk in battle. Indeed, rising budgets cloak limits in US capacity to act militarily abroad. With wars in Afghanistan and Iraq, US military expenditures increased significantly to replenish US arsenals, maintain and repair weapons, and support ongoing military operations, not to augment prewar US military capability.

The point, then, is that controlling most of the "power" in the system does not necessarily permit the dominant state to accomplish even narrowly defined military objectives. As will also become apparent, such power is also of little advantage when the fact of predominance itself exacerbates the limitations of US military capability. For even the strongest of military powers, like the United States, the basic impediments to the effective use of military force are considerable and numerous, for several reasons.

First, US power is *dispersed*. Whereas a major power maintains a "global" outlook and set of interests, it is constrained (more than its local rival) in the share of its resources—human and otherwise—it can invest in any one place and a given time. As Art (1980, 25) puts it, "Great powers have great ambition and, consequently, need to ration their military power among competing goals." In consequence, the United States dedicated only a portion of its firepower—half of its tactical air power, a third of its naval forces, and two-fifths of its combat-ready divisions (Lomperis 1996, 125)—to the fight in Vietnam, at the apex of the US war effort with the outcome still undecided. The United States was concerned, in fact, that its "small" war in Vietnam would hurt US preparedness for a European war. The severity of the overstretch challenge has provoked intense controversies within the military (and between the military and civilians) over the kinds of weapons and doctrines the services should employ.[23]

Although US forces appear to be large enough to handle multiple contingencies, they are less divisible for simultaneous operations than aggregate statistics suggest. Troop strength, for instance, is a deceptive figure given the rotation demands and the necessary length of the troop deployment cycle. Lengthy combat deployments cannot be sustained without sacrificing the preparedness, training, and well-being of troops and the fortunes and stability of their families. For this reason, US military leaders expressed grave concerns, in late 2006, that sending five additional combat brigades to Iraq, as part of the Bush administration's "surge" strategy, would hurt US readiness. Those five brigades were tantamount to fifteen brigades inasmuch as five brigades must stand in line behind the first, and another five behind them, to maintain troop levels over the deployment cycle.[24] The US military is also spread thin because combat is a team effort. US weapon systems (bombers, fighters, electronic warfare aircraft, and aerial-refueling aircraft) join with others to impose heavy logistic burdens, especially involving fuel and maintenance. Likewise, each US soldier in combat is backed by others who fill vacated positions at home stations and provide various services abroad and in the field. In Vietnam, then, allied forces enjoyed a 6-1 numerical advantage but an actual combat manpower advantage around 1.5-1 in the 1969–71 period, a figure that dropped to 0.8-1 with the North Vietnamese buildup for the 1972 Easter Offensive (Thayer 1985, 93–94).[25] Despite US reliance in Iraq on many tens of thousands of private contractors, support-to-combat personnel ratios remained at traditional levels (roughly, 4-1 in the pre-surge period).[26] Indeed, the US support effort in Iraq pinched US and NATO operations in Afghanistan by absorbing key personnel (civil affairs soldiers, engineers, military police) and equipment (helicopters to transport troops and evacuate the wounded).[27] Conversely, with the new priorities of the Barack Obama administration, support demands on the Afghan front took a toll in Iraq.[28]

Overstretch remains a challenge for consecutive, as much as simultaneous, US operations. Although the United States planned in the Cold War decades to fight wars on multiple fronts (witness McNamara's "two-and-a-half war" standard or the "one-and-a-half war" standard to follow) and in the post–Cold War period to fight consecutive wars (the "win-hold-win" standard of the Clinton administration), the actual combat record suggests that these standards were never met. For instance, the United States required six months under President George H. W. Bush to move into position in the Gulf before launching the Desert Storm operation to push Iraqi forces from Kuwait. That the problem remains is indicated, to an extent, by the reverse example. With the signing of the 2008 US-Iraq Status of Forces Agreement requiring all US troops to leave Iraq by 2011, US military officials contended that three years would be required to remove US troops and equipment from the country. Even skeptics assumed the withdrawal would take eight to ten months.[29] Admittedly, these estimates also considered the time required to dismantle US-built facilities and turn US military operations over to US civilian and Iraqi personnel. Still, the timetables speak to a certain "stickiness" to commitments that limits US operations in rapid succession. Indeed, the US shift from Iraq to Afghanistan would *increase* immediate US costs in Iraq and require the re-equipping and retraining of US forces to address the peculiar demands (climate, terrain, and ruralness) of the new battlefront (US GAO 2009b).

The United States can try to cope with overstretch by relying upon its foreign allies for support. But this support comes at a price. As the United States seeks to secure basing rights, overflight privileges, intelligence, troops, equipment, support personnel, or even restraint from an ally to facilitate US military operations, the United States must make various political, economic, and military concessions. The United States footed a large bill to assemble its "Coalition of the Willing" to support the effort in Iraq (Newnham 2008) and received largely symbolic and ephemeral contributions in compensation. For their part, multilateral coalitions require elaborate inter-state negotiations over military strategies and tactics, rules of engagement, command structure, force contributions, offsets and compensation, divisions of labor, national exemptions, and the circumstances that will trigger military action. Coalition formation can prove a formidable obstacle to the United States if potential allies believe that the United States is seeking a pretext for military action, fear that confrontational policies will feed momentum toward war, or harbor concerns about the actual legitimacy or potential consequences of the operation.[30] Moreover, unsuccessful negotiations can prove costly. The failed negotiations over the use of Turkey as a northern invasion route into Iraq in 2003 forced a late adjustment in US war plans and reduced the eventual Coalition presence in parts of Iraq.

The difficulties do not end there. The United States might have to accept significant costs to keep coalition partners on board in the course of war operations. For example, to maintain the Desert Storm coalition in 1991, the United States chose not to pursue Iraqi forces to Baghdad and chose to dedicate significant aerial resources to hunting the Scud missiles being fired at Israel to keep it out of the fighting. The impact of US allies is felt, also, in the inefficiencies of a command structure (as in Afghanistan) that impedes coordination among allied units and dilutes coalition combat strength. It is felt further in the actions and nonactions of allies that run counter to US preferences or contravene US policies. In post-2003 Iraq, Great Britain resisted US entreaties that its forces act more aggressively to reign in Shiite militia activities in the south of Iraq. Likewise, European Coalition members (deferring to domestic antiwar sentiment) rejected US calls to deploy forces in the violent southern and eastern parts of Afghanistan. Even countries (Great Britain, Canada, and the Netherlands) that had participated actively in combat balked at US requests for more troops and threatened to withdraw forces from combat areas unless they received reinforcements.[31] At a minimum, multilateral efforts risk internal friction that weakens a coalition's cohesion—as occurred when the United States blamed its allies for the lagging military performance against the Taliban. US officials claimed that NATO's reliance on air power (to hit geographically dispersed targets and to avoid friendly military casualties) increased the toll on innocent civilians, precluded the holding of territory, and fed local hostility toward the foreign troop presence.[32] That such tension is perhaps inevitable in coalition warfare was conveyed, at the time, by heavy US reliance upon air power and liberal US rules of aerial engagement.[33] After a series of deadly incidents, the chief of the UN mission in Afghanistan called, in mid-2009, for investigating the conduct of US Special Operations teams whose routine response to hostile fire was calling in air strikes.[34]

Second, US power is *deficient* given limits to what the United States (or any other state) can achieve, even with so-called overwhelming force. The world's primary power actually has a finite capacity to project power on an adversary's home turf. "The closer US military forces get to enemy-held territory, the more competitive the enemy will be," as "political, physical, and technological facts . . . combine to create a contested zone—arenas of conventional combat where weak adversaries have a good chance of doing real damage to US forces" (Posen 2003, 22).[35] Whereas US bombers and missiles can hit critical leadership, military, economic, or communication targets with unprecedented precision and discrimination—incapacitating vast networks, disrupting complex economies, and limiting collateral damage (which can undermine US postwar objectives)— impressive US air capabilities are not sufficient for accomplishing many combat goals.[36] Strategic bombing is less effective against non-industrialized adversaries (which lack economies of scale and interdependent communications, military, and economic networks). For that matter, it might even backfire against any government that can rally its public to maintain morale and conduct "business as usual," respond effectively to attack warnings (Posen 2003, 27–28), or protect critical assets through mobility or subterfuge.[37]

The basic problem here is twofold. First, the capabilities of the dominant state are *inappropriate* for certain commitments because powerful states must worry about major threats (and major rivals) and must craft their military capabilities and doctrines accordingly.[38] The military capabilities that the United States has available, then, to address "lesser" threats are often not the right fit for the task. US conventional forces overwhelmed the Iraqi Army easily in 2003 but failed to stem the Iraqi insurgency in the years to follow. Indeed, lead powers have traditionally lacked a significant capability to "project their influence inland" and possessed capabilities that were intended primarily to control the commons, in support of "constrained systemic leadership" (Thompson 2006, 11–12). Second, the capabilities of the dominant state are *offset* by seemingly lesser adversary capabilities. Despite any quantitative or qualitative edge that the United States enjoys in conventional combat (Cohen 1986), US forces are potentially vulnerable under a variety of conditions—when adversaries employ guerrilla style hit-and-run tactics, low-profile platforms, mobile weapons, and explosive devices that are easily manufactured, planted, hidden, and activated. Improvised explosive devices (IEDs) placed on roads or pathways can slow down troop movements and inflict military casualties, just as suicide belts and car bombs can kill soldiers or inflict a high civilian death toll to complicate efforts to bring stability and reconciliation to a country. The Israeli operations in Lebanon in 2006 and in Gaza in late 2008 illustrate the difficulties faced by a technologically "superior" military force against an adversary that knows the local terrain, receives support and refuge from a civilian population, relies upon small and mobile weapons, seeks cover quickly to avoid capture or death, plays for time, and capitalizes politically upon an opponent's "indiscriminate" use of firepower. Even precision-guided weapons are counterproductive when they go awry or generate collateral damage. For that matter, efforts to reduce the vulnerability of US forces in Iraq—by confining troops to fortified bases or moving through areas quickly, en masse, in armored vehicles (or with cover fire) to minimize military casualties—can create grievances that feed an insurgency.

To be sure, states can adjust to their adversary's tactics or find ways to multiply the effectiveness of their weapons. The Army did learn meaningful lessons in Iraq after jettisoning a war strategy that appeared to fuel rather than weaken the insurgency. In consequence, the counterinsurgency mission gained prominence in service doctrine, as reflected in revisions to the *U.S. Army/Marine Corps Counterinsurgency Field Manual* and the selection of Army personnel for promotion.[39] It received an additional boost when the Army Field Manual 3-07 recognized nation-building—that is, "stability operations"—as part of the Army core mission that would shape the service's organization, training, and resource commitments.[40]

Yet, adaptation is often belated, incomplete, and impermanent. Historians and foreign policy analysts have long appreciated that leaders and governmental organizations tend to "fight the last war"—to adopt a strategy that assumes falsely that future engagements will resemble the last.[41] For the US Army, the lesson taken into Vietnam was to fight as if confronting the conventional foe the United States defeated in World War II and then Korea. In turn, the lesson drawn from Vietnam was that the war was an aberration, or mistake, and offered no guidance for future US combat. Just as the US Air Force did not back away from its stance that *more* air power was the appropriate answer, the Army did not reject the idea that US advantages in firepower and mobility could turn the tide against the communist adversary. When General Creighton Abrams replaced General William Westmoreland as commander of the Military Assistance Command in 1968 (Westmoreland's position from 1965), the shift in emphasis at the top—from enemy destruction to population protection—could not overcome a resistant army culture: "Rather than squarely face up to the fact that army counterinsurgency doctrine had failed in Vietnam, the army decided that the United States should no longer involve itself in counterinsurgency operations" (Nagl 2005, 175, 207). Even in the post-surge environment, the battle to change military opinion and culture continued. The secretary of defense, for one, was prompted to warn against "the kind of backsliding that has occurred in the past, where if nature takes its course, these kinds of capabilities—counterinsurgency—tend to wither on the vine."[42] His emphasis on preparing the US military for "irregular warfare" met significant opposition within the US military out of concern that it would lose its traditional edge and ability to compete on the technology front.[43] The leadership of the four services "non-concurred" formally, in 2008, with a classified version of the secretary's *National Defense Strategy*.[44]

The fact is that organizational learning is constrained by organizational culture (Kier 1997). It is impossible to separate what an organization *does* from what it *is*: the Air Force defined itself around strategic bombing just as the Army embraced the equipment and tactics that made it a formidable conventional force (Lebovic 1996). The organizational raison d'etre rests on a deeply held faith that these tools work—or can be made to work—better than available alternatives. Organizational resistance is that much stronger because it is rooted in the arational and dysfunctional tendencies of individuals and organizations *and* the rational need for organizations to resist change. Deference to the past, in the form of rule-abiding behavior, helps make organizations purposeful, orderly, and efficient. Enforcing uniformity and consistency in organizational behavior prevents subordinates from running amok—freely instituting (their own) policies that undermine organizational goals (as articulated by organizational leaders). By drawing from experience, employing available tools, and relying upon familiar procedures, organizations can also cope with novel challenges. Little is gained when organizations try to reinvent themselves to address each new contingency. In fact, much is lost—in efficiency, cost, and continuity—if change reduces organizational cohesion, resolve, and morale or disrupts hiring, training, or procurement plans. Thus, critics of military transformation rightly ask whether the United States should engage in irregular warfare, which places the United States at a comparative disadvantage. Because critics can ask these questions (quite rightly), counterproductive and unhelpful practices are harder to change.

Third, the power that the United States has available for given missions is *depletable*. Increasing the "readiness" of US forces leaves them less able to sustain combat, accept bigger or unexpected challenges, or respond to threats with the passage of time (Betts 1995).[45] In war, US preparedness suffers greatly: the war in Iraq sapped US equipment and manpower reserves, strained procurement and maintenance budgets, and produced military morale problems and manpower shortages.[46] As one former defense official described the tour extension, announced in spring 2007 for active-duty Army personnel heading to Afghanistan and Iraq, "It is setting the Army on a descending spiral. You make the job harder, you make the tours longer, you put additional stress on families—all of which makes it harder to recruit new people."[47]

Problems of exhaustion are potentially contagious across missions: just as the United States could not maintain its forces at full strength in Europe when challenged by an "undersized" adversary in Vietnam, the redirecting of US military and intelligence resources to Iraq in 2003 exacerbated the security problems in Afghanistan in the years to follow. Thus, the seeds for the insurgency in Iraq were arguably sown in 2003 when US military commanders planned for a quick exodus in part to address manpower requirements of the continuing war in Afghanistan (Wright et al. 2008, 28). The competing demands of fighting on two fronts continued to bedevil US efforts on each front. Although the reduced violence in Iraq allowed the services, in early 2008, to consider redeploying to address the growing threat in Afghanistan, they still feared that shifting the focus ever so slightly to Afghanistan would endanger progress in Iraq. Committed to send an additional 3,200 Marines to Afghanistan by spring, while maintaining a 25,000-strong presence in Iraq, the commandant of the Marine Corps insisted that "we cannot have one foot in Afghanistan and one foot in Iraq."[48]

In sum, thinking about US capability in terms of broad aggregates tends to exaggerate the US capability to affect outcomes through coercion or force. Indeed, the current system is militarily unipolar only in the sense that the United States possesses the capability to perform the traditional functions of a hegemonic state. These functions center narrowly around controlling the "global commons," the skies and oceans that ferry global civilian and military traffic. Of course, controlling the commons is not all that the United States can do. The United States can bring massive firepower to bear around the world in short order. Consequently, the United States can deter and deflect major challenges to the *global* military status quo, protect against any and all conventional attacks on the US homeland, and assist in the defense of a set of well-defined vital interests (protecting Europe from attack, safeguarding the sovereignty of Taiwan or South Korea, maintaining access to Gulf oil supplies). It is also well positioned to support multilateral combat or peace operations by providing logistic support, establishing air superiority over the combat zone, and commanding the seas to and from hostile territory. This is a significant—indeed, unprecedented—capability: the United States possesses "more useful military potential for a hegemonic foreign policy than any other offshore power has ever had" (Posen 2003, 9). But the world's primary power has a finite capacity to project power inland, especially when acting outside its traditional spheres of engagement, when pulled at once to support multiple commitments, or when required to sustain costly (and, perhaps, unfamiliar) operations over long periods.

Unquestionably, the United States can ameliorate some of its capability deficiencies with doctrinal adjustments. In particular, the Vietnam and Iraq cases suggest that the United States would have benefited from employing counterinsurgency principles to multiply the effectiveness of US military personnel and support. Yet, as will become apparent, operant conditions do not always support the pure application of these principles, and a pure or hybrid application does not guarantee success given US comparative disadvantages and available capabilities.

As will also become apparent, any US action abroad must be conceived in light of its motivational disadvantages relative to opponents: the global position of the United States imposes constraints on its resolve no less than on its military power. This is the implication of a paradox of power: the more capability a state possesses, the lower is its stake in any given conflict, especially those in which the state has a decided military advantage. The US disadvantage is in competing with parties, then, that can make *total* commitments to goals that have *limited* value to the United States, given its global objectives. However much capability is hypothetically available to the United States to accomplish its goals, it is disinclined to tap its store of capability to address any but the gravest of threats. In 1967, despite years of sacrifice and a realization that a victory was not achievable at current force levels in Vietnam, the Johnson administration was still unwilling to mobilize the US reserve force and thereby take on the disruptive economic and unfavorable political consequences of committing the US public more fully to the war effort. Similarly, in 2007, the Bush administration was hard pressed (with the surge) to send to Iraq an additional 30,000 troops—one hundredth of one percent of the total US population—to rescue the war effort. When the stakes of conflict are that low, the United States will have difficulty imposing its will on a creative and determined opponent that can and will extend a conflict for long-term gains. A reality of contemporary warfare is that "when a state pursues war aims that can be attained with brute force, its material resources and war-fighting capacity relative to that of the adversary are the primary determinants of success and failure." When objectives center on goals that require "target compliance," the advantage shifts in favor of the weak (Sullivan 2007, 502–503, 505).

As will become clear, too, the United States will encounter a variety of leverage challenges in seeking to obtain "target compliance." These include challenges ensuing from expanding the conflict into neighboring states, winning over a host population, and obtaining the cooperation of a host government that is unable or unwilling to assist the United States. In Vietnam and Iraq, the United States had to defeat an adversary that relied upon popular support, while US personnel lacked the requisite skills and legitimacy for the task and the host government had strong incentives to let the United States carry the costs and to avoid reforms that would ease the US burden.

CHAPTER TWO

Leveraging the Adversary's Forces

The Wars in Vietnam and Iraq

In irregular warfare, the United States is confounded by an abundant variety of military limitations—inappropriate US doctrines and capabilities, deficient and counterproductive capabilities, offsetting adversary capabilities, and—perhaps—eventual exhaustion. These limitations are featured in this chapter, first, in a look back at US combat in Vietnam, and then in an examination of the sources, evolution, and challenges of the Iraq conflict. The chapter recognizes that, in both conflicts, the US military capitalized effectively on its superior mobility and firepower but could not overcome the adversary's asymmetric tactics. It concludes, further, that the US shift toward a counterinsurgency strategy in Vietnam and Iraq was not the fix that is commonly supposed. Counterinsurgency principles were not fully applied in either conflict and "worked" in both due to a host of felicitous conditions. Indeed, changes in these conditions eventually doomed the Vietnam effort and could yet reverse US progress in Iraq. Even a dedicated US effort might not provide the United States with the resources to succeed at counterinsurgency.

The Vietnam War

In Vietnam, the United States was severely tested. It fought the war that it was best prepared to fight—playing to US conventional strength—not the war that was arguably appropriate given adversary strategy and advantages. After years of fighting, the United States adjusted its approach to give more weight to counterinsurgency principles. It is debatable, however, whether such attention earlier to rural "pacification" would have ensured a more favorable outcome for the United States. What is apparent is that the United States encountered an opponent that exploited US weaknesses by playing to its own strengths, including the capability and will to wait out the opposition. In the end, the United States was unable to defeat an adversary that increased its reliance upon conventional force. Failure was foretold by the US conduct of the war, in the air and on the ground.

The War in the Air

Throughout the Cold War period, air power advocates argued that wars are won effectively and efficiently by establishing air superiority over opponents and then pounding them into submission. Their case was based on reputed lessons from World War II, when Germany and Japan were subject, soon before their defeat, to massive bombardment in tonnages that dwarfed those in the earlier years of the conflict.[1] The various justifications for the bombing and its questionable effectiveness fueled debate over the role of strategic air attacks in the years to follow. But US policymakers and planners concluded from World War II, as well as the Korean conflict to follow, that the United States must play to its superiority in speed, maneuverability, and firepower.

Reflected first in the Eisenhower administration's declaratory shift to a massive retaliation doctrine,[2] the message was clear: the United States would not allow the enemy to play to its own advantage by choosing the time, place, intensity, and scope of combat. For many military officials, the unforgivable constraint, imposed by US policymakers in the Korean War, was allowing China, out of fear of escalation, to serve as an enemy sanctuary. Unable to target the complete enemy infrastructure, the Air Force dismissed the long and costly Korean War experience as an "aberration" that said little about the basic utility of air power (Clodfelter 1989, 3). If anything, the wartime lesson was that next time the United States must dictate the terms of conflict and capitalize more fully upon overwhelming US superiority in air power.[3]

From the Air Force perspective, this is not what the United States did in Vietnam: once again, the Air Force maintained that it was tied down by civilians. With Lyndon Johnson and Robert McNamara choosing a weekly target list (Gelb and Betts 1979, 137), the administration intended the Rolling Thunder bombing campaign (1965–68)—at least in its initial phases—to send a mixed message of resolve and restraint to North Vietnam. By restricting when, which, and how targets were hit and escalating and deescalating attacks gradually in response to the communist war effort in the South, the administration believed that it could communicate that the United States would do whatever it would take to defend South Vietnam *and* that it wished to settle the conflict without fully investing the United States in the conflict. The idea was to squeeze the enemy but leave it always with more to lose—"to tighten the noose gradually in recognizable and conspicuous ways" but "keep the hostage healthy" (Pape 1996, 179). The Air Force backed a more aggressive approach. With support from the Joint Chiefs of Staff, the Air Force pushed for an expanded and intensified bomb campaign against North Vietnam's imports, supply lines into South Vietnam, and general war-making infrastructure, which included roads, bridges, and rail lines, petroleum storage sites, industries, airbases and air defenses, and hydroelectric facilities. In the military's view, this was the only way the war should be fought: "The military promised much if allowed to bomb heavily, quickly, and without restraint but promised little if bombing was to be slow, limited, and restricted." Rather than a strategy of carrots and sticks, "the military would have preferred freedom to wield the stick with full force and let the carrot take care of itself" (Gelb and Betts 1979, 135, 153). In a word, the military preferred "sledgehammers"—attacking North Vietnam "rapidly, unrelentingly, with overwhelming force" (Spector 1993, 13). It was not satisfied to "threaten" North Vietnam's industrial base, it wanted to "destroy" it (Pape 1996, 180).

The military never fully got what it wanted. Civilian officials pursued an aerial strategy that they believed would leave the door open to a negotiated end to the conflict, keep China and the Soviet Union out of the fighting, and restrain rising US public opposition to the war effort. From the military's perspective, the result was an on-again, off-again bombing campaign that could not bring the enemy to its knees. Restrictions were placed on the weapons that the military could employ: powerful B-52 bombers—the lynchpins of the US strategic bomber force—were kept initially from operating against the North. Restrictions were also placed on when and how the military could strike. Its view, then, was that the air campaign never targeted the right things over a sustained period: it placed far too much emphasis on interdicting supplies from the North at the expense of hitting critical strategic targets in the North. Perversely, the US bombing campaign appeared to respond to political exigencies over military necessity. When the Johnson administration suspended the bombing of North Vietnam, it shifted targeting to Laos and areas south of the DMZ (Kimball 2004, 21).[4]

Champions of air power could take comfort in knowing that progress was fairly immediate once the military engaged in the sustained bombing of preferred targets in the Linebacker I (May–October 1972) and Linebacker II (December 1972) bombing campaigns. The Linebacker II raids were especially intense. They were intended to overcome North Vietnamese resistance to renegotiating the terms of peace, required to placate (and reassure) the Saigon government. US forces flew thousands of sorties against railroad yards, electric power stations, petroleum depots, ports, airports, and so on, and dropped almost as much tonnage on North Vietnam in less than two weeks as in the six months of Linebacker I (Kimball 2004, 275–279). Soon after, in January 1973, the United States and North Vietnam came to terms, in the Paris Peace Agreements, that brought US involvement in Vietnam to a close, suggesting that unrestrained air power could have won the war quickly and decisively. But this compelling interpretation of events also misrepresents wartime conditions in critical respects.

First, the United States *was* engaged in an intensive bombing campaign for much of the war, without significant effect. In the 1966–68 period alone, the tonnage dropped in Southeast Asia exceeded that dropped by allied forces in WWII *in both theaters* (Lewy 1978, 99). Indeed, in the first five years of the Vietnam bombing, the United States dropped nine times the tonnage dropped in the Pacific War, an average of around 70 tons of explosives per square mile of Vietnam (Thayer 1985, 79). This was an ineffective use of bombing inasmuch as it was mainly meant to cut the flow of personnel and resources moving from North to South Vietnam, when the Vietcong insurgency was largely self-sustaining. Not only did North Vietnam provide only a relatively small percentage of communist forces in the South and insurgent war materials and supplies, the communists could sustain themselves with limited resupply over long periods by controlling the pace and conditions of combat and avoiding direct confrontations with US forces (Pape 1996, 192). Cutting the inflow of Northern supplies to a trickle would have had a negligible effect on the communist war effort.

Second, the bombing was a blunt tool against a country like North Vietnam. The bombing disrupted its war effort and imposed hardships on its population, but not enough to matter given its political will, low state of development (and reduced dependence on a transportation, petroleum, and industrial infrastructure), and adaptiveness. North Vietnam took effective measures to counter the US bombing campaign. It offset the shortage of electricity by turning to portable power generators, using manual instead of automated tools, dispersing production, and promoting power conservation (Griffith 1995, 40). It compensated for attacks on the rest of the country's infrastructure by widely dispersing fuel supplies in small storage containers, relying upon ferries and submersible pontoon bridges (undetectable from the air), housing individuals and materials in the country's vast tunnel network, maintaining crews and supplies for rapid road repair, and so forth (Herring 1986, 147–148). Thus, when the Johnson administration "took the gloves off" in 1967 and hit the great majority of industrial and transportation targets located in politically sensitive areas, including targets in and around Hanoi and near the Chinese border (Pape 1996, 184), the bombing failed to produce the desired military or political effects.

Third, the military was not well positioned nor predisposed to assess objectively the success of any US bombing effort. The military *did* want to expand and intensify the bombing in the Johnson years, but it also argued that interdiction *had been* effective in curtailing the flow of resources to the enemy in the South, despite growing civilian skepticism (see Komer 1986, 52–53). The US Air Force (and Navy) marked progress in the air war by pointing to a variety of statistics ("input")—such as sorties flown, tonnage dropped, and targets hit—that spoke little to the impact on intended targets, let alone the effects of air power on the overall war effort. Consequently, the military ignored evidence that US military casualties were not linked to bombs dropped, that enemy supplies were acquired within South Vietnam and rose after the United States started bombing the North, and that the monetary cost of bombing North Vietnam greatly exceeded the return in damage inflicted. In sum, the military ignored the limited effect of bombing a non-industrialized adversary relying primarily upon local resources (Lebovic 1996, 63). Its view was unaffected by executive studies in 1967 that concluded that the bombing had not worked, and might not work, to reduce infiltration (Gelb and Betts 1979, 168) or evidence that the bombing had been counterproductive. Indeed, civilian Pentagon analysts concluded that the United States was effectively airlifting war materials—via the bombing campaign—to the Vietcong to carry out their insurgency. They calculated that each "dud" bomb provided hundreds of pounds of explosives for use in mines and booby traps against US and South Vietnamese soldiers (Schelling 1981, 14; Krepinevich 1986, 201).

Fourth, US bombing became an effective military tool in 1972, only after Hanoi employed its own forces in a major conventional assault. After the launch of the Easter Offensive, the US bombing of strategic and interdiction targets limited the flow of supplies and munitions from the North and the mobility and coordination of North Vietnamese troops in the South—when the offensive itself greatly increased communist resource requirements, dependence upon Northern materials, and reliance upon regular forces.[5] Then, the reputed effects of bombing must also be attributed to US and South Vietnamese ground troops, which took a huge toll on enemy forces as they attempted to capture and hold fixed positions. For its part, the Linebacker II campaign (the "Christmas bombing" of the same year)—often credited with bringing about the 1973 Peace Agreement within a matter of weeks—appears to have had only a limited military and political effect on Hanoi. US bombers attacked targets hit earlier in the year (in Linebacker I), though Hanoi's resource requirements and vulnerability had dropped with the end of its offensive. The US raids compelled Hanoi neither to make major negotiating concessions nor to surrender the ground gained in 1972. For that matter, the raids did not prevent Hanoi from resuscitating its forces quite soon. By late 1973, Hanoi was capable of launching another major offensive. (These conclusions follow from Pape 1996, 197–205.)

Finally, by the war's end, the United States had moderated its goals. The terms that the United States and North Vietnam accepted in January 1973, after Linebacker II, did not differ substantially from those that North Vietnam accepted in October 1972, when the United States had made critical concessions. The United States had legitimized the presence of Hanoi's forces on South Vietnamese territory (by allowing North Vietnamese troops to remain in place) as well as the Vietcong through formal acceptance of the Provisional Revolutionary Government as a legal party to the conflict (Herring 1986, 250–255).[6] Indeed, the United States had arguably surrendered the moral high ground already by committing to "healing the wounds of war and to postwar reconstruction," which Hanoi interpreted to mean that the United States would provide "reparations" to compensate for US misdeeds (Randolph 2007, 335). Thus, US political concessions, not formidable US air power, set the stage for agreement.

The War on the Ground

That successful counterinsurgency rests in acquiring popular support is clear from the strategy's association—in academia and the policy community—with "winning the hearts and minds" of a population.[7] The strategy, which had roots in successful campaigns against communist insurgents in Malaysia and the Philippines at the end of World War II, is associated most immediately with the US pacification effort in Vietnam. Indeed, the failings of the (inappropriate, counterproductive, and unsustainable) early "attrition" strategy are often contrasted with increasing US success at pacification late in the Vietnam War. But the limits to US military capability are clear from the US experience in military combat and in pacification.

Military Combat

The basic US "attrition" strategy in the early years of combat in Vietnam was to go after the enemy, in force, wherever it was found: when located, the aim was "to 'pile on' as many troops as were available, supported by close air support, artillery, and even B-52 strikes, to kill as many of the Vietcong and North Vietnamese Army (NVA) soldiers as possible" (Nagl 2005, 154–155). Thus, the military fought its war—and advertised progress—by focusing on the body count. As long as the enemy toll continued to mount—assuming US casualties could be kept within acceptable limits—the military anticipated a favorable outcome. Surely, the adversary would eventually exhaust itself.

The problem for the United States was, however, that its adversary was choosing the time, pace, and location of combat. Because the United States placed primary emphasis on the external threat—supplies and personnel from the North—it allowed North Vietnamese troops to draw US forces into remote areas like the Central Highlands and away from the populated coastal regions that provided manpower, food, and other supplies that fueled the war effort in the South. Adding to the problem, US forces could not engage the enemy. Attempts to do so were frequently thwarted when enemy units disappeared after detecting the advance warning of slow, methodical, and cumbersome US force movements (Lewy 1978, 60–61); drew fire into evacuated areas; inflicted casualties on US forces with mortars, mines, and booby traps; "clung to the belt" of US troops by fighting at close range to preclude US aerial or artillery support (Arreguín-Toft 2005, 154–155); and kept US forces on the defensive (spreading them thin) with small-scale attacks on roads, waterways, and so on (Thayer 1985, 95). Firefights were routinely initiated by communist forces operating in small units around the country (Thayer 1985, 28), which struck when conditions were propitious and avoided contact altogether when conditions were not (Record and Terrill 2004, 18). Even with the 1968 Tet Offensive (and the 1972 Easter Offensive), when the communists turned to larger (battalion-size) units, the overwhelming share of the fighting involved small communist units (Thayer 1985, 46). It was the pace of attacks by these units—not US attacks on communist forces—that correlated highly with US combat deaths until the Tet Offensive (Thayer 1985, 92–93). Throughout the 1960s, the overwhelming majority of small US operations yielded no enemy contacts, and increases in US military activity did not translate into higher enemy casualties (Lewy 1978, 83). In such asymmetric warfare—when the enemy could avoid fighting to recover its losses and exploit US vulnerabilities and practices—the United States could not achieve the "cross-over point," where enemy forces "attrited" at a faster rate than they could be replenished (Lewy 1978, 83–84).[8] Efforts to compensate for the US strategic disadvantage with superior firepower proved inadequate. Enormous amounts of US ammunition were expended—through sheer "availability"—under conditions of "light or inactive combat" (Krepinevich 1986, 201).

When US forces drove the Vietcong successfully from villages in the coastal regions, the Vietcong returned after US forces evacuated. US special operations units that could help the military clear and hold areas were used, instead, to support conventional operations (in reconnaissance, sabotage, and so on; see Avant 1993). More generally, "counterinsurgency" focused primarily on "counter-guerrilla" operations so that little attention was devoted to depriving the enemy of its indigenous support base (Hamilton 1998, 6–7, 109). The US military thus ignored a key feature of a guerrilla war that defies the pattern in conventional war: "In an insurgency, supplies and support are *at the front, among the people,* and the direction of the logistical flow is *opposite* that of the line of advance (it flows from the "front lines"—the people—to the insurgents' rear bases areas)" (Krepinevich 1986, 9). In failing to direct efforts to these front lines in a dedicated counterinsurgency effort, the US military fell victim to the enemy's *political* strategy: in Kissinger's (1969, 214) famous words, "The guerrilla wins if he does not lose." In other words, the guerrilla does not tally wins and losses in battle; it has its eye on the big picture that unfolds over the course of a conflict. What matters in the end is which side is left standing, as determined by the relative capabilities of the parties and their levels of resolve. Consequently, "Insurgents may gain political victory from a situation of military stalemate or *even defeat*" (Mack 1975, 177).

Illustrating the unorthodox (political) path to victory is the adversary's shift, then, to a *conventional* strategy, in the 1968 Tet Offensive, launched by the Vietcong to capture cities throughout the South. The communists hoped to spur the collapse of the Saigon government and deliver a severe blow to US morale (Elliott 2003, 1046–1047). Instead, they were beaten back in heavy fighting, suffered tens of thousands of casualties, and lost their hold on villages across the country. After

Tet, the Vietcong could no longer stem the Saigon government's territorial gains, nor reverse them in offensives (Hunt 1995, 200–201); for the first time, North Vietnamese regulars—which had been a proportionately small presence in the South[9]—came to supply most of the military manpower there (Record 1998, 27). In this sense, Tet was a military disaster for the Vietcong and their North Vietnamese allies. Yet, Tet—as expressed in its powerful imagery of Vietcong forces attacking the US embassy in Saigon (Johnson and Tierney 2006, 64)—was unquestionably a *political* victory for the US opposition. The communists successfully upped the ante to convince the United States that it faced a critical choice—either escalate or withdraw (Elliott 2003, 1062). The offensive served their long-term purpose of convincing the United States that its wartime goals were not achievable at an acceptable level of commitment. They expected that the United States would rather accept defeat (perhaps in some "dressed-up" form) than invite additional costs that would only improve the *prospects* of victory or delay an inevitable defeat.

Thus, the opposition got what it wanted by challenging existing US assumptions about the likely costs of the war and the credibility of official US claims that the war was being won. The fallout from Tet included a change in the leadership of the US war effort (with the departure of General William Westmoreland),[10] the announcement by President Johnson that he was halting the bombing of North Vietnam as a peace gesture (and, incidentally, would not seek another term in office), a dramatic rise in US domestic opposition to the war, and the recognition on the part of top US policymakers that the United States had to extricate itself from the conflict.[11] The communists accommodated their "defeat," in turn, by avoiding big-unit military confrontations and widening their political activities in the South (Hunt 1995, 200–201, 219–220).[12] Hanoi anticipated, correctly, that its challenge would ease considerably once US forces departed.

Pacification

Counterinsurgency principles were embodied in Vietnam in pacification—the "other war," as it was sometimes known in Vietnam. Counterinsurgency counsels unity in military, political, and economic effort at the local level, with the aim of obtaining support—for the host government—from the large "uncommitted" portion of the population (the portion that otherwise would support the insurgents). By providing economic incentives, political messages, and security from retaliatory violence to the population while relying upon it and rewarding it for support (for intelligence or manpower), the intent is to separate the population from the insurgency. Pacification stood, however, in subordinate and uneasy relation to the main US combat effort in Vietnam. The United States employed military force (a) in place of building popular support for the Saigon government and (b) without considering negative political consequences.

Throughout much of the war (especially under Westmoreland's direction), the United States seemed to do everything it could to undermine pacification. The US military's "search and destroy" strategy gave priority to enemy kills at the expense of cultivating a popular following and inflicted a heavy burden on peasants caught in the fighting, when their allegiance was actually required to uproot the communist infrastructure (see chapter 3). The military had little use for pacification—except as a by-product of enemy attrition (as in, "pacifying the countryside by killing the enemy")—and feared that pacification would absorb scarce personnel and resources and dilute the US war effort. These sentiments were not universally shared. The Army's chief of staff, General Harold K. Johnson, actually championed pacification and—after returning from Vietnam in 1965—commissioned an intensive staff study that identified major failings of the current US approach and recommended its fundamental restructuring around counterinsurgency principles. The massive classified volume, entitled "A Program for the Pacification and Long-Term Development of Vietnam" (PROVN), was completed and briefed, in 1966, to top US civilian and military war leaders. Unsurprisingly, its conclusions were dismissed by General Earl Wheeler, the JCS chairman who argued that "the essence of the problem in Vietnam is military" not "primarily political and economic," and by Westmoreland, inasmuch as the findings "repudiated everything [he] was doing" (Sorley 1998). In their resistance, military officials were joined by officials in various civilian agencies and departments (the Agency for International Development, the State Department) who feared that their prerogatives would suffer if pacification programs were submerged in the centralized bureaucracy. So progress in implementing a pacification program was slow in coming. Short of a unified and dedicated effort, pacification continued to suffer under the weight of problems that included competing bureaucratic agendas, inadequate resources and personnel, changing policies and officials over time, poor coordination between Washington and Saigon, a disconnect between planning and execution, and the outright abandonment of some promising efforts.

That pacification languished was not entirely because of "mere" politics and narrow views of how wars should be won. Civilian officials were rightly concerned about the counterproductive effects should the United States take the lead in counterinsurgency. What message would that convey to the Vietnamese public? That the Saigon government was weak and undeserving of public confidence? They worried, too, that a US-led effort would allow the South Vietnamese government to shift the burdens of yet another program to the United States and to resist making the political, economic, and administrative reforms necessary for pacification to succeed. The unfortunate realities for US policymakers were that the South Vietnamese government and military were neither enthusiastic about pacification in principle nor especially good at it in practice. At best, Saigon's pacification effort was hurt by weak governance at the local (district and village) levels; deficiencies in manpower, resources, and program commitment; and delusions of program success based on inflated statistics. At worst, Saigon's "pacification" effort repelled the very "hearts and minds" that it was supposed to win.

To the authorities in South Vietnam, the strategy would become a familiar one. Recognizing the threat from the communist insurgency, the South Vietnamese government moved into pacification in the 1959–61 period. By relocating villagers into fortified hamlets ("agrovilles"), its intent was ostensibly to build rural islands of security that would render the insurgents progressively unable to obtain recruits, supplies, and cover. Although many of these villages existed only "on paper," as self-interested government officials attempted to inflate their success (Hamilton 1998, 130–131, 143–144), the effects on the ground were disheartening. Peasants were separated from their ancestral lands, left to cultivate undeveloped tracts of land, and required to build their new villages with the false promise of government compensation (Herring 1986, 69; Spector 1985, 333). In the end, the villages—with their discontented and dissatisfied residents—spread so rapidly in number that they could not provide security. Consequently, the fortified-hamlet program did not hinder the communist effort; indeed, it probably helped it.

History repeated itself in the Kennedy years, as the agroville logic was reintroduced through the Strategic Hamlets program. In principle, the program was designed to extend security through the countryside. As "oil spots" spread on cloth, the aim was gradually to acquire the trust and support of the local population, obtain its participation in local security operations, establish overlapping village perimeters, and free military forces to confront main-force units that might mobilize for large-scale attacks (Krepinevich 1986, 14–15). But the programs of Ngo Dinh Diem, the first president of South Vietnam, "were often victims of poor leadership, half-hearted execution, and corruption" (Krepinevich 1986, 24). The effect was a proliferation of hamlets that were neither functioning nor secure, the siphoning of program resources into the coffers of those charged with implementation, and disastrous public relations for the Saigon government and its policies, as screaming peasants were forced from their homes on camera (Herring 1986, 89; Arreguín-Toft 2005, 156). The Saigon government continued to lose the battle of "hearts and minds" to a dedicated Vietcong adversary that knew the value of cultivating popular support.

The pacification effort was hurt further with Diem's assassination in a 1963 coup. Programs were neglected or pillaged in the power struggle that followed (Grant 1991, 216; Hunt 1995, 36), yet forced displacement continued as populations were uprooted to permit unfettered military action or to deprive the Vietcong of its support base. The consistent result was "a conglomerate mass of unhappy and unproductive humanity" (Lewy 1978, 112) with a strong sense of grievance against a Saigon government that was responsible for the conditions of displacement and apparently toothless, given its inability to protect villages where they stood. Indeed, the relocations sometimes brought along the Vietcong infrastructure and created a receptive audience for Vietcong recruiting (Herring 1986, 161). The irony was that pacification efforts "drove a wedge not between the insurgents and the peasants, but between the rural population and the government" (Lewy 1978, 25)—and certainly did not prevent the adversary from building on its gains. By 1964, the Vietcong purportedly controlled 30 percent of the territory and over 15 percent of the population of South Vietnam, including most of the strategic hamlets; by 1965, the US embassy estimated that the Vietcong controlled almost a quarter of the South Vietnamese population, with central government control limited—by day—to areas immediately around provincial and district capitals and major traffic routes (Hunt 1995, 25, 33).

The pacification effort was aided, to an extent, by US and South Vietnamese forces—their bombing and shelling of the countryside—and by the Vietcong, who required ever greater sacrifices from the peasantry. Villagers chose to live in secure parts of the country—in cities and rural villages under South Vietnamese government control—rather than risk their lives and livelihood or submit to the Vietcong's financial, material, and physical demands. Whereas the statistical evidence points, then, to a growing share of South Vietnam's rural population located in secure hamlets—a 43 percent increase from mid-1965 to mid-1967—the percent of rural hamlets that remained contested or communist controlled dropped by only 14 percent in the same period (Thayer 1985, 142). Pacification had succeeded mainly in drawing the population base away from the insurgency—"draining the pond to catch the fish"—neither satisfying popular demands nor building loyalties that could survive the relocating of villagers back to their original homes. The government was increasingly in possession of a displaced population without allegiance to the forces in charge (Elliott 2003, 852–907, 1137).

Pacification was hampered at all levels of policy and implementation: the Saigon government remained reticent to divert military forces to village security; the regular army would not stick around long enough to maintain any gains in local security; paramilitary and police forces were inadequately equipped, trained, and sized to substitute for army troops; and civilian cadres—placed in villages to serve the political mission—were scarce and poorly trained (Hunt 1995, 26–27). For the various parties whose enthusiastic participation was essential for pacification to succeed, the incentive to get involved in the villages was small: the rewards (in the form of prestige and the like) were paltry, the work was hard, and the risks (to personal safety, for example) were great. Those who served often became "part of the problem"—security units helped collect back rent, stole from villagers, and refused to provide security when needed. Although the US military picked up some of the slack, its inability (and frequent unwillingness) to depend upon or coordinate with South Vietnamese officials and personnel—including those that were supposed to hold ground that US forces had cleared—meant that South Vietnamese institutions would stay under-involved in pacification. When villagers expressed a desire for protection by US forces over South Vietnamese troops (Hunt 1995, 37–38, 48), pacification clearly suffered.

The counterinsurgency mission greatly improved in standing and performance when the US Civilian Operations and Revolutionary Development Support (CORDS) program formed in 1967 (see chapter 3) and General Creighton Abrams took over command of US forces in 1968. Even if the purported doubling in official statistics of "safe hamlets" to around 90 percent of the countrywide total in the ensuing years was an exaggeration, there did exist a decidedly upward trajectory (Parker 1975, 356, 361) that registered in a variety of statistics.[13] For all the problems in the abundant metrics associated with the pacification program,[14] they still permitted the United States independent checks, which affirmed the positive military trends (Thayer 1985, 137–153, 173–193). As one program insider (Blaufarb 1977, 270) observed, "The evidence is impressive that a completely changed situation prevailed in the rural areas and that the insurgency in the countryside—the people's war—was effectively contained."

A compelling storyline is that US and Saigon leaders saw the light: they recognized they were fighting the "wrong war" and achieved greater success with a counterinsurgency strategy. This interpretation receives additional backing from evidence of Saigon's growing interest in pacification. Substantial progress was realized when Nguyen Van Thieu became South Vietnam's president in 1967. He supported the US pacification effort by creating a centralized authority that worked closely with CORDS (Hunt 1995, 196). He also promoted meaningful land reform (redistributing millions of landlord-controlled acres to many of the country's tenant farmers) and built up militias that could provide local security. This permitted the Saigon government to claim many villages for the first time and absorb manpower that might have fought South Vietnamese forces. But this interpretation is problematic because extended security in the countryside had a variety of (more) plausible sources. These included the flow of refugees out of Vietcong-controlled areas and the success of the US-led Phoenix Program (see chapter 5)—an aggressive US effort to "neutralize" the Vietcong infrastructure by capturing or killing alleged members (Hunt 1995, 234–251). Most important, the communists had overplayed their hand militarily in the Tet Offensive. After Tet, the Vietcong could no longer halt the forward progress of pacification through attacks, and ever greater amounts of South Vietnamese territory (and people) fell officially under Saigon's control.

Saigon was nominally in control, but the lingering question was whether it had established a legitimate claim to govern. The Saigon government could distribute one major benefit—land reform—but this lost considerable appeal as the war continued: the evacuation of the countryside had curtailed the influence of landlords and their prohibitive rents and increased the availability of land (Elliott 2003, 453). Moreover, government civilian and military institutions remained beset by a host of ills, including corruption, nepotism, insubordination, desertions, failure to report attacks, accommodation with and subversion by the enemy, heavy dependence on US financial support, limits on political participation at the village level, and increasingly nondemocratic practices (on these problems, see Hunt 1995, 258–268, 277). The pacification program's statistics actually provoked serious questions within the US government about whether the Saigon government had established real security (Hunt 1995, 202–203). Rather than being won over by benefits that the Saigon government could offer, the population appears to have acquiesced to the realities of power—which side held it, which side did not, the dangers of being caught in the middle. Opinion surveys revealed that the concepts of "peace" and "security" resonated far more with the South Vietnamese public than did "victory" and "freedom" (Thayer 1985, 177).

True, the Vietcong were *losing* "hearts and minds" after Tet. The weakened Vietcong alienated the local population by imposing a high tax burden on controlled villages and shifting to heavy-handed tactics to mobilize local resources and recruits (Blaufarb 1977, 267; Herring 1986, 213), in part because the "recruiters" were now less closely tied to the villages. Even those predisposed to support the revolution (for instance, those who had benefited from Vietcong-imposed land redistribution) found that participation brought a prohibitive price (Elliott 2003, 651–689). Nevertheless, the conclusion that the peasantry was repelled into the arms of the Saigon government provides only weak support for the principles of counterinsurgency. It begs the question: Specifically, what frightened the population? Notwithstanding the brutalities of the Vietcong, its presence in an area was also associated with the violence of war that threatened the economic and personal security of collocated populations. As Popkin (1970, 662, 663) concluded at the time, "Extensive bombing and shelling, frequent search-and-destroy missions, and defoliation of Vietcong areas have made life outside the 'protection' of [the South Vietnamese government] intolerable." The upshot is that the peasantry "chose to live in villages with the most economic advantages and, ideally, on the side that would predominate in the end." Even villagers who bristled at the harsh demands of the Vietcong were willing to support them to facilitate an end to the war (Elliott 2003, 690). Most villagers were not loyal to a particular side; they hoped only that the shooting would stop—and, if not, to get away from it, if possible. In consequence, falling support for the Vietcong did not yield proportionate increases in support for the South Vietnamese government (Hennessy 1997, 166).

Success at pacification may have been illusory. What is certain is that it was fragile and reversible (as many in the CIA and State Department had long suspected).

A Final Analysis

The United States employed its conventional forces to advantage throughout the Vietnam conflict. Various statistics showed that the United States was "winning" its war of attrition: the United States managed to exact a far greater toll on the adversary than the adversary inflicted upon the United States in return. This edge was most consequential when the communists engaged in all-out offensives that negated their advantages in surprise, subterfuge, and evasion, exposing their troops to the kinds of fighting that the US military does best. The losses suffered by the adversary in the Tet engagements eroded the Vietcong position in vast expanses of South Vietnamese territory and determined the pace and conduct of the war in the years that followed.

But these losses did not determine the outcome of the conflict. The communists accomplished their goal of pushing the United States to the breaking point when it shifted to a conventional strategy in 1968. Despite their territorial and manpower losses, the communists would regain the initiative as US involvement in the ground war decreased. North Vietnam launched the 1972 Easter Offensive, in fact, to expose the conventional weaknesses of the South Vietnamese military and to reclaim Southern sanctuaries (Parker 1975, 361; Randolph 2007, 26). Intense fighting continued in subsequent years as the parties sought to gain, regain, and hold ground: South Vietnamese troop deaths totaled, according to US military estimates, around 39,000 in 1972, 28,000 in 1973, and 31,000 in 1974 (Shawcross 1987, 259). In 1975, North Vietnam launched an all-out conventional assault. South Vietnamese troops, caught up in the confusion of the offensive and the sea of humanity fleeing the North Vietnamese advance, proved unable to redeploy to defend vital central and southern provinces (Kimball 2004, 36). Outmatched South Vietnamese forces, without backing from US forces or aid, were easily routed, and Hanoi achieved a quick and total victory over the South.

The eventual defeat of the South Vietnamese military invites controversy, as principal US policymakers of the period—including Henry Kissinger—argue that their policies worked. They blame the defeat, instead, on a US Congress that prohibited the president from providing essential support to Saigon in its time of need, when "local forces were desperate to resist."[15] In this, they are correct: the South Vietnamese military took control of the war effort. But this sidesteps the relevant issue: whether South Vietnamese forces were up to the task, not whether the United States could have provided additional military support. Even with the 1972 bombing campaigns against North Vietnam, the United States—with Kissinger *at the negotiating table,* no less—conceded a continued North Vietnamese military presence in the South. The United States could hardly have expected the South Vietnamese to have had greater success. After all, US air power in 1971 was required to extricate the South Vietnamese military from its misadventure in Laos (where South Vietnamese forces displayed the lack of coordination and other deficiencies that would portend their defeat in 1975) and again, in 1972, with the Easter Offensive (when US air power inflicted most of the North Vietnamese casualties). In fact, "U.S. air power accustomed South Vietnamese units to rely on air forces to play a primary role in all engagements, large or small, defensive or offensive" (Randolph 2007, 337). With the US exodus, the challenge for Saigon became daunting. It lacked the military technology available to US forces and was desperately short on munitions, spare parts, and fuel, yet it had to contain the same formidable foe, with hundreds of thousands of North Vietnamese troops in South Vietnam and a still large indigenous communist force: "By the end of 1974 [the communists] were in the strongest position they had been in since 1964" (Thayer 1985, 256).

Kissinger is fundamentally correct to conclude that a lesson of Vietnam (for the United States in Iraq) is that "staying power" is an "essential prerequisite" to achieving a political solution.[16] The US strategy did eventually take its toll on US capability and resolve through declining troop morale, depletion of US military equipment, social distress at home, and plummeting US public support for the war effort. It led US policymakers to accept the negotiated terms that their predecessors would have rejected at the start of the war. That the US Congress—long deferential to the executive branch on foreign and defense policy—voted to end all US military action (and limit presidential discretion through the War Powers Act) in 1973 and cut military assistance to the Saigon government in 1974 speaks volumes to the fundamentally unsustainable quality of the US military strategy. The reality is that after a near-decade of fighting a costly and bloody war that took the lives of over 50,000 Americans and hundreds of thousands of South Vietnamese civilians and military personnel (indeed, well over a million Vietnamese), the United States *chose* to negotiate "an agreement that failed to answer the basic question of the war, namely who was to hold political power." In the end, the United States had to accept terms that were bound to bring a continuation or reescalation of the war (Parker 1975, 352). As Karnow (1997, 478) put it, "The war was not a classic conflict between armies pushing back the enemy as they advanced across fronts, but a test of endurance in which the side able to last longer would prevail." Under the circumstances, that was not a war the United States could win.

Certainly, the United States could have done more to win in Vietnam. But the United States can almost always do more: for a major power, resource exhaustion is rarely an absolute and typically a function of the (finite) resources the power is willing to invest in pursuing its goals. In the Vietnam conflict, the various US principals would only invest resources up to a point. The US military was unwilling to reinvent itself to fight in Vietnam and risk endangering the military's competitiveness in Europe or on other fronts. For its part, the Johnson administration would not expand the ground war into Cambodia, Laos, or North Vietnam, nor would it mobilize the US citizenry and economy fully by calling up the reserves. Although the Nixon administration loosened the geographical constraints by invading Cambodia, backing South Vietnamese operations in Laos, and extending the bombing of North Vietnam, it ratified the actions of the preceding administration by commencing a withdrawal of US forces that moved at its own pace and was not tied, in the end, to South Vietnamese self-defense capabilities (Clarke 1988, 498–499, 518). The point is that over the long haul, US policymakers, the US public, and the US military gave exactly *what they were willing* to give, and nothing more.

Could the war have been won, though, with an alternative strategy? A frequent refrain is that victory in Vietnam was possible for the United States had it relied from the start upon counterinsurgency principles (Krepinevich 1986) or, instead, a conventional strategy that cut off infiltration routes and took the war to North Vietnam (Summers 1982). In these views, US exhaustion through its war effort was a product of an ill-chosen strategy and a failure of leadership, not a consequence of a US inability to win wars by working with available capability. These critiques provoke two questions.

First, were resources that were insufficient for one purpose sufficient for another? Some early success (by US Marines) at pacification actually suggests that clearing and holding the villages of South Vietnam to defeat a communist insurgency would have required an enormous early US expenditure in time and resources (Hennessy 1997). Yet the size of the US military force in Vietnam increased slowly at first, due to an understandable reluctance to commit. Furthermore, most US troops were neither trained nor predisposed to supply the dedicated and active village presence needed to obtain the local trust, cooperation, and involvement required for successful counterinsurgency (see Spector 1993, 194–195). Indeed, a substantial US commitment to counterinsurgency training and requirements would have redirected resources from conventional preparedness, which remained central to US global strategy and might still have had to overcome the consequences in Vietnam of continued US reliance upon an attrition strategy that placed enemy kills over the establishment of popular support (see chapter 3). Just as important, such a strategy would have severely tested US patience and resources. It would have required that US civilian and military officials accept "a long war of time-consuming paramilitary, nation-building operations in which conventional military forces would play but a secondary role" (Record 1998, 93).

Second, was the adversary not able to change its strategy to thwart the US effort? If anything, the communists had proven adept at accommodating the changing fortunes of war: they adopted a guerrilla strategy to capitalize on the weakness of the United States and South Vietnamese militaries, moved toward big-unit engagements when circumstances appeared propitious, and then avoided such confrontations to recoup their losses and prepare for the next round of fighting. The main challenge to the United States in Vietnam was not finding the "right" strategy; instead, it was the flexibility and adaptiveness of an enemy that could thwart any opponent that could not do all things well at all times. For US forces, the problem was circular: "clear-and-hold operations were their only long-term solution to the insurgency, but they could not be very successful until search-and-destroy operations had split up and held off the enemy's main force units," whereas "search-and-destroy operations would never succeed until clear-and-hold operations severed the enemy's supply, intelligence, recruiting, and other relationships with the rural and urban populations" (Hennessy 1997, 127). The conundrum was not entirely lost on US military commanders. For his part, General Westmoreland recognized the down side of his strategy: he understood that, by chasing North Vietnamese regulars around the countryside and defending first against a North Vietnamese attack, he was leaving the villages open to Vietcong penetration. He also recognized, however, that he could not successfully pursue both an attrition and a pacification strategy. Thus, he chose to minimize the risks of a devastating conventional invasion from the North and to adopt a strategy that, given US comparative advantages, appeared to offer an efficient return on resources expended (Hennessy 1997, 123–125). The strategy drew resources away from areas undergoing pacification—that was the adversary's intent. But had Westmoreland chosen the alternative course, he would have made the opposite mistake. The military environment in Vietnam became increasingly hostile to small-unit operations as the level of violence increased, and North Vietnam turned to a conventional strategy.

The bottom line is this: despite its large investment, the United States was unable to defeat an adversary that could exploit the US weakness in countering a guerrilla war, that could spread US forces thin, and that could capitalize on the failings of the host government and changes in the US political mood. Nor could the United States defeat an adversary that could change strategies to offset shifts in the US approach and require that the United States do all things well to win. The problem for the United States was not just that it was ill-equipped to fight a guerrilla adversary; it was that the United States would have had to sacrifice resources for the conventional effort to combat an insurgency (and the reverse). Under these conditions, North Vietnam could play for time, knowing all the while that (a) the United States would eventually retreat from the seemingly interminable costs of war, and (b) Saigon could not survive without active US support.

So US fortunes did improve in Vietnam: the revised adversary strategy, giving more emphasis to conventional operations, played to the *immediate* US advantage, and the revised US strategy, giving more emphasis to pacification, improved US performance against an insurgency. In the end, even these favorable developments could not overcome the limits of US military capability—the finite capability that the United States could continue to invest in the conflict.

The Iraq War

In Vietnam, the United States took sides in an ideological conflict. In post-occupation Iraq, the United States placed itself in the middle of an identity conflict pitting Sunni against Shiite, with various factions and groups vying for dominance. Not only was the United States slow, in its rhetoric and military tactics, to concede the communal basis to the conflict, the United States initially fought its post-occupation war in Iraq as if it were back in Vietnam. In word and deed, the United States suggested that its security challenges stemmed from illegitimate actors to be "excised" from Iraqi politics and society. Consequently, the focus of the US war effort was on "foreigners" (specifically, Sunni groups allied with al-Qaeda and Shiite militia linked to Iran), "spoilers" who sought to profit from the resulting tumult, and "dead-enders"—remnants of the dethroned Baath regime, with no place in Iraq's future. The attention to these elements was warranted, for they were acting—at times, conspiring—to destabilize Iraq and increase their own power through force. Yet this focus was also misguided, for it neglected the strong ties between these actors and the communities that supplied the recruits, supporters, and enablers that fed the Iraqi violence. In going after the troublemakers, the US military failed to appreciate that its harsh measures to quell the violence made the United States a party to the conflict, reinforced identities (Sunni and Shiite) that fueled the violence, and created new grievances.

The US military turned to counterinsurgency principles with the growing violence in the first months after the invasion (Wright et al. 2008, 116–136) and then dramatically in late 2006, by which time Iraq was in the throes of a civil war. The shift in the US approach eventually helped produce a dramatic reduction in the level of violence throughout the country. But, as the following discussion of the military conflict suggests, progress came slowly, at great cost, and not from a straightforward application of counterinsurgency principles. These conclusions emerge from examining (a) the backdrop to the insurgency, (b) the growth in violence through 2006 with Sunni insurgent and Shiite militia activities, and c) the eventual reduction in violence after 2006 in the surge period.

Backdrop to the Insurgency

The roots of the postwar security problem originated in large part in the absence of prewar planning for the aftermath of war. As Ricks (2006, 4) notes, the 2003 US operation in Iraq was enabled by "simultaneously 'worst-casing' the threat presented by Iraq while 'best-casing' the subsequent cost and difficulty of occupying the country."

The Bush administration appeared unwilling to slow the momentum toward war by considering complications that might impugn the efficacy of the US war effort. It focused, instead, on the overriding danger of allowing Saddam Hussein to possess weapons of mass destruction and the political promise of a democratic transition in a pivotal Middle Eastern country. True, the US intelligence community had not fully detailed the potential risks of occupying Iraq. It had not predicted a sustained insurgency following an occupation of Iraq, the poor condition of the Iraqi physical infrastructure that would hinder postwar reconstruction and development, or the effective use of IEDs in armed resistance to a US occupation. But the intelligence community accurately predicted key specifics (for example, that al-Qaeda would redirect its attacks to Iraq) and offered a fairly stark and generally accurate assessment of the conditions that would greet the United States in Iraq. One high-level assessment concluded presciently that building "an Iraqi democracy would be a long, difficult and probably turbulent process, with potential backsliding into Iraq's tradition of authoritarianism."[17]

The administration hoped, as well, to limit its costs of war, militarily and economically, in keeping with Bush's expressed disdain, as a presidential candidate, for (invariably long, involved, and disappointing) "nation-building" efforts. In congressional testimony, Deputy Secretary of Defense Paul Wolfowitz dismissed suggestions that a US force in the hundreds of thousands was required to occupy and stabilize a country like Iraq—directly contradicting the earlier testimony of General Eric Shinseki, the Army chief of staff. In Wolfowitz's view, these higher numbers were "far off the mark"—a figure closer to 100,000 troops was appropriate, given the relatively hospitable environment in which troops would operate in Iraq, a country, as he stated, that had no history of ethnic strife and that would welcome an occupation force that "stayed as long as necessary but left as soon as possible."[18] In his thinking, all post-occupation US missions in the country could be served by military units that would derive from the main US force: in his words, "It's hard to conceive that it would take more forces to provide stability in post-Saddam Iraq than it would take to conduct the war itself and to secure the surrender of Saddam's security forces and his army" (quoted in Bensahel 2006, 468). Although concerned that a small invasion force would be undermanned and overexposed, the military also deserves some of the blame for the deteriorating conditions in Iraq. It devised a war plan that left the United States unable to cope with the aftermath of the invasion; it failed to anticipate the manpower needed to establish and maintain order throughout Iraq; and it did not supply sufficient troops trained for that specific purpose, having, since Vietnam, rejected a view of itself as a counterinsurgency, peacekeeping, or constabulary force. In fact, the US military planned for a short and peaceful occupation of Iraq and a quick handover of responsibilities to a new Iraqi government (Wright et al. 2008, 3). It was actually in the process of withdrawing troops and halting the flow of additional manpower and weaponry into Iraq when "major hostilities" came to a close, that is, when the effort to drive Saddam Hussein from power was complete.

The military did not expect to be haunted after the invasion by the efficient conventional strategy that was used to bring down Saddam Hussein. Having identified Hussein as the problem, and his removal from power as the solution, the United States had written the script for the messy aftermath of war. Initially, "the lightning campaign seemed to vindicate an emerging doctrine of rapid, decisive operations ('shock and awe') and its corresponding emphasis on rapidly deployable forces, precision weapons, and long-range strikes" (Mansoor 2008, 107). But by directing a relatively small mobile force to take Baghdad, the "center of gravity" of the regime (Wright et al. 2008, 14), the United States bypassed a sizable portion of the Iraqi military and left large portions of the country unoccupied and generally untouched. The US armored and mechanized infantry units in place were ill equipped to handle post-occupation security challenges and were sorely undermanned for that purpose. The ratio of US military personnel to local civilians was well below that of prior US military operations—in countries with a more compliant public. For instance, the troop-to-civilian population ratios in the Kosovo operation suggest that over half a million troops were required to establish security in postwar Iraq (Bensahel et al. 2008, 17, 84). Not only was the undermanned US force unable to control the local population, it was also unable to keep it from preparing for the next round of hostilities by looting the arms caches that Saddam Hussein placed around the country to guard against threats to his rule (Ricks 2006, 158–165, 191). In that void, the insurgency was able to recruit, arm, and grow.

Neither had the military anticipated that it would assume the lead, by default, in a broad-based effort at military stabilization, economic reconstruction, and institutional development in the "failed state" that Iraq would become. Although the Department of Defense charged the newly formed Office of Reconstruction and Humanitarian Assistance (ORHA) with addressing the humanitarian crisis that might follow the war, the office was short on staffing and resources and had only months to prepare for its assigned task. It was woefully ill equipped, then, to address the challenges posed by a complete breakdown in order in Iraq (Wright et al. 2008, 13–14). It soon handed off its responsibilities to the newly formed US Coalition Provisional Authority (CPA), which was no more prepared to deal with the occupational challenges. Turf battles involving overlapping responsibilities, mutual dependence, and competing chains of command arose between the US civilian offices and the military command. But the CPA eventually had to concede de facto responsibility for much of the Iraqi stabilization and rebuilding effort to a US military that was not up to the challenge. It had no plan for the aftermath of war, was uncertain about its own role in remaking the country, was understaffed and under-prepared all the way down the chain of command, and had to cope with constantly changing US civilian and Iraqi governance structures and a profusion of ill-formed, variable, and competing visions for Iraq within the US government (Wright et al. 2008, 29, 164–165, 181).

Worse, the CPA, led by Paul Bremer, often appeared to be *trying* to exacerbate the security problem that the military would inherit. By defining a larger and enduring role for the United States in Iraq—remaking it into a constitutional democracy—the civilian authority burdened the US military with all the risks and costs of an extended stay. In addition, Bremer ordered the disbanding of the Iraqi military. As a result, the United States lost any hope of fielding an experienced, indigenous force—hundreds of thousands strong—that could exert authority and relieve the US manpower burden across the country.[19] US military plans had assumed, in fact, that the Iraqi military and lower-level Baath officials in government would maintain order and facilitate reconstruction in the country (Wright et al. 2008, 93). Instead, the Iraqi military became part of the problem. Disbanding the military added greatly to the sea of unemployed and disenfranchised—indeed, endowing it with military training and inside knowledge of arms caches (Wright et al. 2008, 97)—available to the insurgency. The Sunnis would be marginalized further, as the United States pushed for democratic representation in a new Iraqi government that would favor the Shiite majority and indiscriminately purged Baathists from government and positions of responsibility. From the Sunni perspective, "de-Baathification" had become "de-Sunnification" (ICG 2006, 10)—a view that was reinforced when the United States engaged in actions to repress a Sunni rebellion (as in Anbar Province) that had the United States tacitly promoting the Shiite sectarian agenda.

American inattention and practices produced a volatile mix—a security vacuum, growing public grievances against the United States and the host government, and a seemingly unlimited supply of arms. Violence, looting, and disorder combined to create an environment in which lawlessness and attacks spread—and insurgent groups and militia organized, operated, and seized control eventually of entire neighborhoods and cities.

The Increasing Violence: 2003–2006

Whether or not the violence was avoidable, it rose precipitously and then exploded through the (mutually reinforcing) actions of Sunni insurgents and Shiite militia groups. This section assesses these groups, their strategies, and the challenge to US forces in the first years of the occupation.

The Rising Opposition

The actions of Sunni insurgent and Shiite militia groups brought Iraq, within a few years, to a state of civil war. With their various goals, tactics, and interests, these groups presented the United States with a formidable security challenge.

The Sunni Insurgents. Even before it turned in on itself, the Sunni insurgency did not much resemble the communist insurgency. The Sunni insurgency was fragmented, highly decentralized (with little connection between local groups and a broader organization), and bereft of a well-developed ideology and political program, apart from crude nationalistic and Islamic appeals of varying emphasis. The insurgency was certainly not jihadist in character: insurgents opposed the US occupation and an Iraq run by Shiites and Kurds, but most did not adopt a fundamentalist Islamic agenda or express much interest in linking Iraq to a bigger, global cause. Contrary to the Bush administration's suggestions in the early US occupation period, the overtly jihadist groups represented but a portion of groups involved in the insurgency, and all drew primarily from the local recruitment pool. The overwhelming majority (90 to 95 percent) of the insurgents were Iraqis, not foreign operatives: even al-Qaeda in Iraq relied principally on locals, which explains the group's success in recruiting, acquiring resources and intelligence, and operating unobtrusively. Indeed, most insurgents came to resent the presence and interference in Iraq of foreign operatives, as well as their harsh jihadist practices. Consequently, Sunni insurgents were aligned uneasily in common cause: groups splintered, alliances formed and dissolved, and umbrella organizations united groups briefly and in name only as part of a larger contest for supremacy within the insurgency. Still, the administration's characterization of the insurgency was more or less appropriate at various times, as the insurgency appears to have unfolded in (somewhat indistinct) phases as outlined by Guido Steinberg (2006).

The first phase of the insurgency, commencing soon after the US invasion, centered around remnants of the Baath regime—former members of Saddam's paramilitary network who had prepared, armed, and positioned around the country for contingencies that threatened the regime (Wright et al. 2008, 103). Attacks were sporadic, weak, and uncoordinated, focusing generally on military targets. But the intensity of the attacks and diversity of their targets increased quickly in the first months of the occupation. In August 2003, the country was rocked by horrific suicide bombings, attributed to Ayman al-Zarqawi, the leader of al-Qaeda in Iraq. The attacks targeting the Jordanian embassy, the UN headquarters in Baghdad (killing the UN chief envoy and prompting the UN exodus from Iraq), and the Imam Ali Shrine in Najaf (killing almost a hundred people, including Muhammad Bakr al-Hakim, the leader of the Supreme Council for the Islamic Revolution in Iraq, or "Supreme Council"). The number of attacks continued to increase—against a robust list of targets—before the second phase began, in earnest, in the early part of 2004. The scope and seeming indiscriminateness of the attacks—on Shiite holy sites and pilgrimages, among other targets—conveyed their various purposes that included undermining the fledgling Iraqi government (by exposing its divisions and ineptness), provoking resistance to the US military occupation force (by revealing its inability to prevent the attacks and indirect culpability for them), and creating massive instability in order to bring new recruits to the cause and help the insurgents, at some point, to seize control.

The deteriorating conditions spurred the United States into action. With escalating violence and areas north, west, and northwest of Baghdad now safe havens for the Sunni insurgency, the United States moved militarily against insurgent strongholds in Samarra (in Salahuddin Province) and Fallujah (in Anbar Province) in the so-called Sunni Triangle.[20] The results were unpromising. The battles for Fallujah—an urban hotbed of Sunni resistance just forty miles west of Baghdad—proved especially egregious demonstrations of the liabilities of fighting insurgents on their own terms. The city was subject in April 2004 to heavy US bombardment most immediately to avenge the ambush killing of four US private contractors, whose bodies were gruesomely mutilated and paraded before the city. US ground forces withdrew from Fallujah after severe criticism of US tactics from members of the Iraqi Governing Council and heavy fighting that left many hundreds of civilians dead—as insurgents held their ground in populated areas, purportedly seeking refuge in hospitals and mosques. When the military pulled back from Fallujah, it was effectively ceded to radical clerics and insurgents, whose symbolic victory sparked an inflow of supporters into the city. As Islamic radicals took refuge in Fallujah and imposed their extremist religious views and practices upon residents, the United States responded decisively in November 2004. After most residents had evacuated, the city was subject to intense US bombardment by gunships, howitzers, tanks, and aircraft. The US operation resulted in the killing and capture of thousands of insurgents and succeeded in breaking the insurgent stranglehold on the city (Wright et al. 2008, 44). Still, many insurgents and their leaders fled the city, and violence spread to other parts of Anbar Province, including its capital (Ramadi) and the neighboring cities of Samarra and Baqubah (Steinberg 2006, 21). Not only did the insurgents increase the intensity of the suicide bombing and assassination campaign, they returned eventually to Fallujah to carry out attacks.[21] By 2006, the chief of intelligence for the Marine Corps in Iraq, Colonel Pete Devlin, was reputedly offering in a secret report a "very pessimistic" prediction of the likelihood of bringing Anbar Province under control—notable in that it contrasted sharply with the relatively upbeat tone of military intelligence (as compared to CIA) reports. The report assessed, in the words of one officer, that the United States had been "defeated politically" in the province.[22] Neither the Iraqi central nor local governments were operating in the area, and the insurgents were effectively in control. In Fallujah, the United States had won the battle but was losing the war.

Yet, the seeds were being planted to reverse the fortunes of the jihadist groups. Their actions gave rise to a reactionary (third) "nationalist Islamic" phase that started in spring 2005 and lasted until early 2006. In this period, groups like the Islamic Army in Iraq, the Mujaheddin Army, and the 1920 Revolution Brigades—forged in the immediate aftermath of the US occupation—rose to challenge jihadists operating now under the umbrella of the Islamic State of Iraq.[23] In a sense, the jihadists were victims of their own "success." Resentment festered within Sunni communities as jihadists targeted fellow Iraqis (Shiite civilians) indiscriminately, sought conformity with their own Islamic practices (for example, banning cigarette sales, forcing woman to cover themselves from head to toe, and killing service workers, such as barbers, for being non-Islamic), engaged in wanton criminal behavior (confiscating property, kidnapping for ransom, forcing marriages, and killing tribal leaders, officials, and policeman), and rejected all Sunni participation in the formal governing process (via elections or service in military and police units). Indeed, tension between Sunni insurgents and the jihadists was apparent as early as 2004 in Fallujah, when it became a magnet for jihadist groups. Insurgents from the area blamed the jihadists for their excesses and for exposing the city to destruction by the US military. As one local put it, "We welcomed them first because we thought they came to support us, but now everything is clear."[24]

The conflict building between nationalist and jihadist groups soon took second stage, again, to sectarian conflict. The intense sectarian violence that distinguished the fourth ("civil war") phase of the insurgency, commenced, in February 2006, with the bombing in Samarra of the Askariya Shrine, one of Shiite Islam's holiest sites. Whether or not the violence in Iraq was technically a "civil war" (Sambanis 2004)—in the United States, the terminology was a matter of considerable debate—no one could doubt the mounting instability in the country and the immense human toll. The carnage was widespread and overwhelming. Suicide bombs delivered by foot, car, and truck killed hundreds of civilians in a single day; bodies bearing telltale signs of torture were found dumped in streets and mass graves in and around Baghdad; innocent Sunnis and Shiites were nabbed at fake checkpoints along the road, pulled from buses, and killed in their hospital beds or at the morgue when retrieving the bodies of family members; Iraqi government officials lived under constant fear of kidnapping or death; Iraqis were killed by the dozens, in bomb attacks, waiting in lines at police and military recruiting centers; IED and small-arms attacks on US troops per week numbered into the hundreds; reconstruction and repair efforts faltered on Iraq's dilapidated infrastructure (which had, itself, become a prime target of the insurgency); and large portions of the country remained under the effective control of insurgents and militia groups. Even Baghdad had progressively fallen under the control of Moqtada al-Sadr's Mahdi Army.

But the result was somewhat unexpected. Whereas a prevailing view of the dynamics of conflict centers on conflict "spirals"—as captured in the notion of "cycles of violence" (Lebovic 2007, 127–131)—an opposing process was apparent throughout Iraq, as it entered the next phase of the insurgency. Rather than conflict feeding on itself, hardening public attitudes, desensitizing populations to the cruelty of their actions, and sucking in ever more people who commit ever worse atrocities, the violence in Iraq crested. The violence, and response to it, were much of the reason.

The Shiite Militias. Coalition forces were tested, from the start, by the Mahdi Army, the militia wing of the Jama'at al-Sadr al-Thani (Association of the Second al-Sadr), under the control of Moqtada al-Sadr. He was the son of a revered ayatollah who paid with his life in 1999 when he used his clerical position to undercut the legitimacy of the Saddam Hussein regime. More so than his father, al-Sadr derived his power from a grassroots base drawn heavily from the sprawling slums of Baghdad's Sadr City. Dismissed early by US officials as a thuggish firebrand who commanded only a small following, he was targeted by the United States for removal. The United States demurred, however, out of fear that killing or arresting al-Sadr would make him a martyr, instead hoping to discredit or coopt him (Wright et al. 2008, 35). The United States accomplished neither goal, as al-Sadr attracted a large and devoted following by positioning himself as a principled voice for the poor and the disenfranchised and an ardent nationalist who opposed both the US occupation and the weakening of the Iraqi nation.

Given his appeal, al-Sadr could salvage victory when he overplayed his hand militarily. Al-Sadr's efforts to extend his control in Shiite-dominated cities to the south of the country resulted in bloody battles with US forces and competing Shiite militia groups, especially the Badr Organization—the military wing of the Supreme Council, the dominant Shiite political party in Iraq, aligned with the Shiite clerical establishment in the holy city of Najaf. His militia was punished severely in April 2004 after attacking US troops, government installations, police offices, radio stations, and other instruments of local power in the Shiite-dominated cities of Karbala, Kufa, Al Kut, and Najaf. With his audacious assault, Al-Sadr's popularity soared, nevertheless, in cities around Iraq (as opinion surveys verified).[25]

The Mahdi Army was dealt a more severe blow when battling the US military for control of Najaf in August 2004. With the loss of territory and thousands of fighters, Sadr agreed to evacuate the Imam Ali Shrine in Najaf (occupied in defiance of Grand Ayatollah Ali al-Sistani, the most revered cleric in Iraq), disband his militia, and surrender heavy weapons to the Iraqi police. The retreat fed optimism among US military commanders that the Iraqi government could establish control over contested urban territory, including Sadr City, and that Sadr's legions would wither (Ricks 2006, 335–338; Wright et al. 2008, 39–41).[26] But the optimism was unwarranted.

Not only did al-Sadr retain a significant following, he amassed an army, second in size to the Iraqi Army, and became a dominant partner in the Iraqi coalition government. There, he would parlay his electoral strength into a strong position within the central government from which to build his political base. For instance, his organization assumed control over the Ministry of Health and then used that position to further the mass appeal of the Sadrist movement by providing social services to the poor. The Mahdi Army also penetrated the national police force, which allowed it to operate with the full authority and protection of the state, intimidating law enforcement personnel who stood in the way (ICG 2008b, 5). Its abuses in uniform served to further the sectarian agenda of a police force that was controlled, at the highest levels, by the Badr Organization (on its actions, see chapter 5).

The Mahdi Army continued its advance on the ground—pursuing its own "clear and hold" strategy. It pushed methodically into the formerly mixed (Sunni-Shiite) neighborhoods of Baghdad with a campaign of threats and violence against Sunni residents. It also enriched itself in the process through expropriation, extortion, and monopoly control of goods and services in Shiite neighborhoods. The Mahdi Army profited greatly, in fact, from its stranglehold on the local economy, its control of a diverse business and public service enterprise that included electric switching stations, rent from houses that the army had confiscated, food and clothing markets, and gas stations (four of which apparently generated $13,000 per day for the militia).[27] Al-Sadr and his supporters pushed violently for advantage, as well, in southern Iraq,[28] where their main Shiite rival, the Badr Organization, sought to consolidate the Supreme Council's position by building on the party's control of a large number of regional governments. The resulting violence forced the British to retreat to the sanctuary of their bases after failing to "clear" the city of militia.[29]

The civil war that erupted in 2006 actually proved a mixed blessing for the Mahdi Army. Although the war "generated considerable material and symbolic resources and enabled the movement to extend its influence beyond its traditional social base," the resources and expanding base also fed corruption and weakened internal cohesion (ICG 2008b, 10). Rather like the Sunni jihadists, Al-Sadr was a victim of his own success. The bombing of the Askariya Shrine in February 2006 produced a massive influx of undisciplined recruits into the militia just as arrests began to deplete its leadership.[30] Its success in gaining control of Shiite communities added another challenge in that it rendered their inhabitants less dependent on the Mahdi Army for protection and therefore more inclined to resist its appeals and demands (ICG 2008b, 18).

Clearly, al-Sadr lost stature when his rhetoric was contradicted in practice: he promoted the cause of national unity and assailed the injustices of the Shiite establishment, while his militia engaged in sectarian cleansing and retaliation and used and abused Shiite citizens under militia control. These inconsistencies only added to the reasons that many Shiites had to view al-Sadr with distrust. As a champion of the Shiite underclass, al-Sadr threatened the Shiite religious and political establishment, which saw him as a pretender. He was derided for his relatively limited religious training and credentials, his crude and unsophisticated speaking style, and his calculated exploitation of his father's reputation. The Shiite establishment, in fact, had ample reason to regard him as an opportunist. He challenged and then joined the government only to withdraw from it, called for ceasefires and then renounced them. Even his "principled" positions appeared to have a basis in political expedience. His belief in a strong central government converged conveniently with his interest in preventing the Supreme Council from capitalizing on its formidable power in the southern provinces, which contain much of Iraq's oil reserves and petroleum infrastructure. He called for an end to the US military occupation but tacitly accepted its presence.[31] Only adding to his problems, Sadr's equivocations—his attempts to balance the political and military requirements of his movement—ended up splintering the movement among proponents of each approach (Cochrane 2009, 18–22).

Al-Sadr was caught in a downward spiral. He was increasingly on the defensive and losing popular support, challenged from within and without his movement and dependent on a militia that was lashing out, with little regard for public relations or a national political program.[32] Still, undefeated, al-Sadr retained his sectarian appeal. Even in September 2006, 81 percent of the Shiite population claimed to have a favorable view of him, compared to just 9 percent of Sunnis.[33]

US Military Challenges

The United States was severely challenged in its attempts to contain the explosive violence and reduce the control of Sunni insurgent and Shiite militia groups in Iraq. The challenges, reminiscent of the Vietnam conflict, were as follows.

First, the United States was once again hampered by its inability to hold territory, now given the relatively small size of the US occupation force, its reticence to inflict the high civilian casualties that occur in urban warfare, and its emphasis upon relocating to engage the enemy. US troops moved into some Iraqi neighborhoods with great fanfare, established some degree of control—and then left. Insurgents responded to US operations by evacuating the city or lying low, only to reemerge once US forces departed. The US strategy came to be known pejoratively as "whack-a-mole," after the amusement park game in which no matter how often you smack the mole in one hole, it will reappear in another. US military operations were actually counterproductive in these cities. As a counterinsurgency advisor to General Petraeus put it, "We would clear an area, encourage people to sign up for government programs, but then we would have to leave and those people would be left exposed and would get killed" (quoted in Ricks 2006, 348).[34]

Second, the United States was challenged, again, by an adversary that played to its own strength and deprived the United States of offsetting options. In Vietnam, the adversary avoided direct confrontations with US military forces. Instead, it drew US forces into battles that would dilute and sap US capabilities and permit the guerrillas a free hand in recruiting supplies and personnel from villages remote from the battlefield. The Iraqi insurgents similarly learned to play to their own strengths and exploit US weaknesses. When incurring heavy casualties in ambush attempts against US army units, as in Sadr City and Samarra in late 2003 (Wright et al. 2008, 111), the Sunni insurgents shifted their tactics. Their weapon of choice was, of course, the improvised explosive device (IED). Planted inconspicuously on footpaths and roads and made to explode at a time and place of the operative's choosing, IEDs proved lethal against US troops while minimizing the attacker's exposure. They also relied on indirect fire from mortars, rocket-propelled grenades, and attacks by operatives wearing suicide vests or driving cars and trucks rigged with explosives (a so-called VBIED, vehicle-borne improvised explosive device). The effect was to offset the overwhelming US advantage in the technology, troop training, force mobility, organization, and leadership that made the US military an effective fighting force.

Adversary weapons and tactics improved over time in various respects. The insurgents incorporated technological advances, learned to use subterfuge and evasion to advantage, capitalized on their understanding of US military practices, and compensated for US countermeasures. So the insurgents hid their bombs in inconspicuous places such as animal carcasses and trash along the roadsides; they benefited from a division of labor, with some operatives digging holes into which others later planted bombs (thereby minimizing the planter's exposure and improving operational efficiency); they developed combined-arms tactics, for instance, attacking US military vehicles after an IED explosion; they devised tactics to increase the vulnerability of US troops, using obstacles or fake bombs to trap or slow vehicles in ambushes; and they answered US countermeasures with bigger bombs, projectiles capable of piercing vehicle armor, and sophisticated triggering devices (for instance, lasers when garage door openers proved prone to jamming). Furthermore, the insurgents shifted their focus to various "soft" targets—diplomats, politicians, government officials, young men lined up at army and police recruiting stations, funerals for those slain in the violence, religious ceremonies, and markets—to increase the challenges for the defense and to maximize the symbolic impact of an attack. Attacks on bridges into the capital were highly disruptive, if only because they provoked heavy security precautions—checkpoints, car searches, and prohibitions on truck traffic—that brought commerce and travel to a halt.[35] The insurgents capitalized, as well, on the fears of vulnerability that these attacks engendered. In September 2005, rumors—perhaps maliciously spread—that suicide bombers would attack countless Shiite pilgrims crossing a bridge over the Tigris River in Baghdad caused a stampede that left around a thousand people dead. Indeed, by relying upon suicide bombers, the insurgents had at their disposal the poor man's "smart bomb"— operatives that could home in on their target, in this case US troops at checkpoints, with no need to plan an escape that could compromise mission effectiveness. Unlike smart bombs, suicide weapons were prized, however, for their collateral effects: the commitment and inconspicuousness of the attackers and the destructiveness and seeming randomness of the attacks sent shock waves of fear, recrimination, and grief through communities to multiply the physical disorder caused by the attack.

Third, the United States was challenged, as in Vietnam, by problems of statistical interpretation. The Iraq conflict—thanks to vast improvements in data collection, processing, and dissemination since the Vietnam War—yielded a profusion of wartime data, estimates, and statistics. Data were generated, compiled, and assessed by governmental and nongovernmental groups on a variety of dimensions. These included casualties incurred by US troops, Iraqi forces, and Iraqi civilians; the number, geographical distribution, characteristics, and effects of enemy attacks; tallies of Iraqi insurgents killed and captured; and the number of enemy weapons and explosives recovered, disabled, or destroyed. Given their questionable reliability and validity, more data were not necessarily better. For instance, the readiness of Iraqi security forces and the direction of underlying trends depended on the opaque meaning behind the host of classificatory terms employed in US defense reports as well as how the data were aggregated.[36]

This problem of dependence upon assumption was hardly any smaller for the calculations involving civilian casualties. Although these figures were often offered within a likely range, the most likely figure from one source could diverge widely from the mark set by another source; indeed, the low point of the likely range from one source might be considerably higher than the high point of the assumed range from another source. The estimated number of civilians killed in the first years of the US war effort ranged from the tens of thousands (according to the organization Iraq Body Count) to many hundreds of thousands (according to *Lancet*, a British medical journal, using survey methods that sparked considerable controversy).[37] A World Health Organization (WHO) survey—using twenty-three times as many locations around the country and five times as many households as in the *Lancet* study and making adjustments for such factors as the fleeing of households with victimization from violence—placed the number of violent deaths in the three years after the US invasion at 151,000.[38] The reliability problems resulted, in part, because no one "collected" the actual figures, rendering all totals sensitive to assumption, and because data suppliers were self-interested. Illustrating both problems are the data available from the Baghdad morgue. It was a useful source of information on sectarian killings, but its numbers included only bodies found and transported to the morgue (the bodies of suicide bomb victims were taken to the hospital); the Health Department, overseeing the morgue, was under orders from the prime minister not to release fatality data after the UN—drawing from reports from local officials, morgues, and hospitals—placed the 2006 Iraqi civilian death count at 34,000, exceeding the official Iraqi government count by a multiple of three.[39] A Health Ministry official refused to offer alternative numbers even after criticizing the WHO study for its excessively high figures.[40] Iraqi sources were not the only culprits here. US defense sources routinely provided numbers on insurgents killed and captured in order to establish US wartime progress, numbers that contradicted those supplied by other defense sources. For example, in early 2005, the top US military commander in Iraq indicated that the United States had killed or captured 15,000 insurgents in the preceding year—a figure that was three times higher than the size of the insurgency, at least as estimated a year earlier by the top US commander in the Middle East.[41]

Regardless of their quality, the data had many plausible interpretations: any given set of numbers could suggest operational success or failure. A rising number of attacks on US forces could be read to indicate that the militia and insurgent groups were striking out of desperation and depleting their ranks or, instead, that these groups were growing in strength, emerging from the shadows, and increasingly willing to take a stand. Likewise, the number of unexploded IEDs discovered could be taken to establish both increased US detection and intelligence capabilities (such as via tips) and the larger number of IEDs being planted to compensate for US defensive improvements. The question, too, was whether analysts were focusing on the "right" numbers. The mass killing of civilians by Sunni insurgents in suicide bomb attacks was an important measure of sectarian tension. But it spoke little to the consolidating of gains by Shiite militia (for instance, in Sunni neighborhoods) as revealed by the location (dumped or buried) and disposition (shot or mutilated) of bodies found around Baghdad. In July 2005, the Baghdad morgue alone received 1,100 bodies—90 percent of them bearing signs of torture or execution. By December, the number stood at 780 bodies, the majority displaying bullet holes and torture wounds.[42]

Fourth, the United States was challenged because the insurgents—much like the Vietcong—were largely self-reliant. Al-Qaeda–linked groups had access to foreign financing, and indigenous insurgent groups had reportedly received funding from rich Sunni expatriates (in Syria, for example). But their profitable illicit dealings within Iraq included robbery, kidnapping, smuggling, extortion, and diversion of oil revenues (Wahab 2006). With their entrepreneurship, these groups could pay operatives for their services—for example, planting IEDs—and maintain and expand their ranks by promising a financial return. The self-reliance of the insurgents owed, in no small part, to their relatively small financial requirements, courtesy of their ties to the local community, small-unit operations, and abundant firearms and bomb-making materials.

Fifth, the United States, as in Vietnam, could not rely upon indigenous security forces for support. Iraqi troops sometimes refused to fight and even defected to the enemy under fire; suspicions about their loyalty (concerns that they were leaking information to insurgent or militia groups or providing false information to lead US troops into ambushes) made them unreliable partners at best. The effectiveness of Iraqi security forces was further hurt by their sectarian allegiances, which colored their behavior toward the local population, which responded to these provocations, sometimes in kind. (The Shiite-dominated Iraqi police force was resented and feared in Sunni communities; the Iraqi Army, though widely regarded as less sectarian than the police force, was nonetheless split among sectarian commands and units.) Without the aid of Iraqi security personnel (their language skills, cultural sensitivities, and potential relationships of trust with the local citizenry), it was difficult for the US military to obtain the knowledge necessary to court favor with the population, to appreciate local sensitivities that might potentially confound military operations, and to obtain the situational awareness that keeps soldiers alive, that is, a sense of knowing "when things just don't look right"—a child standing on a corner with a cell phone, for instance. Heavy rotation of military personnel made acquiring this sort of knowledge even harder. Without the aid of indigenous forces, it was also difficult to "hold" ground. Military operations suffered because Iraqi troops could not (or would not) maintain control of areas of Baghdad, for instance, when US and Iraqi forces went on the offensive there in the summer of 2006.[43]

Sixth, the United States was challenged in Iraq, as in Vietnam, by its inability to win popular support. The obstacles to public acceptance were considerable. These included a reticent and disbelieving public that was predisposed to view foreign troops as an "occupation" force, active insurgent efforts to intimidate the populace and capitalize politically on the US military's missteps, US reliance upon sectarian Iraqi security units, and cultural, religious, linguistic, and physical barriers that bred hostility and misunderstanding between US troops and the local public. Tension and distrust were perhaps unavoidable in the early postoccupation period given the close links between the militants and their popular base. Still, US troops—under some commanders more than others—were far too trigger-happy, aggressive in house-to-house searches, and willing to place the safety of troops over considerations for the norms and mores of Iraqi society. True, early awareness that "cordon and sweep" operations—which amounted to "grabbing whole villages"[44]—were alienating the local population convinced the US commander, Lieutenant General Ricardo Sanchez, to halt them in August 2003 and to shift from large-scale to more precise operations aimed at verified targets (Wright et al. 2008, 122). Moreover, some commanders, including General David Petraeus in Mosul and Colonel H. R. McMaster in Tal Afar, had early success with a counterinsurgency approach (Bensahel 2008, 96). But large-scale military action continued, most notably in Fallujah in 2004; any progress achieved was lost, then, to an overall strategy that emphasized defeating the insurgency. As Kahl (2007a, 174) concludes, "Efforts to protect the Iraqi population were ad hoc, varied tremendously from unit to unit, and were underresourced; most units defined the requirements of counterinsurgency solely in terms of 'the enemy' and deployed overwhelming conventional firepower to kill or capture a growing list of 'former regime elements,' 'anti-Iraqi forces,' 'bad guys,' and 'terrorists.'" The US military did not take a hard look at the positive experience in places like Tal Afar "to discern if the success there might be replicated elsewhere" (Ricks 2009, 160). For many Iraqis, continuing Coalition tactics made the occupation the central issue in the conflict (on this, see chapter 3).

Seventh, the United States was challenged, as in Vietnam, by difficulties addressing the basic demands of the local population. The US military recognized that giving locals a stake in reduced violence was essential for establishing security. So from almost the beginning, it sought, through its stabilization and reconstruction efforts, to provide aid, essential services, governance assistance, and other support to the Iraqi public (Wright et al. 2008, 117–118). These efforts continued, albeit unevenly, throughout the US war effort. For example, after clearing Fallujah of insurgents in November 2004, the US military distributed cash payments to the many residents who had suffered property loss. The test, however, was to provide reconstruction support when the military had a limited capacity to initiate and manage these operations and when security concerns militated against close relationships with the local population, pushed toward inflicting damage rather than repairing it, and diverted personnel to fighting the enemy (see chapter 3).

In the end, the US military struggled to make do with what it had, and what it knew. As in Vietnam, it eventually adjusted its approach. That scarcely made the challenge ahead any less daunting.

The "Surge" Period and Its Aftermath (2007–)

US military challenges in Iraq arguably stemmed from the initial failure to adopt a counterinsurgency approach. But the eventual application of these principles in Iraq does not provide much reason for optimism if US success in war hinges on overcoming the challenges of asymmetric warfare and "winning" the support of a local population. In short, the US experience speaks to the *limits* of US military capability.

This section establishes that the US success in Iraq—even now, of unclear duration—owed as much to a confluence of felicitous circumstances as it did to a US military command with the foresight and flexibility to capitalize on these conditions. This is clear from examining both the challenges and slow progress of the surge and the conditions, peculiar to the Iraq conflict, that worked to the advantage of the United States. The latter include the rallying of former Sunni insurgents in opposition to jihadist groups (the Awakening Movement), the de facto separation of hostile populations in key areas of conflict, and the "standdown" of a large portion of the Mahdi Army. This section concludes by examining the lessons that the surge offers for counterinsurgency.

The Surge in US Forces

As commonly understood, the change in US policy and its ultimate success resulted from a "surge" in US troop activity—when, in early 2007, the United States started deploying approximately 30,000 additional troops in Iraq, bringing the total number of US troops in the country to 162,000 by August of that year. Bush administration officials credited the surge for the reduced violence that followed—quite understandably, after withstanding strong criticism of the announced troop increase; even sympathetic critics had publicly questioned the wisdom of such a modest force augmentation. The additional combat troops represented a small fraction of US forces then in Iraq. Indeed, overall personnel strength in August 2007, when the stronger US force was in place, matched the US totals at the end of 2005, just months before the onset of the civil war.[45] The larger force was still small relative to the size and geographical distribution of the Iraqi population and—more important—the monumental task at hand. Although the United States committed 10,000 troops to the battle against insurgents in Fallujah in November 2004, the US force, then numbering 138,000, proved unable to prevent the migration of insurgents to other parts of the country and back to Fallujah again. Thus, the obvious question was whether the augmented US force—even with backing from Iraqi security forces—was large enough to cordon off key trouble spots, go on the offensive, and hold ground to prevent insurgents from reemerging in the same place.

Unquestionably, the surge contributed to US success. The key evidence in this regard is the slow pace of progress and the tremendous challenge that US forces faced even after the surge force was in place. A lesser force would have been tested more severely—perhaps fatally. Indeed, the extension of US control took considerably longer than predicted in part because US forces were redirected, when required, to reinforce US efforts in other contested areas. So the obvious lack of slack in US troop strength supports the counterfactual logic that US forces would not have achieved their eventual gains without the forces that the surge made available. This is apparent because time was not the ally of US forces: US military commanders had stressed that, given US deployment schedules and global commitments, US forces in Iraq could be maintained at their peak-surge levels for only a matter of months. Of course, the same logic suggests that the eventual reductions in Iraqi violence could not have been achieved had not one or more other factors turned in the US military's favor, as we shall see—a conclusion that is strengthened, again, by prior US failings absent these conditions.

With a boost from the surge, US forces left their barracks in the early months of 2007 to assume positions in and around Baghdad—the natural focus of the initial US effort, as Iraq's main urban area, the seat of the national government, home to Iraq's diverse communities, and "ground zero" of the jihadist suicide bombing campaign.[46] As the US military presence in the capital increased by 10,000 troops over the levels deployed at the beginning of the year, the intent was first, to push back insurgent and militia influence by directly engaging hostile groups; second, to engage in clearing operations (aimed at weapons caches and so on) to secure the gains achieved in battle and then to hold secured areas. Drawing from counterinsurgency principles, the approach was to establish a visible (and vulnerable) military presence in the capital through forward basing and patrol centers and engage in outreach to local leaders, businesses, and residents. The hope was to position US forces to patrol areas where hostile groups had been or could again become active. Once community members became convinced that they were safe from insurgent and militia groups, US forces hoped to obtain their cooperation in targeting and disarming militants and disrupting their attacks. This approach incorporated elements of an urban "ink spot" strategy that harked back to the idea of "strategic hamlets." These passive defensive efforts turned parts of the city into fortresses, with blast walls, roadblocks, and security checkpoints disrupting traffic into (and insurgent activities out of) entire neighborhoods.

The effort in Baghdad emerged as part of a larger and more complex security operation. The United States now sought (a) to attack and disrupt the operations of Sunni insurgents and Shiite militias within Baghdad; (b) to attack the bases of operation, mostly in areas surrounding the capital that housed al-Qaeda personnel, weapons caches, and bomb-making factories, from which attacks on Baghdad were mounted; and (c) to attack al-Qaeda forces in neighboring provinces, including Anbar (long the center of Sunni resistance to the United States) and Diyala, a province to the northeast of Baghdad, in order to deny groups fleeing Baghdad new areas in which to encamp.[47] Inasmuch as US forces had battled a resistance that could easily melt away or move to new areas, the principle was for security forces to stay put, with support from Iraqi troops and police, and to narrow progressively the areas around the country in and from which insurgents could operate. Such a strategy would presumably produce heavy fighting when insurgents ran out of places to hide or achieved the requisite critical mass to counterattack. Predictably, efforts to cordon off Baghdad contributed, for instance, to concentrated insurgent activity in Diyala Province.

The United States gained ground in Baghdad, but slowly and with intense fighting. Three months into the Baghdad security plan, only roughly a third of the city's 457 neighborhoods were secure: 156 were in the "disrupt" phase, in which US forces attacked militants but had not yet established control over the area; 155 were in the "clear" phase, in which the military moved block by block to clear an area of hostile personnel and weapons; 128 were in the "control" phase, in which areas were protected by US and Iraqi forces from a reintroduction of militants; and only 18 neighborhoods were in the "retain" phase, in which security depends more heavily on the Iraqi force contribution.[48] Some neighborhoods proved difficult to hold, as Shiite fighters moved back into areas once US forces moved on to other neighborhoods.[49] US forces could launch attacks to disrupt militant activities but not big enough to clear Shiite neighborhoods in Sadr City, which remained largely under militia control.[50] By the end of June 2007, the US military command determined that only half of Baghdad was under US and Iraqi military control.[51] Even the walled Green Zone that housed the US Embassy and government buildings was increasingly under mortar and rocket attack from surrounding Shiite and Sunni neighborhoods.[52]

The militants were well prepared to respond to the US operation and often seized the initiative. US troops were targeted, with a dramatic increase in roadside bombings, rocket and mortar attacks, and direct fire with rocket-propelled grenades.[53] In Baghdad, the Pentagon calculated, for the month of May 2007, that the violence included 286 instances—almost 10 a day—of "complex ambush" (these suggest a degree of coordination, planning, and tactical adeptness), 1,348 IED attacks (compared to 1,126 IEDs found), 102 vehicle-borne IED attacks, 529 mortar attacks, and 1,499 instances of small-arms fire.[54] Although the authorities claimed progress in the drop in civilian deaths in the capital,[55] civilians continued to be targeted by Sunni insurgents.[56] Suicide bomb attacks moved into parts of Baghdad that had formerly been relatively tranquil,[57] and proved that insurgents could attack anywhere if the targets were sufficiently appealing. An illustration of this was the June 2007 suicide bomb attack on a Baghdad hotel inside the heavily fortified Green Zone where Sunni leaders from the Anbar Salvation Council, which was aligned with US forces, had convened.[58] Equally troubling through the first half of 2007 was the discovery of bodies, bearing signs of torture and execution, that spoke to the less conspicuous—but no less deadly—battle for political and military control of the capital and beyond. In the four months between January and June, an average of 295 bodies per month were found in Baghdad alone—nearly as many as found in January (321), with the numbers trending upward.[59]

Progress in Baghdad was slowed by a need to divert forces to other fronts, as insurgents relocated and directed their attacks to other parts of the country. Consequently, the number of attacks on US forces in Iraq rose substantially above levels recorded in other (post-occupation) periods of similar duration.[60]

US troops and insurgents were engaged in fighting in a full circle around Baghdad. In Anbar, to the west, 4,000 US troops sought to disrupt insurgent attacks on Baghdad and help end insurgent activities in the province.[61] By July 2007, 15,000 US troops were operating southeast of Baghdad and in three southern provinces.[62] Thousands of US and Iraqi troops moved against the Sunni insurgent stronghold of Arab Jabour in Baghdad's southeastern outskirts, where the United States dropped heavy bombs and used ground troops to block escape routes, engage insurgents, and perform house-to-house sweeps for weapons.[63] Further south, US forces were active in the so-called Triangle of Death (mostly Babil Province), a challenging area with a mixed population and battle zones located on fault lines between rival sects and tribes.[64] In Operation Arrowhead Ripper in June 2007, one of the largest operations since Fallujah in 2004, the US military sent 10,000 soldiers to Diyala Province to combat a robust insurgency. Amidst the province's palm groves and orchards, the resistance established its resiliency. The focus of the US effort was Baqubah, the provincial capital—a city of 300,000 people just thirty-five miles northeast of Baghdad and the self-proclaimed capital of the Islamic State of Iraq.[65] There, the jihadists issued decrees from Sunni mosques; closed down barber shops, coffee houses, and music stores; and tried forcibly to marry into the tribal community.[66] Although US forces hoped to cordon off the city and trap the militants inside, the insurgents proved elusive.[67] Most of their leaders and a good number of fighters fled with advance knowledge of the US attack (Kagan 2007, 9), while others hid among the city's residents. Between mid-June and mid-August, however, the neighborhoods of Baqubah were the scene of some of the most intense fighting of the Iraq War (Hamilton 2008, 4). After establishing control in the city, US forces moved against other insurgent concentrations in the province.

In the provincial fighting, insurgents proved well equipped, alert, and savvy. They employed decoy IEDs with recognizable signatures (such as pressure plates) to slow down patrols in order to expose them to coordinated attacks by mortars, rocket-propelled grenades, and machine guns;[68] they engaged in complex attacks on US military outposts and forces (including aircraft) arriving in support after insurgent bomb attacks;[69] and they set lethal traps, such as by wiring houses (so-called house-borne IEDs) to explode in daisy chains after US troops were lured to the premises.[70] The US military was now better prepared, though, to handle such operations. In particular, it became increasingly adept at thwarting IED attacks: by mid-2007, bombers now required six times as many bombs to inflict a single casualty as they needed when IEDs were first employed in Iraq.[71] But the insurgents retained many advantages. They could produce and plant large numbers of inexpensive devices while US troops were obliged to cope with new enemy tactics, to move cautiously to guard against potential traps and explosives, to rely on temperamental and expensive offsetting technologies (for example, explosive-sniffing robots), and to weigh intelligence information obtained from locals of varying degrees of trustworthiness. So the increased US effectiveness in fighting the bombs did not offset the increased effectiveness of the weapons: IEDs—many large and deeply buried—accounted for roughly 70 percent of the approximately 125 US fatalities in May (twice the share of February 2007) and upped the US fatality-to-casualty ratio.[72] In the three deadliest provinces, from February to May 2007, monthly US troop deaths increased dramatically to 50 in Baghdad, 17 in Salahuddin Province, and 26 in Diyala Province, where less than a dozen US soldiers had been killed between October 2005 and October 2006. In Babil, south of Baghdad, 13 troops were killed in May, when no US troop deaths had been recorded in the prior period.[73]

As civilian deaths dropped in Baghdad with the US surge, they increased elsewhere in Iraq.[74] The civilian death toll mounted in part because insurgents picked vulnerable spots, typically in the northern part of Iraq, to inflict mass casualties: the toll in single attacks included 150 fatalities in Tal Afar in March, 140 fatalities in Baghdad in April, 140 fatalities in Amerli in July, and over 250 fatalities in Qataniyah and Jazeera in August.[75] As in prior years, data on civilian casualties varied by source,[76] but the overall civilian toll was staggering. The 1,558 deaths per month recorded in June and July was in line with the monthly average of 1,943 for the prior two months and the 1,758 monthly average for February and March.[77] Based on Pentagon reports, the overall number of Iraqi civilian casualties (including those killed and wounded) remained at relatively constant levels from the start of the surge in February through August 2007.[78]

Military progress was discernible, however, in various statistics. By early June 2007, the military had purportedly uncovered 2,500 weapons caches and killed or captured 20,000 suspected insurgents.[79] By the end of the year, all indicators agreed that the levels of violence toward US and Iraqi security personnel and civilians had dropped dramatically across Iraq. The top US commander in Iraq estimated that the number of weekly attacks—by mortar, sniper, or IED—had decreased by 60 percent from levels in June.[80] By June 2008, monthly civilian death rates were at their lowest point since the start of the war. Indeed, deaths linked to ethnic and sectarian killing in Baghdad in summer 2008 were 2 percent of the levels recorded there in the prior summer.[81] Progress was discernible as well in reductions in the number of foreign insurgents infiltrating into the country (twenty a month in the summer of 2008, compared to over five times that number a year earlier), indications of a shift in al-Qaeda's focus to Afghanistan, and strong recriminations within al-Qaeda in Iraq over its failing leadership.[82]

Still, the insurgency continued through 2007 and 2008 even in places where the United States had conducted operations to disrupt militant activities and hold ground. Diyala remained an insurgent refuge. Consequently, Diyala was again a target of a major US operation (Phantom Phoenix) when, in January 2008, 24,000 US troops, 50,000 Iraqi soldiers, 80,000 Iraqi policeman, and 15,000 US-backed volunteers took the offensive in four northern Iraqi provinces.[83] Despite military operations, in late 2007, that allowed US forces (with Iraqi support) to gain control of the province's urban and rural areas and its roads and rivers, Sunni insurgents and Shiite militia continued to conduct attacks in the province through 2008 (Kagan 2007, 2).[84] Having regrouped in rural areas, the insurgents were still able to project their power into various cities, including Baqubah and Baghdad (Hamilton 2008, 4–5). US forces remained active in other prior battle zones. In January 2008, US B-1 bombers and other aircraft dropped tens of thousands of pounds of explosives to the south of Baghdad—hitting Arab Jabour, again, among the targets. Indeed, Diyala was the target of still another US offensive in July 2008 aimed largely at al-Qaeda–affiliated groups.[85] It was also one of two provinces (the other being Nineveh) where US military officials believed US troops had to retain an active urban presence after June 2009, when the US military was required, under formal agreement with the Iraqi government, to vacate Iraqi cities (see chapter 5).[86]

As long as insurgents could find refuge, the attacks—especially on civilian targets—would never stop entirely. It was simply too hard to defend every vulnerable human target against the notoriously stealthy attackers. This point was driven home in a series of attacks in July 2008, when four female suicide bombers exploited regional customs preventing male soldiers from frisking them and attacked crowds at a Shiite religious commemoration in Baghdad and a political demonstration in the northern city of Kirkuk.[87] For the jihadists, the payoff from these attacks was hard to resist, as their effects resonated beyond the immediate carnage—the hundreds of people injured and killed. The Kirkuk attack—aimed at Kurds who were protesting their "under-representation" in a provincial power-sharing arrangement—fed animosity toward Sunni Arabs who had progressively taken control of the city under Saddam Hussein. Another dozen people were killed, then, in the clashes between Kurds, Arabs, and Turkmens that erupted after the bombing.[88] Therefore, despite the growing calm throughout Iraq, terrorist attacks killed over 5,000 civilians in 2008.[89] Suicide bombings at high-profile targets and mass gatherings continued into 2009. The attacks occurred even in fortified parts of the capital and took an increasing toll as Iraqi forces assumed control of their country's security. In the first third of the year, over a thousand civilians were killed in violent attacks across Iraq. The numbers increased monthly into April, when Shiites were targeted in a suicide bombing campaign that killed over 450 people nationwide.[90] Although the civilian fatality levels recorded for May approached a post-invasion low, hundreds of people were killed across Iraq in bomb attacks in the two-week period leading up to the negotiated US pullback from Iraqi cities on June 30, 2009.[91]

Although the US surge strategy was announced in January 2007 with the goal of turning all of Iraq's eighteen provinces over to the Iraq government by November 2007, only twelve provinces were officially under government control with the US handover of Babil Province in October 2008. The slow progress testified to challenges that would test any military force.[92] At best, the US military could hope that conditions would conspire to assist the stabilization effort. Fortunately for the military, these hopes had been realized in Iraq.

Facilitative Conditions: Explaining Success

The US troop surge allowed the United States to capitalize on these favorable developments: (a) the Sunni Awakening movement, (b) the de facto partitioning of the country through ethnic and sectarian cleansing, and (c) Moqtada al-Sadr's willingness to stand down the Mahdi Army. Each of these factors contributed to the eventual reduction in violence in the country. Significantly, each contributed only by creating conditions that could lead to an eruption in conflict at some point in the future.

The Sunni Awakening. An active US presence in Anbar Province, the stronghold of the insurgency, failed to quell the violence. But the United States started to reap the benefits of the Sunni "Awakening" movement when the Anbar Salvation Council, a tribal alliance, was formed in late 2006 to confront the jihadist groups that had taken hold in the province. Relations between the indigenous Sunnis and the foreign-led jihadists had always been tense, thanks to the question of who would control illicit enterprises such as smuggling, the general secularism of the local Sunni population, and the jihadists' harsh, punitive tactics.

The costs to the locals of supporting the jihadists were not offset by any noticeable benefits, especially after the empty promises of the jihadists were exposed (Biddle 2008b). Their war against the Shiite population in Baghdad had not yielded victory; instead, it was the Sunni masses that suffered most from displacement, as we shall see.

Although US military commanders did not capitalize on tension between the Sunni groups that surfaced years earlier, they made the most of the discovery in late 2006 that groups in Anbar Province were in serious disarray. US military officials seized on this opportunity to play the non-jihadist insurgents against the jihadists responsible for so much of the indiscriminate killing of Iraq civilians (ICG 2008a, 9). With the blessing and promotion of tribal leaders, the US military obtained combat support from militia groups, groups that included former Sunni insurgents.

As insurgents were pulled from the active resistance and the new US-sponsored security groups disrupted jihadist operations, the level of hostility in Anbar declined. What was called the "Anbar model" was then applied widely to other predominantly Sunni parts of the country including portions of Baghdad, Babil Province south of the capital, Salahuddin Province to the north of the capital, and Diyala Province, which had become a prime battleground in Iraq.[93] In Diyala, US forces in Operation Arrowhead Ripper worked closely with former Sunni insurgents, including the Islamic Army and 1920 Revolution Brigades, who helped US forces identify al-Qaeda members and their facilities.[94] The form of the model varied from place to place, given the varied complexion of the aligning groups—their ties to tribes, former insurgent groups, and the local community. In Diyala, for instance, recruitment drew from multiple models and proceeded slowly, due to the absence of a coherent tribal structure.[95] Sometimes tribal leaders negotiated alignments with US troops; other times the new alliances emerged spontaneously, announced in a hail of bullets when US troops happened upon skirmishes between local Iraqis and jihadist fighters. US soldiers would stand aside, try to assess the situation, and offer support when needed.[96] The profusion of these groups was clear from the variety of names assigned to or taken up by them. US officials eventually dubbed them Concerned Citizens Councils, most likely to legitimize and "civilize" them for publicity purposes. By October 2008, when Baghdad took charge of these hundreds of groups, they were widely known by their Iraqi name, the Sons of Iraq.

With good reason, US military personnel were wary of their newfound allies and questioned whether the groups should be supplied arms, made to conform with US military practices in the handling of suspects, or given amnesty for their past attacks on US soldiers. Yet the needs and opportunities of the moment generally won out, and these groups were given the means and license to operate, for one compelling reason.[97] As Nagl (2005, xiv) observes, local forces have an understanding of language, culture, families, tribes, and behavior that allows them to operate more effectively, and face less resistance, than foreign troops can. Consequently, "It is perhaps only a slight exaggeration to suggest that, on their own, foreign forces cannot defeat an insurgency; the best they can hope for is to create the conditions that will enable local forces to win it for them." An alliance with these local elements would give the United States a capability, otherwise unobtainable, to combat the very worst of the insurgents—those responsible for mass killings of Iraqi civilians in suicide bomb attacks. The recruits knew who the jihadists were and where and how they operated—their mode of operation, attack plans, and weapon cache locations. As one US officer described their relative contribution, "We provide capabilities that they don't have. And the locals know who belongs and who doesn't. It doesn't matter how long we're here, I'll never know. And we'll never fit in."[98] At the very least, working with former adversaries promised to reduce the pool of insurgents and their effectiveness (given personal information obtained on the new recruits), should they one day turn on their US allies. So the US military command accepted its good fortune—fighting manpower, with eyes and ears on the violent opposition. It backed the Awakening movement with combat support, equipment (vehicles, handcuffs, ammunition), and salaries to militia members, and it made concessions that included amnesty to former insurgents for their past offenses and releasing detainees arrested for shooting at US troops or planting roadside bombs.[99]

In Anbar Province, dramatic progress from the new effort was visible very quickly. By May 2007, the size of the police force increased from 2,000 to 14,500 officers in large part by drawing on tribal recruits.[100] The growth of the force brought a positive return. In Ramadi, where the number of local police officers increased from 200 to 7,400, attacks decreased from about thirty a day to less than one attack a day by the late summer of 2007.[101] In Fallujah, despite its tumultuous past, relative calm prevailed thanks to a city-wide vehicle ban and the use of concrete barricades to divide the city into districts, guarded by local Sunni police and "neighborhood watch" groups supported and directed by US Marines.[102] It is striking that the violence against US forces dropped considerably in Anbar Province in the months *before* the surge and that US troop deaths in May 2007 fell below the numbers recorded in February 2007, in opposition to the pattern seen in the other provinces adjacent to Baghdad.[103] The effective contribution of the Awakening to the US effort was clear from the contrasting US experience elsewhere, for instance, in Diyala, where the United States had more difficulty recruiting against the insurgency, and Mosul, the capital of northern Nineveh Province, where Sunni Arabs feared Kurdish territorial designs. In Mosul, members of the threatened Sunni Arab majority showed little inclination to cooperate with the US military, the Iraqi government, or Iraqi security forces, which were largely Kurdish in composition.[104] Not only did violence continue in these places, Sunni leaders trying to make peace with Shiites and Kurds were also targeted in suicide bomb attacks.[105]

The eventual success in Anbar and other provinces reduced the competing demands on available US forces and limited the receptive portions of the country where the insurgents could operate.[106] But with this success came new concerns. US officials were increasingly troubled about the long-term future of the Awakening militia, which would number 100,000 by late 2008. Not the least of US concerns was that the Baghdad government was exceedingly reluctant to embrace the movement. Iraqi officials could accept the Awakening in restive Anbar Province, given the movement's tribal roots and the relative distance of the province from the capital. They were loath, however, to accept Sunni militia groups operating in and around Baghdad, where unrepentant insurgents, unbound by tribal affiliations, could act under the cover of these groups (or worse, in police uniforms) to threaten or attack the Shiite population or the central government. Indeed, many Baghdad militia members were former Baathists who had served in Saddam Hussein's security forces.[107] Whereas government officials challenged the principle of a private force operating outside the government, it was nevertheless unwilling to integrate more than a small fraction of militia members into regular Iraqi security units (about 20 percent, according to the Iraqi prime minister).[108] Of the 54,000 Sons of Iraq operating in Baghdad when the Iraqi government officially took control of these units in October 2008, only 6 percent had obtained jobs in regular units.[109] (By the time of the US pullback from Iraqi cities in mid-2009, the Iraqi government had found positions nationally for roughly 5 percent of the Sons of Iraq.)[110]

Ominous signs emerged. A split was apparent in Diyala between the tribally based elements that provided rural security and former insurgents in Baqubah whose loyalty was questioned.[111] Elsewhere in the country, groups were apparently starting to splinter from the allure of lucrative criminal activities.[112] More troublesome was the unabated hostility between Sunni groups and the Shiite

Baghdad government. Former Sunni insurgents expressed animosity toward the central government and its US supporters whose lavish promises to militia members had mostly gone unmet. In February 2008, thousands of Sunni fighters left their posts in Diyala to protest the Iraqi government's failure to replace the province's Shiite police chief for (supposedly) resisting the hiring of Sunnis and for supporting sectarian violence against them.[113] The Iraqi government response was not reassuring to those who hoped that it would accommodate the Sunni groups. The Iraqi government suggested, in word and deed, that these groups had outlived their usefulness. In August 2008, security forces apparently linked to the prime minister targeted Sunni leaders in a violent raid on the governor's office in Diyala Province (Domergue and Cochrane 2009, 8), west of Baghdad, moved against hundreds of insurgents that had allied with the United States.[114] As a wary fighter in Baghdad summarized his militia's position relative to the Iraqi government and al-Qaeda after the handover of the militia to the government, "We are trapped between two enemies."[115] Once the Iraqi government took full control of these groups, suspicions frequently gave way to protest and acrimony as Awakening units complained about unpaid wages, the targeting of group leaders by the government, and the government's "true" intentions.[116]

So the question was whether Iraqi security forces could contain the potential violence that attacking—or ignoring—these groups could unleash. With that concern in mind, the US military sought to prevent the Iraqi government from arresting former insurgents based on old warrants and prepared to provide salaries to group members in the event that the Iraqi government defaulted. Even with the transfer of Sons of Iraq units to the Iraqi government, the US military supervised the distribution of paychecks to the militia and pressured the Iraqi government to reverse its decision to impose a salary cut on members.[117] From the US perspective, the Iraqi government was courting disaster, for what made these militia valuable to the security effort also made them dangerous.[118]

Ethnic/Sectarian Cleansing. Lurking within the statistics on civilian casualties— heavily influenced by the jihadist suicide bomb campaign—were the effects of the less visible but deadly intimidation campaign by Sunni insurgent and Shiite militia groups. Responding to attention-getting killings and threats against local residents, Sunnis and Shiites sought sanctuary in other parts of a city, the country, or the Middle East. The exodus, propelled by the cleansing campaigns, effectively partitioned the country along "ethno-sectarian" lines. In Baghdad, Sunnis were often forced to leave their neighborhoods and coerced into selling their property directly to the Mahdi Army or other Shiite buyers at a fraction of the former property value.[119] Ironically, the United States inadvertently abetted the cleansing of both groups with a crackdown on Sunni groups that limited their freedom to operate and recruit (ICG 2008b, 2–4) and by constructing barriers that trapped some inhabitants within an inhospitable enclave. A concrete wall built around a Sunni district of Baghdad, partly to protect against attacks by Shiite militias, had the unintended effect of freeing the local Sunnis to attack Shiite residents. As the US officer in charge put it, "Amiriyah became one of the safest areas in Baghdad for Sunnis but lethal for the few remaining Shiites."[120] By the end of 2007, the US military estimated that there were 350,000 displaced persons residing in Baghdad alone, 80 percent of whom were original Baghdad residents. The Iraqi Red Crescent Society (IRCS) placed the number of internally displaced persons in Baghdad at 1.4 million.[121] The demographic shifts in the capital reached staggering proportions. Most of the formerly mixed areas, especially east of the Tigris river, came under Shiite control. For their part, Sunnis extended their control over mixed and even predominantly Shiite neighborhoods in western and southern Baghdad.[122]

The demographics shifted dramatically in other parts of the country. Shiites, who once accounted for almost half of the population of Baqubah, accounted for only one fifth of the town's population by early 2007.[123] By the end of 2007, around 150,000 people in Diyala Province had reportedly left their homes—a pattern that was replicated in provinces around Iraq. With 60,000 Iraqis estimated to have fled their homes in each month of 2007, 10 percent of Iraq's population was said to have become war refugees by the year's end.[124] As in other sectarian conflicts, migration resulted in massive relocation of the threatened population into overburdened parts of the country. By October 2007, the head of the local IRCS office claimed that many hundreds of thousands of displaced Shiites were living in Najaf, mostly in squatter towns outside the city.[125] The refugee flow spilled into neighboring countries. Although estimates varied by source, the data were consistent in order of magnitude. In mid-2008, a UN source claimed that well over 4 million Iraqis had fled their homes since the beginning of the war—1.2 million to Syria, 500,000 to Jordan, and 350,000 to Egypt, Lebanon, and the Gulf states. Of the refugees, 2 million refugees were said to be displaced internally within Iraq.[126]

If ethno-sectarian cleansing had an "upside," it was that partitioning kept warring communities apart. As one US intelligence officer noted, murders declined when Sunnis left because, basically, "they ran out of people to kill."[127] For the United States, the upside was a reduced profile of Shiite militia groups in formerly contested areas. With the US surge, especially intense fighting occurred, in fact, in the mixed Shiite-Sunni neighborhoods of western Baghdad, as militants linked to al-Sadr sought to push Sunnis from their areas of control. The 21,000 US troops in Baghdad were most active on "fault lines" between Sunni and Shiite neighborhoods.[128]

The negative effects of a mixed population were clear to the north in Mosul, the second-largest city in Iraq. Even as violence dropped with the surge through-out much of Iraq, tension among a variety of groups (most explosively, between Arabs and Kurds) combined with the limited US presence and unfavorable geog-raphy to complicate the US stabilization effort in that city (ICG 2000a, 8). The United States found it extremely difficult to combat an active insurgency enabled by a partisan population. Although much of the violence in Mosul was initiated by groups with ties to al-Qaeda, various populations were vulnerable to attack amidst the competing claims and overlapping conflicts of contending ethno-sectarian groups. The 60 percent of the population of 2.8 million that was Sunni Arab harbored resentments against the local Iraqi police force, which, like a quarter of the city's population, was largely Kurdish.[129]

After overstaying their welcome elsewhere or simply longing for home, the refugees started to return (Lischer 2008, 107–109). In October 2007 alone, Iraqis were arriving from Syria at a rate of at least a thousand per day.[130] But there was little evidence of a return to heterogeneity in the newly homogenized regions. With their properties expropriated, neighborhoods changed, and fears undimin-ished, the refugee population accepted—at least tacitly—de facto partition of their country. By November 2007, only 20,000 people were said to have returned to their original homes in Iraq.[131] The demographic shifts in Baghdad, which had become "ground zero" in the cleansing campaign, also appeared to harden.[132] In July 2008, the Iraqi government estimated that only around 5 percent of the fami-lies that had fled their residences in the capital had returned. The number of families that remained displaced in Amiriya alone exceeded the number of fami-lies that had returned to their homes throughout Baghdad.[133]

Accommodating the returnees left the government doubly challenged. The government lacked the means to provide essential services to the large homeless population and to mediate the disputes that would certainly arise when people tried to reclaim their former homes and other lost property. The government was not well prepared to adjudicate the potential legal squabbles arising from prior confiscations of property or exchanges made under duress. It also lacked the ca-pability to enforce edicts and settlements, to protect residents from intimidation, or to manage the violence that would ensue when returning refugees encountered residents and militia intent on keeping their neighborhoods pure or protecting their newly acquired possessions. The everpresent danger was that Iraqi security forces would become a party, then, to sectarian conflict.[134] The decidedly Sunni character of the various refugee populations (including those in Syria and Jordan) only increased the danger (Margesson et al. 2008, 18).

The Shiite Stand-Down. Al-Sadr's response to the surge was somewhat unexpected. He did not fight the surge; in fact, he appeared to be in complicity with US forces.

Signs of al-Sadr's public turn from militant sectarianism were increasingly apparent. While his militia were targeted in the surge by US military forces seeking control of Baghdad neighborhoods, al-Sadr disappeared from public view for nearly four months. He also engaged in a housecleaning of his militia force (purging it of rogue elements engaged in activities that damaged the militia's reputation)[135] and tacitly cooperated with the US operation by allowing US troops to establish a base in Sadr City.[136] Then, when the Askariya Shrine's twin minarets (they had survived the 2006 attack) were destroyed in a bomb attack in June 2007, al-Sadr called for a forceful but restrained response—a mass pilgrimage through Sunni-controlled territory to the scene of the destruction bringing a message of "love, peace, security, and construction."[137] He engaged, as well, in outreach to Sunni groups and religious leaders.[138] In his words, "I say to the Sunnis that we are brothers, and the occupier divided us in order to make the Iraqi people weak. . . . I am ready to cooperate with them at every level, I'm stretching my hand out to them."[139]

With the progressive loss of Shiite neighborhoods in Baghdad to US and Iraqi forces, the Mahdi Army, now in retreat, was forced to relocate to southern Iraq, where the Mahdi Army had long vied with other Shiite militias for control. Abductions, bombings, and firefights erupted as the Mahdi Army competed with the Supreme Council and the rival Fadhila party, which had splintered from the Sadrist movement, over control of provincial governance, ministries, local security forces, and lucrative provincial resources—foremost among them Basra's profitable oil sector and various extortion and smuggling operations.[140] The violence escalated in the summer of 2007, when the Shiite militia sought to fill the void created by the retreat of British forces from Basra, Iraq's third-largest city,[141] and reached a critical juncture in Karbala in August 2007. In this holy city, tensions between Mahdi Army fighters and militias linked to the Supreme Council erupted in a bloody shootout that led to the deaths of many dozens of religious pilgrims caught in the crossfire. The resulting outcry from the attacks and the government crackdown on his militia led al-Sadr to announce a suspension in offensive operations. He also expressed his intent to reevaluate the future of his armed forces by directing the Mahdi Army "to suspend all its activities for six months until it is restructured in a way that helps honor the principles for which it is formed."[142] Recognizing that the violence severely hurt his image and that a ceasefire created opportunities to flush out those who challenged his command, al-Sadr gave tacit approval to the US military to target rogue fighters who continued their attacks. The US military arrested hundreds of Mahdi Army leaders and members in Baghdad and the southern provinces of Iraq.[143] In return, the US military command appeared to go out of its way to praise al-Sadr's restraint and stress that it was only after "special groups" that violated the peace and engaged in criminal activities.[144]

The pressure was on al-Sadr. The US military was targeting elements of the Mahdi Army, which was losing ground to rivals, and members complained openly about their inability to respond.[145] His response, in February 2008, was to announce an extension of his ceasefire. The following month, the ceasefire was dramatically threatened, however, when the Iraqi government—with the apparent prodding of the Supreme Council, Prime Minister Nouri al-Maliki's close coalition partner—sent 15,000 Iraqi military and police (against US advice) against Sadrist forces in Basra (Cochrane 2008, 8).[146] The attack was viewed by al-Sadr's supporters as an attempt to weaken him politically before provincial elections that could give al-Sadr clout in governance.[147] The Iraqi offensive proved a near-total disaster for the government forces. With Iraqi government forces apparently battling an equal number of militia fighters, as much as a third of Iraqi troops refused to fight, and some Iraqi police officers joined forces with the militia.[148] Fortunately for the Iraqi government, the United States intervened in force. Still, the Mahdi Army held its ground in days of intense fighting and continued to operate checkpoints around the city and to take the fight to the Iraqi security forces.[149] Despite al-Sadr's ceasefire declaration, the fighting spread to other cities in Iraq, including Baghdad. The number of attacks in the capital in March rose to 631, over two and a half times the level in the prior month;[150] in the same month, civilian fatalities in Baghdad reached almost 500, approaching the levels recorded in September 2007, in the midst of the surge offensive.[151]

The violence subsided after roughly a week when al-Sadr ordered a halt to fighting. As one commentator aptly noted, "Perhaps more important than the manner in which the militia fought is the manner in which it stopped fighting," that is to say, "when Sadr speaks, the militia listens."[152] In the two days prior to the Iraqi government crackdown in Basra, the US military counted an average of 40 attacks on Coalition troops, Iraqi forces, and civilians throughout Iraq and 14 such attacks in Baghdad. Within three days of the crackdown, the number of daily attacks swelled to 138, with 89 occurring in Baghdad. When three days later al-Sadr ordered his militia to stand down, the number of attacks dropped the following day to 53 throughout Iraq and 20 in Baghdad.[153] Mahdi Army fighters withdrew from the streets, and US and Iraqi forces were left in control, both in Baghdad and across southern Iraq.

As the Mahdi Army withdrew from public view, US and Iraqi forces established their first significant presence in Sadr City. They provided services to a population that had depended on Sadrist largess and paid for it in protection money and inflated prices for goods under Mahdi Army control. But al-Sadr did not reject a military option. He threatened to engage in "open war" if the US and Iraqi government did not stop attacking Mahdi Army personnel in Baghdad and Basra, and he agreed to a negotiated end to the fighting in May 2008 only if roads were reopened in Sadr City and raids and arrests targeting the militia ceased.[154] Indeed, in mid-2008, he called for disbanding the Mahdi Army in favor of a small group—what would become the "Promised Day Brigade"—to combat US forces. Among the indicators of potential violence, then, were the Iraqi prime minister's threat of April 2008 to bar al-Sadr's followers from elections unless the Madhi Army disbanded,[155] sympathies toward al-Sadr expressed by Iraqi forces patrolling Sadr City,[156] growing hostility in Sadr City toward Iraqi Army units conducting raids against Mahdi Army fighters (who held their fire only in deference to al-Sadr),[157] and al-Sadr's threats to resume attacks against the US forces that remained in Iraq if the Iraqi government permitted US forces to stay in Iraq until 2011 under the terms of a negotiated agreement (see chapter 5).[158]

In the end, al-Sadr—with the backing of a militia (once 60,000 strong)—was able to dictate whether the country was at war or at peace.[159] In the words of a Mahdi Army commander, "If the Sayyid [an honorific for al-Sadr] ordered us, we would rise up right now . . . nothing would stop us."[160] US military officials tacitly acknowledged al-Sadr's power by referring to him in respectful terms[161] and by maintaining the pretense that the United States was only fighting "special groups" in Baghdad—not the Mahdi Army per se (despite evidence that regular Mahdi Army units were involved in the fighting).[162] As al-Sadr retreated again from public view, the question, as always, was whether he would reactivate his following and push to reassert control when conditions moved in his favor or threats mounted against him.[163] That al-Sadr remained an important force could be seen in January 2009 by the relatively strong showing, in provincial elections in a number of southern provinces, of his sponsored lists of candidates.[164]

A "Less-Than-Final" Analysis: Lessons for Counterinsurgency

The US conventional war on Iraq was a success when measured in narrow military terms. In short order, the United States defeated the Iraqi military and dismantled the ruthless Saddam Hussein regime. But it created an environment—a vacuum—in which an insurgency could grow and spread. Indeed, the same force-on-force tactics that allowed the United States to prevail quickly in conventional war helped create an even bigger challenge for the United States once it moved to suppress an insurgency that enjoyed relatively wide popular support and would likely win a war in which victory was determined by the relative costs invested and the capacity to endure (see chapter 4). Ironically, the United States designed its invasion strategy around considerations of "efficiency," but that choice created the very messy conditions that would require a huge (and potentially unprofitable) US investment in manpower and resources to rescue the effort in the several years to follow.

This is not to say that the United States would have produced a more stable outcome by intervening with a larger force and seeking to hold ground in Anbar, Diyala, Baghdad, and other provinces before the population had turned against the US occupying force. Without doubt, national violence built on its own momentum before eventually exploding when the Sunni insurgents employed tactics that were meant to spark a civil war. Had the United States intervened quickly, with the help of the Iraqi military, before lawlessness and political violence took hold, years of fighting and the staggering casualty levels were conceivably avoidable. Yet a large US military presence spread throughout the country would have been an easy and convenient target, politically and militarily, for those seeking to undermine the new Iraqi government or take the war to the West on the hospitable (home) turf of an Arab/Islamic country.

It is also unclear whether the United States could have prevented violence from erupting in Iraq with an early application of counterinsurgency principles. The al Qaeda–linked insurgents and Mahdi Army might still have enjoyed a wellspring of popular support to bedevil a US occupation force even had they not taken over cities and shown themselves for what they are. What is certain is that the initial US approach failed and that a strategy that drew from counterinsurgency principles worked in certain respects, after conditions in the country had changed. The common take on events is that the US military came to appreciate the mutual interdependence of military and political conditions in Iraq and then focused appropriately on popular needs rather than fighting insurgents. The US military shifted from a strategy that was accepting of even large numbers of civilian casualties to, as Ricks (2009, 7) puts it, "a strategy founded on the concept that the civilian population isn't the playing field but rather the prize, to be protected at almost all costs." The new strategy directed the United States to "hold" territory by establishing an ongoing presence in contested cities and provinces, to provide protection for inhabitants who feared retribution from insurgent and militia groups, to show deference to local culture and practices, to rely on locals for manpower and support (so as to facilitate mutual understanding, capitalize on local know-how, and inject income into a community), to offset hardships and costs imposed by the conflict, and to provide marginalized groups some hope for the future. Still, the new US approach was not the "victory" for counterinsurgency doctrine that is often supposed; rather, it reveals critical challenges in application.

As Kalyvas (2008, 351) notes, counterinsurgency theory is built around "a strategy of competitive state building combining targeted, selective violence and population control, on the one hand, with the dissemination of a credible mass ideology, the creation of modern state structures, the imposition of the rule of law, and the spurring of economic development, on the other." For this, the theory assumes that "identities are malleable" (Kalyvas 2008, 348), that is, that a relatively large proportion of the population is "uncommitted" and that its loyalty can be claimed by those who can provide "superior goods and services, including government-supplied security" (Biddle 2008a, 348). These principles applied in Vietnam, where the US and Saigon government sought to counter an adversary— and its nationalist/egalitarian claims—by offering security and promising a better future. The United States even invoked the terms and symbols of revolution toward that end, in the form of the "Revolutionary Development" of CORDS. Yet, given the "zero-sum" aspects of ethno-sectarian conflict, these principles were a poor fit in Iraq. Because parties to identity conflicts view their losses as gains for the opponent (and vice versa)[165] and because the government in these conflicts is routinely biased toward this or that group, no basis for agreement exists between the "out-group" and the opposition or the government. A vulnerable group will not make concessions (for instance, by disarming) to a government that group members believe seeks to weaken them. Conversely, "many threatened governments are more committed to their own subgroup's interests than they are to some abstract idea of national well-being" and might well see "U.S. sponsored reforms as a greater threat to their personal well-being—or even survival—than the insurgency" (Biddle 2008a, 348).[166]

Given the conflict between the government and the portions of society that must be "won over" in counterinsurgency doctrine, the government is obviously poorly equipped—and likely unwilling—to promote the standard principles of counterinsurgency, as outlined in a classic work. Sir Robert Thompson (1966, 50–62) argues that, among the requisites for effective counterinsurgency, the government must direct its operations toward "a clear political aim," must act "in accordance with the law," and must have "an overall plan." These principles imply that the aim and plan are not perceived by members of the targeted population as injurious to their interests, that laws are not violated by government officials and servants who carry out vendettas or sectarian agendas against members of that population, that the aim and plan are not confounded and diluted when sectarian groups vie for control of the government or when competing factions within a sectarian community disagree over how best to approach the insurgency, and so forth. With these requirements, the application of counterinsurgency doctrine is made problematic by ethno-sectarian competition. Applying the doctrine is rendered that much more difficult with the policies that are required to win a "war for the people." The aim is to control the population and to win its support by establishing the authority of the government by acquiring a reputation for impartial law enforcement and by implementing a *plan* that "must include all political, social, economic, administrative, police and other measures which have a bearing on the insurgency" (Thompson (1966, 55). But if "'winning' the population over to positive support for the government" amounts to "good government in all its aspects" (Thompson 1966, 112), successful counterinsurgency by a partisan government is now arguably impossible by definition.

The constraints on applying a counterinsurgency strategy in Iraq were not lost on top US military leaders (Robinson 2008, 123). It was for these reasons that the United States opted for a surge strategy in 2007 that put US forces in the lead and incorporated tens of thousands of Sunni personnel into US-backed militia groups—in lieu of relying upon Iraqi security forces—and continued to support these groups despite the Baghdad government's lack of support, indeed opposition. Rather than playing on these groups' fears of third parties, the United States capitalized upon their *fears of the government* (Biddle 2008a, 350) by providing them with the backing and resources that the government would not. In the early months of the Awakening movement in Anbar Province, Sunni leaders expressed deep animosity toward the central government and suspicions about its mo-tives.[167] For their part, Shiite and Kurdish officials in Baghdad were highly skepti-cal of US efforts to arm Sunni groups to combat al-Qaeda elements within Iraq. As one Shiite lawmaker put it, "they are trusting terrorists," "they are trusting people who have previously attacked American forces and innocent people," "they are trust-ing people who are loyal to the regime of Saddam Hussein."[168] Iraqi Prime Minis-ter Nouri al-Maliki was only a bit more circumspect in his remark that some American military commanders "make mistakes since they do not know the facts about the people they deal with." Significant barriers continued to forestall the integration of Sunni forces into central governmental and provincial police units.[169] The central government committed only to incorporate small numbers of militia members into the Iraqi police and consistently hindered efforts by the United States to broaden the recruitment pool (see Ricks 2009, 263; Robinson 2008, 321–322). Among Iraq's leaders, the Sons of Iraq issue was "largely viewed as an American concern and an American responsibility" (Serwer and Parker 2009, 13).

In the end, the United States could get neither disenfranchised Sunnis nor Shiites to believe that the central government, as constituted, serves the interests of all Iraqi citizens. On this point, a US military commander noted in 2007, for example, that in a Sunni district (Amiriyah) in Baghdad, the belief was wide-spread that the government was denying residents access not just to security but also to basic services including electricity and trash pickup.[170] Indeed, rather than win the population over per se, the US military capitalized on a Sunni schism to gain cooperation from insurgent groups and tribal leaders—promises of employ-ment, reconstruction assistance, political representation, and security support in tow—to get them to pull others along. It benefited further from the willingness of a radical Shiite leader to call a truce with US and Iraqi government forces un-der very unlikely circumstances. Even then, the United States succeeded only after the outcome of the sectarian conflict was largely decided, with the effect of forcing Sunnis and Shiites apart, to create demographic realities that reduced the potential for violence.

The upshot is that the United States convinced Sunnis and Shiites that *in the short term*, the advantages of acquiescing to a US troop presence outweighed the disad-vantages. The question was whether the parties would return to violence should the United States fail to meet local expectations, the Iraqi government fail to pick up the slack or make demanded reforms, opportunities arise for one or more discontented groups to improve their military position, or the government or any number of these groups react out of feelings of threat. Despite the unprecedented calm, the signs were worrisome. In previously turbulent parts of the country— including Samarra, where the destruction of a Shiite mosque had sparked civil war in 2006—sectarian resentment toward the central government and its security forces continued to fester.[171] Sunnis continued to voice deep suspicions of the Iraqi government, especially its sectarian leadership and purported links to Iran. Indeed, Sunnis appeared convinced that Iran, not al-Qaeda, was responsible for the upswing in national violence in early 2009: they supposed that Iran was trying to manufacture a Sunni insurgent threat to make the al-Maliki government more compliant (Serwer and Parker 2009, 12). Even Shiites had reason not to look to the government for support. In Shiite areas of the country, residents blamed Iraqi security forces for failing to protect them against a 2009 bombing campaign and expressed fears that the militia and violence would return once US troops withdrew (by agreement, in mid-2009).[172]

This does not mean that a counterinsurgency approach reduces to a clear and consistent set of policy directives. On this point, Kilcullen (2009, 183) observes that "there is no such thing as a 'standard' counterinsurgency," that is, "there are no fixed 'laws' of counterinsurgency, except for the sole and simple but difficult requirement to first understand the environment, then diagnose the problem, in detail and in its own terms, and then build a tailored set of situation-specific techniques to deal with it." Viewed accordingly, the United States adopted a counterinsurgency approach in Iraq—a useful one in light of the payoff in reduced violence from wooing insurgents and tribal leaders. Indeed, Kilcullen notes further that counterinsurgency works best by relying on societal influences rather than the economic incentives of tribal members: "In a tribal, traditional society, choices are made collectively (by family, section, clan, tribal, or village units), not by single individuals," so that "winning over key traditional leaders" amounts to winning "the support of an entire village or lineage group at one time, rather than piecemeal" (Kilcullen 2009, 68). Still, the United States had yet to demonstrate a capability—independently or jointly with the host government—to build local security by establishing control over a reticent or resistant population and redirecting its efforts, then, from aiding to combating the insurgency (see Krepinevich 1986, 10–16). Nor had the United States and the host government demonstrated that they could acquire the leverage to secure long-term stability in Iraq, where sectarianism persisted, critical grievances remained unaddressed, and the host government continued to lack legitimacy for much of the disenfranchised population. In the Iraqi case, the "counterinsurgency" approach must ultimately be assessed by whether it provided a firm basis for accommodation among the warring elements of Iraqi society or helped, instead, to support conditions that would buy but a momentary respite before some group or other managed to seize the upper hand, security forces disintegrated to become partisan participants in the fighting, militia recruits opted for the lucrative returns possible from involvement in criminal activities, insurgent violence spiraled out of control, violence triggered by escalating Sunni bomb attacks or increasing ethnic and sectarian tension engulfed large portions of the country—or all of the above.

Conclusions

Clearly, a lesson of the Vietnam and Iraq Wars is that the United States enjoys an overwhelming advantage in conventional warfare: it can inflict far greater damage on an adversary than the adversary can inflict in return, and it is likely to triumph in any conventional military confrontation. The United States established its prowess, in this regard, when the Vietnamese opposition launched major territorial offensives that the United States could thwart by capitalizing on its decisive technological advantage in firepower and mobility. The United States showed its conventional might, as well, when invading Iraq and bringing down its government by attacking its "center of gravity" in Baghdad. Nevertheless, the approach of taking the fight to the enemy was unsuccessful in both conflicts when the United States found itself battling an adversary that could capitalize on its own strengths, exploit US weaknesses, and indeed, turn the strengths of the US military into weaknesses. In particular, US conventional military capabilities were proven ineffective and counterproductive for combating an insurgency.

Although it is tempting to conclude that success against an insurgency lies in a dedicated commitment to a counterinsurgency strategy, the evidence from Vietnam and Iraq provides only modest support for that strategy. In Vietnam, progress attributed to pacification occurred only when the Vietcong suffered a major conventional defeat at Tet. Furthermore, pacification never produced an essential increase in popular allegiance toward the Saigon government, given its slow and incomplete commitment to the program. In Iraq, the United States adopted its own brand of "counterinsurgency." The United States conceded substantial control over local security to former adversaries, never allayed local suspicions toward the US and host governments, and had limited success encouraging the host government to capitalize on hard-won security gains by addressing the demands of the disenfranchised portions of the Iraqi population. Instead, the United States benefited from unusual conditions that played to its advantage—specifically, an assertive tribal leadership, divisions within the insurgency, ethno-sectarian cleansing that effectively partitioned warring communities, and a Shiite opposition that held its fire despite US "provocations." These conditions helped the US effort directly—as well as indirectly, by allowing Iraqi security forces to remain intact (to clear and hold ground), when confronting militia or insurgent groups would have caused units to fragment. The United States cannot assume that similar conditions will permit future US counterinsurgency efforts to succeed, nor even that these conditions will persist in Iraq to protect hard-won security gains. Celeste Ward, a former assistant secretary of defense for stability operations in the Bush administration, describes the situation aptly, observing that "the prevailing interpretations of the surge narrative . . . put the Americans in the driver's seat of history" with the apparent assumption "that the United States, its leaders and the tactics it employed are primarily responsible for the events on the ground, . . . but the decisions of the Iraqis themselves surely made a material difference"—that is, "they stopped fighting, whether due to political calculations, fear or exhaustion."[173] Thus, the United States fell short of meeting the goals of counterinsurgency, in theory, and certainly as defined in the recently published US government *Counterinsurgency Guide* (signed by both the secretaries of state and defense)—"to simultaneously contain insurgency and *address its root causes*" (italics added; US Department of State 2009).

The evidence is not persuasive, then, that the United States would have had greater success in either conflict if it had initially adopted counterinsurgency principles. Although the United States struggled to overcome its initial setbacks in Vietnam, any US strategy might well have failed given the adversary's capability to shift strategies to counter US efforts, the need for the United States to devote its finite human and material resources simultaneously to regular and irregular warfare, and the limited time and resources that the United States could devote to the war effort. In Iraq, a US invasion with a larger occupation force might still not have precluded the alienation of various societal groups or their mobilization in opposition to the US and host government. Indeed, it might have had the opposite effect. Sunnis, not having endured hardships under the jihadists, and the Shiites, not having lost militia battles to US forces, would have had little reason to hold their fire.

Another lesson from Vietnam and Iraq is apparent. Despite a massive counter-insurgency investment in a conflict, the United States might not have the military, economic, and political resources available to succeed and is severely disadvantaged when engaged in counterinsurgency without full host government support. Ethnic and sectarian tension in Iraq certainly exacerbated US counterinsurgency challenges, but they did not create them.

CHAPTER THREE

Leveraging the Adversary's Support Base

States, Populations, and Societies

Given the challenges of influencing adversary leaders and maintaining domestic support for a US war effort, US policymakers understandably look to increase their leverage by turning to various "third parties" that provide active or passive support to the adversary. This chapter assesses US efforts to leverage (a) border states or outside powers that supported US adversaries in Vietnam and Iraq, (b) the populations that fed the Vietnamese and Iraqi insurgencies, and (c) the societal leaders and groups that were key to the US stabilization effort in Iraq. This chapter concludes that the United States was not positioned favorably to improve its leverage by extending the Vietnam and Iraq conflicts to other states and that the United States was unable to acquire the public following required to disrupt insurgent activities. In Iraq, unlike Vietnam, the United States was able to disrupt the insurgency indirectly by soliciting support from various societal leaders and groups. This approach can fail, however, when a society lacks cohesion or conflicts with its government.

States: Neighbors and Allies

The United States can focus on the "supply side" of its security problem and try to obtain leverage by escalating conflict across international borders. By targeting states that provide aid and comfort to the enemy, the US goals, then, are (a) to obtain a capability advantage by destroying the enemy's sanctuaries or infrastructure (training centers, supply depots) outside the immediate conflict zone and (b) to increase the costs and risks to a state that provides support voluntarily or involuntarily to the enemy. Yet, the danger for the United States in expanding the conflict is that it can add new fronts to the conflict or increase the motivation of all parties to resist. These costs become prohibitive in conflicts that are fueled largely "from within."

Aware of these dangers, the Johnson administration took extraordinary precautions to keep the Soviet Union and China out of the conflict and to prevent the conflict from spreading to adjacent states. Officials in the Johnson administration could not help but recall the chain of events, precipitated by the US crossing of the 38th parallel into North Korea, that provoked direct Chinese intervention in the Korean War. The Chinese offensive forced US troops to retreat and ultimately led to a military stalemate and long negotiating impasse.[1] Johnson's concerns were not misplaced. China adopted measures that made its intervention more likely: it moved forces into North Vietnam, including anti-aircraft artillery units that actively engaged US aircraft; prepared airfields in China adjacent to North Vietnam; committed, in principle, to employ planes based in China to defend North Vietnam and to send aircraft and pilots to the country; and tied its intervention to the US crossing of "green lines," such as a US ground invasion of North Vietnam.[2] Advised by the intelligence community that US bombing would not provoke China to intervene (Prados 2004), the Johnson administration still feared the effects of the United States expanding the conflict. So it ruled out a land invasion of North Vietnam, ground attacks on North Vietnamese sanctuaries and traffic routes in Cambodia and Laos, the mining of Haiphong Harbor, and strikes against certain targets (such as surface-to-air missile launchers that had not engaged US aircraft) and certain areas in North Vietnam.[3]

Conversely, the logic of expansion to counter the enemy's military advantages motivated the Nixon administration to move against enemy sanctuaries in Cambodia in 1970 and Laos in 1971 (when the United States provided air support for South Vietnamese troops). Whereas prior US involvement in both countries was limited to covert missions, recruiting and aiding friendly forces, and aerial bombing, the United States invaded Cambodia to engage tens of thousands of North Vietnamese and Vietcong troops and destroy their base areas in the country. At least that was the objective. The practical effect of the operation was to push communist activities further into the interior of Cambodia, to increase North Vietnamese support for indigenous communist (Khmer Rouge) forces fighting the central government of Cambodia, and to remove any constraints that the Vietnamese communists observed in their deployments and operations in Cambodia. Indeed, with the overthrow earlier in the year of the neutralist government of Prince Sihanouk (who became titular leader of the opposition) and the decision by his successor (General Lon Nol), with US encouragement and support, to move against militarily superior North Vietnamese forces in Cambodia, the new government rapidly lost political and military ground to an ever stronger opposition. To say the least, then, the escalation of the fighting did not damage the communist position in Cambodia. The Khmer Rouge quickly extended their hold on the country: "Within months of the 1970 invasion the Communists had isolated Phnom Penh, gained half the country and over 20 percent of the population" (Shawcross 1987, 200). After the invasion, US intelligence concluded that Hanoi retained a significant military capability within Cambodia and could reconstitute losses in supplies in a matter of months (Shawcross 1987, 173). North Vietnam launched its 1972 offensive, in fact, from sanctuaries in Cambodia. The repercussions of the fight for Cambodia were felt, too, in neighboring Laos. As the host of parts of the Ho Chi Minh Trail, Laos became a more important battleground for Hanoi when the Lon Nol government closed the port at Kampong Son (Sihanoukville) to communist supplies bound for South Vietnam (Stuart-Fox 1997, 143).

The conflicts that evolved in Cambodia and Laos were fueled by domestic rivalries and, in no small measure, by outside infusions and provocations that most definitely included Hanoi's large troop presence and offensives in these countries. But Hanoi did not have territorial designs on either country and, in the Cambodian case, was pushed into a strained ideological alliance with the Khmer Rouge that would turn violent when the Vietnam War ended. Hanoi's interest in both countries centered on their importance as conduits of North Vietnamese manpower and materiel to the South Vietnamese battlefield. Thus, the United States provoked Hanoi to increase its military investment in Laos and Cambodia by threatening its military position there. In principle, making the adversary fight on multiple fronts can pay off, if it is obliged to spread its resources thin to the neglect, perhaps, of the main front. Unfortunately for the United States, Hanoi proved more capable at tipping the balances and securing its prerogatives in these countries than the United States was at weakening the communist position in these countries (through bombing, incursions, special operations, and the equipping and training of indigenous anticommunist troops). In this sense, the Cambodian incursion speaks metaphorically to the danger of extending (and escalating) a conflict beyond its existing borders. The escalation that US policymakers hoped would increase the US chances of success and reduce long-term US costs in Vietnam might well have increased the US chances of defeat in Vietnam and certainly raised short- and long-term US costs in Southeast Asia. Because the wars in Cambodia and Laos were fought—in priority and strategy—to support the US main effort in Vietnam, both countries were finally sacrificed to that effort.[4]

With good reason, the Nixon administration exerted more subtle—and equivocal—pressure on rival powers with a stake in the conflict. The administration apparently warned the Soviets that Hanoi's Easter Offensive could jeopardize the Nixon-Brezhnev Moscow summit scheduled for later in 1972 and pressed China to restrain North Vietnam (Randolph 2007, 80–81). But the administration did not press the issue to the point of endangering the emerging big-power triangular relationship when Russia and China claimed, in response, that they had limited influence over Hanoi and refused to cut its supply of arms and materiel (Randolph 2007, 218). Even when intensifying the bombing of North Vietnam, the United States observed restrictions (including those along the Chinese border set by Johnson in Rolling Thunder), though fears of Chinese intervention were now greatly reduced (Randolph 2007, 193).

Likewise, the United States balanced a host of competing interests when confronting Syria and Iran over their direct and indirect support for groups that opposed the US occupation of Iraq. The challenge from Syria was based on its hostility toward Israel, efforts to undermine the Lebanese government, support for various radical groups in the region, and its porous border with Iraq, a preferred entryway for foreign fighters joining the insurgency.[5] The Syrian government had incentives, in fact, to keep the "pot boiling" in Iraq to "pin down" US forces (Yacoubian 2007) and was still working actively, in early 2007, to organize Iraqi Sunni insurgent groups to oppose the Iraqi government.[6] The challenge from Iran was more potent given its prominent regional profile, support for Hezbollah in Lebanon and Hamas in the Palestinian territories, anti-US and anti-Israel rhetoric, possible pursuit of a nuclear weapon, and deep and far-reaching involvement in Iraqi society and politics. The United States was particularly concerned about mounting evidence that Iran had armed and trained rogue elements (so-called special groups) of the Mahdi Army, had supplied the militias with sophisticated rockets and explosively formed projectiles that could pierce US vehicle armor,[7] and had sent members of the al-Quds Force of Iran's Revolutionary Guard (which supported Hezbollah and Hamas) to support the Shiite militias in Iraq.[8] Like Syria, Iran was presumably motivated to promote violent opposition in Iraq to tie down US troops and to trade its services, as a conflict intermediary, to leverage the Iraqi government.

Still, US policymakers recognized the dangers of taking the war militarily to Syria and Iran. Any cross-border attack by the United States risked creating a "self-fulfilling prophesy"—provoking these governments to increase their support for militant groups and their activities, if not to retaliate broadly. These were exceptional risks when weighed against the potential ineffectiveness of a US military strike: given the vast and elusive militant support infrastructure, a US attack on Syria or Iran would succeed only if these governments *chose* in response to end support for militants or to crack down on their activities. These risks appeared prohibitive in light of considerable uncertainty over whether top Syrian and Iranian leaders were backing these groups, the incentives these governments apparently had to *stabilize* Iraq, and evidence that Syria and Iran acted, at times, to stem the illicit flow of personnel and supplies into Iraq.

For Syria, a stable Iraq promised to draw home many of the million-plus Iraqis who had fled to Syria, reduce the radical jihadist presence in Iraq and Syria that could endanger the Syrian regime, lower the probability that a restive Iraqi Kurdish population could inspire and provoke Syria's own large Kurdish population to rebel, and extract US rewards to Syria for its cooperation and restraint. As a proof of their incentives to cooperate, the Syrians had already provided intelligence information to US and Iraqi intelligence services, turned over wanted Iraqis to the United States, and cracked down on militant operations near the Iraqi border.[9]

For Iran, a stable Iraq would speed the withdrawal of US forces from Iraq. This would allow Iran to capitalize on its links to various Iraqi factions and thereby influence the political and economic development of Iraq. Iran maintained religious and political links to the Shiite majority in Iraq (and its leadership under Ayatollah Ali al-Sistani) and remained a source of considerable economic support to southern Iraq, in part via Iranian pilgrimage traffic to holy places in the country. Iran had ties, as well, to Shiite groups including the Dawa Party of Prime Minister al-Maliki and the Mahdi Army of Moqtada al-Sadr. Iran enjoyed a strong relationship, in fact, with the Supreme Islamic Iraqi Council (the Supreme Council, renamed)—having sheltered its leadership from Saddam Hussein and organized and trained the Badr Corps (later, the Badr Organization) from Iraqi exiles in Iran. Given its connections, Iran was understandably reluctant to pin its strategy, and success in Iraq, to Shiite militias (let alone their radical elements) that were potentially resistant to (external) direction and prone to destabilizing violence. Iran had apparently pulled back personnel linked to Shiite militia from Iraq and pressured al-Sadr to end his attacks on US and Iraqi security forces during their offensive in Basra.[10] Iran's ambassador to Iraq went so far as to brand the Sadrist militia in Basra as "outlaws" (echoing the Iraqi government) and refused to credit them for ending the violence there.[11]

So the US government was neither set nor unified in its approach to these countries. By 2007, US military and intelligence officials were conceding, in fact, that insurgent crossings from Syria had dropped significantly and that the Syrian government was targeting al-Qaeda–affiliated fighters.[12] Although tensions with Syria escalated in late 2008, when the United States attacked an alleged al-Qaeda target in the country (an unmistakable warning that the United States would act against terrorists if Syria did not), the United States did not claim direct Syrian culpability for the terrorist presence: the United States merely held that Syria could be doing *more* to slow the terrorist traffic into Iraq and did not appear anxious to escalate tension with Syria further over the issue.[13] US-Syrian relations worsened again, in May 2009, when the US government renewed sanctions against Syria for its support for terror groups and the US military complained that the al-Qaeda network in Syria had strengthened and was funneling an increased number of foreign fighters into Iraq. Yet the US military also acknowledged that the United States lacked evidence that high-level Syrian officials had direct knowledge of terrorist activities.[14] Even greater ambivalence and inconsistency marked the US approach to Iran. In August 2007, the United States announced its intent to designate the entire Revolutionary Guards as a global terrorist group despite resistance from US allies in the Middle East and Europe and an ongoing internal US government debate pitting State and Treasury Department officials against hard-line White House officials and members of the vice president's staff over whether to target the Revolutionary Guards or only its al-Quds Force for links to global terrorism.[15] By October 2007, the US government announced, however, that it would sanction only the al-Quds Force; in the months to follow, US officials conceded that senior Iranian government officials were curtailing their support for violent Shiite militia and shifting Iraqi training operations to Iran.[16] Whereas high-level US officials continued to stress the Iranian threat in Iraq,[17] they conceded—by what they did *not* say and do—that escalating the conflict militarily into Iran was not a good option. US officials understood that Iran could instigate retaliatory violence in Iraq—and beyond—thereby nullifying any security benefits obtained from the strike.[18]

Efforts by the United States to extend the conflict outward would not have been welcomed by the United States's regional or European allies. Regional states were greatly concerned about the destabilizing effects of US policies in Iraq—in refugee flows, jihadism, extremist violence, and escalating US tensions with Iran (Lasensky 2006). As it was, the United States struggled to acquire support for the Iraqi government within the Middle East. The Sunni-led governments of Jordan, Egypt, Saudi Arabia, and other Gulf states were reticent to assist the fledgling Iraqi government (or even establish diplomatic representation in Baghdad), as they were determined to avoid the appearance of endorsing the US-led invasion of Iraq and a Shiite-led Iraqi regime with close ties to Iran.[19] The Saudi government—long a supportive pillar of US Middle East policy—was actually funding the Sunni groups in Iraq, failing to stem the flow of Saudi nationals (the largest national contingent) to the insurgency,[20] and voicing a fairly uncharitable view of the Iraqi prime minister and his ties to Iran.[21] Half a decade after the US occupation of Iraq, the Saudis still refused to send an ambassador to Iraq or forgive the billions of dollars loaned previously to the Iraqi government of Saddam Hussein.[22] Only in 2008, under US pressure, did a host of US-aligned countries from the region, including the United Arab Emirates, Kuwait, Jordan, and Egypt—send, or announce their intention to send, ambassadors to Iraq (Katzman 2009, 18).

In the end, the United States could not effectively employ pressure "from without" to change the fundamental realities of the Vietnam and Iraq conflicts. US efforts to leverage Hanoi by destroying its sanctuaries and supply lines in Cambodia and Laos were insufficient to end hostilities on US terms and appear to have backfired on the United States in significant respects. The experience suggests that anything less than a full US military commitment is potentially insufficient to dislodge a well-entrenched adversary. It suggests further that the adversary—with its perimeter position threatened—might seek to fortify and extend its territorial control, ally with an opposing indigenous group, and bring down the host government should it prove too weak to resist. By helping turn Cambodia and Laos into battlefields of the Vietnam conflict, the United States helped create an even less hospitable environment for prosecuting the main war in Vietnam and helped turn both countries into casualties of the main conflict.

The limits of an outside-pressure strategy were apparent, too, when the United States sought Soviet and Chinese help to end the Vietnam conflict and, in Iraq, Syrian and Iranian support (or acquiescence) to stabilize conditions. Soviet and

Chinese leaders proved unwilling to bear the ideological and strategic costs of abandoning an ally (more so with the intensifying Sino-Soviet rivalry) or to back down from the United States and suffer a potential loss in face and reputation, especially since these leaders knew that the United States was *depending on them* to cooperate on various issues of mutual concern. The same applied to the Syrian and Iranian leaders, who retained the option of responding to any punitive US actions by reciprocating in Iraq merely by exercising less *restraint* on militant groups or by acting out there or elsewhere. For instance, Iran could employ Hezbollah as a proxy to destabilize Lebanon or militarize the Arab-Israel front, or it could harden its stance to outside demands that Iran abide by the terms of the Nuclear Non-Proliferation Treaty and open the country's nuclear facilities to international inspections.

Thus, the United States prosecuted both wars within constraints imposed by outside states and ignored these constraints (in Vietnam) at its own peril. If anything, the United States depended on states bordering the Iraq conflict to limit the violence (as when Iran brokered a ceasefire with Sadrist militia), and found itself trying to prevent groups within Iraq from provoking outside intervention. These spillover effects were front-and-center, for instance, when Turkey moved its forces into northern Iraq in 2007 to attack the sanctuaries of the many thousands of Kurdistan Workers' Party members (that had waged a violent campaign in Turkey).

Local Populations

The success of any US leverage strategy aimed at winning popular support is determined by the strategy's negative and positive dimensions. In negative terms, the United States must avoid tactics that permit insurgents to tighten their hold on a local population; in positive terms, the United States must provide incentives and political justifications to induce a population to shift its support to the US military and host government. In Vietnam and Iraq, the United States was challenged significantly on both these negative and positive dimensions of policy.

Avoiding Estrangement

Throughout much of the Vietnam and Iraq Wars, separating insurgents from their popular support base was subordinated in US military strategy to killing the enemy. Thus, the military employed tactics that failed to curtail—and may well have boosted—the flow of supplies, recruits, and intelligence to the insurgency.

In Vietnam, the US military's "search and destroy" strategy alienated the peasants whose allegiance was required to uproot the communist infrastructure within the South. Not only were allied forces unable to provide security to local villages to undercut Vietcong inducements and intimidation, they also employed tactics that imperiled civilians and exacerbated their grievances against the US and Saigon governments. These tactics included the widespread use of napalm and defoliants (in part, to deny the Vietcong their food sources), the forced relocation of populations from insecure areas, and the leveling of villages believed sympathetic to the Vietcong (Herring 1986, 88; Lewy 1978, 64–65, 70–72). They also included the indiscriminate use of force, as indicated by evidence from US military reports. Although it is impossible to know how many of the hundreds of thousands of civilian fatalities incurred over the course of US involvement in Vietnam were inflicted directly by US forces—in part because civilians were often caught in firefights between US and enemy forces and because US troops were generally not held accountable for civilian deaths—the high US counts of "enemy kills," participant testimony, and circumstantial evidence suggest a large US-inflicted toll. For example, US military officials claimed to have killed over ten thousand Vietcong troops in a Mekong Delta operation in 1968–69 while only recovering hundreds of weapons (Nagl 2002, 172).[23] The United States was not alone in inflicting large numbers of collateral deaths: to minimize their exposure to hostile fire, South Vietnamese troops relied on heavy firepower in populated areas and operated aggressively in areas assumed to be friendly to the Vietcong (Elliott 2003, 752–753). A high civilian death count was the inevitable result of a US military reward structure built around maximizing kills of an enemy often living and fighting in close proximity to populated villages and visually impossible to distinguish from noncombatants.

In inflicting damage in populated areas, allied forces were abetted by enemy tactics. The Vietcong often fired on US units to draw fire onto villages for political effect—expecting residents to blame their plight on the *proximate* source, that is, the party that dropped the bombs or fired the mortars that hit the village. "American units repeatedly fell for the ruse and returned fire out of all proportion to what they received" (Hennessy 1997, 125), apparently with the intended political effect. Admittedly, the peasants did not always attribute their misfortunes to US or South Vietnamese troops: peasants targeted by allied forces apportioned responsibility on the basis of operant circumstances, for example, whether Vietcong were present in the village or had drawn fire (Elliott 2003, 748–750, 1160). But the United States, as a foreign party and backer of the ("illegitimate") government in Saigon, operated from a disadvantage in the opinion war: "Even those who were indifferent or hostile to the 'VC' accepted that, whatever its faults, it had a monopoly on 'independence,' and—for better or for worse—'independence' was synonymous with a revolutionary-controlled South Vietnam tied to the North" (Elliott 2003, 1110). The United States was not helped, then, by its military tactics that conveyed to villagers that the United States saw little difference—or cared little about the difference—between active combatants and their passive supporters or involuntary civilian hosts. Nor was the United States helped by its own insensitivity to the alienating effects of these tactics. Indeed, the US military could put a positive spin on indicators that suggested the United States was losing the battle of "hearts and minds." For example, huge flows of refugees from the fighting were seen to suggest that people were fleeing the communists (and taking their "hearts and minds" with them). This led to the declaration of "free-fire zones" (Krepinevich 1986, 225–226) in which the military could employ indiscriminate tactics that played further into the hands of the insurgents.

It is hard, given limits of the data, to draw firm conclusions about cause and effect pertaining to "winning hearts and minds" in the country. In surveys conducted through the US pacification program (Thayer 1985, 183), less than a third of the South Vietnam's rural population indicated, in 1972, that it believed that its government was doing an "adequate" job (with another quarter expressing no opinion or indicating that government performance was "inadequate"). Of those surveyed, the largest share (41 percent) expressed the view that the government was performing "as can be expected under the circumstances." Inasmuch as circumstances can be external or internal—reflecting what a government is capable of doing given its fundamental proclivities and competencies—this cannot be taken as rousing support for the "other war" in which the United States and the host government were engaged.

The South Vietnamese public *did* recognize a positive contribution of US forces (Thayer 1985, 187, 190). In 1971, 60 percent of the rural population acknowledged that the US presence was at least somewhat beneficial;[24] only 2 percent of the population believed that the US presence had a "bad effect." Complementing these views were indications, in that year, of a local affinity toward US personnel: 37 percent of the rural population indicated that they liked Americans, with another 52 percent indicating no worse than neutral feelings.[25] Yet rural residents (in a sample slightly biased *toward* "secure" hamlets) did not view US forces as a necessary or desirable presence within South Vietnam: in 1970 and 1971, a clear majority thought it "wise" for the United States to withdraw troops from the country. Even with North Vietnam's Easter Offensive, the number believing it "unwise" for the United States to withdraw remained roughly unchanged.[26]

Taken together, these data suggest that South Vietnamese villagers had not warmed to their government or its performance.[27] Although the data also suggest that a sizable share of the peasantry was not antagonistic toward US troops,[28] the findings indicate that the peasantry concluded that the US presence was generally doing more harm than good. Still, the South Vietnamese appeared to welcome US forces compared to respondents in Iraq, where the United States had to overcome strong nationalistic opposition to the US occupation. The United States did not initially rise to the challenge: US tactics were again inadequate and self-defeating, in several ways.

First, the United States could not override the incentives that even the uncommitted had to cooperate with the insurgents. Because the United States ceded control of neighborhoods to Sunni insurgent and Shiite militia groups, people had little reason to refuse the militants' entreaties and cooperate with the United States (on the public's calculations, see Kalyvas and Kocher 2007b). Disloyalty to the militants invited high costs (death), and cooperating with them offered potentially attractive benefits, including residency in confiscated homes, employment, and protection from rival groups. Although groups demanded a monopoly price on goods and services, committed thievery and extortion, and dispensed punishment mercilessly, these costs of supporting the militants were insufficient for most people to risk challenging them—and certainly to do so alone.

Second, the US military, in pursuing its offensive strategy, was not sensitive enough to declines in public support. For instance, in targeting Sunni insurgents and their support structure, General Raymond Odierno—the Army commander who headed the 4th Infantry Division in Anbar Province (the so-called Sunni triangle) in the first year of the US occupation (and, in 2008, replaced General Petraeus as commander of Coalition forces in Iraq)—was accused of employing divisional tactics that fueled opposition to the US presence *before* the formation of an organized resistance. Military investigations concluded that his troops adopted aggressive measures despite the relative calm in the province, used weapons too freely, and seized control of entire villages and their inhabitants.[29] Military investigations also raised serious questions about the command attitude among the Marine leadership in Iraq, which allegedly depreciated the importance of avoiding civilian casualties. Marines were prosecuted for the killings in 2005 of two dozen civilians in Haditha and were accused of executing eight insurgents in Fallujah in 2004—indeed, the two cases involved the same company.[30]

Undoubtedly, there were security gains for the United States in invading homes and holding terrified families at gunpoint, allowing male soldiers to conduct searches of women, and forcing Iraqi men to lie on the ground handcuffed in front of their families. There were also gains to be had by rounding up men in entire villages that fit the insurgent profile, incarcerating tens of thousands of men suspected of knowing of or participating in insurgent activities, and holding suspects in overcrowded prisons where—as at the notorious Abu Ghraib prison—they were subject to what most certainly qualified as "cruel, inhumane, and degrading treatment."[31] These harsh tactics exposed enemy arms caches, led to the killing or capture of those who participated in (or might have joined) the insurgency, and produced actionable intelligence.[32] But any gains in security that were obtained were negated by the growing popular unwillingness to cooperate with occupying forces and a desire (as a matter of family honor) to avenge the death of relatives and to punish the United States for these indignities (Baram 2005, 7–8). The harsh tactics and limited outreach to local populations and tribal leaders made it impossible for the US military to mount an effective counterinsurgency operation, which required an accepting *and forgiving* attitude toward the local population, including the prison population.[33] Thus, well into 2007, conditions looked bleak for the United States. As one US intelligence expert involved in US operations bluntly put it, "We have lost the fight for public and political support, so no matter how successful we are militarily we are being led to failure."[34]

The US military was similarly challenged when relying upon air support. In strict military terms, US forces were justified when, in the months following the Basra offensive launched in March 2008, they responded to escalating Shiite militia attacks with missiles, rockets, and bombs against militia targets in densely populated neighborhoods of Sadr City.[35] The military was correct that aerial attacks allow for a quick response and save the lives of ground troops. But, taking in the larger view, the critical question is whether the collateral *and political* damage inflicted by these attacks outweighed their military effectiveness.

Clearly, the US military gave far greater priority to avoiding collateral damage and civilian deaths in Iraq than it had in Vietnam. The reasons include improvements in technology, such as smart bombs and munitions, that allowed for more precise targeting of adversary assets and the internalization of norms of war through changes in US military procedures and personnel training (Kahl 2007b).[36] The priority shift also reflected an appreciation on the part of the United States that the densely populated, urban environment in which militants in Iraq operated necessitated greater caution to avoid collateral effects, that communications technology magnified the political impact of damage inflicted on civilians, that winning the battle of public opinion was critical in unconventional warfare, that a US "occupation" of an Arab/Islamic country is a sensitive political issue, and that collateral damage hindered efforts at reconstruction and development necessary for long-term security within the country. For that reason, the number of civilian casualties inflicted by the United States in Iraq was extremely low by historical standards (Kahl 2007b).[37] But to say that casualties were lower in Iraq is not to say that these casualty levels served US goals or that US forces handled these deaths with appropriate sensitivity to local opinion. When challenged by journalists, civilian witnesses, or Iraqi government officials over civilian deaths, the US military was reluctant to drop its version of events. The standard US military refrains were that the United States could not independently corroborate opposing claims, that an incident in question was "under investigation," that the victims at issue had engaged in suspicious or menacing behavior (carrying weapons or driving quickly toward a US military checkpoint), and that the United States does not deliberately cause civilian deaths and takes all possible measures to avoid them.[38] On the occasions that it did actually acknowledge civilian casualties, the military sought to deflect responsibility by asserting that the insurgents, who hide among noncombatants, are ultimately to blame. In the words of an official military spokesman commenting on civilian casualties inflicted in Sadr City in April 2008, "The sole burden of responsibility lies on the shoulders of the militants who care nothing for the Iraqi people."[39] Valid or not, these arguments are unlikely to persuade many people in the target population, especially those disinclined to accept the US version of events.

Third, the US military failed to appreciate that even measures not directed specifically at the local population can reduce its tolerance for a US military presence. These measures included security precautions taken to protect troops that *distanced* and *distinguished* them from the local population. US troops appeared callous, reckless, and hostile to the local population when US military forces were housed in bases fortified against the suicide bomb attacks that afflicted city dwellers, drove quickly and aggressively to foil snipers and ambushes, rode on sidewalks to avoid roadside bombs, operated in large groups and fired warning shots (or worse) to keep locals at bay, and traveled in armored vehicles while Iraqi troops traveled in pickup trucks. Indeed, by protecting themselves, US forces could well have been seen to have been *increasing* the vulnerability of the civilian population: when US troops made themselves less inviting targets (through confinement to military bases in the first years of the US operation), Sunni insurgents shifted their emphasis to "soft" civilian targets, including Shiite mosques, Iraqi police, and marketplaces. Even measures meant to enhance the security of the civilian population were not always popular. The construction of walls around Baghdad neighborhoods in 2007 to protect against suicide car-bomb attacks drew comparisons with the security wall that Israel had constructed to seal off Israeli (and Israeli-claimed) territory from Palestinian attacks, fueled complaints about the prison-like atmosphere and isolation of communities, and created delays at access points where Iraqis had to provide identification and were subject to searches.[40] For that matter, US troops were blamed, in general, for having placed Iraq on the path of death and destruction. As a grieving Shiite villager exclaimed after losing much of his extended family in a suicide bomb attack in July 2007, "We were wiped out mercilessly, and we blame the Americans, the Iraqi government, the criminals and all the politicians who brought us catastrophe and destruction."[41]

Fourth, the US military failed to appreciate the cumulative and disproportionate effects of the many or the few whose habits, practices, and impulses can undermine a security effort. To levels unknown in Vietnam, the effects of shootings, bombings, and acts of abuse were enhanced through technological transmission (primarily the internet) and the suspicions of a local population inclined to presume the worst of US troops based on personal experiences and prejudices. The Abu Ghraib prison-abuse scandal had an immediate and explosive effect in Iraq (and throughout the world) as pictures of prisoners being taunted, intimidated, and humiliated by US troops—in one of Saddam Hussein's most infamous prisons, no less—reinforced a public's assumptions about US deviousness and malevolence. According to one survey, half of Iraqis attributed the events at Abu Ghraib to fundamental deficiencies in the American character (as in, "all Americans are like this").[42] The problem of guilt by association was made worse, of course, by the US decision to shift military responsibilities to civilian contractors.[43] US officials understood the distinction between US military forces and private contractors *in the employ* of the US government, but the behavior of these private entities reflected on the behavior of all US personnel in Iraq. The notorious actions of (some of) the tens of thousands of private contractors employed by firms like Blackwater USA—unprovoked killings of Iraqi security personnel, attacks on US military personnel, gratuitous shootings of civilians, and hair-trigger and disproportionate responses to perceived "threats" in populated areas— embroiled the US government in controversy, placed inordinate pressure on the Iraqi government to reign in the perpetrators, and made it much more difficult for the US military to counter accusations that US troops were engaging in indiscriminate violence. The unwelcome situation arose in large part because private entities focused narrowly on providing services under contract, not on serving the broader political and military mission: security firms were hired "to get 'the package' safely from point A to point B," which meant that they were acting in "terms of their contract" even "if they forced civilian traffic off the roads or even killed an Iraqi civilian in the performance of their duty" (Mansoor 2008, 78). The situation was exacerbated by lack of cooperation between contractors (and their firms) and official US investigations of these incidents, a seeming lack of legal accountability for crimes committed, and a reluctance in parts of the US government (especially the State Department) to challenge firms upon which those agencies depended.[44] The lack of US military control over these contractors, and their unresponsiveness to US security plans, tested US policies in Iraq more severely as the US military shifted toward a counterinsurgency strategy (Ricks 2009, 270).

Fifth, the US military failed to appreciate that it had a fleeting window of opportunity to win over the Iraqi public. Quick and extraordinary measures were necessary to provide the security for Iraq that was essential for restoring essential services, protecting the public from criminal action, and acquiring public trust. The failures to provide basic services, prevent the looting, and control the violence were seen by the public as stemming from US indifference at best and malevolence at worst. From the public's perspective, surely the United States had the ability to fix these problems *if it chose to do so* (Wright et al. 2008, 91, 281). Expressed more graphically, "The Iraqis would ask why the Americans could hit a tank hiding between two buildings from 3,000 feet away, but they couldn't turn on the electricity. . . . They assumed the reason had to be something sinister."[45]

Public opinion polls taken in the weeks after the US occupation suggest that Iraqis in Baghdad believed that the United States was right to invade Iraq. They were generally thankful that Coalition forces had liberated Iraq from Saddam Hussein's authoritarian rule and were not pressing overwhelmingly for a rapid troop withdrawal.[46] But any gratitude that the Iraqi public felt toward the United States quickly dissipated with the increasing violence in the country, the breakdown in order, the rampant looting of Iraq's infrastructure, and the harsh realities of life that clashed with high public expectations in the immediate aftermath of the invasion. Coalition authorities had "assumed their success depended on persuading Iraqis that they would experience quick and dramatic improvements in their lives." Unfortunately for the United States, "Iraqis judged the coalition's performance on the basis of its promises" (Henderson 2005, 7). They could clearly see the negative consequences of a US troop presence; they had trouble "seeing positive progress on the issues that matter to them most" (Bensahel et al. 2008, xxvi). Half a year later, the State Department's intelligence branch concluded that most Iraqis thought of US troops as "occupiers" rather than "liberators."[47] Fifteen months after the US invasion, in the summer of 2004, this view was clearly prevalent: 92 percent of respondents in five major Iraqi cities judged Coalition forces as "occupiers" when given choices that included "liberators" and "peacekeepers."[48] In a nationwide survey conducted in early 2006, an overwhelming majority of Iraqis (Kurds, Sunnis, and Shiites) expressed their belief that the United States planned to set up permanent bases in Iraq and would not withdraw even if requested to do so by the Iraqi government.[49] By September 2007, even Shiites were unsure whether the initial US attack on Iraq was wrong or right: 52 percent of Shiites asserted that the invasion was either somewhat or absolutely wrong.[50]

Apart from their status, Coalition forces were believed incapable or unwilling to provide security for the Iraqi public. In April 2004, 87 percent of Iraqis expressed no confidence in Coalition forces.[51] Indeed, Iraqis came to *attribute* the security problems in Iraq to the Coalition presence.[52] With Iraq in the midst of a civil war in early 2006, a clear majority of respondents believed that violent attacks, inter-ethnic violence, and the presence of foreign fighters would decrease with a withdrawal of US forces. For that matter, Iraqis indirectly held Coalition forces responsible for the many hardships in the country: 67 percent of Iraqis thought that electricity, schools, and public services would improve, and 73 percent of Iraqis believed that parliamentary factionalism would decline once US troops left Iraq.[53] In August 2007, large numbers of Iraqis continued to view US troops as a problem, and not the solution: 69 percent of Iraqis asserted that the presence of US forces was making the security situation worse and 77 percent indicated that the US role in Iraq was generally negative.[54] Thus, Sunnis and Shiites overwhelmingly favored a timeline for US withdrawal.[55] Although attitudes softened a bit in the extreme violence that precipitated the Awakening movement in late 2006,[56] 91 percent of Sunnis still wanted the United States out of Iraq within a year, and 97 percent of Sunnis continued to believe that the US military presence was provoking more violence than it was preventing—a view shared by 82 percent of the Shiite population.[57] At the height of the surge, almost half of Iraqis wanted an immediate US withdrawal.[58]

Even these negative numbers mask an Iraqi antipathy toward Coalition forces. In a January 2006 survey, 88 percent of Sunnis and 41 percent of Shiites voiced approval for attacks on US-led forces in Iraq (despite overwhelming opposition to the targeting of Iraqi civilians and very mild support among Sunnis for attacks on

Iraqi security forces).[59] In September 2006, 92 percent of Sunnis and 62 percent of Shiites expressed approval of attacks on Coalition forces;[60] at the height of the US surge (August 2007), 93 percent of Sunnis and 50 percent of Shiites believed that attacks on Coalition forces were acceptable.[61] Indeed, these attitudes appeared most prevalent in Anbar Province, the center of the Awakening movement: at the start of the surge, 100 percent of Anbar residents (compared to 50 percent of Baghdad respondents and 42 percent of Basra's largely Shiite population) believed that "attacks on coalition forces are justified."[62]

It cannot be inferred from these data that negative attitudes resulted directly from encounters with US forces. Negative attitudes were prominent in places where US troops were active, but US troops were active in these places for a reason—specifically, the insurgent activities that were promoted with public support. Yet it is possible to conclude from considerable anecdotal evidence that the civilian casualties and damage inflicted by US troops in confrontations with Iraqi militants galvanized opposition to the US presence and even led to some unity of effort between Shiite and Sunni militants (Malkasian 2006, 438–439). It is also possible to conclude that, for much of the Iraqi public, US troops came to symbolize the insecurities, hardships, and indignities that followed the US occupation of Iraq. Negative views formed and spread quickly, resisting change even in the face of a dramatic reduction in Iraqi violence, attributable in part to the surge. Once the Iraqi forces lost faith in Coalition forces, confidence levels never recovered.[63] Coalition forces appeared to get little to no credit for the improving security and reduced violence in the country. By March 2008, 79 percent of Iraqis expressed little to no confidence in Coalition forces (compared to the 56 percent that expressed at least some confidence in the Awakening Councils), and 61 percent of Iraqis continued to believe that the US military presence was a threat to security. (In a perverse victory of sorts for the Coalition's stature in Iraq, *only* 42 percent of Iraqis believed that attacks on Coalition forces were acceptable.) By the time the violence had abated, Iraqis were inclined to read the worst into US actions, magnify US misdeeds, and hold the United States responsible—indirectly, at least—for their country's problems. At that point, these views were so deeply held that the United States could not realistically expect to change them. The US military itself had concluded, from its own studies, that virtually all Iraqis believed that Sunnis and Shiites had coexisted peacefully in Iraq before the US occupation and that the occupation was responsible for the ensuing problems in the country.[64]

If Iraqis believe that the problems of Iraq are not indigenous to the country, that is good news, ultimately, for the US effort. Indeed, animosity toward Coalition forces did not preclude public support for Iraqi security institutions. By and large, Iraqis believed their own security forces were best equipped, despite their deficiencies, to handle Iraq's security problems. In March 2006, with violence raging in the country, 78 percent of Iraqis indicated they placed primary trust for security either in the Iraqi Army or police (compared to 1 percent who received primary comfort from Coalition forces).[65] Unfortunately, the positive sentiments were not shared by many Sunnis: compared to populations elsewhere in Iraq, residents of Sunni provinces and northern Arab regions had significantly less faith in government forces (only 42 percent of the former group trusted Iraqi security forces for personal security the most).[66] Moreover, the positive view of Iraqi security forces belied negative popular sentiment toward the central government. In early 2008, only 48 percent of Iraqis expressed ("quite a lot" or "great") confidence in the Iraqi government.[67] As expected, then, Sunnis expressed little support for the Shiite-led government of Prime Minister al-Maliki or the Shiite-dominated security forces under the Interior Ministry, and few Sunnis (11 percent) thought the ouster of Saddam Hussein was worth the price.[68]

Addressing Humanitarian and Economic Needs

Obviously, leveraging a population involves convincing it that it is better off aligning with the US or host government rather than the insurgents. The US goal, then, is to convey to a public that the net benefits of realignment outweigh the costs—whether in lost benefits (land reform, security, employment) or retaliation for disloyalty from the insurgency. For that reason, US leverage derives from success of a combined military, political, and economic effort that has the United States providing humanitarian assistance, employment opportunities, political empowerment, and reconstruction and development support to the population. The underlying principle is enshrined in the notion of "clear, hold, and build" (the mantra for US counterinsurgency in Iraq) and the US military's conception of counterinsurgency as one aspect of stability operations. Indeed, the new Army/Marine Corps Field Manual shows an understanding that troops conducting counterinsurgency operations must move beyond traditional military functions—assisting in nation-building, infrastructure development, development of rule of law, and so forth—to perform tasks traditionally assumed by civilian (governmental and nongovernmental) agencies.

In Vietnam, the US position vis-à-vis South Vietnam's rural population improved with the formation of the CORDS program. As a combined military/civilian enterprise, the CORDS effort centralized US pacification under US military control (under the immediate direction of a civilian, Robert Komer) and paired military and civilian personnel down the chain of command to the thousands working (in close contact with South Vietnamese teams) at the village level. CORDS personnel were involved in diverse activities ranging from training and advising regional and local militia to providing assistance and support for education, medical care, and infrastructure development (Wright et al. 2008, 53). At one point, the effort was assisted directly in Vietnam by 6,464 military, 1,137 civilian, and 223 third-country advisors (McNerney 2005–6, 43–44). Nonetheless, there is considerable doubt whether CORDS succeeded in its basic mission despite the monumental effort and substantial indicators of progress on the ground (see chapter 2). As one program official concluded, the Saigon government was still viewed by the peasants as "a government of 'them,' remote, arbitrary, and often abusive" (Blaufarb 1977, 271–272).

Though small relative to its Vietnam-era counterpart, when the US effort in Iraq is measured in terms of personnel dedicated to the program in the field, it attained immense financial proportions indeed. Billions of US assistance dollars were eventually channeled to Iraq through programs aimed at assisting Iraqi reconstruction and development from the macro to the micro levels. Among numerous applications, aid was allocated to rehabilitate Iraq's dilapidated oil, electricity, water, and sanitation systems; build up Iraqi security forces; promote local governance, law enforcement, and civil society; help small businesses; and compensate those who had lost family members or suffered property damage in the conflict.

Despite its scope, the assistance program was largely improvised, evolving through necessity and default given the lag in Iraqi oil revenues, the dire state of the Iraqi infrastructure and economy, and the Iraqi government's sluggish budgetary response. The US government was simply unprepared to staff, organize, coordinate, and manage the far-reaching programs that US civilian and military officials had initiated in the hopes of stabilizing conditions in Iraq. The effort suffered enormously, as well, from a delayed and then incomplete US military response to the security challenge in Iraq. The military gave priority to combat operations that were not designed to support a broadly conceived counterinsurgency effort in which combat and reconstruction were mutually supportive goals.[69] At the same time, the US military inherited much of the burden for supporting and managing projects at the provincial and community level through the distribution of Commander's Emergency Response Program (CERP) funds and the assisting and staffing of Provincial Reconstruction Teams (PRTs).[70]

Billions of dollars in CERP money allocated (through 2009) gave lower-level military commanders flexibility to fund a variety of reconstruction and development activities without the usual contracting hurdles.[71] The idea was to get things done, as quickly as possible. Funds were distributed to pay for the salaries of Sons of Iraq, the construction of schools, major sanitation projects, micro-grants for starting businesses, compensation to families, and various other programs intended to "win hearts and minds" over to the US and Iraqi government. A half million dollars was expended, for instance, to purchase action figures made to look like Iraqi Security Forces, almost $13 thousand dollars was spent on pools to cool bears and tigers at a Baghdad zoo, and so forth.[72]

In turn, Provincial Reconstruction Teams (PRTs) originated with the US mission in Afghanistan, where these small (largely military) units helped local governments provide basic services and increase effective governance.[73] The PRTs of Iraq, introduced in 2005, were considerably larger units. They were meant to combine hundreds of personnel under the lead of a State Department official, with representation from various US government departments and a largely civilian composition. Early team performance was hampered by the assortment of problems expected of a novel enterprise operating in a challenging wartime environment: telephones and basic office supplies were in short supply; an unwieldy organizational structure impeded outreach to local populations; the recruiting of competent civilians (ideally with expertise in democratization, agriculture, and police operations) proved exceedingly difficult; significant turnover in staff compromised mission continuity; local authorities feared cooperating (or publicly interacting) with US personnel; coordination between military commands, civilian government agencies, and private contractors proved difficult; and bureaucratic infighting (often between civilian and military personnel) stalled assistance until matters of funding, responsibility, and direction were resolved. Indeed, military officials battled with civilian officials at all levels over the priority to be given the reconstruction mission and the paltry contribution (especially by the State Department) of qualified civilian personnel to the teams: before 2006, the United States had virtually no civilian presence in Iraq outside of Baghdad's walled Green Zone.[74]

With the 2007 surge, the PRTs were expanded in number (from ten to twenty-five) to include smaller teams, involving 8 to 12 persons each, embedded (ePRTs) in brigade combat teams under the lead of a brigade commander. Unlike the traditional PRTs, which focused on improving local governance, the ePRTs complemented the US military effort directly by addressing the immediate needs of residents in hot spots like Baghdad, Anbar, and Diyala Provinces.[75] The operations of the ePRTs, though initially constrained by the violence,[76] expanded greatly as conditions stabilized in the country. The ePRTs proved flexible vehicles for assessing conditions in communities, reconciling conflicting groups, facilitating contacts among Iraqi governing units, training local leaders, promoting political participation, and injecting funds (including CERP monies) quickly into communities (Perito 2008a).

The CERP-funded and PRT activities were critical features of the US mission and had an undeniable positive effect on Iraqi recipients. The funding gave a large and diverse set of recipients an incentive to turn from violence and to invest psychologically and financially in the future. But the funding did little, it seems, to soften the general public's attitude toward Coalition forces or Sunni attitudes toward the Iraqi government. Moreover, flexibility and speed in assistance exacted costs in accountability, project oversight, and inter-project coordination. Serious questions remained, in fact, over the long-term effectiveness of the aid given the turnover in military supervisory personnel, the lack of prior military experience in providing such support, the absence of a grand plan for reconstruction and development, the use of funds designed for small, short-term projects to fund large, longer-term efforts (Tarnoff 2008, 40–42),[77] and the paucity of available materials, financing, and know-how needed to sustain projects once US personnel and resources departed. Many projects undertaken with CERP funds were later abandoned by national or local Iraqi officials, due to their lack of interest or support capabilities, and the future of at least one major project—a hotel funded in part to house prospective foreign investors—was compromised by looting.[78] Indeed, the economic outlook for Iraq dimmed significantly with the departure of US forces. The US withdrawal coincided with a severe (global recession-induced) drop in petroleum prices—which depleted formerly flush Iraqi government budgets—and an increase in violence that deterred direct foreign investment.[79]

The Challenge

Neither the Vietnam nor Iraq conflicts offer compelling evidence that the United States can "win over" a population that is indifferent toward the US presence or the host government, let alone hostile openly toward both. The United States made substantial progress in stabilizing Vietnam and Iraq, as measured convincingly— after years of struggle—by the constricting battlefront in South Vietnam and decreasing violence throughout Iraq. But the evidence is far from conclusive that these populations were "won over," in any sense of the term. A more likely explanation is that they grew weary of the costs of supporting or tolerating the insurgency.

In Iraq, the public turned on insurgent groups without accepting the legitimacy or the good intentions of the US or Baghdad governments.

The United States operated from a severe disadvantage in its "hearts and minds" effort. In both conflicts, although in Iraq more than in Vietnam, the United States had to overcome a profound and widespread belief that the United States was an occupying (or "imperialist") power and that conditions were better before the United States arrived and would improve if the fighting would just stop. In Iraq, the United States had to contend with a belief, as well, that the ostensibly neutral support that the US and host government provided actually aided the opposition. Certainly, the United States helped its cause by providing local populations (political and economic) incentives to support the US-led mission. But these incentives depended for their effectiveness on a huge, enduring US footprint in the country—to assess the needs of the population, to monitor distribution and quality, and to coordinate development. The nagging questions, then, were whether a smaller US footprint would do much good and whether even a massive and lasting US effort would be undone by its negative effects—when US aid and support provoked resentment against the foreign presence, produced unrealistic popular expectations, generated unsustainable projects, created new sets of haves and have-nots, and fostered black-market profiteering within the country.

The Vietnam and Iraq conflicts presented different popular challenges for the United States. In Vietnam, the United States encountered ideological resistance but a population that was typically less hostile to the US occupation than it was desirous that the fighting end. In Iraq, the United States encountered strong sectarian-based resistance and widespread resentment toward a US presence, reinforced by US ties to an unpopular host government. In neither conflict was the public convinced, however, that the US or host government acted in the country's best interests.

Societal Leaders and Groups

The United States was able to rely on "intermediaries" to build a popular base of support in Iraq. Rather than swaying the public directly, the US military eventually capitalized on the anti-jihadist sentiment that had developed among various tribal leaders and nationalist Sunni insurgent groups, to convince them to align with the US military against the al-Qaeda affiliates. A similar alignment option—coopting societal leaders and organized groups representing some portion of the population—was unavailable to the United States in Vietnam.

The heterogeneity of Vietnamese society had some impact on the US military effort in Vietnam. The "fixed" (ethnic and religious) identities of a good portion of the Vietnamese peasantry pushed them to join forces either with the communists or with the government. (In this sense, the Vietnam War was not the pure "identity war" of counterinsurgency theory, as discussed in chapter 2.) In particular, minority religious groups were inclined to support the government, while Buddhist areas were ripe for communist recruiting.[80] In Vietnam's Central Highlands, US Special Forces recruited members of the (largely Christian) Montagnard minority to fight the Vietcong despite their hostility toward Saigon. The US military worked, as well, with members of the Cao Dai and Hoa Hao religious sects that once controlled large amounts of South Vietnamese territory, and their own private militias. Still, their defeat by the Diem regime and questionable loyalties (many were also fighting for the Vietcong) limited their effectiveness as a third force against the communist insurgency. In the final analysis, the competing loyalties within South Vietnamese society probably hurt more than helped the US mission. Buddhist monks, by immolating themselves in public places to protest religious discrimination, precipitated a train of events that led to the overthrow of the (Catholic) Diem government in a military coup. They continued to rally opposition to the Saigon government and created instability in the South that the communists could exploit.

In Iraqi society, by comparison, the United States was aided by groups and leaders with strong social standing. The generally cooperative US relationship with the dominant Shiite party in Iraq (the Supreme Council) allowed the United States to exert leverage indirectly on the Shiite public to quell the violence. Moreover, the United States benefited because Ayatollah al-Sistani was committed to a united and nonviolent Iraq and pivoted among the feuding Shiite factions.[81] His useful efforts included pushing al-Sadr toward restraint and cooperative engagement.[82] Still, al-Sistani was hardly a reliable "agent" for promoting the US agenda (Rahimi 2007a). He accepted the temporary US occupation of Iraq as a practical matter and refused direct meetings with US government officials, who were then left to work around his edicts. For example, when the CPA planned for a managed transition to democracy, it was forced to compromise in deference to unanticipated opposition from al-Sistani, who pushed instead for the direct election of a national legislature that would oversee the drafting of an Iraqi constitution. Furthermore, al-Sistani was not viewed favorably by the Sunni minority and could not bridge the sectarian divide (except, perhaps, as a force for moderation and calm within the Shiite population) that threatened the stability of the country.

Lacking an authoritative counterpart to al-Sistani among Sunnis, the United States eventually built an alliance around a network of tribal and militia groups. But the factors that led to US success in connection with the Awakening also made for a tenuous peace, suggesting the challenges that could arise in future conflicts. This is true for a number of reasons.

First, the US-led alliance system depended on the influence of leaders who had limited authority over their heterogenous "tribes" (on the Iraqi tribal structure, see Eisenstadt 2007). Single tribes often subsumed people of different religions and ethnicity, and tribes varied in their tightness and authority structures. Tribes could fragment, then, when political, economic, and military circumstances pulled the membership apart and its leaders could no longer maintain their tribal stature by providing benefits to their followers.[83] Tensions developed within Anbar Province, then, when the US troop withdrawal in 2009 deprived some tribal leaders of the financial means to secure a following. These embittered leaders lost their base of political support; indeed, they feared for their lives for having exposed themselves as US "lackeys"—a charge that was given weight by their change in fortune with the US exodus.[84]

Second, the US-led alliance system was vulnerable to internal divisions.[85] The alliance system that the United States forged was always threatened by fragmentation, based in tribal rivalries, conflicts of interest, and political or religious differences. It was these very divisions that prevented the Anbar model from taking hold quickly in provinces with heterogeneous populations, like Diyala,[86] where conflict was rooted in societal tensions that predated the arrival of al-Qaeda–linked groups.[87] For example, in the area south of Baghdad known as the Triangle of Death, al-Qaeda had a relatively small direct role in the violence that erupted largely along tribal and sectarian lines.[88] The alliance was also threatened by warlordism, as various groups established criminal fiefdoms.[89] Many of the tribal groups that the United States had embraced in Anbar were involved in smuggling and banditry and were passing compromising information about rivals to US forces to eliminate the economic competition.[90]

Third, the alliance system threatened to create new social divisions—between haves and rival have-nots who had benefited unequally from US support. Conflict was made more likely because the United States had supported a "newer" generation of tribal leaders who could point to benefits (salaries and aid) received from the United States under their leadership to build a tribal support base.[91] One possible result was to foster jealousies and feed suspicions that these leaders (and their friends and relatives) were benefiting unfairly from the largess.[92] At the very least, the newly empowered leaders and groups threatened the existing national and provincial power balance, to create a potential for violence. For example, severe tensions surfaced in Anbar Province between the Awakening groups and the Iraqi Islamic Party—which had participated in 2005 provincial elections despite a widespread Sunni boycott.[93] These tensions threatened to erupt in violence after the Islamic Party's surprisingly strong showing in the January 2009 provincial elections: when tribal leaders claimed that the Islamic Party had stolen the election, the tenor of the accusations and threats reportedly stunned even Iraqi officials.[94]

Fourth, the alliance system could potentially turn on the central government or its Shiite backers. The Sunni recruits and their leaders expressed strong suspicions of the Shiite-led government and its Iranian connection. In observing that a Sunni reconciliation with US forces did not amount to a reconciliation with the central government, an American general captured the prevailing sentiment: "We hate you [the United States] because you are occupiers, . . . but we hate Al Qaeda worse, and we hate the Persians [the Shiites] even more."[95] The question, then, is whether these groups would continue to renounce the use of violence against the government should US money and support run out[96] or should the Iraqi government decide that it had no further use for the groups.[97] Tensions between the al-Maliki government and Awakening Councils rose dramatically, then, with the US handover of these groups to the government. Awakening group members complained about their lack of pay and unpromising future and expressed deep suspicions that the government had targeted them, *as Sunnis*, for arrest. The situation exploded in March 2009, with the high-profile arrest in Baghdad of an Awakening leader, ostensibly for his criminal activities, leading to intense battles between Awakening fighters and Iraqi government forces backed by US troops.[98] Such battles reinforced suspicions on both sides and promised further increases in violence and instability.

Thus, the United States had managed to pull a sizable and powerful share of a hostile population away from the insurgency, but the issue remained whether the resulting alliance could survive unfulfilled promises and a downturn in economic fortunes with the departure of US troops. That the US appeal to these groups and leaders rested on immediate interests—and even then, on the pecuniary interests of the few more than the many—brought the long-term stability of the alliance into question.

Conclusions

For the United States, success in asymmetric conflicts might well depend on its capability to leverage outside states, indigenous populations, and societal groups and leaders. The Vietnam and Iraq conflicts suggest, however, that the United States has less leverage over these critical conflict participants than is often assumed. A lesson from these conflicts is that the United States will encounter significant constraints, risks, and costs and realize limited benefits when leveraging various third parties is required to achieve US goals. This is true for various reasons.

First, the United States might find it difficult to acquire leverage by extending conflicts to border states and outside powers. In Vietnam, the Nixon administration shed Johnson-era constraints when it moved massively against enemy sanctuaries in Cambodia and Laos and signaled to the Soviet Union and China that the United States expected their help to secure an acceptable peace. Yet the administration acted with restraint against the Soviet Union and China, paired its horizontal expansion of the war with a US troop withdrawal from Vietnam, and escalated the air war against North Vietnam while reducing US negotiating demands. In Iraq, the United States warned Syria about its indirect support for Sunni insurgents and Iran about its direct support for Shiite militia groups, in part by arresting Iranians in Iraq for supporting the militias and trumpeting evidence of Iranian complicity with these groups. The United States nonetheless resisted temptations to extend the war into Syria or Iran, knowing that an expanding war would undermine the precarious US position in Iraq.

Second, the United States was challenged in winning over the indigenous populations in Vietnam and Iraq. The US military strategy tended, at critical junctures in these wars, to alienate the very people whose allegiance was required to disrupt insurgent activities. These problems were especially apparent in Iraq. The strong and enduring negative public attitudes toward Coalition forces suggest that Iraqis were quick to attribute the trials and tribulations of post-occupation Iraq to occupying forces and were opposed, perhaps, to all but a fleeting US military presence within the country. Iraqis came soon to assume the worst of US behavior and intentions. Although the US military came, as a consequence, to appreciate its strategy's negative effects, it could not undo its earlier mistakes. Indeed, its belated response speaks to a military insensitivity to political matters when sensitivity is required—above all in the early stages of a conflict.

Third, the United States was challenged when it tried to drive a wedge between the insurgents and various societal leaders and groups. In Iraq, the United

States ultimately succeeded in building bridges to tribal leaders and in recruiting groups away from the insurgency. Unfortunately for the United States, this recruitment strategy depended on felicitous conditions—not present in Vietnam—specifically, a hierarchical social structure and coherent groups willing to ally with US troops. Even the strategy's success in Iraq should give pause to those seeking its applications to future US military engagements. The strength of the alliances between the US military and its former adversaries owed much to animosities that developed *over the course of the conflict* toward a *foreign* (insurgent) presence within the country. The US insurgent recruitment strategy might not work when the United States is itself the outside party to the conflict. Regardless, any alliance between the United States and indigenous parties is likely to be fragile when the essential demands of these leaders and groups go unsatisfied and deep hostility and distrust separate them from the host government.

CHAPTER FOUR

Leveraging the Adversary's Leaders

The Balance of Resolve and US Exhaustion

In asymmetric war, a combatant's weapons or doctrines offset the overwhelming advantages of a qualitatively or quantitatively superior force. In "asymmetric conflict," a variety of factors—including military capabilities *and* psychological or political "intangibles"—could permit a combatant to thrive under adversity. Its strength lies in knowing, then, that a materially stronger opponent will accept an unfavorable compromise or defeat when it appreciates the costs of persevering.

The leverage balance between the United States and its adversaries does not reduce to simple capability ratios—qualities and quantities of personnel and hardware that are available to one side versus the other and determine the relative ability of each to inflict costs upon the other. Leverage also ensues from differences between the combatants in their willingness to use their human and material resources, to lose them—and to risk losing more of them. It makes sense, then, to view leverage partly as a function of resolve—the relative willingness of contesting parties to tolerate the "damage" that an opponent can inflict and more generally to "absorb costs" (Mack, 178). Whether on the battlefield or in negotiations, outcomes are greatly affected by "who wants it more"—a common sports phrase meant to suggest that teams triumph by overriding pain ("digging deep") to tap their capability reserve. Such resolve draws, at least in part, from the perceived benefits of persevering.[1]

True, victory in conflict is often predicted—correctly—for the side with relative capability advantages (military, economic, or otherwise). Wars between unfairly matched opponents—for instance, the United States and Grenada—are won by the side that can employ a minimum of effort to overwhelm an opponent's capability to resist. When victory is effortless, however, it is reasonable to ask whether the stronger party will fully engage itself in the fight: after all, a hopelessly weak opponent is not much of a threat, in a world filled with bigger threats. Thus, it is useful to think of the leverage balance that decides outcomes between two opponents as a ratio of the products of each party's anticipated costs (economic, political, and military) and cost tolerance.[2] Together, costs and cost tolerance determine whether, when, and how one party influences another.

Unfortunately for the United States, it was severely disadvantaged in this battle of resolve in Vietnam and Iraq despite employing various compensatory strategies. Most important, the United States fought an uphill battle in its efforts to maintain support, at home, for prosecuting both wars.

Adversary Resolve: US Relative Disadvantages

The United States is unquestionably advantaged over likely opponents because of US technological advantages and the large population pool from which the United States can draw military personnel. Probable wartime scenarios have the United States imposing higher (absolute and relative) fatality levels on opponents than those opponents can inflict in return. The same applies to economic resources. The many billions of dollars that the United States poured into Vietnam and Iraq to sustain its war efforts far exceeded the offsetting amounts that US opponents mobilized in return. But, as long as the adversary *could avoid defeat*, to capitalize on declining US resolve, its loss tolerance compensated for such capability deficiencies. The United States lost over 50 thousand men in Vietnam; by comparison, Hanoi claims to have suffered force losses, in the US combat period, in excess of *one million*—constituting over 5 percent of the population of North Vietnam and communist-controlled areas in the South at the time (Record 2007, 5)—on top of an exceedingly high civilian toll. The adversary's loss-tolerance advantage—in Vietnam and Iraq—drew from the adversary's higher relative stakes in the conflict. The adversary built on this advantage by effectively communicating its cost tolerance to the United States.

Relative Stakes

The adversary's higher relative stakes have two (somewhat counterintuitive) sources. These are the adversary's aggregate capability deficiencies and standing as the target of (compellence) demands. Both work to the US disadvantage.

The Benefits of "Weakness"

The advantages of the weak relative to the strong draw from a paradox of power: with power comes responsibilities that tax the capabilities of a preponderant party and reduce its stakes in "small" conflicts.[3] Consequently, the strong must accommodate the weak when, all other things being equal, the strong can dominate the weak.

Accommodation—the idea that, despite an overall capability edge, stronger parties will allow adversaries to achieve some level of military success or to drag out conflicts for political gain—informs a key paradox in realist thinking: the capabilities that states employ to further their interests also free those states from having to react, or indeed require that they not react, to each and every adversary provocation.[4] The cumulative contribution of realist writings lies in the nuance of their claims. They do not insist that the central actors avoid conflict at all costs any more than they assert that actors match adversary conflict, act for act. Instead, they acknowledge that, under certain conditions, powerful actors accept some price to avoid conflict: for instance, A may not respond with conflict toward B when B is more of an annoyance than a serious threat or when a conflictive response would compromise A's ability to react to provocations from powerful states in other parts of the world. Wolfers (1962, 111–122) notes, for example, that "whenever two great powers are locked in serious conflict they can spare little if any of their coercive strength to deal with minor offenders and to impose their will on them over issues that have no direct bearing on the major struggle in which they are involved with their equals."

Thus, drawing out the fighting is a winning strategy for a weaker party, like an insurgent group, that can exploit the paradox of major power status: for the insurgents, the war is "total" when, for the intervening power, it is "necessarily limited" (Mack 1975, 181). Whereas a major power maintains a "global" outlook and set of interests, it is constrained, more than its local rival, in the nature and share of its resources—human and otherwise—it can and will invest in any one place and time. US leaders seek to avoid investing too heavily in a "small war" that will distract the United States from its more critical obligations—or worse, require the US military to reinvent itself and thereby diminish its capabilities to address the threats that the military is structured ("meant") to address (see chapter 1). The irony, then, is that the weaker party might retain the initiative—control the pace and severity of the fighting—to capitalize on constraints that inhibit the "stronger" party from engaging fully, and so prolong a war to secure a more favorable *negotiated* outcome (Pillar 1983; Wagner 2000). It has an added incentive to do so because escalating and extending a conflict allows the weak to demonstrate its strength. On this point, Wagner (2000, 477–478) argues that, by displaying its true capabilities in combat, "a weak state can hope to gain concessions from a strong state even though it would be unable to disarm the strong state." Similarly, Pillar (1983, 48) embraces the somewhat counterintuitive notion that a state "will be more likely to seek negotiations when the military situation is favorable." For example, Hanoi might have avoided peace negotiations with the United States in the early 1960s out of fear that it could not yet negotiate from strength (Duiker 1996, 223–224; McNamara et al. 1999, 126–127); years later, North Vietnam adopted a hardline stance in peace negotiations after the devastating damage to the Vietcong in the Tet Offensive, apparently to allow time for insurgent forces in the South to recuperate (Elliott 2003, 1132; on fighting as bargaining, see Werner 1998, 322).

As a global power, the United States is further disadvantaged knowing that its gains in one conflict invite costs in others. In Vietnam, US leaders adopted tactics that included foregoing a land invasion of North Vietnam so as not to provoke Chinese or Russian intervention. In the Iraq conflict, the United States was deterred from attacking Iranian facilities, used to support Shiite militia, by the likely effects should Iran retaliate on one or more fronts (see chapter 3). Indeed, the resulting instability in Iraq would have prevented the United States from transferring troops to Afghanistan. The United States only appears positioned, then, to employ massive force cheaply to affect the adversary's capability and resolve. Toward that end, the United States could have used nuclear weapons against North Vietnam or bombed its dikes to flood the countryside (and destroy its agricultural economy).[5] Such wanton destruction can break a population and its government *at some point*, just as a scorched-earth policy will eventually hurt an insurgent movement that draws its sustenance from an indigenous population. Yet the United States is unlikely to impose these costs on a hostile population (except to avoid catastrophic troop losses or imminent military defeat): a high civilian toll might undermine norms of war that serve US purposes in other parts of the world (by constraining the behavior of other states), might weaken the moral or political standing that the United States requires to pursue its (national, regional, or global) objectives, and might offend the sensitivities of vocal domestic constituencies that are present within the United States, as a democratic nation (Merom 2003, 50).[6] Accordingly, the US military went to great lengths to minimize civilian distress and deaths in Iraq. Although it inflicted many hundreds of civilian deaths in trying to take Fallujah in April 2004, it withdrew from the city with heavy civilian casualties (and a realization that efforts to safeguard civilians would take a toll on US troops). Thus, the United States—here and elsewhere—found itself in a lose-lose situation. The adversary could benefit—militarily—if the United States held its fire or refrained from hitting certain targets and—politically—in claiming credit for compelling the United States to back down or for deterring a US attack. Should the United States have attacked these targets and inflicted human cost (collateral damage), the adversary can point to the "indiscriminate" attack to demonstrate to a receptive domestic or global audience that the United States is malevolent. In consequence, the United States has the worst of both worlds—unable to commit to combat or to withdraw from it. In such a no-win position, the United States inevitably inflicts casualties sufficient to harm the United States politically but not enough to help the United States militarily, that is, to bring the opponent to its knees.

The United States is also disadvantaged because, as a global power, it must surrender home-field advantage. The United States is engaged globally in conflicts that pit the United States against leaders that can paint the threat to local populations in grand terms that arouse popular passions, evoke fears, and justify national sacrifices to mobilize offsetting resources. The North Vietnamese and their Vietcong allies did this with great success, as did Sunni insurgents and Shiite militia leaders in Iraq. By comparison, US leaders must struggle to keep a public on board that cares little about international affairs and becomes increasingly unwilling to sacrifice to achieve military goals with mounting expenditures of blood and treasure, as we shall see. The pressure on leaders only increases when the feared costs of war include the sacrifice of domestic programs (for instance, the Johnson administration's Great Society programs) or economic stability (the meltdown of the global financial system in the last months of the Bush administration) and when changes in the global political system (US-Soviet detente and fractionation of the communist bloc in the Vietnam era) undermine the assumptions that provoked a war's initiation. As Reiter and Stam (2002, 178) conclude in a study of the statistical evidence from the last two centuries, "When democratic leaders make accurate forecasts of how the war will unfold, they fight wars that are short, low-casualty, and victorious. When they guess wrong, however, and the war does not end quickly, they eventually must give up on their hopes for victory and seek a draw in order to exit sooner rather than later."

Given these advantages, the "weaker" party enjoys a relatively high rate of success: over half of wars fought in the last half of the twentieth century were won, in fact, by the weaker actor (Arreguín-Toft 2005, 4).[7] The major powers failed to accomplish their primary political goals through military intervention in almost 40 percent of cases since 1945, with the United States exhibiting only a slightly better success rate (Sullivan 2007, 519). A single painful experience is sufficient, however, to make that point: "What we witnessed with Vietnam was the end of the era in which one could believe that a great industrial power is *bound* to win when it fights a small, poor, backward country" (Schelling 1981, 9). For all its mobility and firepower, the United States was disadvantaged if its intent was to break the will of North Vietnam and sap its strength. As Record (1998, xiii) concludes, "In the end it was America's will, not North Vietnam's, that faltered, and it faltered because Hanoi recognized, if Washington did not, that a condition of enduring military stalemate, given American impatience and North Vietnam's far greater stake in the war, would ultimately produce an American withdrawal from the fight." North Vietnam's legendary defense minister, General Vo Nguyen Giap, recognized as much when he observed that the United States would fail inevitably in Vietnam because US strengths were "limited" and its weaknesses were "basic" (quoted in Currey 1997, 259). The irony is that US policymakers identify threats of sufficient magnitude to justify US military intervention but of insufficient magnitude to warrant staying the course once the attendant costs are belatedly appreciated.

Resisting Compellence

The balance of resolve works against any intervening power because it is likely to encounter "compellence" problems rather than the "deterrence" problems that preoccupied US leaders during the Cold War (on the distinction, see Freedman 2004, 109–112; Schaub 1998). With deterrence, the challenge is preventing an adversary *from doing* something; with compellence, the challenge is getting an adversary *to do* something.

The distinction is not merely semantic: compellence problems place the United States at a strategic disadvantage. Compellence is more difficult than deterrence in part because the latter comes with plausible deniability: in response to a deterrence threat, the target can always justify its inaction by claiming that it had no intention of taking the controversial step in the first place. With compellence, the target has limited opportunities for a graceful exit. In conceding to a compellence demand, a target state or militia group will have to vacate territory, disarm, or observe a ceasefire, among possible concessions that the target must fear will undermine its bargaining position by impugning the target's capabilities or resolve to an all-important domestic or foreign audience. The United States might be disadvantaged from the start in attempting to compel change in another's behavior. Psychological research indicates that people tend to place more value on what they have than what they do not yet possess (Levy 1997). Individuals are much more likely to take risks and incur costs to hold onto their possessions or to retrieve what they have lost than to pursue new gains (to undermine deterrence). The costs to the challenger of conceding to a compellence demand only increase once the challenger has invested significantly in a course of action, for example, by announcing its ambitions to a supportive public. It is hard to back down once expectations for action are created without being accused of hypocrisy and a lack of commitment and risking a loss in support to extremist elements (on the "audience cost" issue, see Fearon 1994). Parties are bound as much by their own earlier behavior as their rhetoric. Once a party fights with a particular level of commitment, decreasing it can incite constituent fears that the conflict is being lost or signal to the adversary that it holds the military or political advantage. Similarly, backing down or deescalating a conflict is not a viable option for leaders who believe that their group (or movement) requires forward progress to survive— that inertness will deplete the ranks of the organization, create a loss in focus, or deprive the leader of the moral authority that stems from adopting an absolutist, uncompromising stance. Under these conditions, leaders are motivated—if anything—to *increase* their commitment to a course of action. Even deterring these leaders becomes problematic, then, because it amounts to *compelling* them to abandon their power or goals. In this regard, it is useful to note the retrospective comments of one Hanoi official who was involved in the Paris negotiations. He criticized the US failure to pay "closer attention to the minimum objectives and requirements" of the opposition by observing that "no matter whether you say you are demanding the other side to surrender, this is the way you will be interpreted" (quoted in McNamara et al. 1999, 228).

In Vietnam, the United States faced a challenging compellence problem— inducing Hanoi to accept a settlement that left the Saigon government in military and political control of the South. For North Vietnam's leadership, compromise involved costly concessions. Compromise risked the appearance that Hanoi's leaders were "caving into U.S. pressure" and were abandoning their brethren in the

South (McNamara et al. 1999, 187, 228). It would also undermine the legitimacy that these leaders obtained from the unapologetic nationalism that was essential for these leaders to acquire mass support, in the North and South, for the war effort. Concessions opened these leaders to charges that they were making empty claims and promises and were forcing the public to make needless sacrifices. Almost as damaging, compromise required reopening internal debates over the wisdom of pursuing unification through force and overturning decisions that had long guided Hanoi's war strategy. The effect would have been a loss in policy direction and a shift in the intra-governmental power balance against those who had championed the prior approach (Thies 1980, 256, 262, 276–278). Such concessions would not come easily to Hanoi's leaders, especially when they believed they were winning the war and would ultimately prevail.

The compellence challenge—even if not recognized as such—figured more decisively in US calculations in Vietnam than did the deterrence challenge. Without question, the United States wanted to deter military intervention by the Soviet Union or China. But the United States mostly sought to *avoid* provocations that would cause these powers to up their military commitment in Vietnam and hoped in the final years of the war that the Soviet Union and China would intervene, cooperatively, by getting Hanoi to settle on US terms. The United States actually had good reason to deemphasize the deterrence dimensions of the conflict: given its technology advantages, the United States relished a war that raised the profile of North Vietnamese regular forces or brought the Vietcong into direct conflict with US troops. In fact, the US attrition strategy depended on it: the United States made substantial military gains after the Vietcong tried to seize ground throughout South Vietnam in the 1968 Tet Offensive.

By comparison, deterrence had a central role in post-occupation Iraq when the United States confronted Sunni insurgent and Shiite militia groups. Unable to defeat them, the US approach was to *deter* these groups from engaging in deadly and destabilizing actions and to *deter* individuals who might be recruited or intimidated by these groups from providing them with aid, comfort, and manpower. By attacking strongholds of Shiite militias and Sunni insurgents, the United States sought to send a clear message to Iraqis that the costs of suicide bomb attacks on civilians or assaults on US forces are severe and that the future is in working with the Iraqi government and US forces, not against them.

At first glance, this is a relatively straightforward deterrence problem. Yet the deterrence problem is inseparable, here, from a compellence problem because the United States intended also to convince these groups to demobilize, disarm, and enter the political process and because the United States sought to deter these militant and militia groups from *continuing* or *escalating* their violent operations and effectively to compel them, in consequence, to *reduce* their public presence and therefore, in essence, to back down. Thus, unfortunately for the United States, it requires targeted-group leaders, in such situations, to make costly concessions that open them to charges of selling out (Pillar 1983, 65). These leaders risk delegitimation from compromising core principles, paying the price in a loss in organizational control through splintering, reduced organizational resolve, or a cynical ethos that pulls members toward self-interested (in some cases, criminal) behavior. That price was apparently paid by Moqtada al-Sadr when, by observing a ceasefire with Coalition forces, he precipitated the fragmentation of the Mahdi militia.

The costs of concessions are made still more onerous when parties—like those involved in the sectarian conflict of Iraq—are caught in a "security dilemma" (Snyder and Jervis 1999). Its compelling logic, drawn from the realist literature in international politics, has parties trapped in a war for survival. The logic is threefold (a) under anarchic conditions (when governments are unavailable for protection), parties must provide for their own security; (b) parties are wary, then, of their standing relative to others and must act to offset their rising capabilities; and (c) any gains achieved in defense for a "threatened" party will present "offensive" challenges to others requiring that they, too, adopt offsetting measures.[8] For realists, the dilemma is not the irrational one of misperception, growing hostility, and an explosion, perhaps, into war. The dilemma is that competing parties have no choice but to act in ways that perpetuate conflict: given uncertainty about the intentions of others and their willingness to do the "right thing" in the face of temptation, parties do what they must to defend themselves. Compromise is impossible for leaders of threatened groups if they believe that concessions (territorial or otherwise) will ultimately weaken their security position vis-à-vis the occupation force, rival groups, or the government. Indeed, compromise is especially difficult in a domestic security dilemma given the close geographical proximity of opposing parties, personal grievances against members of a rival group that boost security concerns, and the reticence of groups to disarm, as required for national reconciliation, when this will expose them to attack and give opponents a lethal edge by retaining hidden caches of arms. Always fearful that opponents are seeking and acquiring an advantage, leaders become wary of losing the initiative through compromise and instead seek opportunities to grab resources, extend their support base, and weaken the opposition.[9] Given the security dilemma, it is hardly surprising that Shiite and Sunni militants repeatedly sought to militarize the conflict and avoided concessions that were necessary to foster long-term national stability.

In sum, the problem of compelling change in the behavior of adversary leaders is that they avoid concessions from positions of both strength *and* weakness. Strong leaders feel no need to concede; weak leaders cannot (see chapter 5).

Communicating Intent

The strong resolve of an adversary can give it a significant bargaining advantage. This assumes, however, that the adversary can communicate its resolve to outside parties.

From the adversary's perspective in Vietnam, the United States was but one in a succession of powers that sought to dominate the people of Vietnam and control its resources. Strengthened by the rightness of its nationalist cause and the formidable symbolic backing of North Vietnam's president, Ho Chi Minh (who led the fight for liberation against Japan and France), the adversary was uncompromising in its pursuit of unification. Yet strength of commitment is not always sufficient to communicate resolve. The Johnson administration consistently underestimated Hanoi's dedication to national unification. In essence, in demanding that North Vietnam end its military efforts and support for guerrilla activities in the South, the administration sought precisely what Hanoi would never concede.

To compensate, parties seek to boost their apparent resolve, either to exaggerate their resolve or to communicate their *actual* resolve to the adversary (Fearon 1995).[10] Hanoi did just that by fighting with a seeming indifference to its own casualties over the course of the Vietnam conflict. As John Mueller (1980, 512) described the attitude of General Giap toward his own high body count, "It seems to be an unimportant part of his military strategy." Indeed, Giap was callously dismissive when commenting on the human toll of his war efforts (Karnow 1997, 20). This show of indifference played to prejudices within the US policy establishment about the willingness of Asian adversaries to withstand pain, as conveyed by Douglas MacArthur's suggestion that China and North Korea have a "gross indifference to human loss" and John Foster Dulles's warning about wars of attrition with Asian countries that were "glutted with manpower" (as quoted in Gartner 1998, 247). Yet Hanoi was potentially advantaged in the contest in resolve from the start for having chosen to challenge the status quo against a materially stronger foe (Paul 1994, 17). The adversary that attacks and "keeps coming" when, by existing wisdom, it should have lost can benefit from the fact of low prior expectations:

the stronger foe might later compensate for its error of judgment by exaggerating the opponent's resolve or capability. Conversely, the adversary can benefit if it can appear to hold the superior position and therefore needs to do less to win. The United States was politically disadvantaged in Vietnam, then, to the extent US officials embraced the view of the PROVN study that "the VC do not have to deliver until they win," where the United States has "to deliver in order to win"— indeed, to do so allied with a host government "that cannot validly claim the active loyalty of a majority—even a significant minority—of the people" (US Army 1966).

By elevating the perceived costs to the United States of continuing to fight, Hanoi realized success, then, when Secretary of Defense Robert McNamara— the principal architect of the US war strategy—confessed to a congressional committee in 1967, shortly before his departure from office, that intense bombing had not broken the will of the North Vietnamese (who were "accustomed to discipline and were no strangers to deprivation and death") and was unlikely to bring them to the negotiating table (Karnow 1997, 522–523). Hanoi's work was hardly done. It planned the Tet Offensive knowing that it, by itself, would not lead to a US defeat. Hanoi meant the offensive, instead, to convince US policymakers that they must escalate US involvement in Vietnam and incur even greater costs— economically, politically, and militarily—that might still not bring the conflict to a successful conclusion. Under these conditions, the United States would presumably prefer to withdraw (Elliott 2003, 1049–1050). To be sure, Hanoi's leaders did not agree when assessing what their forces could accomplish militarily. Most notably, General Giap argued for a "protracted war" in which communist forces would avoid all-out confrontations with US troops, and he opposed the Tet and Easter Offensives. Yet, even Giap acknowledged that the 1968 Tet Offensive had exposed the limits to what the United States could accomplish through force and would speed the eventual US defeat (Currey 1997, 261–274). Hanoi's leaders had actually constructed a continuum of "victory" scenarios before Tet that included, albeit at the low end on the victory scale, a US troop *increase* and *expansion* of the war (McNamara et al. 1999, 363).

In Iraq, attacks and battles meant to convey strength and resolve were behind much of the militant violence. In 2004, the Mahdi Army went on the offensive in Najaf intending to capture the center of Shiite religious authority in Iraq; Sunni insurgents—extolling their major victory over US occupation forces in Fallujah— made it a rallying center (cry) for foreign insurgents and their jihadist allies in the country. Not only did they believe that the victory demonstrated their own strength and superiority over Coalition forces, but moderate Sunnis were also apparently convinced that the United States had suffered a defeat—that they had to placate the militants because the United States could not offer protection (Malkasian 2006, 444–445). The tactics of militant groups were actually intended for maximum political impact. The Sunni jihadists attacked the Asmara Shrine in Samarra in 2006 and other Shiite places of worship throughout the country in an effort to land a symbolic blow to spark a civil war; Shiite groups retaliated, for further political effect, with attacks on Sunni mosques and Sunnis of all walks of life. Indeed, rockets and mortars fired from Sunni and Shiite neighborhoods fell continuously on Baghdad's Green Zone, the center of US authority in Iraq, as militants from various groups sought to communicate to US officials that they were vulnerable *anywhere* in the country. These attacks on high-profile targets in well-fortified parts of the capital continued, even as Iraq entered a period of increased stability. In one week in March 2009, suicide bombers killed scores of people in attacks on gatherings of police recruits and on a reconciliation meeting of tribal leaders.[11] The deadly Baghdad vehicular-bomb attacks of August 2009 were aimed in part at Iraqi government ministries. Such attacks continued to serve a variety of specific purposes—to instill popular fear, to establish the ineptness of Iraq security personnel, to exacerbate sectarian tension, to provoke US retaliation to expose the dark side of the US occupation, and to generate support from a "receptive" public. But the fundamental purpose was always to magnify the apparent capability and resolve of the attackers to affect critical opinion.

The adversary might nevertheless exercise restraint if it is seeking to accomplish its goals with an economy of force. Its dilemma is simple: if it is insufficiently forceful, the United States will doubt its will; if it is too forceful, it risks depriving the United States of an easy way out of the conflict. The United States might not leave if it feels that its primary goals are threatened, that US credibility globally is compromised by a hasty retreat, or that the adversary is not negotiating in good faith. In fact, the United States might escalate its involvement, which could increase the costs to the adversary even should it ultimately emerge victorious. Thus, the adversary might choose to communicate somehow that it is not wedded to maximalist goals—without narrowing its options. Hanoi did just that throughout the 1960s with its perplexing demand for an unconditional US bombing halt. Was it a sign that Hanoi might renounce its maximum goals with the "right" deal or a propaganda ploy meant to make the United States seem uncompromising in rejecting the demand? Although the demand was arguably a face-saving device meant to pave the way for meaningful North Vietnamese concessions or even a sincere offer meant to test the US willingness to compromise, the nature of the demand also provided strong reasons to suspect Hanoi's motives. Why would Hanoi demand an *unconditional* bombing halt? Hanoi was implying that it denied the fundamental legitimacy of US claims and actions, and wanted a major—perhaps, primary—US concession up front (Pillar 1983, 76). Hanoi benefited, nonetheless, from the pretense of making perfectly reasonable demands. As Pillar (1983, 71) puts it, "By skillfully dangling the juicy plum of peace while calling for a reduction of the U.S. military effort—particularly a halt to the bombing of North Vietnam—they could portray themselves as peace-lovers, encourage anti-war forces in the United States, and make it appear that the Johnson administration was deliberately passing up opportunities for negotiation." Hypothetically, such a strategy could convince an opponent to disengage or undercommit until it is exhausted. At the very least, it renders the opponent vulnerable to an effective negotiating strategy.

In negotiations, the United States is disadvantaged by its desire to make a deal. In dribs and drabs, by simply waiting out the United States and feigning a compromise posture, the weaker party can accumulate what amount to "irrevocable" concessions. Any concession—even those that are meant as "peace feelers" or that are reputedly "no longer on the table"—are essentially nonretractable and build on prior concessions. This is because any offer contains information about what the conceding party is willing to give (or give up) to consummate a deal. With such information, the recipient is positioned to try to improve upon the offer, that is, to hold out or to increase the pressure in the hopes that the other party is willing to give still more for a deal. Once the United States communicated a demarcation line to Pyongyang with the hope of ending the Korean War, the line became the basis of an armistice agreement—but not without protracted negotiations over contentious issues (for instance, prisoner repatriation) and costly North Korean offensives aimed at bettering the final terms.[12] The US death toll in the negotiating period exceeded the previous toll (Iklé 2005, 89–90). The adversary strategy worked better in the Vietnam War period. In its first three years, according to Paul Pillar, "the Nixon administration had softened several times its position on military disengagement, electoral arrangements within South Vietnam, and the timing of these with respect to each other and a prisoner release, while receiving very little in return" (Pillar 1983, 113). When any offer is nonretractable—and when the adversary is not losing ground militarily (or politically)—the United States could only hope to seal a deal with additional concessions. With an eye to the exit and viewing each of its concessions as an incremental departure from the preceding one, the United States found that later concessions come easier than the first.

Eventually, Hanoi accepted terms, in the 1973 Paris Peace Agreement, that it had long rejected: it acquiesced to President Thieu retaining the presidency of South Vietnam and no longer pushed for a coalition government (in the South) that included the Vietcong (as of 1969, the Provisional Revolutionary Government, or PRG). But Hanoi could tolerate a ceasefire short of achieving its political or military goals because it assumed that the United States was seeking to withdraw from Vietnam and would not reengage with a reescalation of the conflict and because Hanoi's position was not compromised militarily and politically by the agreement. Indeed, the Paris Agreement explicitly prohibited the return of US forces to Vietnam, sanctioned North Vietnam's military position in the South, legitimized the PRG by recognizing it as one of "two South Vietnamese parties" with equal standing, acknowledged the 17th parallel as a "provisional" boundary (separating North from South Vietnam), and referenced Vietnam's "unification" as an end goal (of a peaceful and consensual political process). As Snepp (1977, 50) surmised, "The peace of Paris was no peace at all," for it "imposed no limitation, or obligation, on either side [North or South Vietnam] that could not be nullified through the unanimity principle, and apart from the withdrawal of U.S. forces, all major provisions were subject to reinterpretation and further debate." In other words, the accords did nothing but open the door for a decisive North Vietnamese military offensive once US troops had withdrawn.[13]

In Iraq, the United States was equally anxious to explore the opening that Shiite militia and Sunni insurgents provided in their conditional willingness to accommodate a US presence in the country. But in respecting a ceasefire with elements of the Mahdi Army and allowing Sunni groups to "switch sides," the United States had to accept the accompanying risk that al-Sadr was simply marking time and waiting for a propitious moment to flex his muscles and that Sunni insurgents would return to violence as soon as they became exasperated by the Baghdad government's intransigence. The upshot is that agreement was made possible in Iraq—as in Vietnam—by the adversary's initial relentlessness *and* apparent willingness ultimately to compromise. Lacking viable military options, the United States was anxious to consummate agreements (formal or otherwise) to end the violence that did not significantly constrain the other negotiating parties.

US Counter-Strategies

To acquire offsetting leverage, one possible US response is to expand or intensify the conflict. Escalation is advisable for the United States if it can win at a higher level of violence and the adversary is unable to escalate the conflict further to compensate.[14] Escalation can also work, in principle, if the United States employs its forces to obtain a motivational edge in a "competition in risk taking" (Schelling 1960). If the United States is more willing than its adversary is to accept the costs of a conflict spiraling upward or extending outward, the United States is positioned to obtain concessions from an adversary that permit a reduction in violence. The danger for the United States is, however, that the opponent will not concede and that the United States must then live with the consequences of its strategy.

The problem for the United States was that it was not well positioned, for much of the Vietnam and Iraq conflicts, to make escalation work. So the United States chose to bolster its position by (a) increasing the stakes ("creating interests") to justify the US investment, and (b) signaling US resolve and restraint to the adversary. Indeed, signaling was a defining feature of the US air war in Vietnam.

Manipulating the Stakes: Linkage

If US adversaries doubt that the United States will stick to its goals given the costs, the United States can compensate by redefining its goals to increase the US stake in the conflict. More specifically, by linking one conflict to another or to a grander struggle, the United States gives itself more to gain from persevering and more to lose from conceding.

US Cold War strategy illustrates this. For most US policymakers, there was no such thing as the "wrong war, at the wrong place, at the wrong time, with the wrong enemy"—the famous critique of the Korean War by Omar Bradley (then chairman of the Joint Chiefs of Staff). By embracing the domino theory—its depiction of a single-minded communist enemy with global ambitions—US leaders argued that a strike by communists anywhere in the world was tantamount to an assault everywhere. In consequence, leaders could mobilize domestic public opinion and justify the immense resources and time invested in small conflicts around the world, from the Dominican Republic and Lebanon to South Korea, Taiwan, and South Vietnam.

By the late 1960s, the principal dominos—the Soviet Union and China—appeared at least as likely to topple into each other.[15] But the US stake in Vietnam did not decline accordingly: the *fact* of the US commitment became the key justification for persevering in Vietnam given the potential consequences of a US defeat. Lyndon Johnson (1971, 147–148) could not have articulated this assumption any clearer than his statement to his cabinet in 1965, in which he warned, "If we run out on Southeast Asia, there will be trouble ahead in every part of the globe—not just in Asia, but in the Middle East and in Europe, in Africa and Latin America. I am convinced that our retreat from this challenge will open the path to World War III." This position retained prominence in US thinking as the fear of a monolithic communist adversary diminished. For Henry Kissinger, less important than the reasons the United States went into Vietnam (to fight communism) were the political ramifications of leaving: the United States could not renege on its commitment to Saigon without causing US allies and adversaries to question US resolve.[16] In this view, US allies would capitulate rather than fight, unable to trust US assurances, and US adversaries, having exposed the emptiness of US commitments, would press for advantages.[17] This possibility gave the United States reason to stay the course in Vietnam—while giving Hanoi reason, presumably, to believe that the United States would do just that.

US policymakers focused similarly on the broader implications of the Iraq conflict, in part to bolster the US stance. US leverage arguably increased when US officials identified al-Qaeda as the principal threat to Iraq,[18] and when US officials trumpeted the links between Iran and al-Sadr's Mahdi Army (and, later, the "special groups" that defied al-Sadr's calls for a ceasefire).[19] As these threats subsided, US policymakers remained attentive to "grander" threats. US policymakers warned, again, of a domino effect by which instability in Iraq could spread beyond its borders and create opportunities for US adversaries to exploit and, too, of the consequences should the United States fail to stand behind its commitments.[20] Yet the strategic reasoning behind manipulating conflict "linkages" is unsound in various respects.

First, with a focus on linkages, US policymakers can overcommit US resources to a conflict. In consequence, they might dilute US resources by spreading them thin among conflicts or avoid making the tough (but necessary) choice to extricate the United States from a conflict. It is one thing to identify the negative consequences of retreat; it is quite another to suggest that avoiding these consequences is reason to stay the course. A perverse effect of US policies in Iraq was actually to *create* global linkages among groups (for instance, between Iraqi insurgents and al-Qaeda) and to distract the United States from its efforts against groups (for instance, the Taliban in Afghanistan) that were linked more directly to al-Qaeda.

Second, by virtue of these linkages, US policymakers are compelled to adopt a military strategy that reflects the grand conception of the strategic problem. For example, by asserting that the Vietnam War was fueled first and foremost by North Vietnamese intervention, the United States would make aerial strikes on

North Vietnamese troops and supply lines a key element of the US military strategy, to the neglect of indigenous sources of personnel and resources that fueled the war effort in the South. Likewise, with similar assumptions, US officials ignored the domestic origins and orientation of Sunni insurgent and Shiite militia groups—their reliance on local resources and personnel and pursuit of national over international (for instance, jihadist) goals. Consequently, US officials discounted the possible effectiveness of securing the loyalty of a local population over combating the enemy and the counterproductive effects of US tactics on local opinion.

Third, US policymakers are inclined to see, and act on, linkages that are not meaningful to US adversaries, even when the linkage approach assumes that adversaries appreciate these linkages. The historical record offers little evidence, for example, that the Soviet Union read lessons about US resolve into US actions throughout the developing world (Hopf 1994; see also Mercer 1996). In other words, despite grave US concerns, the reverberations of the US defeat in Vietnam were not widely felt. The Soviet Union, no less than other US adversaries, appeared to appreciate that US behavior is conditional—that US actions change as circumstances require, given broad US security goals and capabilities to support them (see Press 2005). Most definitely, US adversaries have read negative lessons into US retreats under fire. Saddam Hussein and Osama bin Laden supposedly concluded from the hasty US exodus from Lebanon in the early 1980s and Somalia in the early 1990s that the United States would not tolerate mounting casualties (see Gordon and Trainor 2006, 66; Trager and Zagorcheva 2005, 104). Still, it is not clear that the United States could have avoided being perceived as soft by some Islamic militants given their predisposition to believe the best of their own capabilities and the worst of US intentions and character. Their message is, after all, that time is on their side—that the sacrifices of followers are for noble and achievable goals. These predispositions and claims position militants to take credit for any US retreat and to read it to signify relative US weakness.[21] Conversely, it is also unclear that any amount of US sacrifice and policy rigidity could have convinced the militants of the strength of US resolve. As Shannon and Dennis (2007, 289) conclude, "Acts of firmness are discounted, reinterpreted, or situationally attributed to preserve the paper tiger image" among militant Islamists of their powerful nemesis.

Finally, US policymakers are overly selective when depicting linkages among conflicts. In the world of policy, detecting linkages is not a politically neutral exercise that draws from a dispassionate understanding of conflict dynamics; to the contrary, it is based on an ideologically driven view of an adversary that is constantly probing for weaknesses that can be turned to advantage. As Fettweis (2007–8, 621–624) notes, linkages based on the "credibility imperative" typically draw from a hawkish perspective on international politics that pushes for "action" rather than "inaction," results in exaggerated rhetorical claims, and surfaces when the immediate stakes at issue are grossly insufficient to justify the costs that the United States has invested in a conflict. Perversely, then, claims that US credibility is endangered are likely to appear most strident when the economic, political, and military advantages of getting involved or staying the course in a conflict are most limited. That a withdrawal under these conditions might actually enhance US credibility—that a prudent redirection of US resources might boost the apparent willingness of the United States to back its more vital interests in other parts of the world—is not usually up for discussion. The fact is, however, that withdrawal from Vietnam might have strengthened the US reputation for resolve in defense of its interests: "If anything, many of Washington's closest allies seemed relieved when the war ended, since many of them had doubted its importance in the first place and had feared that it distracted the United States from other more pressing issues" (Fettweis 2007–8, 614).

Ultimately, a linkage strategy in the Iraq War—as in other conflicts—was only as effective as the validity of the depicted connections among ostensible fronts in the conflict. Whether US linkage strategies were appropriate depended on whether Iraq served as a "lightning rod"—drawing in combatants who otherwise would have attacked the United States (or its interests in third countries)—and not an independent battlefield, largely disconnected from the "global terror network," or a terrorist "breeding ground" providing training—and inspiration—for terrorist operations in other parts of the world. Of these three possibilities, the lightning-rod thesis had the weakest evidentiary basis in the violent civil-war period.

Signaling: Communicating US Intent

Given the limitations of linkage and escalation strategies, the United States put greater relative emphasis on a signaling strategy in Vietnam and Iraq. In Vietnam, the United States intended to squeeze the enemy militarily and to send messages of US capability and resolve to affect Hanoi's will to resist. In Iraq, the United States intended to disarm insurgent and militia groups by force and to send a message that these groups could not expect to win. (Eventually, the United States would send a more conciliatory message—that the United States would provide security and support to those who stood up against groups that continued to lash out against US forces, the Iraqi government, and the Iraqi civilian population.) The problem was that these signals often got lost in transmission. The reasons are as follows.

First, a signal is distorted when it means different things to those who *send* it. It is easier for policy officials to agree that signals are useful than to agree on the nature of the signal to send. Johnson's advisors advocated bombing, in the early years of the Rolling Thunder campaign, by arguing that it could strengthen the morale of the Saigon government and its willingness to reform, show Hanoi that the United States would stand by the Saigon government, and increase US bargaining capabilities relative to a Saigon government that was not doing its part to assist the war effort (Clodfelter 1989, 45; Gelb and Betts 1979, 119, 252; Herring 1986, 124). The problem for the United States was that bombing could not accomplish all of these goals at once. In fact, some US policy officials feared that bombing, if it emboldened the Saigon government, would reduce its inclination to make concessions to the United States. It could also spur new challenges to the government by exacerbating tensions within South Vietnamese society or by provoking a Vietcong attack (see, for instance, Herring 1986, 127). That bombing appeared collectively within the policy community to serve irreconcilable goals should have indicated to policymakers that bombing might serve none of these goals: after all, each of the intended recipients of the signal (the Saigon government, South Vietnamese people, the Hanoi government, and the Vietcong) could assign it multiple interpretations. For example, bombing might signal the Saigon government that it could implement reforms without fear of US abandonment, that Saigon had unqualified US support that obviated the need for reform, or that the United States would discontinue its effort if Saigon failed to pull its weight. Which message was Saigon supposed to read? If the message of conditional US support, how was Hanoi expected to respond, then, if it "intercepted" that message?

For that matter, communication problems arose because the same signal *was meant* to send a different message to each of the parties that received it. Nixon and Kissinger believed, for instance, that Vietnamization and de-Americanization of the war worked in tandem to send useful messages to the Hanoi and Saigon governments. Vietnamization communicated to Saigon that it could carry the war effort without substantial US assistance. In turn, de-Americanization signaled both to Hanoi and Saigon that the United States was serious about withdrawing. The United States hoped to encourage Hanoi to seek a peaceful settlement of the conflict and to warn of the pending consequences to Saigon if it failed to strengthen its military capability and domestic political base (Kimball 2004, 13). It was likely, however, that Saigon "read" the message that was intended for Hanoi, and vice versa. The Saigon government was quite concerned about a US betrayal in secret peace talks between the United States and North Vietnam; in turn, Hanoi was apparently convinced that the United States was ready to withdraw and was passing the military burden to Saigon. Viewed in these terms, Vietnamization was but a function of de-Americanization and could only signal that Hanoi's military burden was about to lighten. If policymakers can send a different message with a single act to multiple parties, or cannot agree on the message that is sent to any single party, the likelihood increases that the target will misread a signal.

Second, a signaling strategy is problematic because of unintended messages. Many US policymakers of the 1970s and 1980s sought, through a signaling strategy, to avoid the catastrophic effects of an all-out nuclear war between the United States and the Soviet Union. They assumed that the Soviet Union—even in the fog of war—could appreciate the "limitations" inherent in US missile attacks of less totalistic severity that could still produce millions of Soviet deaths.[22] Such thinking about limited military options and limited war had early origins in the academic scholarship and policy analysis of the 1950s and 1960s that informed US military strategy in Vietnam (see, for instance, Schelling 1966). Drawing from these ideas, early in the conflict the United States relied on light mobile forces to signal Hanoi that the United States wanted to avoid sustained intervention and escalated and deescalated the aerial bombing of North Vietnam, within constraints, throughout the war. The viability of the US strategy hinged on the dubious assumption that bombing could simultaneously communicate resolve and restraint to the adversary. Resolve is perhaps appreciated from the act of escalation itself but restraint is judged from subjective reference points and is arguably missed entirely by an adversary under attack: its focus quite naturally is on what has been destroyed, not what remains standing. In the aftermath of the terror attacks on the World Trade Center in New York and the Pentagon in Washington, D.C., few Americans responded by exclaiming in relief, "It could have been so much worse!"—for instance, had the attackers hijacked six and not four planes. The question is, how do you signal restraint so that it is not drowned out by the signal of resolve? Clearly, US policymakers did not find the answer in repeated bombing pauses which the United States meant as a "carrot" to Hanoi but which it could easily have read either as an ultimatum (given the not-so-subtle suggestion of the stick, in the pending resumption of the bombing) or a propaganda ploy that allowed the United States to sugarcoat its violent and destructive actions. Conversely, given the subjectivity of reference points, "resolve" might have been lost to the message of restraint. Indeed, by relying on signals, the United States arguably signaled that it did not believe it was strong enough to *impose* its will upon the target. If sending signals to Hanoi through bombing was a transparently "cheap, low-risk approach" (Rosen 1982, 91), it might have communicated that the United States was unwilling to commit itself to the conflict—to do what was required to win. In early 1965, "Hanoi seems to have concluded that [Rolling Thunder] was just a desperation holding action that would not amount to a major U.S. commitment to fight and win a ground war in Vietnam" and that the best way to respond, then, was to escalate the fighting (Elliott 2003, 741; see also Record 1998, 110). Johnson-era policymakers assumed, nevertheless, that their preferred interpretation would get through to Hanoi.

The Johnson administration was not alone in its thinking: if anything, the Nixon administration was more inclined than its predecessor to overstate the value and clarity of signals that the United States was sending. A powerful example of a failed attempt to send a dramatic signal was Nixon's early effort to communicate to the Soviet Union and, indirectly, Hanoi that the newly elected president was capable of doing *anything*, including using nuclear weapons, to bring a rapid end to the Vietnam War. In 1969, the United States flew eighteen B-52 bombers—loaded with nuclear weapons—toward the Soviet Union and back in an orbiting pattern over the polar ice cap. The message was paired with the alerting (and dispersal) of US bombers at home to suggest that the United States was prepared for a counterattack should the Soviet Union respond with force. The perversity of this frightening move—which stemmed from Nixon's belief that the Soviets would not fool with a "madman"—was that it could not communicate any particular message to Soviet leaders about US intentions in Vietnam. The strategic bombers were directed at the Soviet Union, not Vietnam (and were launched from bases in the United States, not Guam—the source of aircraft for the Vietnam air campaign); the Soviet Union was preoccupied with a military confrontation with China, not US problems in Vietnam; and the US move was accompanied by a global US alert that included US bombers in Europe.[23] Soviet leaders appeared confused by the gesture and dismissed it accordingly. (On the alert, see Sagan and Suri 2003; Suri 2008.)

The Nixon administration was undeterred, however, by its earlier failure at signaling. It escalated the bombing at key points in negotiations to communicate that the United States would do whatever it took to obtain concessions from

North Vietnam. Yet the United States arguably ended up sending the opposite signal. Even the intense Linebacker bombing campaigns of 1972 focused on specific targets with the intent of limiting collateral damage; the final Linebacker campaign was accompanied by a relatively generous US negotiating offer to settle the conflict (as revealed in the terms of the final agreement). Consequently, any escalation could easily have been read by Hanoi as indicating not that the United States would stand firm but rather that the United States would incur risks and costs to expedite an exit from Vietnam. Ironically, the bombing could have been taken as an act of US desperation—a sign that the United States would do whatever it took to *leave* Vietnam. This very possibility had been anticipated by influential members of the Johnson administration (Thies 1980, 174).

The sending of unintended messages featured, as well, in the Iraq conflict, as US officials took symbolism into account when crafting US military tactics. For instance, the top US military commander sought to involve the Iraqi Army in battles against insurgents in Fallujah, Samarra, and Sadr City, with the hope of driving a wedge between the militants and their supportive population (Wright et al. 2008, 178). It hoped that the Iraqi public would respond positively to these forces and might come to view the battle against insurgent and militia groups as their own. The problem, of course, is that the use of these troops sent other signals, including (a) a sectarian message when Kurdish and Shiite units were employed in Sunni-populated areas, (b) a condescending message when under-equipped Iraqi troops were made to accompany well-equipped US troops, and (c) a counterproductive message when Iraqi troops proved deficient. Clearly, the wrong message was sent in the first battle for Fallujah when Iraqi forces refused to fight and when the United States eventually turned over security responsibilities for the city to a Baathist officer whose units quickly dissolved. Similarly, US attempts to signal Moqtada al-Sadr, to secure his cooperation, that the United States was only targeting "special groups," not mainstream units of the Mahdi Army, were confused by the US conduct in these operations. The message of US restraint was contravened by the targeting of individuals and units that were allegedly close to al-Sadr, attempts by US and Iraqi government forces to establish control throughout Baghdad and the southern provinces of Iraq, US actions that weakened al-Sadr's physical position vis-à-vis the Supreme Council, and Baghdad's insistence that it retain a monopoly on military force within the country.

The challenges of sending unambiguous signals in Iraq (and Vietnam) were compounded by a compellence problem. It was hard for the United States—as the compelling party—to communicate convincingly to the adversary the terms that the United States found satisfactory. In the deterrence case, the status quo serves as a clear reference point around which the expectations of all parties can converge: for instance, by deploying troops in a volatile region, the message is clear that the United States will be caught up in any violence and will respond to adversary transgressions that threaten the peace. Compellence comes without actions that send signals with clear reference points. The question becomes, then, what will it take to satisfy the compelling party? Should US restraint in targeting Mahdi militiamen—even praise for al-Sadr's cooperation and moderation in standing down his forces—be taken as signals that al-Sadr had met US demands? Can he maintain his militia if controlling its actions and, at least for now, eschewing violence?

Third, the environment can drown-out the signal. Leaders often carefully craft signals without recognizing that signals do not stand apart from "noise" and that seemingly "obvious" messages do not get through to the recipient. Put differently, the tools of war are inherently blunt instruments: they are designed for combat, not messaging.[24] They frequently convey much more and much less than the messenger intends. The precision-guided weapons of the Iraq War were no exception: any misses, inconsistency in targeting, and collateral damage become "part of the message," that is, the "noise" *was* the signal for the targeted leader or group. If innocents are hurt in a blast that kills the intended target, if a missile goes astray and hits people in a crowd, if multiple blasts destroy a military target while a coincident explosion wrecks a neighboring hospital or school—in all of these cases, the human cost can overwhelm any message that the signaler seeks to convey. That the missile was precision-guided, that the attack occurred at night when streets were uncrowded, and that innocents were warned about an impending attack is often lost on those with a view on the ground. It is easy to observe the *effects* of an attack; people can only guess about the *intent*. Ironically, that care is taken to avoid casualties could well feed suspicions that the attacker knew what it was doing and thus that the damage was intended.

A distorted signal is made more likely because government signals are inherently noisy: they are typically sent via government agencies that act on their own agendas and internal logic. So it was hard to see how Hanoi could ever conclude that it was subject to a "slow squeeze" at the hands of the US military or to any particular strategy that was meant to suggest that Hanoi's behavior was driving the attacks. Even if the strategy was sound in principle, the actual bombing patterns were far too ambiguous to communicate a clear message. In part, the incoherence stemmed from the magnitude of US attacks: by the fall of 1966, US aircraft were flying up to 12,000 sorties per month over North Vietnam when these sorties had numbered in the hundreds in the early part of the prior year (Thies 1980, 213). Indeed, as Robert Pape has written, "In 1966, the Johnson administration permitted complete freedom for armed reconnaissance and restrikes of previously released targets throughout all of North Vietnam except for small areas around Hanoi, Haiphong, and the Chinese border" (1996, 186). Over successive years, bomb tonnages increased at a rapid rate—starting at 63,000 in 1965, more than doubling in 1966, almost doubling again in 1967 (Pape 1996, 185). In part, the ambiguity was due to the indecipherable patterns. The US military consistently focused its bombing on interdicting manpower and supplies bound for the war in the South; it bombed targets both near and distant from Hanoi with regularity and on schedule; it bombed targets as they were identified not for their relative value; it adopted tactics meant specifically to maximize bombing sorties, to increase the efficiency of US aircraft, to avoid bad weather, and to minimize the danger to US aircraft without intending to send any particular message; it anticipated bans on certain targets by accelerating attacks on them; and it conducted its bombing campaign without considering effects on the negotiating environment (Thies 1980). In point of fact, US military leaders "hoped that graduated pressure would evolve over time into a fundamentally different strategy, more in keeping with their belief in the necessity of greater force and its resolute application" (McMaster 1997, 328). Communication was hampered, too, because US civilian leaders pursued strategies with differing emphases (without necessarily appreciating the contradictory underpinnings): the early Rolling Thunder campaign of early 1965 was based directly on "slow squeeze" principles; the bombing in mid-1967 was intended, in the end, to destroy Hanoi's military and economic assets (Pape 1996, 182–184).[25]

In reality, the signaling effort was bound to suffer as long as the US civilian leaders simultaneously regarded bombing as a military tool and signaling device. Certainly, a forceful bombing campaign can send the powerful signal that the United States does not care about sending signals—that the United States will accomplish its goals one way or the other. But the United States is challenged in signaling both that the United States can impose its will and depends on the adversary to make the "right" choice. Inasmuch as the second signal contradicts the first, a deescalation of the bombing had to signal that the United States did not believe bombing could work. If it actually held the upper hand, the United States would continue to bomb until the adversary capitulated.

How likely is it, then, that US signals rang through the clamorous environment in which Iraqi militants and their support base lived? Whatever the message of hope and progress that the United States intended to send, Iraqis also read messages into the slow receipt of electricity production, failed efforts at reconstruction, the deteriorating security environment, their day-to-day interactions with US troops, and the much-publicized actions of a few soldiers who acted outside the rules of engagement or engaged in criminal behavior. Indeed, "new" messages had to compete with "old" messages, when circumstances forced US civilian and military officials to change their approach (toward, for instance, Shiite militia, the Iraqi government, or the Sunni insurgents); furthermore, "official" messages had to compete with other "official" or "unofficial" ones, by virtue of disagreements within the US government or the unsanctioned actions of US troops and private contractors.

Fourth, a signal must overcome the prior beliefs of the recipient that bias any interpretation of new facts. Because audiences accept messages that they are predisposed to accept, Hanoi missed the meaning behind seemingly obvious signals—for instance, that the Johnson administration had, as it claimed, launched its early Flaming Dart aerial bombing raids with the intent of punishing Hanoi for attacks in the South that had killed US soldiers at Pleiku. That the United States was acting in "reprisal" for communist actions was lost on Hanoi (McNamara et al. 1999, 190, 213–217). The predispositions of North Vietnam's leaders were bound to color their perceptions of US actions. For instance, a temporary cessation of US bombing was viewed as an ultimatum by Hanoi because it simply could not concede ground. It had to conclude, then, that the United States was not seriously interested in negotiating and was looking, instead, for North Vietnam to surrender (McNamara et al. 1999, 303–305, 406).[26]

Predispositions colored the interpretation of messages sent by the United States from the war's start, including the sequence of events that led up to full-scale US military intervention. The United States unleashed its first set of aerial retaliatory attacks on North Vietnam in response to what the Johnson administration claimed were unprovoked attacks by North Vietnamese torpedo boats on the USS *Maddox* and *Turner Joy* in the international waters of the Tonkin Gulf. The two attacks led to a congressional resolution that amounted effectively to a declaration of war under the US Constitution. In short, it authorized the president "to take all necessary measures to repel any armed attack against the forces of the United States and to prevent further aggression." The situation was apparently viewed differently by North Vietnam's leaders. From North Vietnam's perspective, the first attack was initiated in response to the ship's assumed involvement in surreptitious intelligence-gathering and sabotage operations against

North Vietnam that *were* under way (islands had recently been attacked off the North Vietnamese coast).[27] The second attack must have been viewed as entirely a US fabrication: the "attack" was based on a misreading of radar and sonar information by the US Navy, which falsely assumed that other vessels were in the vicinity (Herring 1986, 119–121). A US aerial attack that was purportedly launched as a response to these events could only be interpreted by North Vietnamese leaders as a premeditated attack launched under the cover of retaliation. Rather than communicating the modesty of US goals, then, such an attack could only communicate US "treacherousness" and "aggressiveness." At a conference of participants many years after the war, when former secretary of defense McNamara mentioned Hanoi's possible "misinterpretation" of the Tonkin events, General Giap replied, "Excuse me, but we *correctly* understood you—what you were doing in the Tonkin Gulf. You were carrying out sabotage activities to create a pretext that would allow you to take over the war from the Saigon government, which was incompetent" (quoted in McNamara et al. 1999, 23–24). The United States was not only escalating the conflict militarily, it was seeking to place North Vietnam in the worst possible light to foreclose any possibility of resolving the dispute peacefully (on the Tonkin events, see Karnow 1997, 379–387; Lewy 1978, 32–36). Ironically, the US military response to the Tonkin Gulf incident appears to have silenced those within the Hanoi leadership who wanted to avoid a direct confrontation with US forces (McNamara et al. 1999, 186–187).

In Iraq, US policymakers were similarly challenged in overcoming existing viewpoints. Despite their desire to set the right tone through symbolic acts—including the destruction of the Saddam Hussein statue in Baghdad *by Iraqi citizens*, the passing of sovereign control to an interim Iraqi government, the holding of national elections, and efforts to rely more on Iraqi security forces for delicate missions (for instance, taking control of mosques)—US efforts to send messages were confounded by preexisting popular beliefs. The US presence could not be taken by much of the Iraqi population as anything but a prolonged US occupation, given strong suspicions of US motives and little indication that US forces intended to leave the country. It is telling that, according to opinion polls, for instance, popular attitudes toward the United States were most negative among Sunnis, given their sectarian ties to the toppled Saddam Hussein regime, and never really softened (as discussed in chapter 3).

Finally, a signaling strategy suffers against an adversary that is reading messages to achieve victory on its own terms. An irony of the US slow squeeze is that the tepidness of the early US bombing campaign appears to have convinced

Hanoi's leaders that they needed to increase their military effort in South Vietnam to secure gains before the United States had fully committed itself—indeed, in the hopes that the United States might never fully commit itself (Thies 1980, 270–271, 281). As the United States escalated the bombing, Hanoi viewed it in the context of its own strategic goals, which were "to continually deny Washington its objectives, as it proceeded up the rungs of the ladder of escalation, until U.S. leaders at some point made a sensible, rational decision to cease and desist and, at last, to withdraw" (McNamara et al. 1999, 174). Their interpretative emphasis was not on how to stop the bombing but how to survive it, mitigate its effects, and respond in a way that signaled Hanoi would not concede defeat. Consequently, Hanoi increased its shipments and infiltration into the South purportedly as a political response to US bombing of the North (McNamara et al. 1999, 408).

In fact, Hanoi appears to have relished the US desire to send signals that effectively placed the United States at a military disadvantage. The battle for Khe Sanh just across the DMZ, near the Laotian border, is a powerful example and serves more generally as a microcosm for the entire Vietnam intervention. There, in late 1967 and early 1968, US Marines were encircled by North Vietnamese troops in a long and bloody siege. For US military and civilian leaders, the battle, which took the lives of hundreds of Americans and thousands of communist troops, provided an opportunity to inflict heavy damage on enemy forces and to signal US resolve. For top US leaders—including the president—the tempting analogy of the French surrender at Dien Bien Phu made it imperative that the United States win the engagement despite the limited strategic significance of the fortress, which the United States in fact abandoned after its victory. The North Vietnamese were hardly impressed by the show of US *resolve*—in fact, they were *pleased* with it: the battle was a diversion intended to draw US forces away from the coast to open it to the Vietcong's massive Tet Offensive. Tellingly, General Westmoreland believed that Tet was a ruse to distract the United States from its important work at Khe Sanh (Currey 1997, 265–266; Karnow 1997, 552–555).

Thus, the deficiencies of a signaling strategy were apparent in Vietnam and Iraq: signals are often faint, ambiguous, and contradictory, and they are not easily crafted with due sensitivity to the target and its likely interpretations. As Thies (1980, 219) noted about the Johnson administration's bombing campaign, "What is perhaps most remarkable about the Administration's strategy is *how little* it knew about the targets of its strategy." (For more on US failures at signaling in Vietnam, see George 1971.) The failings of the US signaling strategy were only aggravated by the serious US motivational disadvantage. From its weak position, the United

States established that even the "best threats" fail when the target dismisses them as a bluff or decides that it can live with the threatened consequences.

US Resolve: The Politics of Exhaustion

One major failing of US strategy in Vietnam and Iraq was that US policymakers neglected the time dimension of the conflicts—their potential endurance—in early operational planning. US policymakers intervened in Vietnam expecting that Hanoi, under military duress, would seek an end to the conflict. In 2003, US policymakers were even more sanguine about the consequences of invading Iraq given the quick and relatively easy victory in the US-led Desert Storm Operation in 1991. If anything, the George W. Bush administration anticipated less difficulty the second time around, given the deteriorating state of the Iraqi military. The general optimism was expressed by a prominent administration supporter in his much-cited (and later regretted) prediction of a US "cakewalk," in a war with Iraq.[28] Unfortunately for the United States, the prediction was inaccurate *over the long-term*, as circumstances between the two operations differed greatly. The 1991 operation ceased once Iraqi forces withdrew from Kuwait, where Coalition forces *were* welcomed as liberators; the 2003 operation started at Iraq's borders, where the 1991 operation had ended. Contrary to the suppositions of key policymakers in the George W. Bush administration, most Iraqis welcomed their liberation (from Saddam Hussein) but rejected the "liberators."

The United States was taxed severely once it overstayed its (brief) welcome because time is not the natural ally of a "predominant" power when engaged in small wars. When these conflicts endure, US leaders must seek to maintain public support for a war effort, confront societal limits on available manpower, and cope with dwindling support for a war strategy within government. In other words, these leaders must bolster their leverage against adversaries by leveraging support at home.

Public Support

The conventional wisdom in US public opinion research is that war support declines nonlinearly with mounting casualties (specifically, the logarithm of cumulative casualties). These studies assume that public support for a war declines rapidly and then steadily as casualties accumulate because people "are sensitive to relatively small losses in the early stages, but only to large losses in later stages." Those with a soft commitment fall easily when the first battle deaths are recorded;

strong war supporters drop their support only with a much higher toll (Mueller 1971, 367). (The logarithm assumes, nonetheless, that the first death compared to the thousandth has a greater cognitive impact.)

The conventional wisdom regarding the downward public support trend provoked contentious debate. For those who dissent from that wisdom, what goes up—public support for an operation—can stay up. After all, the public thought highly enough of the operation to support it in the first place. The US public must believe, however, that its country's goals behind an operation warrant sacrifice. In this view, the public's tolerance for cost is a function of "beliefs about the rightness or wrongness of the war, and beliefs about a war's likely success" (Gelpi et al. 2005, 8). The case for a supportive public is strengthened by various evidence.

First, the case is strengthened by evidence that the public responds positively to leadership cues. Indeed, the US public rallied in support of escalated US bombing in Vietnam: by 1967, around 55 percent of the US public supported escalation, whereas less than 10 percent of the US public favored withdrawal (Lunch and Sperlich 1979, 22, 26).

Second, the case is similarly strengthened by evidence that the public responds positively to good news. During the Iraq War, public support rebounded (a bit) with the transfer of sovereign control of Iraq to its government (Gelpi et al. 2005, 18). The supportive public thesis is reinforced backhandedly, then, by evidence that support for US war policy declined with indications of wartime failure. US support for the president's war policies dropped significantly, for instance, after the Vietcong's surprise Tet Offensive in 1968 and after the ill-fated South Vietnamese Laos offensive in 1971, which yielded photographic evidence of South Vietnamese fighters fleeing the combat by hanging from military helicopters (Randolph 2007, 18–19). Along the same lines, the thesis is reinforced by evidence of declining support when indications of progress are absent. After the early optimism that greeted the Iraqi election in January 2005, there was little good news to boost the public's confidence that the war was going well—albeit lots of reasons, also, to suspect that it was not including the slow progress of Iraqi security forces, continuing secular violence, and a stalemated central government (Gelpi et al. 2005, 9). By mid-2005, the percent of the public voicing disapproval of Bush's handling of the war fluctuated roughly between 60 and 70 percent (Klarevas 2006, 191).[29]

Third, the case is strengthened by evidence that certain kinds of military missions receive relatively strong public backing. Research has indicated, for example, that the public is "prudent" in the sense that it supports intervention to achieve some foreign policy goals—force used against adversaries "engaged in aggressive actions against the United States, its citizens, or its interests"—more than others—force employed to serve humanitarian goals or bring internal political change to a country (Jentleson and Britton 1998, 397). Thus, US public support for the president remained strong throughout World War II.

Fourth, the case is strengthened by evidence that even declining public support eventually levels off: a portion of the public will continue to support any war effort, perhaps for partisan reasons. US public support, which dropped with China's entry into the Korean conflict, nevertheless remained constant for the remaining years of the war (Mueller 1971, 361). Similarly, from early 2004 through early 2008, the percent of the US public that wanted to keep US troops in Iraq until conditions in the country stabilized did not change much (remaining around 40 percent).[30]

Finally, the case is strengthened by evidence that residual support for a war effort is hidden in apparent opposition. In the months after China's intervention in Korea, the share of the public that favored escalation as opposed to withdrawal increased dramatically when respondents could choose from a broad set of options that included intensifying the fight against Red China and using atomic bombs.[31] During the Vietnam War, support for US military action was also stronger than it might appear. Although less than half the US public expressed support for the Vietnam War in the period leading up to the Tet Offensive,[32] overall public support for escalation greatly exceeded support for withdrawal. Likewise, in 2006, around half of the US public wanted US troops to remain in Iraq until conditions there had stabilized, though only around a third of the public voiced approval for Bush's handling of the Iraq War (Gelpi and Reifler 2006, 196). For that matter, almost 60 percent of Americans opposed efforts by the Congress to deny funding for sending additional troops to Iraq, with the start of the surge in February 2007, even when roughly an equal proportion opposed the surge.[33] By 2008, only around a quarter of the US public supported immediate withdrawal, when most Americans wanted some time limit on US action in Iraq.[34]

That war support can masquerade as opposition is clear from a popular misinterpretation of some well-known facts surrounding the 1968 electoral campaign. It is widely known that Lyndon Johnson announced that he would not seek a second full term in office after he had won a narrow victory (as a write-in candidate) in the 1968 New Hampshire Democratic primary over Eugene McCarthy, a peace candidate. What is less widely known is that McCarthy drew substantial support from people opposed to current US war strategy in Vietnam, not to the war itself. McCarthy supporters who desired a "harder line" position against

Hanoi outnumbered withdrawal advocates "by nearly a three to two margin" (Converse et al. 1969).[35] History repeated itself. In the 2008 New Hampshire primary, over half of Barack Obama's support came from voters who preferred that US forces remain in Iraq. Obama, who had made much of his early opposition to the Iraq War, received less support from withdrawal proponents than did the other two major candidates (Hillary Clinton and John Edwards).[36]

Despite its misgivings about a given US military operation, the public is apparently reluctant to accept defeat, or a less than honorable end to a US operation that could negate the sacrifice of American troops.[37] Nevertheless, leaders have a hard time bucking the downward trend in public support, for a number of reasons.

First, the public becomes increasingly inattentive to war events, including the leadership cues and "good news" that, in theory, might boost public support. The Iraq War was not a pressing issue in the 2008 presidential election, even before the global financial meltdown grabbed the headlines, nor was it a subject of much public interest. On the eve of the election, only 9 percent of the US public rated it the most important issue affecting their vote (compared to 51 percent that rated the economy their top priority).[38] By early 2008, only around a quarter of the US public could correctly guess the number of US soldiers that had died in Iraq (in thousands). This represented a dramatic decline in awareness from six months earlier (across demographic groups).[39] The media outlets do not prevent the public from redirecting its attention: news from Iraq dropped off the front pages of daily papers and nightly television broadcasts exactly as US and Iraqi casualties *were mounting*. An analysis of news coverage of four major US newspapers indicates that coverage of Iraq dropped dramatically from 2003 to 2008 (though leveling off in the violent 2005–6 period), even declining in 2007 despite the violence that accompanied the US surge. Indeed, Iraq news declined fairly consistently, as a percent of total coverage, throughout 2007 (though spiking with the congressional testimony of General David Petraeus in September). Iraq stories were down by two thirds in 2008 from 2003 levels in the *New York Times* which, of the four papers, had given the most coverage to Iraq, with around a thousand stories in 2003.[40]

Second, accumulating casualties, themselves, are arguably "bad news" that combines with related bad news to undermine the perception, irreparably, that a war is succeeding. Indeed, such bad news is likely to trump any "good news" obtained from the jumble of nebulous indicators that point to success in asymmetric conflict. US fatalities in the 1968 Tet Offensive were potentially among the compelling indicators that turned US public opinion irrevocably against the Vietnam War by revealing both the likely cost to the United States of continuing to fight *and* the ineffectiveness of the current US war strategy.[41] Gelpi et al. (2005, 23) concede, in fact, that casualties can undermine public support for a war effort, once the public's confidence in victory is "shaken."[42] The portion of the US public that believed the United States made the "wrong" decision when intervening in Iraq rose fairly consistently through 2007 and into 2008 despite an overall increase in the share of the public, in the last half of 2007, that believed the war was going fairly or very well.[43] Indeed, there was a twenty-point jump (to 50 percent) between September 2007 and 2008 in the percentage of the US public that believed the troop surge had improved the situation in Iraq, but this development brought with it virtually no change in the percentage of the public that believed the United States should have "stayed out" of Iraq.[44] By then, improvements on the ground were not boosting the public's confidence in victory, at least at an acceptable cost.[45]

Third, remaining support for a war is likely unenthusiastic and increasingly confined to a small percentage of the population. In the last years of US combat in Vietnam, over 70 percent of the public favored withdrawal; by the time of the 1973 Paris Agreement, almost 80 percent of the US public opposed reintroducing US troops even "if North Vietnam were to try to take over South Vietnam" (Lunch and Sperlich 1979, 25, 28). The reality is that factors that sustain public support for a war effort have not typically countered the effects of factors that produce a marked decline in US public support over time across various demographic groups (Lunch and Sperlich 1979, 38–43).

This is not to say that public support declines per the conventional wisdom. Changing public support appears not to follow the nonlinear pattern of logged cumulative casualties. During the Vietnam War, withdrawal sentiment remained low in the early years despite tens of thousands of US fatalities and became increasingly sensitive to casualties in the later years of US involvement. Public support for the Vietnam War declined less rapidly between 1965 and 1967 than after the costly Tet Offensive (when US soldiers were dying at a rate of over 500 per week) despite *declining* US casualties in the aftermath of the offensive. After Tet, negative sensitivity to casualties increased threefold (Gelpi 2006). During the Iraq War, opposition increased dramatically in the first year and remained at fairly constant levels, despite mounting casualties, before increasing again slightly in 2007 and 2008.[46] Furthermore, conventional judgments about the effects of casualties are influenced heavily by the homogenizing effects of logging the casualty variable: World War II, the Korean War, and the Vietnam War produced very different monthly fatality patterns but yielded virtually the same "transformed" pattern[47]—which is itself a near-linear function of the passage of time, for instance, the date in which deaths occurred (Gartner and Segura 1998, 282). Thus, cumulative fatalities in a model predicting support for a war effort are potentially expressing the effects of any of a large number of variables that change value monotonically over time.[48] These include global developments that impugn the war's justification (for instance, growing detente during the Vietnam War), mounting economic costs, the evaporation of the rally effect, and growing public skepticism over government policy (as impugning information becomes available, opposing policy voices are heard, and success appears elusive). Strong evidence suggests that the public responds to cues from informed partisan elites who impose their own political beliefs and ideologies when interpreting events and seek political gains from challenging the administration's war strategy (Berinsky 2007).[49]

Taken together, the overall evidence suggests a public that is generally indifferent to global events: it reluctantly sacrifices domestic for foreign policy benefits and has little knowledge of or interest in international affairs. It responds, then, to appeals for support from leaders who can tap patriotic sentiment and sell military action as a fundamental security threat—perhaps a battle against "evil" (Saddam Hussein, Osama bin Laden). But such a public is hard to keep focused and committed and will come to doubt the necessity of sacrifice as costs mount, progress slows or reverses, and skeptical elites reject the war's demands in blood and treasure. Indeed, maintaining public support appears tougher now than it used to be: public support declined much more quickly and dramatically for the war in Iraq than for the wars in Korea and Vietnam (Mueller 2005). The share of the public that viewed the US war in Iraq as a "mistake" almost doubled (from 23 percent) over the first year of the conflict; by April 2008, the 63 percent of the public that held this view topped the highest share (61 percent) recorded for this judgment about the ongoing war in Vietnam.[50] In principle, the public might stay on board and continue to tolerate costs with signs that a mission is succeeding. The question, however, is whether these signs are palpable in asymmetric conflict, where evidence of progress is mixed and policy goals are frequently modified or contracted. For that matter, the question is whether these signs are likely to be appreciated, in any small conflict, when the tolerance for cost is low from the start and accumulating costs signal that the war's price will continue to grow.

Societal Constraints

As important to the long-term success of US strategy is whether US leaders can prosecute wars within the constraints that society imposes on available resources. The Vietnam and Iraq Wars were fought to reflect the US leadership's view of resource demands that the American public would tolerate.

Lyndon Johnson recognized that exceeding a public tolerance threshold could bring extraordinary domestic pressure for a change in US war policy. So he sought to minimize the public impact of the Vietnam War despite its huge financial cost and negative economic effects on the national inflation rate and budget deficit. Although Johnson ultimately had to accept an unpopular tax increase (Karnow 1997, 501–502), he refused to cross a critical labor threshold in pursuing his war strategy. Johnson ruled out mobilizing the US military reserve force (which included National Guard units) and chose instead to rely heavily on conscripts to meet the demand for ground forces in Vietnam. From Johnson's perspective, mobilizing the reserves would extend the demographic reach of the war, as the draft drew—more than the reserves—from less advantaged groups within US society. A mobilization would also heighten the profile of the war by putting the nation politically on a war footing. A mobilization, he feared, would bring unwanted attention to the US prosecution of the war—that is, the (in)effectiveness of Johnson's war strategy—and would reduce the political support that Johnson required to pursue his Great Society agenda (Downes 2009, 45–46). Compared to World War II, the demands of Vietnam were arguably small, but not for Johnson, who "feared that even the slightest accommodation to the war would compel him to sacrifice some of his domestic programs—and, more critically, awaken the public to the costs of the commitment" (Karnow 1997, 501). [51] When it became clear to Johnson that he could not hope to win in Vietnam without tapping the reserves to meet the military's latest troop request, he rejected the request and pushed instead, through conciliatory gestures, for peace negotiations with Hanoi. Johnson preferred freezing the war in place over adopting a course that could have politically calamitous effects.

In hindsight, it seems odd that drafting young men—principally for Army service—was a less contentious option for the administration than relying on a volunteer force, given the radicalizing effect of the draft on US college campuses of the 1960s and early 1970s. The administration clearly made a "lesser of two evils" choice. Whereas the draft, long a "fact of life" in the United States, had come (courtesy of the baby boom after World War II) to impose decreasing societal demands (Spector 1993, 29), equity concerns led to stricter conditions for granting deferments and a random selection of conscripts through a lottery.[52] These reforms guaranteed that the political, social, and economic effects of the draft would resonate (more) broadly. The draft, and its two-year military obligations, induced fears and uncertainty among those eligible to serve, motivated men who would otherwise avoid service to enlist (to exert more control over their military future), and produced disgruntlement among the eventually conscripted. Resistance to military service only contributed to the travails of a US military in Vietnam that was weakened from within by rampant drug abuse, breakdowns in discipline (including assaults on unpopular officers), desertions, skyrocketing casualties (physical and psychological), and a deficiency and depletion of (qualified) mid-grade officers and NCOs (Herring 1986, 243; Lewy 1978, 154–161). The return home from the war—relatively quick for draftees—fed social distress as former soldiers shared tales of brutal combat and struggled to adjust to civilian life. The effects—for families—were worse, of course, when loved ones did not return and were made worse, still, by the unkind demography of death. The war hit the conscripted population hard: in 1969, at the peak of US war involvement, an Army draftee was twice as likely as an enlistee serving in Vietnam to be killed (Spector 1993, 32). It took its toll on the young: almost 60 percent of US soldiers killed were 21 years old or younger; over 80 percent were 25 years old or younger. It consumed the inexperienced: 40 percent of troops died in the first *three* months of their tour.[53]

Ironically, the Bush administration was placed in the opposite position. It recognized that the return of the draft was a nonstarter: neither the public nor the military was predisposed or prepared to accept the return of conscription. Indeed, any public discussion of conscription would create huge misgivings about the direction of US war strategy in Iraq and turn up the heat on the administration to withdraw US troops. The administration had to rely, then, on an all-volunteer force that included reserve and national guard units; moreover, the administration pushed plans initially for a small invasion force so as to limit manpower demands and avoid raising the operation's (domestic societal) footprint. As the war dragged on, the military increased the pressure on available US troops, to support operations in Iraq and US military commitments worldwide. To meet force requirements, the military had to extend deployments in Iraq from 12 months to 15 months, issue "stop-loss" orders that prevented soldiers from leaving the service at their retirement or re-enlistment dates (a "back-door" draft, to critics), limit the training for missions other than counterinsurgency, send troops to Iraq on multiple tours, and reduce the deployment cycle so that soldiers spent less time at home and in training.[54] The war took its toll on troops, in morale, broken marriages and families, trauma, depression, even suicide.[55] The uninviting prospect of lengthy and repeated service in Iraq led to an exodus of experienced personnel from the military. The Army was negatively affected, for instance, by the departure of junior officers in critical specialty areas such as military intelligence and aviation (leading to a projected yearly shortfall of thousands of captains and majors). It sought to compensate by offering unusually large cash bonuses as a reenlistment incentive and promoting captains more quickly to the rank of major.[56] To attract recruits, the military coped in part by offering attractive enlistment bonuses, lowering educational standards, and lifting service disqualifications for some with criminal records.[57]

Thus, both administrations were forced to fight their wars around critical societal constraints. In theory, the United States possessed immense power, in material resources and labor, for prosecuting the small wars in Vietnam and Iraq. Only a finite portion of that capability was available, however, for a military operation that did not threaten US security interests directly, greatly, and unambiguously. Johnson dealt with the constraint by freezing the US commitment in place and accepting that he could not achieve US objectives militarily in Vietnam. Bush dealt with the constraints by imposing greater demands on available personnel and accepting that the capability on hand was adequate, at best, for securing a precarious peace in Iraq.

Governmental Support

But how much does rising dissatisfaction actually affect policy? The evidence from the Vietnam and Iraq conflicts is mixed. The Congress is arguably more susceptible to public pressure than the president. Individual legislators can please their constituents (for electoral benefits) by opposing current war policies, hoping that other legislators will carry the political burden of supporting the president or will provide cover for a dissenting vote by standing together. Still, the Congress, as a body, was extremely reluctant to challenge executive prerogatives in Vietnam and Iraq, having moved expeditiously to authorize the president to initiate wars in both countries.

The Vietnam War generated contentious legislative debates and increasingly frequent amendments to constrain presidential action. In 1964, the Congress passed the Gulf of Tonkin resolution quickly and overwhelmingly (with a 466-0 vote in the House and a 88–2 vote in the Senate) to give the president virtually unchecked power to pursue the war (from the text of the resolution, "to take all necessary steps, including the use of armed force, to assist any member or protocol state of the Southeast Asia Collective Defense Treaty requesting assistance in defense of its freedom"). Although the Congress wrote in an option of repeal through a concurrent resolution, it did not rescind the resolution until January 1971, as US involvement in Vietnam was coming to a close. The repeal came years after the administration's version of the Tonkin Gulf events was impugned in Senate hearings, prior efforts to rescind the resolution had failed, and the Senate (in 1970) had defeated the McGovern-Hatfield Amendment, which would have forced the withdrawal of US forces from Vietnam by 1971. Congressional efforts to employ the power of the purse to restrict presidential prerogatives were similarly belated and tepid. Responding to the 1970 invasion of Cambodia, the Congress passed a modified version of the Cooper-Church Amendment later that year proscribing the use of defense funds to reintroduce US troops into Cambodia. This was a landmark action: for the first time, the Congress moved to restrict the wartime powers of the president. Yet the resolution passed many months after a stronger version of the amendment failed (in the House) and US forces left Cambodia; moreover, the resolution did not prevent the president from continuing the ferocious air campaign in the country. Not until 1973, after the signing of the Paris Peace Agreement, did Congress pass the Case-Church Amendment (by a veto-proof margin)—to end, as of August 1973, all US combat in Southeast Asia. (In 1974, the Congress followed up by cutting military aid to the Saigon government.)

Congressional reticence featured, again, in the Iraq War, once the Senate and House passed the Authorization for Use of Military Force Against Iraq Resolution of 2002, albeit with a less resounding vote (77–23 in the Senate and 297–133 in the House) than for its Vietnam-era predecessor. The resolution gave the president the authority to employ the military "as he determines to be necessary and appropriate" to "defend the national security of the United States against the continuing threat posed by Iraq" and to "enforce all relevant United Nations Security Council resolutions regarding Iraq." By the end of Bush's term in office, despite strong public opposition to the war and aggregate war costs in Iraq and Afghanistan nearing a trillion dollars, Congress turned back various efforts to impose a troop withdrawal timetable in Iraq or to force an end to US operations in that country through funding cuts. Although legislative reticence owed in part to a strong perception that war funding was necessary to ensure the security of US troops, the Congress also rejected restrictions—such as the proposal to require longer troop rest periods between deployments—framed in the language of force protection.

In sum, the Congress was reluctant to constrain presidential prerogatives in Vietnam and Iraq when the president is presumably positioned—by merit of relative resources, the chain of command, and tradition—to judge how a war is best prosecuted (and ended). At most, Congress constrained the president by giving voice to growing public concerns about the war and declining legislative support (bipartisan or otherwise) for the presidential agenda and perhaps by helping to legitimize opposition to the nation's war strategy.[58] Thus, the effect of exhaustion on US war policy in Vietnam and Iraq was felt most, not through formal checks and balances of legislative intervention, but directly in the executive branch as the president and his advisors came to recognize the limits of US military power, that is, the prohibitive costs of continued escalation given societal constraints on available resources and rising public opposition.[59]

Key policymakers—their beliefs and political capabilities—certainly mattered. Policy shifts had much to do with a turnover within administrations in critical personnel—for instance, when General Abrams replaced General Westmoreland in the Johnson administration and Secretary of Defense Gates and General Petraeus replaced Secretary of Defense Rumsfeld and General Casey, respectively, in the Bush administration. Important policy shifts also occurred across administrations. Departing from its predecessor, the Nixon administration hoped to convince Russia and China to pressure Hanoi to negotiate on US terms, and it escalated the fighting significantly by sending ground troops across Vietnam's border into Cambodia in 1970 and intensifying the bombing in and around Hanoi and mining Haiphong Harbor in the years to follow. The change in administration also brought new intra-governmental disputes. Secretary of Defense Melvin Laird, for one, challenged the wisdom of expanding the ground war into Cambodia and Laos, escalating the air war over North Vietnam, and adopting policies that undermined US efforts to Vietnamize the war and downgrade US involvement in Southeast Asia (see, for instance, Randolph 2007, 114–115, 169).

But intensifying policy disagreements and personnel changes within and across administrations were attributable in large part to exhaustion, in the form of a growing and widespread dissatisfaction with the handling of the war, which increasingly constrained US leaders. The Nixon administration appreciated the

Vietnam War's harsh realities—the limits to what the United States could accomplish militarily, with available capabilities, and what the public would continue to tolerate. Accordingly, it set the United States on the path of disengagement, and committed increasingly to it. In turn, the Bush administration had to acknowledge that its military options had dwindled. In late 2006, Bush's push for a large-scale troop surge encountered stiff opposition from US military commanders and the Joint Chiefs of Staff, who argued that US military forces were stretched to their breaking point and were without a secure fallback position should the operation fail.[60] The US troop surge in Iraq was accompanied in fact by a reduction in US goals for the country, just as the Nixon administration had escalated the bombing of North Vietnam in 1972 to facilitate (and, perhaps, cover) a US exit from the conflict. Increasingly, the Bush administration focused on the short-term goal of containing violence within Iraq and managing the handover of military operations to Iraqi security forces. The administration conceded, through its behavior, that it had but limited capability to force Iraqi policy reforms, engineer changes in Iraqi governing institutions, and disarm groups that could challenge the government or threaten the peace.[61] These downsized aspirations informed the approach to follow of the Obama administration. Within weeks of the inaugural, the administration announced an accelerated timetable for a US troop withdrawal (ending the US combat mission by August 2010) based on the supposition that the United States will have met its "achievable goals."[62] That a new chapter had begun was clear in Vice President Joseph Biden's purported remarks in Baghdad within days of the June 30, 2009, US pullback from Iraqi cities. In essence, he was said to have stated to Iraqi officials that future US support was contingent upon their resolving long-standing conflicts and that the United States would not rescue the country if it descended, as before, into violence. As a senior administration official summed up the remarks, there "wasn't any appetite to put Humpty Dumpty back together again."[63] The top US commander in Iraq was among those expressing concerns that, due to declining US public interest (and the redirected focus to Afghanistan), US troops would leave Iraq before their work was done.[64]

Conclusions

That the United States persevered under duress, in its wars in Vietnam and Iraq, is perhaps more notable than that the United States lost steam over the course of these conflicts. But time worked decidedly against the United States—given the high and accumulating costs of US involvement relative to the foreseeable benefits that the United States was likely to obtain from staying the course.

In Vietnam, the United States relied on linkage and signaling strategies that could not compensate for adversary advantages in resolve. In Iraq, the United States was less attentive to "symbolic action" but was increasingly incapable of defeating insurgent and militia elements without the active or tacit support of those who had once fought US troops. In such conflicts, the US military and political disadvantage lies, ironically, in the immensity of US capability. This capability limits the US stake in any given conflict and requires that the United States marshal its resources to serve a global set of objectives and the military commitments that follow. As a major power, the United States is prone, then, to "accommodate" its adversaries by not engaging fully in a conflict.

True, the stakes for the United States will likely increase once it is engaged, to counter exhaustion. This can occur when policymakers quite rationally consider the "reputation" effects of failing to honor a military commitment or yield to an illogical tendency to retrieve sunk costs—"too many lives have been lost to quit"— and accept costs during an operation that would have been unacceptable at the start (Levy 1997). Few in 2003 would have regarded thousands of American lives and expenditures nearing a trillion dollars as an acceptable price for stabilizing or democratizing Iraq. A war that was hard to justify a priori, absent an Iraqi weapons of mass destruction threat, eventually became a "war we cannot afford to lose." The commitment to existing policy is furthered by political considerations. Government officials reject options that amount, in their view, to "losing" (Gelb and Betts 1979)—an admission of failure that will not appease opponents and could alienate supporters. Neustadt (1981, 18) expresses doubt, for instance, that "the U.S. government ever seriously studied the option of getting out of Vietnam. Nobody insisted on having that option seriously explored. It was always taken to be unacceptable on the face of it."[65] If anything, US policymakers choose to deepen US involvement when existing policies fail. Indeed, a politically unpopular leader might "go for broke" by incurring high risks to end a conflict on favorable terms or by escalating a conflict with the hope that a "rally-around-the-flag" effect (an outpouring of patriotic fervor and support in crisis) will strengthen the leader's domestic backing (Oneal and Bryan 1995). If so, leverage is potentially derived from the precariousness of the leader's position—that it has, in the adversary's view, "nothing left to lose."

Yet even these tendencies are insufficient to bulk up US resolve over the long term. For one thing, leaders almost always have something left to lose—honor, a tarnished legacy, ridicule, the defection of close advisors and remaining supporters, a narrowing of policy options, and growing costs, risks, and domestic opposition should escalation fail to accomplish its purposes. For another, missions become hard to support when they expand beyond their original parameters, with newer tasks accreting to older ones.[66] With such "mission creep," policymakers recognize—rationally, it seems—that military problems cannot be "solved" without addressing economic, social, and political ones. They fail, nevertheless, to ask whether the benefits of expanding US operations are worth the price of a broadened US commitment—as in Somalia in 1992–93 and Iraq after 2003. This only makes the mission harder to sustain.

Consequently, when devising military strategies, US leaders must anticipate exhaustion, a weakening of US resolve due to declining domestic support, the consumption of a finite supply of available societal resources (especially manpower), and the growing reticence of government officials to persevere in the face of adversity. Approaching exhaustion in Vietnam, the United States held its ground but settled ultimately for a face-saving solution that positioned the communists for a final takeover. Challenged similarly in Iraq, the United States accepted an outcome that left critical issues of the country's governance unresolved and a precarious peace among competing factions. Whether a more substantial initial commitment would have changed US fortunes in Vietnam and Iraq is debatable; what is not in question is that a reticence to commit can further reduce the capabilities of a party by increasing the future costs of employing force. In Vietnam, the US preference for slow engagement was meant to signal Hanoi that it could avoid an all-out war; instead, the United States convinced Hanoi and its allies in the South that they needed to *escalate quickly* because the United States would eventually commit—or might never fully commit. In Iraq, the United States sought initially to minimize its ground presence by relying on small mobile forces both to capitalize on superior US training, troop quality, and technology and to avoid troop casualties that sap militaries of fighting strength and undermine support for the war effort at home. Yet the US desire to avoid a large footprint arguably produced these very consequences once the United States was left without a force that could maintain order or convince opponents that resistance was useless. Thus, early US decisions not to commit fully might have increased the US military challenge as the conflicts endured.

US leaders were far better positioned domestically to influence the adversary in Vietnam than in Iraq given strong national backing for the global fight against communism, based in wide acceptance of the domino theory. The Bush administration had no such luxury: the Iraq War was a "hard sell," absent an Iraqi WMD threat. Indeed, the administration had to fight a growing public perception that the war in Iraq was instigating terrorism, not combating it. In the end, even the Johnson administration depleted its domestic political capital to fight the Vietnam conflict. What is striking, then, is that domestic support for the Vietnam and Iraq conflicts was high at the start, dropped more rapidly for the Iraq than the Vietnam War, but ended up in the same lowly place—a belief that the war was a mistake and that the United States had to find its way out of the conflict.

In principle, the adversary might tire before US resources are depleted: all parties can be coerced if they have a "breaking point" or can be convinced to compromise by potential costs of staying a course. Such compromise is facilitated when parties share certain objectives and view the same outcomes as beneficial. It is facilitated, most definitely, because the instances are rare when parties are involved in a zero-sum conflict that precludes cooperation (because gains for a rival amount, by definition, to one's own losses) or in a "deadlock" scenario in which the largest payoff for each party arises from reciprocated conflict (that is, when the rivals would rather fight than win by default or through the concessions of another). The relevant question, then, is typically not whether A can be compelled or deterred but rather whether A can be influenced with resources that are available to B, within what B views as an acceptable timeframe. Although B has available to it a host of signaling mechanisms that presumably multiply the effectiveness of those resources and permit B to resolve a conflict more quickly, on favorable terms, these mechanisms are possibly insufficient to overcome conditions that motivate A to resist. The evidence from Vietnam and Iraq is that these mechanisms cannot compensate when A is favorably situated by merit of resolve and can outlast B.

Given the US global position, the lesson is clear. Relative to its adversary, the United States is disadvantaged by its weaker resolve and small (human and material) resource share invested in a small conflict. This does not mean that the United States will lose when engaged in conflicts with ostensibly weaker adversaries, only that the United States must compensate for its disadvantage (in resolve and capability) with a larger (absolute) resource investment or greater quality of investment (for instance, in technology). Should the United States have resources to spare, it must still work around another important lesson: the US government and public will lose resolve when anticipated costs grow in a "small" conflict.

CHAPTER FIVE

Leveraging Host Governments

The Challenges of Institution-Building

US officials knew that their success in Vietnam and Iraq ultimately hinged on the host government taking control of the conflict. They also knew that transferring "ownership" was impossible absent security gains and stronger host-government institutions. Yet these officials came to recognize that by taking the lead in both conflicts, the United States gave host-government leaders reason to "shirk," that is, to allow the United States to carry the security burden, to forego costs of institutional development, and to resist reforms.[1] In consequence, the United States bore a disproportionate *share of the costs* of the US-led mission in the country. Host-government leaders passed on the costs to the United States because it was wedded to its goals, could presumably achieve them without the host government's assistance (or would not achieve them even with the government's aid), and would pursue these goals even if bearing the costs alone (on the "free rider" problem, see Olson 1965). These leaders actually had everything to lose from accepting these costs if they included a loss in political capital or control over the instruments required to retain and extend their power.[2] Their behavior owed, then, to a paradox of governing power: a weak leader is *unable* and a strong leader is *unwilling* to accept costs of a policy—regardless of its desirability—when the intervening government can and will.[3] Predictably, then, US relations with Saigon and Baghdad were often distant, sometimes confrontational, and a consistent threat to the US-led, security effort.

The United States did eventually acquire significant leverage over the South Vietnamese government. The United States compelled Saigon to assume the lead in the war effort by employing a credible threat to withdraw US forces and leave Saigon vulnerable to an existential threat from communist forces. By comparison, the political challenge for the United States in Iraq was great, in the short and the long term. In the short term, the challenge was that Iraqi leaders would not incur the costs necessary to serve US goals because these leaders accepted one or more of the following premises: (a) they lacked the power to satisfy US demands over strong internal resistance, (b) US demands required costly political, economic, or security concessions, (c) their strong power base protected them from US retaliation, or (d) the United States would carry the load alone if necessary. The challenge only increased because US goals and actions shifted leverage to Iraqi leaders to resist US demands when compliance would reduce the power of these leaders or increase their costs. Over the long term, the challenge was that an ever more capable host government would claim an increasing *share of benefits*—exerting greater independence on matters of politics and security— because the United States would not be able to impose sufficient costs in retaliation. Importantly, in neither conflict did the United States possess sufficient leverage to push reforms that host-government leaders believed would weaken them politically, nor did it have the leverage to overcome formidable (political, economic, and social) institution-building challenges. These conclusions follow from assessing the US institution-building challenge, first, in Vietnam and, then, in Iraq.

Institution-Building in Vietnam

In Vietnam, the United States sought to promote democratic institutions and political-economic reforms to legitimate the Saigon government so that it could compete more successfully with the communist opposition for popular support. The United States also sought to build the capabilities of government institutions in South Vietnam—in particular, indigenous security forces—to take over the war effort. The United States had mixed success. Although the United States could not overcome Saigon's incentives to maintain the existing distribution of power and wealth within the country, the United States had more success inducing

Saigon to develop its combat and pacification capabilities. The reasons emerge from examining US leverage in the pursuit of each set of goals.

Democratic Institutions and Political-Economic Reform

US officials never committed to building a model democracy or an egalitarian political-economic system in South Vietnam. A task of that magnitude would have exceeded meager US capabilities and risked creating instability in host governance that would undermine US strategic goals. Yet US officials frequently acknowledged that their primary goal of achieving military success in South Vietnam ultimately depended on increasing participation in national and local governance, closing the gap between the haves and have-nots in the countryside, and building effective public institutions. As their involvement in the country deepened, the challenges of juggling these goals were painfully apparent to US officials.

In the prelude to direct US military intervention, US officials recognized that the imperial and corrupt practices of the Ngo Dinh Diem government were alienating the peasants and driving them to support the communists. Diem's attempts at legitimizing his presidency in the mid-1950s through democratic procedure were farcical. On American advice that he pull off a credible victory in a national referendum (pitting Diem against Bo Dai, the former emperor of Vietnam), Diem orchestrated an impressive victory: by the official returns, he obtained nearly 100 percent of the vote—a total that (extrapolating from the absolute vote) included 150 percent of eligible Saigon voters (Herring 1986, 55). Despite his desire to inflate his popular appeal, he seemed to go out of his way to alienate his public. His unpopular efforts included feeble attempts at land reform (allowing landlords to retain large and prime acreage and impoverishing peasants who could secure government loans to procure land; see Spector 1985, 309), rewarding loyalists with positions of power over communities to which these officials were unconnected (Arreguín-Toft 2005, 148), tolerating widespread corruption (Hamilton 1998, 117), and quashing all resistance.

Diem had some success. He defeated a principal armed threat to his rule when he violently confronted the Hoa Hao and Cao Dai politico-religious sects that controlled private armies, commerce, and government activities within the country (including Saigon), and he killed and incarcerated many communist leaders and operatives. But his heavy-handed methods and antidemocratic instincts and practices (closing newspapers, stifling dissent, and purging government officials) repelled a large portion of the population (Herring 1986, 63–70; Spector 1985,

335), pushed opponents into alliance with communists in the National Liberation Front, and may have convinced Hanoi, in the late 1950s, to regain ground and capitalize on growing disenchantment by increasing support for the insurgency and attacks on troops and government officials in South Vietnam (Herring 1986, 67–68).[4]

With the Buddhist revolt rallying public support for democratic reforms, the United States was awkwardly positioned and under pressure to act. Although the United States wanted Saigon to broaden its political base, it could not coax its leaders to reform and feared that their overthrow would produce a less capable or compliant government. Consequently, US officials were not of one mind on how best to deal with the problem—whether the United States *must* or *could* push Diem to adopt reforms that included empowering the legislature, diversifying his leadership circle, establishing a meritocracy, and engaging in land redistribution. The problem was that "reforming meant sharing power and wealth, but to share some would be to jeopardize all" (Gelb and Betts 1979, 63).[5] The Kennedy administration put pressure on Diem to accept reforms; it was unwilling, however, to back demands by curtailing economic and military aid when Diem resisted out of fear that such measures "would fray the ties of those loyal to him" (Hunt 1995, 14). Inasmuch as reducing US aid and military support would imperil US efforts to engage Saigon in the war effort and deprive the United States of a mechanism for influencing the actions and development of the South Vietnamese military, Diem recognized that he had much to gain and little to lose from stonewalling and deflecting challenges for reform. Predictably, Diem resisted US efforts to link aid to political and military reforms (Herring 1986, 77, 84–85, 103), and the United States softened its approach (Smith 1971, 109).

Leverage problems vis-à-vis the South Vietnamese government did not end with the assassination of Diem in 1963 in a coup condoned by the United States. With its "neutralist" stance, Diem's replacement proved far less agreeable to the United States on essential issues of war and peace. The junta, under the control of General Duong Van Minh, resisted the US bombing of North Vietnam, a greater US military role in the country, and the very idea that the war in the South was winnable militarily. Instead, it preferred a political settlement with the united opposition—the National Liberation Front—in the belief that it was not controlled by the communists (McT. Kahin 1979–80, 648, 654). The administration was thrust in the ironic position of supporting the overthrow of Minh (McT. Kahin 1979–80, 672), when the United States had opposed Diem for endangering the overall war effort. For a period, worst-case fears of instability were realized as one government fell after another. These governments lacked a stable power base or claims to legitimacy from which to draw popular support. Indeed, all future governments would have to overcome the stigma of being US "puppet regimes" for having replaced Diem. Despite his enormous failings, Diem was a nationalist and a formidable political presence. That he lost power, when he fell out of favor with the United States, was bound to taint future governments. In turn, US government officials had to carry the burden of having helped to unseat Diem. As the PROVN study noted, "The feeling that President Diem's downfall in 1963 was hastened by threatened US withdrawal of support has further sensitized Americans to the issue of 'intervening' in the sovereign affairs" of the South Vietnamese government. Given the stakes, the study implored the US government to "override fear of the stigma attached to such labels as 'colonialist' or 'imperialist'" and employ its influence when necessary to push the South Vietnamese government to adopt measures to gain popular support (US Army 1966).

The challenges for host governments, and in US efforts to leverage these governments, were exacerbated by the power structure that evolved quickly with the "decapitation" of the Saigon regime. Successive rulers had to contend with the military factionalism and devolution in authority that came with Diem's removal, as generals grabbed power and then safeguarded and extended it through an elaborate military patronage system. The generals remained hyper-vigilant to potential reorganizations and personnel changes in the government bureaucracy that could unfavorably redistribute power. Conditions did stabilize, after 1965, when Nguyen Cao Ky and Nguyen Van Thieu became prime minister and president, respectively, in a military-led South Vietnamese government. But power plays and considerations were never far from the surface in a government in which authority was shared by members of a military Directory. Its members ruled collectively on promotions and appointments yet pursued their own individual policies through their control of regional military forces and political positions (Clarke 1988, 20–25). As top US military and political officials in South Vietnam were quite conscious of the ruling generals' "narrow basis of political support and the deep divisions within its own membership, . . . the danger of political turmoil colored almost every bit of advice they tendered to their Vietnamese counterparts" (Clarke 1988, 127). In this, Ky played explicitly on US fears of military rebellion to promote his bureaucratic agenda (Clarke 1988, 129–130).

As the new government consolidated its hold on power, it sought to legitimate its position through elections. Although the elections threatened to expose the regime's narrow military base and exacerbate the longstanding rivalry between

Ky and Thieu, the generals ruling the country addressed part of the problem with a joint ticket combining President Thieu and Vice President Ky. That did not convince some US officials that the election was anything but a step backward for reform: both leaders represented the old military guard and lacked a substantial popular base, and their election would inevitably raise questions about the fairness of the vote. Their election, in 1967—and with a mere 35 percent plurality at that (albeit a refreshingly low number, given recent electoral history)—was engineered by keeping popular candidates (including Duong Van Minh) off the ballot. The prevailing US position was, again, that these leaders were best equipped to bring stability to the government and ensure its commitment to the war effort (on the election, see McAllister 2004).

The rivalry between Thieu and Ky continued in the aftermath of the election, as each sought to alter the military bureaucratic structure and to make personnel changes to strengthen his own relative position within the government and country. With such competition, US officials in the country were reluctant to push Saigon to reform. They thought that empowering civilians could provoke the country's military leaders to respond or produce a weak—even if popular—leadership. US officials worried further about the unsettling consequences of moves that might disturb the fragile balance within the country's military leadership (Clarke 1988, 256–261). Such an outcome would presumably threaten Saigon's military performance, invite domestic instability, and show the American public, growing weary (and wary) of the war, the narrowly based military leadership for what it was.

Through purges of opponents, suppression of dissent, and skillful maneuvering, Thieu soon established himself as the primary leader in the country (Clarke 1988, 308–313). With a stronger hold on power, Thieu had sufficient confidence and clout to promote reforms (most prominently, in land redistribution)—at least up to a point. President Thieu was well aware of the political dangers of reform: broadening the popular base of the Saigon government could bring *long-term* stability to the country only by undercutting existing support from the haves and empowering the have-nots. The harsh reality of South Vietnam's political system was that Thieu had to give first priority to placating his primary constituency— the military. As Blaufarb (1977, 273) notes, "If he attempted to strip it of power and privilege and access to wealth, he risked the development of a serious opposition to his leadership within the armed forces which could eventually bring him down." As always, stability had its price: whether or not US officials wanted the Saigon government to do more, they remained aware that it could probably be pushed only so far, and possibly further than it should. Therefore, to the extent that Thieu made personnel changes that pleased US government officials, it was Thieu who decided when and how they would occur (Clarke 1988, 502). To the end, the military retained its hold on the government, as "South Vietnamese Army officers continued to monopolize province and district posts; military units continued to have territorial police responsibilities; and corps commanders continued to act as regional governors" (Clarke 1988, 504–505).

In sum, US leverage over Saigon remained limited. The balance in leverage favored Saigon as long as its leaders believed their interest lay in avoiding reforms and the United States valued a Saigon government that was strong and anticommunist above all else. It also favored Saigon when it realized that the United States could not disengage easily, would not push Saigon if it might push back or make concessions that threatened national stability, and would ultimately cast its lot with the Saigon government in place. Although a stronger Saigon government was more open to some progressive policies, it was not amenable to surrendering governmental power. Indeed, Thieu sought to extend his base within the civilian government in lieu of building a popular following outside of it (King 1971, 402–403); he "managed to isolate, fragment and finally outlaw" most rival political groups (Snepp 1977, 56) and, in the wake of the 1972 Easter Offensive, acquired the power (from the National Assembly) to rule by decree. He used this power to call off village elections and close down newspapers that had criticized his government. A stronger Saigon leadership, more secure in its position, did not need to concede its prerogatives.

Institutional Capacity

The United States increasingly sought to build up the Saigon government's capabilities in combat and pacification. The United States was challenged persistently on both fronts.

As a nationalist, Diem resisted an increased US presence in his country, but he was not well prepared to combat a communist insurgency. Under Diem, the military fielded a fighting force that was no match for disciplined communist forces; troops were "poorly organized, trained, and equipped, lacking in national spirit, suffering from low morale, and deficient in officers and trained specialists such as engineers and artillerymen" (Herring 1986, 58)—let alone officers who "shared, or even understood, the American officers' belief in coordination, teamwork, loyalty to superiors and subordinates, skill, and delegation of authority" or understood the need to subordinate their efforts to those of a larger functioning entity (Spector 1985, 345). Positions were distributed on the basis of political allegiances and reliability in a military system that was *designed* to impede quick, efficient, and coordinated military operations, to shield the government against coups (Spector 1985, 278–280). At all levels, military personnel capitalized on their positions to engage in illicit dealings and outright thievery against local populations.[6] Thus, US aid was often lost to fraud or usurped to serve the political needs of the Diem leadership. For instance, Diem adapted the Civil Guard (backed by the United States for counterinsurgency) as a private militia and sought to arm it with US-supplied tanks, artillery, and helicopters (Spector 1985, 322–325).

Once the United States intervened directly in the Vietnam fighting, it faced a profound dilemma: it wished that South Vietnamese troops would assume a greater combat role but, having little faith in their capabilities and commitment, relegated these troops to supporting US combat operations and pursuing less demanding missions. By the same token, US officials recognized that these missions would not improve South Vietnam's fighting skills, would hurt the morale of these troops, and would foster an attitude of dependence and resignation within the South Vietnamese military that impeded its emergence as an independent and effective combat force (Hunt 1995, 34–35).[7] To the extent that US forces "stepped up" throughout the 1960s, South Vietnam's forces appeared to "step down," judging from enemy contacts and kills and US casualties incurred.[8]

US military officials tried to improve the fighting performance of the South Vietnamese military with a dedicated advisory effort and coordination and joint operations between US and South Vietnamese units; they also performed quantitative evaluations of the military effectiveness of South Vietnamese military units. These measures proved insufficient, however, in overcoming problems deeply embedded in local culture and practices due in part to US operational deficiencies that included the unevenness of the advisory effort and the inconsistencies, bias, and disconnects of a rating system that showed unit improvements "on paper" that did not translate into performance in battle.[9] Then, US officials eschewed dramatic measures fearing their consequences. US officials worried, for example, that an integrated US–South Vietnamese command would provoke local resentment and make the South Vietnamese military even more dependent on the United States (Clarke 1988, 501). They worried also that restructuring the South Vietnamese military for improved performance would backfire in Saigon, where personal loyalty and power were valued above professional competence and military effectiveness.[10]

The United States sought to increase the relative South Vietnamese contribution to the war effort through Vietnamization, a term introduced by Nixon's secretary of defense, Melvin Laird. Through training and equipping the South Vietnamese military on a massive scale, the policy tried to achieve the twin military goals of reducing US involvement (and casualties) and increasing the relative combat role of South Vietnamese forces. Vietnamization proved a formidable challenge, however, given the litany of longstanding South Vietnamese military problems—the woeful lack of capable officers, the class divide between officers and soldiers, the absence of rigorous and sustained training, the low morale and high shirking and desertion rates, the lack of accountability for poor performance, and the tendency to reward political loyalty over military competence. In combat, these problems translated into poor performance—tactical rigidity, a lack of military aggressiveness (for instance, leading to the use of excessive force in populated areas), and a dearth of initiative (Lewy 1978; Thayer 1985, 59–77). Not the least of the challenges was rampant corruption—manifest, up the ranks, in a full range of nefarious activities from stealing chickens from local peasants to selling military positions, black-market profiteering, and siphoning government funds by collecting pay for fictitious personnel (the "ghost payroll"). The effect was to drain the military of resources, damage its efficiency, and undermine its legitimacy for a good portion of the South Vietnamese population.

Importantly, these problems were not specific to the South Vietnamese military; they were failings of South Vietnamese (civilian *and* military) institutions more generally, including those integral to the pacification effort. Indeed, to overcome these problems, the 1966 PROVN study had recommended the construction of an integrated civil-military advisory "scaffolding designed to stand alongside the weak [South Vietnamese governmental] structure" so that "leverage" could be employed "at all levels," along "a continuum from subtle interpersonal persuasion to withdrawal of US support" (US Army 1966, 56–58). Yet up until the defeat of the Saigon government, traditional problems continued to plague the pacification effort—official intransigence and corruption, a lack of intra-governmental coordination and data sharing, the redirecting of policies in implementation, and an unwillingness of personnel to serve in programs that brought neither "glory or promotions" (Blaufarb 1977, 243–278).

There is no better example of (some of) these failings than the Phoenix Program. The joint US–South Vietnamese program (under US direction) was intended to disable the communist network by identifying and "neutralizing" (that is, capturing or killing) elite Vietcong agents (Kalyvas and Kocher 2007b, 192). It succeeded at disrupting Vietcong operations in South Vietnam but with a significant economic and social cost. As always, South Vietnamese officials siphoned

US aid from the program while those charged with implementation inflated statistics (body counts) to show progress toward meeting program goals (Karnow 1997, 617). The program also suffered from misdirected effort: belying the program's purpose of targeting important agents, three-quarters of those neutralized "operated at the village level or lower" (Thayer 1985, 208). More troublesome is that program goals suffered from the effects of greed and personal vendetta: innocent villagers were rounded up to fill quotas, bribes were secured to obtain the release of Vietcong suspects, and punishment was dispensed with specious evidence of a suspect's illicit activities (Karnow 1997, 617). One rigorous analysis of post-1970 program data suggests that, of the roughly fifteen thousand suspects that were killed over the course of the program, a significantly higher relative and absolute toll was taken on suspects for whom confirmatory evidence was the weakest: "in a truly awesome process of perverse selection, those under low suspicion were almost five times more likely to be killed than those under high suspicion"—indeed, the former accounted for almost 97 percent of those killed. The unavoidable implication is that large numbers of innocent people were targeted (Kalyvas and Kocher 2007b, 194, 201).

Despite institutional failings, noteworthy progress did occur. The South Vietnamese government eventually made a huge personnel commitment to various national and regional security forces that were integral to the pacification effort. Furthermore, Vietnamization resulted in the substitution of South Vietnamese for US troops in combat: accordingly, US casualties declined, South Vietnamese military casualties rose; moreover, there was no tendency for South Vietnamese casualties to track US casualties (Gartner 1998). Given the challenges of Vietnamization, including deficient US leverage, what explains the success in getting a large South Vietnamese force into battle? There are a number of plausible answers. The Saigon government had consolidated its political base and was positioned to make allocation decisions with the aim of combating communist forces; it was operating in the permissive post-Tet security environment that facilitated mobility in the countryside and the use of a large draft pool for military service; and it benefited institutionally from the huge infusion of funds and resources that the United States offered to support pacification and Vietnamization. It is unlikely, however, that these factors alone would have convinced Saigon to carry the massive security burden if Saigon had believed that its self-reliance would provoke the United States to withdraw from the country. The US withdrawal would actually bring South Vietnamese military casualties many times greater than those suffered previously by US troops, severe economic hardships (inflation, unemployment), and a growing political challenge from key elements of South Vietnamese society (on the latter, see Elliott 2003, 1354). With these potential costs, it made little sense for Saigon to improve its capabilities—to seek autonomy or make the United States think that Saigon could act autonomously—unless independence was inevitable, as it appeared to Saigon after Tet. With US domestic support for the war plummeting and a new US administration looking for a way out, the "writing was on the wall" that Thieu would soon have to go it alone, despite US assurances that troop withdrawals would be based on local conditions and progress in the Paris negotiations (Hunt 1995, 209–210). He thus had strong incentives to improve South Vietnam's capabilities to compete for military and political control of the countryside.

By the same token, the United States lost some leverage over Saigon, as the pending US withdrawal (and secret US negotiations with Hanoi) reinforced Saigon's fears of abandonment. Once Saigon recognized that it would be largely on its own, it had every reason to try to pull the United States back into the fighting. The problem for the United States was that Thieu defined South Vietnamese security in broad and uncompromising terms. In fact, his rejectionist policies were popularized as the "four no's"—"no coalition, no sharing of land with the communists, no neutralism, and no legal activities of the communist party" (King 1971, 419). Thieu was hypersensitive to the possibility that he would lose sovereign control over some South Vietnamese territory and refused even to acknowledge that the Vietcong held de facto control of parts of the country. For instance, he rejected the notion of a "contested" area that was used by US pacification officials to designate places where the Vietcong retained an ongoing presence: for him, a hamlet under "VC control" was instead a "hamlet not yet fully controlled by the government" (Hunt 1995, 193–195). He agreed, in fact, to participate in the talks with Hanoi only after receiving assurances that the United States would not recognize the National Liberation Front as a separate political entity and thereby undermine Saigon's claim to sovereignty over any and all territory in the South. Thieu feared—with good reason, it turns out—that the United States would capitulate on the basic terms of a settlement and allow North Vietnamese forces to remain in place to legitimate the communist position in the South. So by playing the "spoiler," Thieu maintained some leverage over US policies.

Thieu was positioned to create political difficulties for US policymakers by challenging their pretense to having negotiated an honorable exit from the conflict. By charging the United States with a "sellout," Thieu could undermine the Nixon administration's efforts to choreograph an exit that would signal US allies and adversaries that the United States had upheld its commitment. Thieu also had the power to challenge Hanoi militarily on the battlefield and undercut a ceasefire agreement. So Nixon and Kissinger chose to placate Thieu to avoid the appearance that he was being shunted aside. Indeed, deference to the Thieu government over the acceptable terms of an agreement—and the resulting increase in US negotiating demands—created the negotiating impasse with Hanoi that Nixon and Kissinger sought to bridge with the Christmas bombing of North Vietnam.[11] The terms of the Paris Agreement did not differ markedly from those that had precipitated the bombing, but the administration felt that by escalating the violence, it made its point with Hanoi, reassured Thieu (and others) of the US commitment to Saigon, and received the best possible terms, under the circumstances. For his part, Thieu remained unconvinced. With his recalcitrance, the Nixon administration threatened to negotiate a separate peace with Hanoi and to cut off all military, economic, and diplomatic support to Saigon. Thieu "held out to the last possible moment" and relented when the United States promised broad military support for South Vietnam and a return of US bombers should Hanoi violate the agreement (Randolph 2007, 333). In other words, he conceded his position only when he recognized that he had done all that he could and that further resistance would be self-defeating. Even with the agreement, Thieu continued his campaign on the ground. He sought to extend his territorial control militarily— challenging areas first under the control of the Provisional Revolutionary Government and then base areas for North Vietnamese forces (Parker 1975, 365–366).

In the final analysis, it must be said that even Thieu's strong security commitment was insufficient to prevent a communist victory. Ultimately, any leverage that the United States exerted on Saigon was limited given the counterweight of South Vietnamese culture and practices, the inherent weaknesses of South Vietnamese institutions, and the monumental divide (and hostility) between segments of society and their government. What can be said with certainty is that the United States used what leverage it could and that was not enough. The South Vietnamese military still suffered from a high military desertion rate, problems recruiting competent officers, a discernable reluctance to engage the enemy, a lack of cohesion under fire, and woefully deficient air attack capabilities.

Thus, former secretary of defense Melvin Laird was not wrong, in his defense of Vietnamization, to argue that "[General Creighton] Abrams carried through magnificently on our plan for having a trained and ready South Vietnamese force in place when the U.S. withdrawal dates arrived. And this force never lost a battle from the time of our last withdrawal of combat forces until our government went

back on its word to continue interim military support to the South Vietnamese."[12]
His argument does beg some fundamental questions: how do you define success?
Was Vietnamization successful if South Vietnamese troops were incapable of operating effectively without active US support and relied heavily on US financial
and military assistance? Despite evidence that these troops often fought well,
valiantly at times, they failed their first true test, their solo performance in 1975.
With initial losses, the South Vietnamese military proved incapable of strategic
retreat and recovery—and largely self-destructed. As one former Defense Department official concluded, "They were a fairly good fighting force of more than
1 million troops by the time the last American troops pulled out, but they were
not good enough" (Thayer 1985, 75).

With additional leverage, the United States might have pushed the Saigon
government to accelerate and broaden its institution-building effort to compete
successfully with North Vietnam and the Vietcong and to organize the military
more effectively to deflect the challenge from communist forces. Yet, it was apparently not within the power of any South Vietnamese leader (or set of leaders)
to spur the governmental and societal changes that could yield success. For that
matter, neither the threat of imminent US withdrawal nor, later, imminent defeat
could rally the South Vietnamese military to fight as required to safeguard the
nation's security. Its defeat was likely preordained. Under US guidance, South
Vietnamese troops adopted the same organization, equipment, and tactics that
the United States had employed to fight to a stalemate.

Institution-Building in Iraq

With the US occupation of Iraq in 2003, US goals turned ambitious, by any standard. The US plan to topple the Saddam Hussein regime and destroy its alleged
non–conventional weapons capabilities was quickly transformed into a vast and
intensive US nation-building exercise. The US institution-building and support
effort—like the US military plan—drew initially from a flawed assumption—that
Iraqi government structures were functioning and effective. US officials assumed,
for instance, that Iraqi police would maintain law and order in the country (Rathmell et al. 2005, 11). The effort drew, in fact, from the same assumption that
produced a flawed military plan—that Iraqis would greet US troops as liberators.
This led US policymakers to expect the best and prepare accordingly—that is,
underprepare: "If Iraqi citizens welcomed American troops and helped them in
their mission, and US officials would only need to assist functioning ministries

for a short while, then reconstruction would only be a minor task for incoming forces" (Bensahel 2006, 457–458).

Although these assumptions were impugned by mounting evidence—the looting, destruction, and violence that erupted after the US occupation—US officials chose to prolong and expand the US mission in the country. The US goals were now to turn Iraq into a showcase of democracy, inclusiveness, and institutional competence (among Iraq's promised characteristics) in a region of the world renowned for authoritarian governance, brutal internal security measures, and bloated bureaucracy. The institution-building effort was, at best, a mixed success, as revealed by examining US leverage challenges, over the short and long term.

Short-Term Leverage: Building Democracy, Inclusiveness, and Capacity

The United States expanded its goals under challenging conditions. The US government entered without a working plan; enough qualified personnel on hand to oversee the effort; a clear chain of command to ensure consistency in program goals and to monitor progress; adequate contact between officials in Washington and Baghdad and with operations in the field; financial, technical, and human resources to reconstruct the damaged and decaying Iraqi infrastructure; essential prerequisites for democracy in a country that knew only authoritarian rule (see Moon 2009); and a backup plan, should the original plan prove unsound or demanding (Bensahel 2006, 458–465). Developing open, inclusive, and competent Iraqi institutions would have been difficult, even without a major insurgency.

Throughout its effort, the United States was confounded by fundamental challenges inherent in the nation-building enterprise. These included (a) the constraining effects of early decisions, (b) onerous tradeoff decisions, (c) intractable societal maladies, and (d) interdependent national problems. These challenges tested the capability and resolve of the United States and increased its difficulty acquiring host-government cooperation for achieving US policy goals. Host-government leaders acquired leverage for resisting US demands from the ambitions of US goals and various US actions that affected the power of host-government leaders and the costs of conceding to US demands.

The Tyranny of Early Decisions: The Origins of Political Stalemate

In the engineering of any complex system, early decisions bind future choices. In Iraq, early US efforts to build an inclusive government and accept popular elections had irreversibly negative consequences. US actions produced an Iraqi leadership that was *insufficiently diverse* to appease or address the demands of the country's increasingly disenfranchised Sunni minority and *sufficiently inclusive* to produce a stalemate that would impede reforms. Once in place, the host government's actions worsened societal tension and increased the barriers to political compromise.

The Coalition Provisional Authority, under Paul Bremer, initially rejected an early transition to Iraqi self-governance. It reversed prior US efforts (under the Office for Reconstruction and Humanitarian Assistance, led by Jay Garner) to boost electoral participation at the local level and prepared for an extended stay in an Iraq under US tutelage. CPA officials were justifiably concerned that an appointed Iraqi leadership would try to grab power and that popular elections would favor leaders who could capitalize on and exacerbate ethno-sectarian divisions. Political maneuvering and growing social divisions were the result, however, when the CPA appointed the Interim Governing Council (IGC), which held the power to appoint key officials and to develop procedures for writing an Iraqi constitution. Despite its broad membership, the IGC favored organized groups, apportioned disproportionate strength to exile leaders, and disenfranchised Sunnis tainted by their association with the former Baath regime. Its decisional problems forewarned of political challenges to come. Decision-making in the IGC proved cumbersome, to say the least, given the rivalry and mistrust among its members. Even simple decisions proved complicated, and issues were resolved by distributing benefits ("horse-trading" or "dividing the spoils"), not through compromise meant to realize shared interests. For instance, when asked by the CPA to pick a leader, the IGC opted, after lengthy negotiations, to have nine leaders rotate through the position monthly, in alphabetical order (Bensahel et al. 2008, 169). National leadership positions—such as vice presidencies and many ministry positions—were assigned on an ethno-sectarian basis. Unsurprisingly, the IGC had trouble agreeing on procedures for drafting a constitution (Diamond 2005, 49–52).

With security conditions deteriorating in the country, and pressure mounting nationally and internationally to transfer authority to an Iraq government, the United States reversed course. It decided to transfer sovereignty, in mid-2004, to an Iraqi transitional government to be selected through provincial caucuses. This attempt to ease the democratic transition and limit popular input provoked resistance from Ayatollah al-Sistani, who maintained that an Iraqi government and constitution must reflect the will of the Iraqi people (and, as it happens, its Shiite majority). Although the United States was slow to appreciate al-Sistani's formidable influence from the sidelines in Iraqi politics, a solution was eventually devised and incorporated by the IGC into an annex of an interim constitution (the Transitional Administrative Law). It required the transfer of sovereignty to the Interim Iraqi Government (IIG)—with designated powers—in advance of the January 2005 elections for a permanent, 275-member National Assembly that would elect government officials and oversee the drafting of a constitution. So the authority granted the IGC by the United States would greatly influence the course of Iraqi politics. The IGC had the first opportunity to address critical issues, such as the role of Islam, the form of Iraqi governance, and the political standing of "regions" as provincial conglomerates (that would give the Kurdish population significant control over its security forces, finances, and so forth). It also affected the constitutional process by merging the National Assembly and the constitutional convention into one body and, more ominously, by giving Kurds an effective veto over the Constitution—permitting its rejection with a (two-thirds) "no" vote in any three Iraqi provinces—thus, the three Kurdish provinces (Diamond 2005, 140–178).

Marred by violence and boycotted by Sunnis and Sadrists, the January elections limited voter choices. Seats in a National Assembly were assigned proportionately on the basis of national votes cast for a "closed-list" ballot, which restricted choices to "political entities"—parties, party coalitions, and so forth (Katzman 2008).[13] Thus, the elections furthered the heavy bias toward the organized interest groups that were part of the new Iraqi power circle, permitted various Shiite groups (especially the Supreme Council) to strengthen their hold on power, and reinforced existing political and social schisms. The Constitution was drafted, with little Sunni participation, by a committee appointed by the Assembly and was adopted by referendum in October 2005, with substantial electoral opposition in Sunni-dominant provinces (but just short of the two-thirds vote in three provinces, that would have derailed ratification).[14] It left key issues largely unsettled, including the power of the central government relative to various regions, the powers of the presidency, the future of disputed territories (containing much of Iraq's oil reserves) including Tamim Province (which contains the city of Kirkuk, claimed by Kurds as part of their region), and the regional distribution of oil revenues and power to control oil reserves in the country. (The Constitution was accepted by the dominant Sunni legislative party only with the promise of future amendments.)

The legislative distribution of power was enshrined in the executive branch, where ministries were assigned to parties on the basis of their electoral strength (following the consensus approach of the IGC). A consequence was that the Iraqi government amounted to "a collection of separate ministries, run mostly as individual fiefs with little sense of belonging to a national government, whose ministers have not developed the habit of collaboration with fellow ministers on national issues" (Marr 2007, 4). The profusion of these rival power centers undercut the power of the prime minister, who was constrained further by severe legislative divisions—first in the National Assembly and then in the Council of Representatives, the permanent legislature elected in December 2005, under the new Iraqi constitution.

The tenure of Iraq's prime ministers proved short, that is, until May 2006, when Nouri al-Maliki was named Iraq's third prime minister of the post-Saddam era (Kurds and Sunnis had opposed his predecessor, Ibrahim al-Jaafari, who had served from April 2005). Yet his position remained vulnerable both because he relied heavily on loyalists from his Dawa Party and because the party had a limited popular following and depended for support on a fragile and volatile coalition called the United Iraqi Alliance. The governing coalition was repeatedly threatened in mid-2007 by walkouts or departures by ministers and parliament members loyal to Moqtada al-Sadr, the (Shiite) Fadhila Party and the (Sunni) Iraqi Accordance Front. (At one point, a third of cabinet posts, including the minister of justice, were unfilled.)[15] The broad impasse in the legislature kept the Iraqi government from moving on a variety of constitutional reforms that would affect the power, role, and performance of the central government. Sunnis sought a strong central government (in which Sunnis were adequately represented) that would control oil resources located primarily in Shiite- and Kurd-dominated regions of the country; Shiites linked to the Supreme Council sought to decentralize power in Iraq to capitalize on the party's strength in the south of Iraq. In turn, Kurds favored a strengthening of regions and sought to grab authority (for an independent Kurdistan, according to critics) that was not granted explicitly to the central government by the Constitution. Consequently, negotiations dragged on for years over a national oil law that would determine authority for developing and managing Iraq's oil resources. (When unable to secure a legal right to negotiate oil contracts and reach agreement with opponents on the distribution of oil revenues, the Kurds passed their own regional oil law in August 2007.)[16] The relative power of the central government was the basis of a large variety of issues, both old and new—electric power sharing (when some provinces refused Baghdad its required power allocations, it caused shortfalls and blackouts in the capital; see US GAO 2007a, 29), the authority of the Kurdish Regional Government to negotiate arms contracts (after it was revealed that the Kurds were importing arms from Bulgaria), and so forth.

With considerable delay, the legislature moved forward on some issues. In February 2008, the Iraqi parliament finally passed a law that established the relationship between the central and provincial governments, but only as part of a political "package" involving an amnesty law and annual national budget (Gluck 2008). Provincial elections were postponed until 2009 because some parties were concerned that they would lose power in the voting and because elections were tied to other divisive issues—in particular, control over territories coveted by Kurds for their region. Even this progress was incomplete: the Kurds remained opposed to provisions in a July 2008 law that placed provincial security forces under central government control and gave Arabs, Turkmens, and Kurds an equal vote in the Kurd-controlled Tamim provincial council.[17]

So in building an inclusive representative democracy in Iraq, the United States moved faster than it preferred, faster than a country with an underdeveloped civil society (of organized interest groups) and democratic norms (of tolerance for opposing views) could support. The effect of the initial US appointment of an "inclusive" government followed by early elections was to reinforce divisions within Iraqi society that worsened a stalemate in governance. The sectarianism that had assumed a "benign" form in the country (ICG 2006, 6), given layers of connectedness (familial, tribal, and regional) within Iraqi society, became malignant when newly empowered leaders manipulated sectarian identities to their own advantage and Sunnis were deprived of power (and their livelihood) in the name of de-Baathification. Once battle lines were drawn, the resolution of any issue was complicated by its connection to others—big and small. Parties viewed compromise on key issues, then, as tantamount to conceding power. The effect was to leave key issues unsettled and to reinforce the ethno-sectarian underpinnings of all disputes. The latitude for government action—and US leverage—were increasingly constricted, then, by the intense politicization of conflict.

Although the politicization fed on itself, its origins lay, fundamentally, in a problem of inadvertent empowerment. To legitimize the US position in the country and move it toward self-governance, the United States had to delegate responsibilities to Iraqi leaders. The problem for the United States was that delegation, by its very nature, concedes powers to nominal subordinates who can use their newfound power to operate from an enhanced position of strength.[18] In Iraq, US deference to certain individuals and groups (starting with initial US appointments to an advisory Leadership Council) positioned them to affect the selection of the Interim Governing Council (Diamond 2005, 42–43) and, more generally, to pursue their political agendas and grab power at the expense of opponents. Having acquired power, these leaders jealously guarded and actively promoted it—by trying to control the selection of caucus members that would elect the transitional assembly, seeking recognition for the IGC as the interim government of Iraq, negotiating Council members into key positions in the interim government, taking control of key ministries, and so forth (Diamond 2005, 81, 258–264).

Useful insights into empowerment at work are obtained by examining individual cases, like that of the remarkably resilient Ahmad Chalabi. Chalabi ingratiated himself to the US Defense Department in the buildup to the 2003 war by providing "information" on Iraqi WMD programs to help make the case for war. Appointed to the IGC, he soon fell out of favor with his former US supporters for his alleged criminal activities, the phony prewar intelligence he supplied to the United States, and his leaks of sensitive information to Iran. But Chalabi survived the US challenge to become a significant obstacle to political reconciliation from his new position as head of the country's de-Baathification commission—created by the Iraqi Governing Council to implement the CPA de-Baathification edict (as discussed below). In leading a commission renowned for its power and secretiveness (ICTJ 2008, 5), Chalabi apparently blocked efforts to allow lower-level Sunni party members from returning to their prior professional positions.[19] The de-Baathification Commission is alleged to have intentionally brought false charges against Sunni officers to purge them from military units (US GAO 2007a, 68–69). Of course, the United States did more than empower figures on the margins of power in Iraq—the United States installed the country's top leaders, who would then exert their autonomy.[20] Their influence and rivalries would bring to power a succession of prime ministers who would stymie the United States by wheeling and dealing and playing to particular constituencies. By 2007, the United States came to view the al-Maliki government itself as a significant source of the country's problems but lacked a viable leadership alternative. It resigned itself to working with al-Maliki because replacing him would only add to the turbulence in government and set the stage for the next Iraqi government to fail—and to fall.[21]

A potential US response was to nurture rival power centers and thereby induce al-Maliki to compromise. For example, by supporting the Awakening movement over the concerns and resistance of the Iraqi government, the United States put the al-Maliki government on notice that the United States would not depend on Baghdad to adopt more inclusive policies and would force the government's hand by empowering opposition groups—economically, militarily, and politically. But a balancing strategy carried the risk of political stalemate (or worse) if an in-group became disinclined to concede ground to an out-group that now poses an even greater threat.[22] A potential effect of the strategy was, then, to leave the United States with even less room to maneuver among uncompromising parties or perhaps even to lay the groundwork for another power struggle. Ironically, the strategy might "work" only if the US-supported party established its nationalist credentials by distancing itself from the United States: in the January 2005 elections, even parties that had worked closely with the United States campaigned hard on pledges to remove US troops.[23] Indeed, various parties might compete for political advantage by employing this strategy, as al-Maliki did with considerable success. Al-Maliki earned grudging respect, in early 2008, for his alleged leadership skills in seizing the initiative and launching a surprise offensive against the Mahdi Army in Basra. He also improved his nationalist credentials by pushing the United States hard on the terms of a US withdrawal (as discussed below) and then advertising "his" political victory.[24]

Under the circumstances, top US government officials were not of one mind on how best to approach the Iraqi government. US officials in Baghdad, including Ambassador Ryan Crocker and General David Petraeus, did not shy from confronting Prime Minister al-Maliki. But they did so knowing that he could not be pressed to the limit—that US leverage was limited given the absence of a viable replacement government to which the United States could throw its support. Their efforts were diluted further within an administration that preferred to deal with al-Maliki with gestures of encouragement and support. Not only did Bush consistently oppose leveraging the Baghdad government, he also adopted rhetoric and held to practices that the al-Maliki government could interpret as unconditional support. For instance, by emphasizing repeatedly that the United States stood with the Iraqi government and maintaining biweekly teleconferences with the Iraqi prime minister, Bush reinforced al-Maliki's perception that the United States would not incur the risks and costs of pressuring the Iraqi government or of seeking to replace it. Inevitably, these practices appear to have shifted leverage to the al-Maliki government, as Bush administration officials feared that reducing the regularized contact with al-Maliki would hurt US influence on him.[25] The Iraqi government benefitted in bargaining from an implicit threat of becoming even *less* cooperative.

This is not to say that the US would have succeeded with a hardball approach. Overall, the United States was without available pressure points: no single leader had the power to push through a narrow set of reforms, no necessary majority of like-minded leaders was available to press through a full package of reforms, and no leader was willing to compromise and risk weakening his bargaining position vis-à-vis his political rivals (none of the potential candidates were women). Simply put, the leverage challenge for the United States was that like-minded leaders were too weak to push the US agenda, and the rest were too strong for the United States to challenge given the absence of useful leadership alternatives.

Tradeoff Decisions: Making Hard Choices

In the aftermath of its occupation, the United States discovered an Iraq in need. The country lacked governmental institutions that could effectively deliver essential services (electricity, sewage, water treatment, trash collection), stimulate economic growth and investment, provide educational and medical services, adjudicate disputes and enforce the law, repair the country's roads and bridges, and rehabilitate the country's petroleum facilities to fund Iraq's reconstruction and development. Iraq had suffered severely under the combined effects of international sanctions, Saddam Hussein's authoritarian priorities, and war; it suffered again as Iraqis turned on one another in the looting, political violence, property damage, and thievery that followed the destruction of the Baath regime and its security institutions. The United States was left to help build Iraq's social, political, and economic infrastructure under the worst possible conditions—when security threats took priority over all else, human and material resources were unavailable, time was of the essence (with the pending transfer of sovereignty to the Iraqi government), and progress was often temporary or elusive. Inevitably, US officials came to recognize that pursuing their objectives involved tradeoffs—that accomplishing some worthy goals hurt or prevented the achievement of others.

First, US officials encountered tradeoffs between their short- and long-term goals. On the one hand, the emphasis on short-term goals had deleterious long-term consequences. For instance, by pushing the Iraqi police—which had been a "neglected, secondary player" under Saddam Hussein (Rathmell et al. 2005, xii)[26]— into the field early, the United States created graver security challenges in the country. Employing the Iraqi police as a front-line public security and counterinsurgency force fostered unit disintegration and allowed units to form and operate that were decidedly sectarian in composition and disposition.[27] But the reverse held too, as the emphasis on long-term goals brought unwelcome short-term consequences. By bringing diverse groups into government to ensure its inclusiveness and by bowing to demands for early elections to move toward democratic representation (absent a developed civil society, democratic norms, and critical constitutional compromises), the United States empowered groups to pursue their self-interested agendas. The effect was to produce a stalemate in government, to increase levels of societal conflict, and perhaps to impede *long-term* development of an inclusive Iraqi democracy.

Second, US officials encountered tradeoffs among a basket of political, economic, and security goals. Therefore, when placing Iraqi security first, the United States compromised its reconstruction and development objectives. Absent security measures tailored to meet these goals, it was impossible to get civilian personnel into the field to enable reconstruction, engage in civic action to build local governing institutions, and to construct an infrastructure to support long-term national stability—let alone to get the local population to assist these efforts.[28] Conversely, when emphasizing economic considerations, the United States jeopardized security. For example, an absence of security in reconstruction zones created material and human targets for the insurgents and drew security personnel for protective missions away from offensive and other defensive operations. Likewise, an emphasis on political considerations endangered security. An unappealing effect of the draconian de-Baathification policy adopted by the United States was that the civilian and military institutions were stripped of competent officials, leaving the rehabilitated security force vulnerable to a vetting process for officers and recruits that was open to abuse and error (Rathwell et al. 2005, 35). Indeed, holding all those who served the Baathist regime or held party membership equally liable had the effect of pushing Sunnis—Baathists and non-Baathists—into the active (violent) opposition.[29]

Third, US officials encountered hard decisions involving the balance between building strong central government institutions or dispersing power to subnational entities. A strong central government in Baghdad risked a monopoly of power that could benefit some groups at the expense of others, but fragmenting central authority risked reinforcing ethnic and sectarian grievances (among groups that were dispersed geographically). The United States discovered that all efforts to build central authority or empower local entities are inherently threatening to those who view national politics through the lens of group interest. For instance, US support for the Sons of Iraq challenged those in Iraq's Shiite leadership who wanted the central government to obtain a monopoly on force—to protect, in part, against the Sunnis. The debate over federalism was itself a source of ethnosectarian and political tension in Iraq. A devolution of power to subnational entities encountered deep resistance from those in Iraq (and throughout the Middle East) who viewed federalism (albeit eventually recognized in the Iraqi Constitution) as alien to the region and a threat to the coherence and future of an Iraqi state (on the internal tensions of federalism, see Elkins and Sides 2007). Whereas the Kurds and Shiites, linked to the Supreme Council, sought to strengthen regional authority, Sunnis and other Shiites, linked to Moqtada al-Sadr, pushed for a strong central state.

Fourth, US officials encountered tradeoffs between the goals of managing Iraqi affairs and promoting Iraqi self-reliance, as when employing US troops to provide security rather than depend on Iraqis to fill the void. This tradeoff was central to the thinking in 2006 of top US military commanders in Iraq who opposed a proposed US troop surge. They believed that a US troop increase would only lead Iraqis to assume that the United States would solve Iraq's problems, reduce US leverage over Iraq's government to gain its compliance, and offer a temporary solution, at best, that would not survive the eventual withdrawal of US troops (Ricks 2009, 53). In turn, by employing US private security contractors in lieu of local personnel, the United States ensured the political loyalty and military training of personnel charged with protecting US officials, equipment, and goods, but they also fielded a force that was unaccountable to any national government and operated with great insensitivity to the political requisites ("winning hearts and minds") of the overall US mission in Iraq. Likewise, funding US firms to deliver infrastructure projects in Iraq kept US officials on familiar turf (and generated profits for US companies) but also tied Iraq's future to expensive, gold-plated products delivered at a greater cost, over a longer period, and with lower performance than promised. Illustrating these deficiencies was a high-profile wastewater treatment project in Fallujah, which had been pushed by the US embassy to assist "national reconciliation" at a time when US forces were battling insurgents in the city. The project was eventually completed at three times the cost ($100 million dollars) and in twice the time predicted while serving only a third of the target population.[30] That the US-funded reconstruction and development effort was faltering was clear from the conclusion of a report by the US Special Inspector General for Iraq that, despite tens of billions of dollars invested in Iraq by late 2008, oil production, electricity, and supplies of potable water remained roughly around prewar levels. Accordingly, the US GAO (2009c, 27–28) concluded that, by the end of 2008, available electricity met 52 percent of demand and safe drinking water was available reliably to only 40 percent of Iraqi children. Many "successful" projects seemed unsustainable, in fact, once US financial and technical support had ended. Here as elsewhere, short-term solutions would fail over the long term if they did not build on Iraqi capabilities—and accept their limitations.

Finally, US officials encountered tradeoffs when deciding between working with existing institutions and building entirely new ones. Iraqi ministries were notoriously over-centralized, uncoordinated, and slow-moving. Yet, recreated institutions would not necessarily perform better, with the limited resources that the United States could invest in Iraqi institutional development. When the United States opted for a "fresh start"—specifically, in the rebuilding of the Iraqi military—the United States eventually came to appreciate the costs. The United States understood the risks of relying upon *preexisting* institutions—staffed and structured to keep Saddam Hussein in power; it also came to recognize the opposing liabilities of bottom-up rebuilding once the United States had dismantled the Iraqi Defense Ministry and Armed Forces, as mandated by CPA Order No. 2, and purged the senior ranks of Baathist officials, in the language of CPA Order No. 1, "by eliminating the party's structures and removing its leadership from positions of authority and responsibility in Iraqi society." The order directly targeted the top four ranks of the Party but also full party members "holding positions in the top three layers of management in every national government ministry, affiliated corporations and other government institutions (e.g., universities and hospitals)." The immediate effect of the order was to push 140,000 party members out of their jobs (including 11,000 teachers).[31] One major practical effect of both measures was to strip the government of its institutional memory and know-how.

What the United States got for its particular effort to remake the Iraqi military was a force that was exceedingly slow to assume security responsibilities. The Iraqi military looked stronger on paper than in the field.[32] Units stood well below full strength—at 60 to 75 percent strength at any given time, as troops traveled home to deliver their paychecks, wounded soldiers counted on active rosters so that they could collect their pay, and so on. For soldiers, in combat operations outside their usual deployment zones, absenteeism was a severe problem—as high as 50 percent for some units. Moreover, a high annual attrition rate (15 to 18 percent) damaged the overall skill and experience level of active duty personnel, betrayed a severe problem of morale in the ranks,[33] and required the redirecting of resources from improving military proficiency to basic training (Jones 2007, 55–69).[34] In a true test, in battle, the Iraqi military was short on performance. For that matter, units crumbled on their way into battle. On being directed to Fallujah in April 2004, one Iraqi Army battalion refused to proceed when it came under fire in Baghdad; of Iraqi security personnel participating in the fighting, about half actively participated, another 40 percent deserted, and another 10 percent defected to the opposition (Bensahel et al. 2008, 147). The performance of these forces remained uneven through the US surge offensive in 2007. The Iraqi government struggled to provide brigades of sufficient strength to the capital to support the Baghdad Security Plan, in relatively brief, ninety-day rotations. By late summer of that year, the Department of Defense reported that, of the nineteen Iraqi units that had participated, only five had performed well, while some others performed poorly, and then worse over time (US GAO 2007a, 41). Although Iraqi security forces joined US troops successfully in patrol operations, they often proved unable to hold territory to prevent its reacquisition by militant groups. Their offensive capabilities also remained suspect. In early 2008, Iraqi security forces proved overmatched against committed Mahdi Army fighters in the Basra offensive, prior to the arrival of US troops and air support.

The Iraqi military improved in standing and performance over time. By the end of 2008, the Iraqi Army was several hundred thousand strong, operating with over half its units in top tiers of readiness, teaming successfully with US units, controlling formerly violent parts of the country (for example, Anbar Province), drawing from Iraq's various communities, and benefiting from experienced leadership (Biddle et al. 2008; see also Dubik 2009). An upward performance trajectory was clear even in early indicators: by mid-2006, Iraq Security Forces were taking an ever larger proportion of the troop casualties—a percentage that climbed steeply with the onset of the surge. By mid-2007, these forces recorded twice the casualties of US troops. Iraqi military professionalism was bound to grow further in the post-surge environment: national stability would inevitably reduce ethnic and sectarian tension within the military (and between it and various segments of Iraqi society) and lessen corruption that resulted from theft and extortion of military funds and equipment by militant groups. Still, far-reaching progress in building an effective military force did not erase its deficiencies. The Iraqi military had not proven that it could rise above the various maladies that afflicted Iraqi society and governance. The Ministry of Defense had repeatedly been cited, in official US and Iraqi reports (referenced in the next section), for its corrupt practices and ability to fend off investigations; meanwhile, the military was implicated, throughout the ranks, in corruption, one of many problems that hindered military performance.[35] These problems—including corruption, sectarianism, political interference, cronyism, lethargy, poor management, and a lack of professionalism—were the subject, for instance, of a scathing indictment of Iraqi military performance, written by a senior US military advisor in Iraq in the aftermath of the US pullback, in June 2009, from Iraqi cities (on sectarianism in the Iraqi military, see al-Jabouri 2009, 4).[36] Moreover, the Iraqi military had yet to prove it could operate satisfactorily on its own, even in a defensive capacity: its capabilities were shown to be deficient by various high-profile lapses in security, including a failure to prevent six coordinated vehicular-bomb attacks in August 2009 in Baghdad (the first in a series) that left 100 people dead, 500 people wounded, and the Foreign and Finance Ministry buildings severely damaged.[37] Exposed breaches in security triggered recriminations—in heated accusatory exchanges among Iraqi leaders—in lieu of a commitment to bridge the organizational divides that contributed to these lapses.[38] Even then, Iraqi forces remained critically dependent on US advisory, logistical, armor, aerial, intelligence, and fire support, and they lagged severely in various support functions—maintaining supply stocks, ensuring delivery, and equipment maintenance and repair.[39] A US General Accounting Office (2008, 28) study released in mid-2008 concluded that only around one in ten Iraqi Army battalions could operate independently in counterinsurgency operations. The prospects for sustained improvement appeared dim. The Iraqi budgetary crunch, induced by plummeting oil prices, promised to arrest forward progress—most directly through a hiring freeze—and to exacerbate shortfalls by furthering the local tendency to perform only dire equipment maintenance (rather than risk losing equipment, fuel stipends, and so on) and to deplete stocks by cannibalizing units to compensate for poor inventory management.[40]

In the end, the United States had far less control over outcomes in the complex, unpredictable, and challenging Iraqi security environment than the notion of a "tradeoff" implies. US decisions were often made out of necessity, or by default, that is, without considering the relative payoffs of competing choices or the acceptability of the resulting costs.[41]

A better understanding of available choices and their consequences could have increased US leverage over the Iraqi government by leaving it to act in place of the United States when appropriate or necessary to ensure programmatic success. Instead, by taking the lead, the United States gave the host government strong incentives to shirk. For instance, by assuming the lead in providing Iraqi security, the United States gave the host government little reason to create a nonsectarian security force that could operate effectively in Sunni communities or to take other measures (including enlisting the Sons of Iraq into government service) that might facilitate national reconciliation. Similarly, by pouring billions of dollars of reconstruction and development assistance into Iraq, the Iraqi government was under little pressure to release Iraqi government funds to aid the US effort.[42] In 2007, the US General Accounting Office (2007, 64) concluded that while the United States had obligated most of the $40 billion that the United States had allocated since 2003 for Iraq reconstruction, the Iraqi government spent less than a quarter of the nonprovincial capital projects and reconstruction budget, spent under 3 percent of the billions allocated for oil reconstruction in 2006, and had shown little improvement in releasing these funds through much of 2007. The office concluded that the Iraqi government had a cumulative budget surplus approaching 50 billion dollars at the end of 2008, a year in which Iraq's central government ministries spent less than a quarter of their investment budgets (US GAO 2009b, 25–26).

Furthermore, a better understanding of choices and their effects would have increased the efficiency and effectiveness of US policies. Instead, by pushing an ambitious agenda, the United States made it more difficult to accomplish its goals, which only discouraged the host government from becoming a full participant in the US-led mission. The host government was understandably reticent to assume any costs of a mission that promised limited gains and came with high risks.

Confronting Intractable Problems: Sectarianism and Corruption

That the United States chose not to delegate some responsibilities to the Iraqi government was understandable given its seeming inability to act. No less troubling was that delegating meant that policies would be subverted by sectarian and corrupt Iraqi government officials and practices.

At all levels of the Iraqi government, positions were disbursed on the basis of ethnicity, religion, and partisan loyalty, not professional competence. Indeed, sectarian practices (and ethnic and partisan biases) drove out professionalism, as charges of sectarianism were used, for instance, to rid the Iraqi military of competent Sunni officers (US GAO 2007a, 68–69). Worse still, state security institutions were employed by parties to conduct their sectarian campaigns. US officials were left, then, to work with (and around) Iraqi security forces that *contributed* to the Iraqi security problem.

The challenge for the United States was no greater than when it had to cope with the multiple security services within the Iraqi Interior Ministry. Although the CPA purged the Interior Ministry of mid- to senior-level officials,[43] it assumed that the ministry would perform a (politically neutral) policing role and did not try to remake the institution from the bottom up. Instead, the US approach placed quantity above quality: it pursued ambitious goals for expanding Iraqi security forces (for instance, adding 30,000 policeman over a thirty-day period) without due regard for the competence and trustworthiness of the recruits or their oversight within the ministry (Perito 2009, 4). Not only did the CPA have insufficient numbers of qualified advisors and trainers on hand, then, to guide the development of police units,[44] it allowed the ministry to become a prize in a ferocious competition among sectarian groups. The recruiting of US trainers and advisers for the Iraqi police suffered significantly as violence worsened across the country (Perito 2009, 5).

Sectarian partisanship in the Interior Ministry worsened dramatically when the United Iraqi Alliance of Shiites and Kurds won a majority of legislative seats in the January 2005 elections. The Supreme Council took control of the Interior Ministry and thus much of the nation's police force. Bayan al-Jabr, a former leader of the Badr Organization, became interior minster (in the newly elected government of Prime Minister al-Jaafari) and placed Supreme Council members in critical ministry positions and staffed counterinsurgency units with Badr Organization militia members. Subsequently, police units linked to the Badr Organization were implicated in a systematic wave of terror that included the torture and murder of Sunnis. The abuses received considerable public attention when, in 2005, US troops uncovered a secret underground prison, linked to the Interior Ministry, where Sunnis were harshly confined and abused. As one report described the gruesome pattern that implicated the Badr Organization, "Carried out during curfew hours in the dead of night and reportedly involving armed men dressed in police or military uniforms arriving in cars bearing state emblems, raids in predominantly Sunni towns or neighborhoods appeared to cast a wide net. Those seized later turned up in detention centres or, with a disturbing frequency, in the morgue after having been found—hands tied behind their backs, blindfolded, teeth broken, shot—in a ditch or river" (ICG 2006, 3).

With the arrival, in mid-2006, of a new prime minister, al-Maliki, the ministry was nominally brought under the nonpartisan control of Jawad al-Bolani and his principal deputies, which were drawn from three of the country's major contending groups. Police personnel were subject to more deliberate screening and training, and Interior Ministry personnel were purged, including brigade commanders in the National Police (assembled from paramilitary groups that had operated under the auspices of the Interior Ministry) and thousands more implicated in the violence (Jones 2007, 30; Perito 2008b). Yet the problems in the ministry continued. Although the Coalition announced that it had met its goal, by the end of 2006, of training and equipping almost 200,000 Iraqi policy and border patrol personnel, its "success" spoke neither to the actual quantity of personnel and equipment in active service nor to the quality of service that was actually provided (Perito 2009, 6). A number of high-profile US government studies—including reports by the Iraq Study Group and the Independent Commission on the Security Forces of Iraq, also known as Jones Commission (Jones 2007)[45]— concluded that Iraq's vast Interior Ministry force was sectarian and corrupt to its core. These studies offered a broad indictment of Iraqi government performance inasmuch as the Interior Ministry controlled a force, many hundreds of thousands strong, with responsibility for the Police Service (for instance, traffic and patrol police, at the provincial level), the National Police, the Department of Border Enforcement (with partial control over land, air, and sea access into the country), and the Facilities Protection Service (independent security units intended to protect various government ministries).

If anything, "sectarian" and "corrupt" are kind descriptions of an organization housed within a disharmonious eleven-story structure in which positions and responsibilities were divided among Iraq's warring factions: armed guards and escorts protected heads of departments from one another, officials shied from the elevator to avoid making themselves an easy target, and disputes were settled by assassination as officials entered or exited the building (so that many chose to live in the building).[46] The Facilities Protection Service (FPS) was an especially egregious case of a "good idea gone bad" through corruption and sectarian influence. Under US prodding, the FPS was conceived as a modest effort to provide security guards for government buildings (to free up US security personnel); it would become a collection of rogue private armies (and patronage jobs), with over 150,000 personnel divided among the ministries to help their leaders pursue their nefarious agendas (Perito 2008b). The Mahdi Army apparently had a strong position among its personnel (Jones 2007, 30). Its use of FPS personnel made headlines in late 2007 when legal charges were brought against a deputy health minister and the official responsible for Health Ministry and hospital security. They were accused of operating a 150-person militia that—under the guise and protection of the Health Ministry (employing ambulances to deliver weapons, and so on)— engaged in a multi-year campaign of sectarian murder and kidnapping that targeted Sunni staff, hospital patients, and relatives who came to visit the sick or injured or to recover bodies from the morgue.[47] The Mahdi Army was certainly not alone in employing these forces for partisan and private gain. For instance, the Fadhila Party employed the FPS as a private militia in Basra, where its tasks included smuggling and collecting kickbacks to help the party.[48]

By the end of 2007, significant progress had apparently occurred toward ending sectarianism in the Interior Ministry. Late in 2007, US commanders reported that the 27,000-member National Police—the most problematic entity within the ministry—had reformed sufficiently that it did not have to be disbanded, as the Jones Commission had recommended. Yet, Shiite militias continued to exercise control over Interior Ministry operations, and corruption continued to drain ministry resources at the central government and provincial levels (Perito 2008b). Even US officials who argued against disbanding the National Police acknowledged that sectarianism was a persistent—perhaps inevitable—problem given its roots within Iraqi society.[49] (Retaining existing forces was, in fact, a tacit admission of the inevitability of the problem.)[50] Officials who were "purged" for abuse were allowed to operate in other official capacities, and those who had conducted themselves professionally were purged along with the wrongdoers (Robinson 2008, 336).

For its part, corruption in Iraq was, in the words of a senior US State Department official, "real, endemic and pernicious."[51] Corruption—an enormous problem in some government ministries, such as the Petroleum and Trade Ministries[52]—was deeply rooted in the fabric of Iraqi governance, in part because corruption and sectarianism were mutually reinforcing evils. Corrupt practices financed a sectarian agenda; the corrupt were tolerated when politically loyal.

The United States took measures early to combat Iraqi corruption. In 2004, the CPA mandated the creation of the Commission on Public Integrity (CPI) to investigate major corruption cases and the appointment, in each ministry, of an inspector general (Rathwell et al. 2005, 58).[53] These measures proved inadequate, however, to address such a monumental problem. In mid-2007, the underresourced CPI staff was apparently handling 2,000 cases amounting to $5 billion in potential theft.[54] By late 2008, a former chief investigator for the CPI claimed that over $13 billion in US funds for Iraqi reconstruction had been lost to fraudulent activities.[55] Judging from a copy of a draft report by the US embassy in Baghdad that was leaked to the press in September 2007, the magnitude of the problem was apparent to the US government.[56] The report painted a grim picture of the challenges facing the Commission beyond its small staff, modest resources, and limited mandate. The report detailed the CPI's difficult relationship with various ministries (and their inspector generals), a judicial system that was too overburdened and weak to handle corruption cases, and severe staff intimidation: many CPI personnel had been killed in the line of duty and expressed deep concerns about the personal consequences of investigating the Interior Ministry.[57]

Existing policing mechanisms failed if only because corruption enjoyed governmental protections: unless the prime minister decides otherwise, Iraqi ministers (and former ministers) enjoy immunity from prosecution—and, within their ministries, can further immunize select employees.[58] Although the prime minister himself referred often to the fight against corruption as the "second war in Iraq," the draft report acknowledged that "the Prime Minister's Office has demonstrated an open hostility to the concept of an independent agency to investigate or prosecute corruption cases" and noted instances in which the government attempted to influence the outcome of cases involving members of the governing coalition (pp. 3, 65). The al-Maliki government had long been accused of turning a blind eye to Shiite militia activities and favoring Dawa party loyalists.[59] (It was alleged also to have removed Iraqi civilian and military officials from their positions through the Office of the Commander in Chief, who had acted against partisan army and national police commanders.)[60] In November 2008, the al-Maliki government moved to purge the inspector generals: anywhere from a third to a half of these officials were apparently dismissed from their positions—guilty, it seems, of performing their professional duties.[61] Al-Maliki had consistently expressed a distaste for the former head of the CPI: after repeated corruption investigations of his government, al-Maliki's office supported corruption charges against the head of the Commission.[62]

True enough, the al-Maliki government instigated some positive changes. In early 2009, it launched a major anti-corruption offensive that targeted almost a thousand officials for arrest. In April 2009 alone, with al-Maliki's blessing, the CPI supposedly issued arrest warrants for 387 government personnel, including over 50 department heads. (The campaign netted the Iraqi trade minister, who resigned under duress.)[63] Significant reforms occurred, even in the Interior Ministry. But reforms did not come easily and were enabled by a confluence of factors. These included al-Maliki's hope to break the dominance of rival Shiite parties in the Interior Ministry and neutralize a major Sunni grievance against the government. They were facilitated primarily by the perseverance of Iraq's *sixth* interior minister (al-Bolani), who was uniquely positioned to undertake the reforms. He was dedicated to building a professional security force, had established a reputation for nonpartisanship and professional competence, and was not beholden for his position to the prime minister. Still, the ministry continued to suffer under the influence of sectarianism, corruption, and politicization of justice (as discussed below).[64] By its performance, it suggested that government institutions meant to pull societies in new directions are products of those societies, for good and for bad. When the bad—in the form of sectarianism and corruption—triumphs so completely over the good, progress becomes slow and always reversible. Correctives have little effect: the CPI claimed that only 34 members of Iraq's

275-member parliament elected in 2005 had submitted their *mandatory* financial disclosure forms *by 2009*.[65] Or else, the correctives become part of the problem. Illustrating this is the official reliance on "underspending" (failing to spend government budgets) to prevent monies from being lost to corruption or sectarian activities, as well as corruption charges made by corrupt and sectarian officials in order to hurt their competition, keep investigators busy, or impugn the integrity of honest investigators to weaken their effectiveness.[66]

Without question, the United States possessed some leverage for reforming the Iraqi Interior Ministry and other government institutions. By distributing some benefits contingently, the United States involved itself in the oversight and direction of the ministry, at various levels—from advising the interior minister to training police personnel. Yet US influence was fundamentally limited. As a top US military official put it, "The only reason they listen to us is we give them equipment and money. Once we pull out, much of that stops."[67]

Ultimately, the United States had limited leverage to press host-government leaders to act decisively and effectively when the government was weakened by sectarianism and corruption: progress on a wide variety of issues was impeded because resources were pilfered to serve sectarian or corrupt interests, host-government leaders had limited leverage themselves to confront the sectarian and corrupt or were themselves biased or corrupt (and obviously disinclined to back US demands), and the mechanisms devised to combat these problems were weapons in the employ of the sectarian and/or corrupt. As these conditions increased the costs to Baghdad's leaders of complying with US demands, necessary improvements and reforms were stymied and exceedingly slow in coming: by mid-2009, six years into the effort, corruption and sectarian remained serious problems in the Interior Ministry.[68] As important, progress in the Ministry was eminently reversible, for it remained a "leadership-led" institution that would rise or fall with the professionalism of its leaders, not a "bureaucratic-led" institution, with traditions and practices that could overcome or outlast the failings of its leadership.[69]

Problem Interdependencies: Narrowing US Goals and Using "Benchmarks"

US officials came to appreciate the mutual interdependence of military, economic, and political problems in Iraq, that is, the difficulty in achieving progress when success always requires some prior achievement. Security was impossible without addressing public demand for jobs, economic opportunities, and government services; in turn, jobs, opportunities, and services required reconstruction and development in a secure environment. Lacking security, US government personnel and contractors would not travel to much of the country; Iraqis who could assist US personnel would avoid contact with them so not to become insurgent targets; and firms could deliver their products only with a multifold increase in costs (and with delays), as work was halted, financial resources were diverted into security, and the rebuilt was itself rebuilt, again and again. Likewise, the absence of security throughout the country exacerbated the political tensions that stalemated the government and pushed sectarian groups to obtain control of Iraqi security forces. The circle was completed when these conditions contributed, in turn, to deteriorating security in the country. Sectarian government security units within a rival community reinforced identities on which the insurgency fed, and they sometimes disintegrated when confronting members of their own community, with the effect of handing over the resources of the state (trained soldiers and their equipment) to the violent opposition.[70] A circularity challenge was apparent, as well, in plans to reform Iraqi governing institutions. Trying to build responsive and efficient institutions that respect the rule of law could add fuel to the fire (that is, increase sectarianism and corruption) when these institutions were left unprotected from malevolent societal forces. For example, the centralization of planning, programming, and budgeting creates openings for nefarious individuals or groups to seize control of these institutions and redirect their purposes.[71]

Taken to its extreme, the idea that progress is inevitably impeded by interdependencies presents an implausible logic—a möbius strip in thinking—where every condition is endogenous to the system and none stands outside the loop. So the US official response was understandably to look for ways to move the Iraqi political system beyond the impasses. The response took two basic forms.

First, US officials looked for interdependencies in "virtuous cycles." The US hope was to engineer conditions to spur positive spillover effects. Accordingly, US officials focused initially on a top-down (political) strategy. They assumed that pulling leaders from conflicting groups into government to address national problems and promote the common interest would facilitate societal reconciliation. As the government proved incapable of bridging impasses and violence subsumed the country, the United States adopted a bottom-up (security-driven) approach, meant, with the US troop surge in 2007, to create opportunities and incentives ("breathing space") for governmental compromise.[72] The hope was that establishing local security—in part through accommodation with insurgents—would lay the groundwork for national reconciliation and integration.[73] US officials were correct that the mutually reinforcing aspects of the conflict were impeding progress and that establishing security was *necessary* for bridging the impasse in government. Unfortunately, establishing security was not *sufficient* for bridging the governmental impasse: improving security might actually have created "breathing space" for leaders to act irresponsibly rather than compromise (for example, on the future of the Sons of Iraq), which led to new grievances, as Sunnis now vied for a greater role in government.

Second, US policymakers implicitly sought to circumscribe or override the interdependencies. They did this by trying to reduce the US focus to a set of manageable tasks and by pushing the Iraqi government to make progress simultaneously on multiple fronts. Both solutions received considerable attention within the US policy community when they were recommended in December 2006 by the Iraq Study Group, a bipartisan panel of ten people appointed by the US Congress and headed by former secretary of state James Baker and former congressman Lee Hamilton. The Iraq Study Group called for cutting, by roughly 50 percent, the US troop presence in Iraq and shifting the US focus from a combat to a training and support mission. These recommendations dovetailed with recommendations from within the Bush administration that the United States pull out of the fighting and narrow its mission to training Iraqi forces, securing Iraq's borders, deterring Iranian involvement, and preventing Iraq from becoming a terror haven.[74] The Iraq Study Group also supported tying future US economic and military assistance to Iraqi progress as measured by various performance criteria known as "benchmarks."[75] Unfortunately for US policymakers, interdependencies among policy goals would limit success, whether the United States shifted its focus to a *narrow* set of objectives or held the Iraq government to a *broad* set of policy goals.

Narrowing the policy focus makes considerable sense. Why not move from an active US combat role to patrolling Iraq's borders and training or supporting the Iraqi Army? Doing so could help Iraqi troops to gain practical experience, extend their combat role, and accept most of the casualties. The problem is that narrowing the US focus and passing responsibilities to the Iraqi government makes sense only if the Iraqi government can assume the burden. Given the societal conflicts and influences that impair the performance of the Iraqi military and the institutional infrastructure upon which a military depends, the government appeared poorly equipped to handle increased combat responsibilities, even with US advice and support. If it could not take on these duties, the danger was that US forces would get caught in the crossfire or would have to pick up the slack later, from a weaker military and political position after conditions in the country had spiraled out of control. So in 2007 the all-important question was whether "middle-ground options leave [the United States] with the worst of both worlds: continuing casualties but even less chance of stability in exchange."[76] One answer, provided retrospectively by the US general then in charge of training Iraqi security forces, is that "developing indigenous security forces" is not an "exit strategy from conflict." Instead, it is a long-term, multidimensional, and multilevel institution-building effort that is best nurtured in an environment of improved security.[77]

It also makes some sense to hold the host government accountable for progress on a broad front through the use of benchmarks. Why not pressure the Iraqi government to perform by withholding aid for noncompliance? Does not that give the government strong incentives to meet US demands? Indeed, of the two basic approaches in the Iraq Study Group report, the idea of holding Iraq to benchmarks developed the most backing in the US policy community, though arising from concessions (in June 2006) by the al-Maliki government that it be evaluated for its ability to accomplish a specific list of goals. The list was lengthened by the Bush administration[78] and given formal weight by the US Congress, which added performance criteria of its own. The list was attached to a supplemental appropriations bill (signed into law in May 2007) which tied future US assistance and strategy in Iraq to its progress in meeting the benchmarks. The president was required to certify formally that the benchmarks were met in an interim report in July 2007 and in a comprehensive assessment in September 2007. In consequence, future US support for operations in Iraq was ostensibly linked to whether it met key goals that included completing a constitutional review, enacting and implementing legislation to disarm militias, ensuring that Iraqi security forces enforced the law evenhandedly, increasing the number of Iraqi security forces that could operate independently, enacting and implementing legislation to facilitate the formation of semi-autonomous regions, and spending ten billion dollars in Iraqi funds for reconstruction (US GAO 2007b).

The problems in implementing the approach are twofold. For one thing, the approach assumes that solving problems jointly is no more difficult than solving problems individually—that the Iraqi government can make wide-ranging progress when it found it difficult to accomplish the various single benchmark goals. Although the joint resolution of problems is enabled through logrolling strategies that put "something in the deal" for everyone, the challenges in resolving multiple issues rise dramatically when addressing these issues together requires that the parties resolve fundamental issues that divide society. Under these conditions, no party will concede on any issue, fearing that it will lose ground in the bigger struggle. No issue can be addressed without first resolving fundamental conflicts—and that is impossible without some progress (for example, in resolving specific issues) that conveys to the parties that the gains from cooperation outweigh the costs. For another thing, the benchmark approach assumes that the United States would actually withhold aid from a government if it failed to meet the benchmark goals. This was unlikely when withholding aid would obviously have the effect of making it more difficult for the Iraqi government to meet these (and other) goals that were critical to the success of the US mission. Perversely, withdrawing US aid might make it harder, then, for the United States to limit its military role in Iraq.

The United States was caught, as a result, in a treacherous middle: it could not credibly threaten to reduce the US profile in Iraq because a US retreat would likely create conditions that were even less hospitable to reform, reconciliation, institutional development, and national stability. Indeed, efforts to "engage" Baghdad by negotiating or dictating terms that, if met, would allow the United States to continue supporting the host government might have backfired if convincing it instead that the United States is stuck—that it really had no viable options but to offer unqualified assistance to Baghdad.[79] That was the likely result because incentives, no less than threats, require credibility to work, that is, the bargaining partner must believe that the United States will follow through on its promises. To convince Iraqi leaders of the benefits to be had from compliance, the United States had to establish that its promised actions were not merely "cheap talk." So to establish its commitment to Iraq, the United States had to allocate and spend money, hire private contractors, and gain the support of other governments for the US-led effort. These measures do not come with an easily manipulated "on/off" switch. Signals that the United States will retract a commitment, if believable, could have detrimental consequences for the entire support program by creating doubt about the long-term willingness of the United States to stay the course. These signals might lack credibility, paradoxically, for that very reason.

Of course, the United States could conceivably finesse all these challenges by credibly moving to withdraw forces from the country, to end the US military mission there (Katulis et al. 2007). Accordingly, one analyst (Lynch 2008) argued that the US military "protects Iraqi leaders from the consequences of their choices" and that removing the crutch "would give Iraqi politicians a self-interest in political accommodation—accommodation reached not to meet foreign demands but to ensure their own survival."[80] But this implicit threat can produce results, again, only when the parties within the host government are willing to put aside their differences to avoid US sanctions and, if not, the United States actually *is* willing to follow through by cutting its losses and leaving the country. Both developments were unlikely as long as rival leaders viewed themselves as parties to an existential conflict—a belief that could lead to a disintegration of the government and open warfare should US forces depart. Indeed, an unconditional withdrawal "strategy" mistakenly assumes that, if a basis for internal compromise existed, it is likely to be found after the United States has threatened to withdraw support and leave indigenous parties to fend for themselves. Under a security dilemma, it is more likely that a credible withdrawal threat will feed insecurities, provoke defensive behaviors, increase tensions, and generally make matters in the country considerably worse (see Biddle et al. 2008).

Unsurprisingly, the Bush administration (which had not embraced the Iraqi Study Group's recommendations) did not challenge the Iraqi government with mounting evidence that it would not meet established benchmarks on time. Without discernable progress toward meeting most of the goals, the Bush administration claimed that fluid circumstances in Iraq prevented an evaluation using the established criteria. Thus, in July 2007, the administration offered its own "benchmarks"—ad hoc measures against which US policies had fared well. Although violence in the country remained at high levels, the administration emphasized that tribal leaders in Anbar Province were turning against al-Qaeda units, pointed out that Iraqi leaders had collectively managed to urge calm to prevent an escalation of violence with the second major attack on the Samarra mosque in June 2007, and that the number of sectarian killings had dropped (that same month).[81] The administration continued its line of reasoning as the September deadline drew near, and the indications were that few of the benchmarks were going to be met (as was confirmed shortly thereafter with the September 2007 release of a study commissioned from the General Accounting Office).[82] The administration's point was that the established benchmarks were grossly insensitive to the actual progress that was occurring in the country[83] and that new benchmarks were necessary to keep pace with progress as it occurred.[84] (Eventually, the administration issued a waiver to permit the expenditure of the Economic Support Funds that the Congress had tied to the benchmarks.)

To be fair to the Bush administration, even a firm set of US expectations was insufficient for US leverage when no single Iraqi leader was positioned to compromise politically and the United States had everything to lose from acting on its

threat.[85] Under these conditions, rather than locking onto established benchmarks selected to accomplish goals that *had proven elusive*—building in a bias in
favor of failure—it was perhaps useful for the United States to encourage progress
outside the benchmark framework. In this sense, US officials were correct to
emphasize progress in the form of "Iraqi solutions to Iraqi problems"—how Iraqis
worked through or around problems identified by the formal benchmarks even if
falling short of meeting them (for instance, Iraqis still managed to distribute oil
revenues in the absence of an oil law).[86]

A downside in pushing benchmarks against the social and political currents
in Iraq was, in fact, that its government met benchmarks in letter and not in
spirit—as the United States discovered when it pushed for a less stringent de-
Baathification law. The Iraqi legislature responded to US pressure, in early 2008,
by passing the Justice and Accountability Law. Its focus was considerably less on
helping Sunnis who had unfairly lost their livelihood—none of the law's eight
formal justifications referenced Sunni employment—and more on the Shiite victims who had suffered "persecution, oppression, and deprivation" under Saddam
Hussein.[87] The law continued to make individuals account for their Baath Party
membership rather than hold particular individuals responsible for specific actions under Hussein's rule.[88] Moreover, it gave grounds for stripping thousands of
additional government employees of their jobs.[89] By one interpretation, the new
law barred former Baathists from employment in various ministries—Foreign,
Defense, Interior, and Finance—in which they were currently employed.[90] Indeed, Chalabi's reading of the new de-Baathification law was that it was even
harsher than the CPA order that the law was meant to replace. In his ominous
words, for those who hoped that the law might facilitate Sunni-Shiite reconciliation, "be careful what you wish for."[91]

The point is not that the United States would have been better off abandoning
benchmarks and letting the Iraqi government determine the pace and direction
of progress. The point is that the United States would have better off had it pursued a more modest (obtainable) set of goals from the start. Once the United
States placed itself in the impossible position of having to secure progress *everywhere* to obtain it *anywhere*, US opportunities for securing useful leverage over
Iraqi government leaders declined enormously. These leaders' incentives for passing the burden to the United States were great: no leader (or coalition of like-
minded leaders) was positioned to address the problems, and the United States
could not credibly threaten to reduce its role in Iraq.

Long-Term Leverage: Trying to Hold On

With violence raging, the financial and human costs of the US mission mounting, and no end in sight to US involvement in Iraq, the Bush administration was increasingly under public and legislative pressure to find a way out of the conflict. Its challenge was devising a sustainable intermediate path—somewhere between immediate and total withdrawal and the open-ended US commitment to Iraqi reconstruction, development, and security that the US operation had become. Once security conditions in Iraq had improved, the administration settled for a gradualist "holding" strategy—seeking to maintain peace in Iraq while building up its security institutions, facilitating reconstruction, and prodding contending groups toward accommodation. But the administration eventually had a) to concede the scope and timing of the US exit to the Iraqi government given its negotiating advantages and (b) to contend with an increasingly assertive Iraqi government.

Negotiating Withdrawal: The Status of Forces Agreement

Legal authorization for US military operations in Iraq was provided by UN Security Council resolutions, first passed in October 2003. In 2007, as conditions in the country stabilized, the Iraqi government sought to replace the yearly UN authorization (set to expire at the end of 2008) with an agreement negotiated directly with the United States. The broad parameters of a bilateral agreement were acknowledged formally by President Bush and Prime Minister al-Maliki when they signed a "Declaration of Principles" in November 2007. But the agreement left key issues unresolved, including the position and role of US military forces in Iraq and the "whens" and "ifs" of a US withdrawal from the country.

With the two sides holding largely incommensurate views of an acceptable compromise, the resulting negotiations were protracted and contentious. The Iraqi government sought primarily to acquire sovereign control over the activities of US military forces, to limit their discretion and independence in Iraq, and to ensure their expeditious departure from the country. In its view, a long-term US troop presence undermined Iraq's sovereignty and autonomy and weakened the Iraqi government politically by suggesting that it was overly deferent toward the United States. Conversely, the United States sought mainly to retain legal control in Iraq over US troops, to safeguard their operating autonomy, and to make their withdrawal contingent upon improved conditions on the ground. Thus, the ensuing negotiations placed the United States in the somewhat ironic position—from a Vietnam-era perspective—of trying to maintain an active US military presence in the country over its government's opposition. Some basis of agreement between Washington and Baghdad did exist on the issue of a longer-term commitment to defend Iraq against external threats (Iran, primarily). The statement of principles noted, in fact, that a long-term relationship between the two countries would involve "security assurances and commitments" to "deter foreign aggression against Iraq." But even these principles were a basis of disagreement, as both sides sought to minimize the domestic political costs of a security agreement: the Iraqi government, seeking to avoid opposition charges of a sellout, would commit neither to an enduring US troop presence nor to permanent US bases in Iraq; the Bush administration, seeking to avoid a treaty ratification debate in the Senate, would not commit to wording that suggested that the United States was making a permanent defense commitment to the country. Accordingly, the Bush administration stressed that the "nonbinding" agreement would not specify US troop levels, authorize permanent bases, or commit the United States to Iraq's defense.[92]

Most contentiously, the negotiations centered on a "status of forces agreement" (SOFA) that set the rules for US military operations within Iraq. Whereas these agreements are routinely negotiated with governments hosting US troops to cover relatively mundane matters (including the use of radio frequencies, customs, issuing of drivers licenses, and the wearing of uniforms), the contours of the agreement provoked intense bargaining between the US and Iraq governments.[93] The negotiations were bound to bring intense scrutiny to all aspects of the US-Iraq political and security relationship given the Iraqi sensitivity toward the US troop presence, the improving security conditions in Iraq, and the growing capabilities of Iraqi security forces. The Iraqi government was unwilling to write rules for US operations in Iraq without a firm US commitment to end those operations, place such operations under sovereign Iraqi control, and withdraw (sooner rather than later) from the country. Controversy was inevitable, as well, because such agreements can create political and security realities, as US negotiators appreciated. In specifying conditions under which US troops would operate in Iraq—powers of arrest and detention, operating autonomy, immunity from prosecution, locations of bases, and the timing and terms of a US withdrawal—the agreement also implicitly constricted the US mission, determined the risks and costs US forces would incur, and influenced their capability to respond to threats.[94] Initially, the Bush administration announced that negotiations would center on a "strategic framework agreement" pertaining to the broad dimensions of the US-Iraqi relationship and a status of forces agreement to provide the basis for continued US operations in Iraq (Weed 2008). With the negotiating deadlock, the latter agreement eventually had to address the full set of issues confounding the US-Iraq security relationship.[95]

In resolving these various issues, the United States was disadvantaged, for a number of reasons. First, the United States was hurt, when negotiating, by its long-term interest in Iraq's defense. Baghdad could push its terms on the United States knowing that Iraqi security forces were increasingly equipped to handle internal threats and that the United States had a long-term interest, regardless, in maintaining stability within Iraq and protecting it from foreign threats: "The Iraqis needed and wanted the United States to continue to provide a security blanket, but they knew the administration was just as eager to stay" (Robinson 2008, 334). Thus, Baghdad could expect US forces to back up Iraqi forces over the short term (on request, if necessary) and to maintain an offshore military presence to deter outside aggressors over the long term.

Second, the United States was disadvantaged by the unfavorable timing of the negotiations. The growing likelihood that Bush would be succeeded by a Democrat, Barack Obama (who had campaigned for president on the promise of bringing US forces home quickly), pushed the administration to consummate an agreement that would bind Bush's successor.[96] The Iraqi leadership was not similarly pressed by a closing window for an agreement. Although it did not relish asking the UN to reauthorize the US presence in Iraq (especially when it became clear that the Security Council would only reauthorize the existing mandate),[97] the al-Maliki government did not see this as the last opportunity to negotiate. Even if the negotiations dragged on well into 2009, the Iraqi government could continue to press its terms. By comparison, US forces would not have a legal basis to remain in Iraq without an agreement (or a UN resolution). Predictably, US officials tried to employ that fact to obtain negotiating leverage. As the US ambassador to Iraq put it, bluntly, without an agreement, "we do not operate"—"that means no security operations, no logistics, no support for Iraqis on the borders, no nothing."[98] That US officials found it necessary to emphasize to their Iraqi counterparts just how dependent the Iraqi government remained on US financial aid, technical support, and security assistance—and that US officials acknowledged, then, how vested the United States was in the entire Iraq mission—backhandedly suggests how likely it was that the Iraqi government would win this game of "chicken."

Indeed, impending provincial elections positioned the al-Maliki government to reject terms that would expose the government to domestic criticism for having capitulated to the United States in the negotiations.

Third, US leverage in these negotiations was hurt, perhaps significantly, by the nature and level of the domestic pressure exerted on each of the two governments. Baghdad's bargaining strategy drew from the principles of a "two-level" game (Putnam 1988) in which government leaders attempt to *limit* their flexibility in international negotiations by capitalizing on domestic constraints, and vice versa. Strong domestic resistance in Iraq to a visible, enduring, and extralegal US military presence in the country positioned Baghdad to press the US government repeatedly for concessions, while the US government could not act similarly to decrease its own room to bargain.[99] The Bush administration's leverage was undercut both by Baghdad's maneuvering and by strong congressional resistance to any long-term troop commitment to Iraq. For that matter, Baghdad improvised successfully on the two-level game by tacitly allying with Bush administration policy critics. By demanding a US withdrawal date, the Iraqi government strengthened the political position of those in Congress who were pressing for an early US exit from Iraq. Furthermore, it muted charges by John McCain, the Republican presidential candidate, that his opponent, Barack Obama, was soft on US defense for not supporting the administration's contentions that a fixed withdrawal date would send US troops home prematurely and would signal hostile parties in Iraq that they could effectively hibernate until US forces left the country.

The Bush administration was left to bolster its negotiating position by trying to limit congressional interference. It did so by arguing, for example, that any agreement with Iraq would simply articulate US interests (not constitute a binding commitment), that Congress had consented to the terms of a negotiated agreement, back in 2002, by having authorized the use of force against Saddam Hussein,[100] and that, by only providing "help" to the Iraqi government, the United States had not reached the threshold of activity that would require Senate approval.[101] More frequently, the administration sought to minimize the novelty of the agreement by portraying it as merely one of many dozens of executive agreements with friendly countries that the US negotiated without congressional approval.[102] It maintained that the United States was simply moving to a "normalized" relationship—"an arrangement that is more in line with what typically governs the relationships between two sovereign nations."[103] But the administration could not affect the Iraqi prime minister's decision to obtain formal approval of any agreement from the Iraqi parliament, the timing of the agreement to coincide with pending provincial elections, or the effective veto wielded by Ayatollah al-Sistani who was insisting that any agreement must have widespread popular support.[104] It could also not halt Moqtada al-Sadr's strong stated opposition to anything but a complete and immediate US withdrawal from the country. Such opposition would force the United States to concede al-Maliki's tough demands for a strict US withdrawal timeline.

Although both the US and Iraqi governments gave ground, the United States appears to have retreated the most from its opening negotiating stance. The United States apparently pressed initially to retain fifty-eight long-term bases in Iraq,[105] control over Iraqi airspace, and protection of US military personnel from Iraqi legal jurisdiction while not committing to Iraq's protection against foreign aggression. Purportedly, it relented, however, on a number of critical issues—that private contractors would no longer have legal immunity, that detainees would be surrendered to Iraqi authorities after combat operations, that US forces would operate only with the approval of the Iraqi government, and that US forces would not launch attacks from Iraq on other countries.[106] Nevertheless, by July 2008, the negotiations were at a standstill: Iraq was publicly demanding a specific timetable for a US troop withdrawal, whereas the United States was focusing on the "conditions" that would prompt US forces to remain.[107] The Bush administration conceded additional ground with vague public references to a "time horizon" and "aspirational goals" for a US withdrawal that fell short of a rigid schedule.[108] By August 2008, the administration was allowing for a pullout of US combat brigades, but not US military advisors, special forces, and air support—conditions permitting—in 2012 or 2013.[109] The negotiators split the difference between opposing proposals and settled on a 2011 departure date, with indications that the United States and Iraq were moving toward a "condition-based" US withdrawal that would allow many tens of thousands of US noncombat military personnel to remain in Iraq.[110] Yet, once again, the United States was pressed to retreat. Within days, Prime Minister al-Maliki claimed that the United States and Iraq had agreed that no foreign forces—meaning noncombat troops as well—would remain in Iraq after a firm deadline of 2011.[111] He then abruptly dismissed his negotiating team, replaced it with his close advisors, and reiterated his demand for a complete US pullout by 2011 (with a US redeployment to combat bases located outside of Iraqi cities by June 2009).[112] A continuing matter of dispute remained the US insistence on legal jurisdiction over US military and civilian Defense Department personnel when the Iraqis insisted on jurisdiction over soldiers who commit crimes outside military operations.[113]

Because the battle lines were drawn so emphatically and because the United States held its ground on key issues for so long, it is clear that issues were resolved largely on Iraq's terms. Indeed, after the draft document was circulated among the Iraqi cabinet, it was further modified to include a prohibition on the use of Iraqi territory to launch attacks on other states, a firm deadline for the withdrawal of all US troops by December 2011, the removal of language suggesting that US troops can remain in Iraqi cities after June 2009, and the inclusion of language indicating that the Iraqi government must grant permission to US troops to search Iraqi homes.[114] For that matter, al-Maliki publicly threw his support behind the agreement in November 2008 only once the various amendments were accepted and the agreement had gained political support.[115] (Once al-Maliki committed to the agreement, it was in his best interest to ensure that it receive strong support. The agreement was passed overwhelmingly by the cabinet, signed by US and Iraqi officials, and submitted to the parliament for consideration.)[116]

Of course, the United States might still have had to accept more stringent terms. Given al-Sistani's insistence that any agreement have broad public backing, the parliament yielded to Sunni demands for a public referendum on the agreement within the next six months. Under the terms of the deal, a public rejection of the agreement would necessitate a US withdrawal within a year of the vote (to be held, by stipulation of the parliament, on July 30, 2009).[117] When the agreement passed Iraq's 275-seat parliament with 149 positive votes (and opposition from all 30 members of al-Sadr's voting bloc), al-Sistani increased pressure on the Iraqi government for the referendum.[118] Once again, the future of the US relationship with Iraq was in limbo: the United States faced the prospect of being forced to withdraw from Iraq even sooner than it had planned.

The United States held its ground on some critical issues. The agreement provided only a vague security guarantee to the Iraqi government from foreign threat and, though the Iraqi government acquired jurisdiction over US troops that commit offenses "outside agreed facilities and areas and outside duty status," the United States had the right to determine whether an "alleged offense arose during duty status." But the terms of the agreement spoke largely to dwindling US influence over the Iraqi government as security conditions in Iraq improved. There is no more compelling evidence of this than the final title of the agreement—"the *Withdrawal* of United States Forces from Iraq and the Organization of their Activities during their *Temporary* Presence in Iraq" (italics added).

In the end, the Iraqi government sought an early and relatively complete US exit on its own terms. The United States had limited leverage with which to resist.

The Iraq Government, Assurgent

Even before the negotiated exit, the Iraqi government had increasingly asserted its sovereign prerogatives in ways that challenged US military and political preferences in the country. As the position of the Iraqi leadership strengthened and security conditions in the country improved, signs of the leadership's newfound confidence abounded.

Politically, al-Maliki was emboldened. The al-Maliki government retracted measures meant to curb corruption (which undercut government allies) and moved to grab power at the expense of political opponents. He called for amending the Iraqi Constitution to increase the powers of the central government (over the provinces and regions) and organized and funded Tribal Support Councils, tied directly to the prime minister's office, in Baghdad and various other provinces, with a stated wish to extend the councils into Kirkuk and Mosul, where the Kurds desired more influence. Although al-Maliki claimed that these councils were comparable to the Awakening Councils (to deflect criticism that these councils were an extralegal assumption of power), opponents feared—with good reason—that the councils were meant to buy votes from tribal participants for al-Maliki's Dawa Party in the 2009 elections and to provide armed support for the prime minister, if needed.[119]

He also unambiguously signaled his increasing independence on matters of security. Evidence of al-Maliki's increased assertiveness emerged in 2007, when the prime minister sought to concentrate military command responsibilities within the Office of the Commander in Chief, which al-Maliki had created, and used his powers to hire and fire commanders, reputedly based on their political loyalties.[120] It was also visible when he issued a directive, in the same year, to create the Counter-Terrorism Bureau (CTB)—outside the Ministries of the Interior and Defense and answering directly to him—to control thousands of elite Iraqi special force troops and again in 2009 when he sought legislation to formalize the arrangement.[121] The Jones Commission (2007, 53) had advocated the abolition of both problematic entities, given the separate chain of command created. It noted that, "At the *very least*, there now exists the appearance that a senior elected official can bypass existing military command structures for sectarian reasons" (emphasis added). An even stronger message was contained in the Jones Commission's association of the command structure—at least in appearance—with the Saddam Hussein regime. Al-Maliki's hand was visible, too, when a new Iraqi

Army Brigade, the Baghdad Brigade, reporting directly to the prime minister, assumed control of the Green Zone in the capital.[122] The Baghdad Brigade was placed under the formal control of the Defense Ministry only after the Iraqi parliament voiced its strong disapproval of the existing control arrangement.[123]

Suspicions were rampant within the Iraqi government, in fact, that al-Maliki was employing special paramilitary units to weaken political opponents. Indeed, CTB units under al-Maliki's control were employed in August 2008, in what the Iraqi government claimed was a "rogue" operation, to raid the offices of the provincial governor and, in November 2008, to disrupt what al-Maliki's office alleged was a Baathist plot (in the traffic police, of all places) against the government organized by dozens of Interior Ministry officials (Domingue and Cochrane 2009, 8). In the latter incident, suspicions were fueled by changing government explanations for the raids, tight government control over relevant information, suggestions that the accused were poorly positioned to pull off a coup, and claims by Jawad al-Bolani, the interior minister, that those arrested were innocent victims of political conspiracy ("outside hands")—in his words, "it is a big lie."[124] (The interior minister had opposed the raids and was out of the country when the arrests occurred.)[125] Evidence of the al-Maliki government's independence was apparent on other security fronts. The government refused to move swiftly and broadly to integrate members of the Sons of Iraq militia into government employment, targeted leaders of the Awakening movement for arrest, attempted to undermine the organized Sunni and Sadrist political opposition through intimidation and arrest (purportedly prompting intervention by the US commander in Iraq),[126] engaged in near-violent confrontations with Kurdish security troops in northern Iraq over the control of disputed territories,[127] and, against US advice, sent Iraqi security forces into Basra to confront the Sadrist militia. Telling is that the US military was sufficiently concerned about Iraqi assertiveness that it employed satellite reconnaissance, normally reserved for US adversaries, to keep track of Iraqi units.[128]

The Iraqi government exerted its prerogatives, most notably, through controls over US combat forces under the new security agreement. As of January 2009, US forces could no longer arrest Iraqis without a warrant issued by an Iraqi judge, were made to conform to stringent requirements to obtain these warrants, and were required to coordinate all missions with Iraqi security forces.[129] In fact, the Iraqi government moved to assert its authority by challenging the legality of US military actions that apparently fell within the letter of the negotiated agreement and by demanding legal recourse that violated the explicit terms of the agreement. This was the case when the Iraqi government reacted to a deadly raid on Shiite militiamen in the city of Kut by denouncing the action (which apparently had been approved by Iraqi military officials) as "a violation of the security agreement," arresting the Iraqi military commanders who had given permission for the raid, and demanding the prosecution of US soldiers in Iraqi courts (which had jurisdiction only for premeditated actions committed off-duty—a status to be determined by US officials).[130] In addition, the government took actions that compromised US security efforts in the country. After arresting the supposed head of al-Qaeda in Iraq in April 2009, the Iraqi government refused to allow the US military to question him, apparently fearing that the interrogations would expose the arrest as a charade. (The government had trumpeted the arrest of "Abu Omar al-Baghdadi" as a sign that Baghdad could fend for itself, but many US analysts considered his very existence a fabrication, created by the insurgents to give them an "Iraqi" character.)[131] More troubling to US officials was that, despite the continued violence in parts of the country, the Iraqi government refused to relax the terms of the agreement to allow US combat troops to remain in some urban areas beyond June 30, 2009.[132] As the deadline approached, the US and Iraq governments continued to debate the definition of "combat troops." The Iraqi government appeared unmoved, although US officials expressed severe doubts about whether Iraqi security forces could pick up the slack were US troops to withdraw from critical locations.[133] As a senior US military official bluntly described the situation, just weeks before the scheduled hand-off, "They are not ready for us to give over the cities. . . . If we do, and all indications are that they will *make* us leave, we will be in a firefight to get back in and stop the violence" (emphasis added).[134] Recognizing that the Iraqi government had made much domestically of the anticipated US withdrawal, the US military capitulated to the political realities of the situation. It conceded the closure of US bases that it had formerly strongly argued should remain open (including bases in Sadr City and Mosul, to the north) and dramatically contracted its urban presence: in 2009, as the deadline approached, approximately 85 percent of US urban bases and outposts were closed.[135]

US military prerogatives were curtailed further, in the post-June security environment, whereupon the Iraqi government offered a stricter interpretation of the security agreement that went into effect at the start of the year. In the new environment, US troops were threatened with arrest when engagements with militants led to civilian deaths, were repeatedly involved in checkpoint confrontations with Iraqi forces, were impeded in operating (for lack of Iraqi troop escorts) in various parts of the country,[136] and were prevented from engaging in joint patrols in Baghdad under the orders of Iraqi military commanders.[137] Under the revised interpretation, the US military was prevented from engaging even in activities that, in the US view, amounted to exercising the "right to legitimate self-defense" under the agreement. From the perspective of the US commander in Baghdad, at least, the Iraqi stance amounted to a significant departure, in "spirit and practice," from the months prior to the June deadline.[138] His words were emphasized by various Iraqi government actions that contradicted US military policies, hopes, and expectations. These actions included a spike in arrests of leaders and members of Awakening militia, the forcible occupation (perhaps at the behest of the Iranian government) of an Iranian opposition group encampment (in Diyala Province) that had been protected by US forces,[139] the prime minister's announced intention to rid Baghdad, soon, of the concrete blast walls that the US military had constructed around the capital to inhibit the movements and activities of militia and insurgent groups,[140] unsubstantiated charges of Syrian government complicity in terrorist attacks in Iraq that damaged relations between the two governments,[141] and posturing that brought the long-term future of the agreement into doubt. Despite US lobbying efforts and assumptions that the issue was dead (as the July 30 deadline had come and gone), the al-Maliki government announced in August 2009 that a public referendum on the US-Iraq security agreement would be held, with the national elections (scheduled for early 2010), to decide the future of a US troop presence. His apparent aim was to turn these elections into a referendum on the US troop presence—an issue that he believed worked to his political advantage (Pollack 2009, 15). A negative vote would force US troops out of Iraq a year ahead of schedule.[142]

The evidence mounted that Iraqi government leaders, freed from a security threat and generally more self-reliant, would promote a peculiarly Iraqi national agenda—more to the point, their own political agenda—and compromise the broad goals that directed the US institution-building effort. Although checks on the power of the prime minister were in place (for instance, the prime minister could not appoint government ministers, and provincial councils exerted some authority within the country), the danger was that fledgling government institutions would surrender professional neutrality, to the extent it existed in Iraq, to become agents for the country's leadership. These apparent dangers only increased when Prime Minister al-Maliki proved adept at translating his military achievements against the Sadrist militias in the 2008 confrontations, and public dissatisfaction with the religious parties, into a major success at the ballot box in the January 2009 provincial elections.

Most certainly, US officials recognized that they were losing influence over al-Maliki. General Raymond Odierno, General Petraeus's replacement as US commander in Iraq, believed that al-Maliki had confused his *political* triumph over Sadrist forces (in 2008) with a military victory. Consequently, he developed a full briefing for al-Maliki on what the United States had actually contributed to the battle in Basra and just how dependent Iraq remained on US support (Ricks 2009, 286–287). That such a briefing was deemed necessary, despite Iraq's material reliance upon the United States, could only portend decreasing US leverage as Baghdad's capabilities improved. With the scheduled US pullback from Iraqi cities approaching, US military officials continued to worry that the Iraqi leadership did not understand just how dependent Iraqi military forces still were on the United States for training, technical support, logistics, and backup.[143] Their concerns were likely reinforced when al-Maliki assembled hundreds of his top military commanders, ostensibly to discuss the US military pullout. With national elections looming, his political agenda was clear at the gathering in the speeches that made scant reference to US troops, in the fawning salutes to the "commander in chief," and in the absence of US representation. Indeed, a senior US military officer was turned away at the door. The US pullback, after all, was an Iraqi occasion: in al-Maliki's words, a "great victory"[144]—no less than "a heroic repulsion of the foreign occupiers."[145] Not only did al-Maliki proclaim June 30, 2009, as "National Sovereignty Day" in a call for festivities and celebration,[146] he also conspicuously avoided public reference to US military contributions and sacrifices over the prior half-dozen years.[147] In addressing the Iraqi people on the occasion of the pullback, he congratulated his government and its security forces for *their* successes against the insurgency.[148] He was no less direct in his message to US leaders. Days later, his response to Vice President Joseph Biden, on a mission to Iraq as President Obama's special representative to promote national reconciliation, was that the issue was a domestic matter and that US interference was unwelcome.[149]

The question, then, was whether al-Maliki would press his advantage rather than compromise with opponents (at home and abroad). Whereas al-Maliki moved to build a post-election coalition (in 2009) with former rivals—including Sunnis—to outmaneuver his former allies, he had not allayed distrust of his motives.[150] Thus, his opponents were only too willing to turn on him as security conditions deteriorated in the country, the public blamed the government for the security breakdowns and performance lapses, and national elections (scheduled for early 2010) presented an opportunity for leadership change.[151] Yet, the problems of Iraq—including the authoritarian temptations of public office—were bigger than any one person and would likely flourish even under new national leadership.

Conclusions

The United States was consistently disadvantaged when attempting to leverage the Saigon and Baghdad governments. In consequence, the United States carried a disproportionate share of the security burden and had problems influencing these governments across a wide variety of issues. Although the level, nature, and endurance of the threat to the host government differed in South Vietnam and Iraq, the United States was unable to pressure either host government to adopt critical political and economic reforms and had to push both governments hard to get them to develop the security institutions that would relieve the United States of its security burden. Indeed, it is striking how much the internal US governmental debates over the pros and cons of leveraging the Saigon government anticipated the controversies to follow in the Bush administration as it sought to build the Baghdad government's commitment to the US-led mission in Iraq.

The intergovernmental dynamics of the two conflicts differed in critical respects. In Vietnam, the United States correctly assumed that Saigon would rise to the challenge once it had to provide for its own defense: as the US withdrawal proceeded at its own pace, the size and capabilities of South Vietnamese security forces grew to fill the vacuum created by the exodus of US forces. In this, the United States exerted substantial leverage (though still insufficient to push Saigon to soften its security stance and uphold political reforms). By reducing its commitment, the United States could leverage Saigon to bear the costs of the war effort because the United States, of the two, was relatively more willing to accept the risk of a communist victory. In Iraq, the United States lost leverage on multiple fronts with improving security conditions and growing host-government security capabilities and self-reliance. In consequence, the Baghdad government became increasingly independent on matters of governance and policy and imposed its own plan and schedule for a US troop withdrawal from the country. The United States was probably unable to increase its leverage with a threat to withdraw US troops from Iraq. The Baghdad government knew that US policymakers believed that acting on the threat would intensify ethno-sectarian conflict in Iraq, which would harm US interests. Although government leaders would likely have "stepped up" with a US withdrawal from the country, that was actually the problem. Unlike in Vietnam—where the US and Saigon governments generally agreed on the nature of the security threat—the threat in Iraq lay in the eye of the beholder.

Certainly, the United States might have obtained additional leverage over the Baghdad government had the United States pursued a more modest agenda and not pushed for thorough de-Baathification or disbanded the Iraqi military—moves that fed Sunni grievances and facilitated the breakdown in order in the country. Sunnis would not have been disenfranchised, and Shiites would not have rushed to fill the institutional security vacuum created by the Sunni exodus and the downward spiral into civil war. In a more stable Iraq, with a more inclusive government, the United States could conceivably have pushed more effectively for societal accommodation and institutional reform. Still, it is difficult to argue assuredly that things would have been different in Iraq had the United States not made critical mistakes. The plausible price of accepting a large Sunni presence within government was Shiite dissension and stalemate (again)—if not rivalry within or between Iraqi government institutions that eventually blew them apart. The United States might *never* have had adequate leverage over Baghdad leaders to move them to democratize and reform or leverage over Iraq's government and society to overcome profound societal impediments to institutional capacity-building.

Put simply, the initial US decision to invade Iraq was most crucial for determining (the lack of) US leverage. But the United States did not help its cause in Iraq by choosing haphazardly to "reinvent" it, that is, by pursuing goals that severely strained available US capabilities and by making grand decisions with inadequate deliberation. In this, US officials failed to grasp some basic truths about nation-building—that early decisions are irrevocable; that the "right" choice is consistently elusive; that solutions to problems frequently depend on solutions to others, and those to still others (especially when goals are ambitious); and that time, effort, and resources are lost to societal maladies (sectarianism, corruption) that defy solutions and redirect national institutions toward ignoble purposes. A negative practical effect of US inattentiveness was to reduce US leverage by empowering host-government leaders, limiting host-government accountability, and worsening already intractable problems.

In sum, important lessons from the Vietnam and Iraq conflicts are as follows: (a) the host government will accept a disproportionately small share of the costs of combat and institutional development, (b) the United States can inadvertently create conditions that transfer leverage to host governments and further reduce their incentives to accept these costs, and (c) the United States will encounter formidable challenges when building host-government institutions requires accompanying changes in societal values, attitudes, and practices. Adding to these lessons is an important one from Iraq: once the host government can handle its own security, it will grab a disproportionate share of the benefits.

CHAPTER SIX

Conclusions

Vietnam and Iraq, Afghanistan, and the Future

O ne lesson from the Vietnam and Iraq Wars outshines all the others: any US victory in "asymmetric conflict" is likely incomplete and may always depend on conditions that the United States cannot manipulate. With its finite capabilities and resolve, the United States is seriously challenged when its goals include winning in combat and maintaining and extending support for US policies at home and abroad. The challenges increase enormously when US goals also include building open and effective host-government institutions, establishing local security, and promoting reconstruction and development in a war-torn country.

Lessons from Vietnam and Iraq

Whereas US institution-building goals were more ambitious in Iraq than in Vietnam and the military challenges were greater in Vietnam than in Iraq, fundamental similarities outweigh dissimilarities in lessons drawn from the two conflicts. The common lessons are as follows.

Lesson 1a: The United States enjoys an overwhelming military advantage in conventional but not irregular warfare.

Lesson 1b: Conventional strategies are ineffective and counterproductive for combating an insurgency.

Lesson 1c: Despite a massive counterinsurgency investment in a conflict, the United States might not have the military, economic, and political resources available to succeed and is severely disadvantaged when engaged in counter-insurgency without full host-government support.

Both conflicts provide compelling evidence that, with their enormous advantage in mobility and firepower, US forces will emerge as the net winner in a conventional military confrontation. The United States can draw on assets that follow from being a global power—as well as, today, the intelligence-gathering, data-processing, communications, and command and control capabilities that go along with being the world's preeminent power—to secure a victory in confrontations that play to traditional US strengths. Given its advantages, the United States imposed high relative troop losses on the adversary throughout the Vietnam War—and certainly in the major communist offensives in 1968 and 1972—and orchestrated an invasion of Iraq in 2003 that dealt a quick death blow to the Saddam Hussein regime.

Unfortunately for the United States, its conventional advantage was decisive only in certain phases of these conflicts and left US forces vulnerable in critical respects. The United States was stymied when its Vietnamese adversary feigned a conventional strategy to protect a guerrilla effort, and when its Iraqi adversaries capitalized on a deficient US national presence to recruit, arm, and conduct a deadly bombing campaign against US military forces, Iraqi governmental personnel, and Shiite civilians. In both conflicts, the US response was ineffective and self-defeating. By targeting the (Vietnamese) villages and (Iraqi) cities where the adversary was lurking and acquiring resources, the United States increased local grievances against the United States and host governments. The United States made significant headway against Vietnamese insurgents and Iraqi militias only when they went on the offensive. The evidence from both conflicts is that conventional strategies and tactics do not work in irregular wars—that the stronger party, in conventional terms, can fail when employing the wrong doctrine. In Vietnam and Iraq, the United States engaged in asymmetric wars against opponents that played to their own strengths, avoided US military strengths, and exploited US military (and especially political) vulnerabilities.

Yet the evidence does not indicate that the United States would have won either war with a counterinsurgency strategy. Early victory through counterinsurgency in Vietnam would have required a huge US investment in manpower and resources and could have been realized only against an enemy that did not nimbly shift its strategy (to a big-unit offensive, for example) to compensate. At no time did the United States have the human and material resources available to win both a conventional and unconventional war in Vietnam. Indeed, the evidence is unconvincing that the United States would have succeeded in either effort. US forces fought North Vietnamese regulars to a stalemate and could not bring the South Vietnamese military to perform even to that standard. In turn, reputed US success at counterinsurgency in Vietnam—as measured by territory and people under Saigon's control—was attributable not to gains in popular support, a key to success in counterinsurgency doctrine, but rather to insurgent losses in a conventional offensive. The United States could not overcome its significant disadvantage—its dependence on a Saigon government that was slow to embrace the counterinsurgency mission and support political and economic reforms. In turn, counterinsurgency "worked" (in 2007–8) in Iraq only when the doctrine is defined, in the broadest terms, to include capitalizing on preexisting disputes among rival insurgent groups, relying on key societal leaders and groups (and not a population per se for support), and reducing violence—without ending hostility—toward the United States and host governments. The evidence is that (a) US success was consistently undermined by a lack of competent and professional Iraqi security forces to relieve US troops in combat, hold territory cleared of hostile personnel, and put a local "face" on the stabilization effort, and (b) neither the key leaders and groups nor the local population were ever "won over" to the US or Iraqi government in any meaningful or permanent sense. In the end, the United States—as an outside power aligned with an unpopular government—could not create the political conditions that counterinsurgency doctrine requires.

In theory, the doctrine might have worked effectively in both conflicts. In practice, the United States was not positioned to manipulate the factors that determined popular support, a key to the doctrine's success. The question remains whether the United States, by virtue of its global interests, is positioned to excel in wars with limited stakes that require heavy, long-term US investments in human and material resources.

Lesson 2: The United States will encounter significant constraints, risks, and costs and realize limited benefits when leveraging various third parties in order to achieve its goals.

With severe challenges in Vietnam and Iraq, the United States was forced to reevaluate its position and tactics vis-à-vis various third parties—outside states, host-country societal groups and leaders, and indigenous populations. The United States did so with mixed success.

The United States eventually shed its concerns about expanding the Vietnam conflict. The Nixon administration took the war directly to the border states that served as sanctuaries, resource conduits, and attack platforms for the war in the South. Accordingly, the United States sent US troops into Cambodia, backed South Vietnamese troops in Laos, and escalated the bombing of both countries. It also increased pressure on Hanoi's major-power backers, the Soviet Union and China, to compel Hanoi to negotiate on US terms. These efforts produced limited success: Russia and China proved generally noncompliant, and the expanding war eventually brought all of Southeast Asia under communist control.

In the Iraq conflict, a US escalation threat arguably prevented key border states—Syria and Iran—from increasing their support for militant groups. In fact, both states contributed to the stabilizing of Iraq—Syria, by providing intelligence information to the United States and clamping down on al-Qaeda–linked groups, and Iran, by supporting the militia *covertly*, limiting its own operations in Iraq, and pressing the militia to hold its fire (as it did in 2008 by brokering a ceasefire between Baghdad and the Mahdi Army in southern Iraq). Yet these countries also had their own reasons for seeking stability in Iraq and were disinclined to do more in this regard, as a response to US pressure. Syria could not be pressed to take aggressive measures to prevent the country from serving as a terrorist conduit into Iraq, and Iran could not be pressed into ending its support for Iraqi Shiite militia groups. An implicit US threat to take the matter into its own hands by attacking the militant-support infrastructure in Syria and Iran, to gain these states' acquiescence to US goals in Iraq, was unlikely to succeed given the costs to Syrian and Iranian leaders of capitulating to US demands and US disincentives for acting on these (veiled) threats. Ultimately, the United States was deterred from expanding the war out of fear that it would intensify (internal and external) resistance to the US stabilization effort in Iraq.

To be sure, one aspect of the US "third-party" approach in Iraq does stand out. The United States reduced the violence in Iraq by packaging aid, support, and concessions (for instance, amnesty) to placate Sunni tribal leaders and members of various insurgent groups. The United States also managed a ceasefire with the "mainstream" elements of the Mahdi Army even when aggressively pursuing its elements ("special groups") that the United States charged were conspiring with Iran. Still, the United States was unable to "win over" the Iraqi population to its government, let alone the US mission. Indeed, the United States might have succeeded only in convincing its former adversaries that the short-term advantages of accepting a US troop presence outweighed the disadvantages, when all options remained open.

> *Lesson 3a: Relative to its adversary, the United States is disadvantaged by its weaker resolve and smaller resource share invested in a small conflict.*
> *Lesson 3b: The US government and public will lose resolve when costs accumulate in a small conflict.*

In Vietnam and Iraq, the United States struggled to adapt its strategies and capabilities to combat a low-tech adversary that was committed to its goals and could capitalize on the US inability to devote resources to achieve the short- and long-term goals of the military effort. The US disadvantage ensued from a paradox of power: the more capability a state possesses, the lower its stake in any given conflict. The United States had to compete with parties that could make *total* commitments—politically, psychologically, socially, and materially—to goals that had *limited* value to the United States, given its global objectives. The United States certainly tried to compensate for its disadvantage in both conflicts: the United States employed linkage and signaling strategies (especially in Vietnam) to show that the United States would do what it would take to win. Yet in neither conflict did signals from the United States or its attempts to manipulate the stakes of the conflict matter more to the outcome than the US ability, through force or material inducements, to control conditions on the ground.

True, the adversary's advantage is arguably also a disadvantage: the adversary's greater relative resource commitment increases the adversary's costs in conflict, with the effect of sapping the adversary's will. Still, the evidence is unpersuasive that the adversary—short of catastrophic losses in military assets or popular support—would have conceded defeat in Vietnam or Iraq before the United States tired of these engagements.

Although US leaders maintained relatively strong and enduring domestic support for prosecuting the war in Vietnam, that support did not survive a downward turn in events (the Tet Offensive) that signaled to US audiences—policymakers and public alike—that a near-term, US victory in Vietnam was unlikely and that winning was impossible without prohibitive cost. Conversely, the adversary tapped nationalistic sentiment and maintained sufficient capability to outlast the United States secure in the knowledge that it would, in time, exhaust itself. The United States lost in the end because victory meant more to Hanoi than it did to the United States: a US defeat was foretold by competing demands on US power in the world, the relatively limited US stakes in Vietnam, the reticence of the US public and its elected representatives to invest resources in the fight, and the challenges of building host-government institutions that could sustain the war effort.

The United States was similarly disadvantaged against Sunni insurgent and Shiite militia groups in Iraq. With the US troop surge in 2007, the United States reached the limits of its available military capability and would have been forced to accept a change in strategy, or even a persistent state of conflict in Iraq, had the violence not abated. The US willingness to concede that its prior military strategy was not working, to provide resources to Sunni insurgent groups to gain their co-operation, and to promote a ceasefire with Shiite militias, when these groups had not disarmed, are critical indicators of waning US capability and resolve over the course of the Iraq conflict.

> *Lesson 4a: The host government will accept a disproportionately small share of the costs of combat and institutional development.*
> *Lesson 4b: The United States can inadvertently create conditions that transfer leverage to a host government and further reduce its incentives to accept these costs.*
> *Lesson 4c: Once the host government can handle its own security, it will grab a disproportionate share of the benefits.*

The challenges for the United States worsened because it depended on the actions of host-government leaders who could capitalize on a US commitment and fail to make hard choices (in the form of political and economic reforms) that would ease the US financial, political, and military burden and facilitate an eventual US withdrawal from the conflict. These leaders, both in power and in the opposition, placed their own political, economic, and security needs first because the United States had the capability and interest to persevere, in the short term, even without host-government support. Not only did these leaders pass the various costs of the conflict onto the United States, the leaders of Iraq and, to a lesser extent, South Vietnam also imposed their preferences on national institutions (constructed with US support) when these leaders could, or had to, provide for their nation's security.

In principle, the United States can acquire leverage over host-government leaders by threatening them with reduced US support. Yet the host government might acquire leverage to resist US entreaties owing to various conditions that the United States itself creates. First, host-government leverage increases when the United States empowers host-government leaders, with the effect of immunizing them from US retaliation. Paradoxically, US leverage declines when host-government leaders develop a strong support base to resist US demands but also when the same leaders are weak and vulnerable and must placate their support base by challenging US demands. In the latter instance, the United States must concede ground to *help* these leaders deflect charges that they are US "stooges" or puppets (knowing that these leaders exaggerate their political vulnerability to reduce US pressure).[1] For that matter, US leverage declines when the host government "weakens itself" by manipulating threats to advantage. For instance, the US bargaining position suffers vis-à-vis a host government that can provoke coup fears (as Vietnamese leaders did) or domestic violence (as the al-Maliki government did in early 2008, when assaulting the Mahdi Army in Basra). Second, host-government leverage increases when the host suspects that US goals are unrealistic or overly ambitious. If the host government believes, for instance, that local security institutions devoid of corruption and sectarian bias are noble but elusive goals, the host is unlikely to commit sufficient resources to allow the program to succeed (a "self-fulfilling prophecy"). Furthermore, US leverage declines when the United States pursues ambitious goals that require progress on multiple, interdependent fronts and excuse the host government from acting within its areas of competence. When the United States intends to do all things—underutilizing host-government capabilities—the United States sacrifices opportunities to exert leverage. Third, host-government leverage increases with a growing US commitment. Leveraging the host becomes harder when the United States sees no easy way out of the conflict—whether because US policymakers are "chasing sunk costs" ("we can't give up now"), US involvement has exacerbated the conflict or reduced the host government's role (to increase the costs of disengagement), or the United States is concerned about damaging its reputation by failing to honor a commitment. Fourth, host-government leverage increases when the host confuses a US commitment to the war effort for unqualified support of the host government. Scholars have recognized the "moral hazard" that ensues when assisting allies allows them to shirk or engage in behavior that compromises security.

Allies are betting that their patron will not end its support or shift it to rivals because of the attendant risks and costs.

> Lesson 5: *Apart from the question of leverage over host governments, the United States will encounter formidable challenges when building host-government institutions requires accompanying changes in societal values, attitudes, and practices.*

The US effort in Vietnam ultimately floundered because even massive infusions of US support and assistance were inadequate to compensate for traditions and practices that weakened the performance of South Vietnamese civilian and military institutions. In Iraq, the challenges were that much greater due to an ambitious US agenda and the severity of the country's problems. The United States sought to promote reconstruction, economic opportunity, and democratic institutions within Iraq despite its severe and unstable security environment; dilapidated physical infrastructure; paucity of technical and economic resources; limited public institutional capacity; intense sectarian rivalry for control over the assets required for national development; deeply rooted societal grievances; longstanding traditions that bred corruption, inefficiency, and sectarian bias; absence of civil society to nurture fledgling democratic institutions; and widespread public intolerance for other religions, groups, and views. The United States learned in Iraq just how difficult it is to address any single dimension (political, economic, or military) of a country's problems—or to focus US strategy on a manageable set of problems—when solving any one requires the solution of others. Indeed, the United States learned how difficult it is to solve problems when doing so creates and exacerbates others.

Afghanistan: Lessons Applied and Relearned

As the United States reduced its military profile in Iraq, the Obama administration moved to fulfill its campaign promise to devote US military resources to the fight in Afghanistan, in order to offset the mistakes of the prior administration. The Bush administration did not foresee the United States returning in force to Afghanistan after removing its Taliban-led government from power in 2001 with relative ease. The administration appeared to have succeeded, when intervening powers of the prior century had failed to impose their will in the country. The administration redirected its military resources to Iraq, in fact, with the assumption that the war in Afghanistan was effectively won.

Administration officials—including Secretary of Defense Donald Rumsfeld—surmised that the war in Afghanistan demonstrated that the United States could employ its technological and operational advantages to surmount US quantitative constraints. For them, the war was a decisive victory for US air power—a robust US arsenal of reliable and precise smart weapons of varying potency tied to a responsive US intelligence, communication, and command network—performing in lethal synergy with mobile ground units. In future engagements, these units could identify and spot targets for aerial attack, clear or control areas that were targeted from the air, neutralize key personnel and seize critical facilities (when air attacks were inappropriate or ineffective), and rally indigenous forces to press enemy ground forces or pursue them in retreat.[2] In their view, the general lesson from Afghanistan was that wars could now be fought on favorable terms: the United States could quickly insert itself into conflicts, employ its forces economically to bring down governments, and reduce the undesirable (collateral) effects of combat. Indeed, given these efficiencies, the United States could move from one battlefield (country) to the next to address perceived threats.

Of course, the US victory envisioned in Afghanistan was incomplete, to say the least. True, the Taliban proved no match for US air power in the fighting: the Taliban lost much of its fixed military assets in the early bombing campaign and concentrated its forces in vulnerable pockets outside the major cities (O'Hanlon 2002). In defeat, the Taliban demonstrated, however, that it could have achieved greater success by playing to its own advantages—an ability to capitalize on US cost and casualty aversions and to rely on its own peculiar links to the local population.[3] Indeed, Taliban forces proved a formidable opponent once they adopted the strategy of the "weak," which amounted to playing for time in an insurgency campaign. The Taliban entrenched itself in hospitable parts of the country and the sparsely governed tribal territories of northwestern Pakistan, where it recruited, trained, and planned attacks against the Afghan government and its US and NATO supporters. By the end of the Bush administration, the limits of US military capability registered clearly in Afghanistan in rising national violence, an absence of central government authority throughout much of the country, and dangerous regional spillover effects. Increased Islamic radicalism in Pakistan—as blowback from governmental support for Islamic groups operating throughout South Asia (including Afghanistan)—threatened its government and a war with India, when that country was targeted in an Islamist bombing campaign.

The new US administration faced an enormous political, economic, and military challenge. It harbored no illusions, however, about the difficult task ahead (as registered, within the administration, in contentious policy debates).[4] In the words of the State Department's new special envoy to Afghanistan and Pakistan, it was "going to be much tougher than Iraq."[5] Given the lessons of Vietnam and Iraq, this was likely an understatement, as the administration increasingly recognized. The struggles in the first months of the administration to devise a workable strategy, no less than the interrelated military, economic, societal, and governmental challenges of operating in Afghanistan, speak volumes about the short- and long-term limits of US military capability in the asymmetric conflict in which the US was engaged.

Once more, the United States was drawn into a conflict with insurgents who knew the local terrain, shared identities with the indigenous population, chose the time and place of fighting, melted away when confronted, and capitalized on its military advantages. Worse still, US policymakers struggled to apply, to Afghanistan, the experience gained and "lessons learned" from Iraq and lacked the resources—again—to apply a traditional counterinsurgency strategy to an ongoing conflict. The US disadvantages in this asymmetric conflict were considerable and numerous.[6]

First, the US effort was challenged by the Taliban's ethnic ties to the Pashtun population. Although divided tribally, geographically, and politically, the Pashtun constituted half of Afghanistan's citizenry and accounted for much of the population in southern and eastern Afghanistan and the tribal regions on the Pakistani side of the Afghanistan-Pakistan border.[7]

Second, the US effort suffered because recruiting local populations and their leaders was difficult but essential for success insofar as the insurgents lacked a "central leadership that can be dealt with, co-opted, or eliminated" (Kilcullen 2009, 48). Any recruitment strategy had to contend with Pashtun resistance to intrusions in their affairs and the strong popular backlash to Coalition military operations that inadvertently hurt civilians. US recruitment was hurt further by feuds, turf battles, and criminal interests within the target population that prevented the United States from sponsoring local militia groups to fight the insurgents.[8] Thus, tactics inspired by the US experience in Iraq—providing training and arms to indigenous groups—risked increasing instability and violence in the country and weakening the national standing of the Kabul government.[9]

Third, the US effort was hampered because the Taliban had resources to conduct an insurgency. The Taliban capitalized on the opium trade and a wide variety of other illicit dealings to finance operations and to build its support base.[10] UN officials estimated that its proceeds from the opium trade alone amounted to

$125 million dollars a year.[11] The Taliban became more adept at safeguarding its own forces and inflicting Coalition casualties. It exacted an increasing toll on opposition forces with hit-and-run tactics and improvised explosive devices, relied upon small units to attack vulnerable targets rather than risk large units in costly confrontations, employed indirect fire to concentrate US troops to render them vulnerable to follow-up attacks with guns and grenades, timed attacks to end before US air support arrived, and hid within populated areas to reduce US retaliatory options.[12] With its improving weaponry, available manpower, and growing mastery of asymmetric military tactics (Kilcullen 2009, 55–58), the Taliban was prepared for a war that would be won through endurance.

Fourth, the US effort languished from the institutional failings of a Kabul government that could neither lead the counterinsurgency effort nor provide significant ancillary support. Afghan security forces were poorly led, ill equipped, overstretched, undersized, -trained, -educated, and -motivated.[13] On top of these deficiencies, the Afghan police were notoriously corrupt, at all levels.[14] Given these problems, the rapid expansion of these forces—deemed necessary to hold territory to serve a counterinsurgency mission—risked doing more harm than good, by exacerbating popular grievances against the Afghan government.[15] Civilian government institutions fared no better in serving their population. These institutions lacked the capacity to promote economic and political development in the country. In 2008, Afghanistan ranked second (behind Somalia) on the Brookings Institution's Index of State Weakness in the Developing World and seventh (out of 177 countries) on the Foreign Policy/Fund for Peace Failed States Index.[16] The roughly ten billion dollars that the United States planned to spend in 2009 to improve security, aid development, facilitate governance, and combat the narcotics trade in Afghanistan amounted to almost half the country's total GDP for 2008 and over ten times the country's annual tax revenue.[17] The Afghan government even lacked the capability to distribute assistance from abroad. Its weakness was reinforced when the United States chose to work around the government by dispensing aid through private contractors, the United Nations, and nongovernmental organizations.[18]

Fifth, the US effort suffered because the United States had to tolerate the malfeasant Afghan leadership. Once again, the United States had to carry the burden of a broad-based security mission, rather than allow it to flounder, at the price of letting the host government off the hook. By deferring to Afghanistan's president, Hamid Karzai, appreciating his difficult political situation, and acknowledging and reinforcing his authority, the Bush administration allowed him to shirk responsibilities and engage in behavior that undermined the US-led mission. For instance, Karzai refused to fire corrupt and ineffective officials and fired reputedly effective ones—seemingly because they *were* effective.[19] The Obama administration had hoped that the Afghan elections of August 2009 would bring a change in national leadership. But the administration also recognized that, for the present, Afghanistan lacked strong leaders who could replace Karzai and that a weak replacement government could not act boldly and swiftly to assist the US-led mission.[20] This left the United States without a credible threat to redirect US political support in order to leverage the Karzai government.

Sixth, the US effort was hurt because the Afghan central government was viewed as *the problem* by much of the rural population. The Kabul government's continuing weakness abetted corruption as the government tolerated unprofessional conduct in exchange for political loyalty. Consequently, Afghanistan continued to rank near the very bottom—176th out of the 180 countries surveyed—on Transparency International's 2008 Corruption Perceptions Index (in tight contention with Haiti, Iraq, and Myanmar for the distinction, again achieved by Somalia, as the world's most corrupt country).[21] Its weakness also induced the Karzai government to attend to the requisites of maintaining power (over building an inclusive government) by constructing a base from weak or isolated tribes that could not threaten the government (Kilcullen 2009, 51), by building alliances with regional commanders (indeed, notorious warlords) who could deliver local votes,[22] and by relying upon the fraudulent practices of his political machine to obtain an electoral majority.[23] The conduct of the August 2009 election—marred by low voter turnout, ballot-box stuffing, voter intimidation, and questionable tallies—could not help provide the legitimation that the central government so sorely lacked.[24] By the same token, a stronger Afghan government—that, in principle, would serve the counterinsurgency effort—was not an appealing prospect for much of the Afghan population. Such a government would likely increase taxes, divert local resources to corrupt officials, and interfere in tribal affairs.

Seventh, the US effort was challenged by the severe underdevelopment of the country. Poverty, illiteracy, inadequate medical care, a lack of basic services, and limited economic infrastructure afflicted much of the population. These deficiencies imposed heavy demands on a counterinsurgency mission that premised national stability on development. Foreign development assistance, centered in numerous Provincial Reconstruction Teams, was hampered by understaffing, limited penetration to the district level, the decidedly military composition of the teams, and lack of coordination among national missions.

Eighth, the US effort was impeded by the unfavorable neighborhood of the conflict. The United States was hindered by its inability to get resources to the conflict zone: attacks on military supply lines from Pakistan exacerbated supply problems due in part to the closure of the US base in Uzbekistan.[25] It was hindered even more by the fluidity with which Taliban resources moved freely into Afghanistan from Pakistan. In the first months of the Obama administration, it appeared, in fact, to US policy officials that Afghanistan and Pakistan constituted a single front, in multiple respects: all the challenges to US counterinsurgency in Afghanistan extended into Pakistan—public opposition to US aerial attacks that were inflicting civilian casualties, indigenous security forces that were ill suited for counterinsurgency, a widespread willingness to accommodate Islamists with the hope of reducing violence, popular disenchantment with the inefficiencies of the national government, an increasingly emboldened insurgency that sought to extend its control, and a weak host government.[26] Parts of the Pakistan military and intelligence establishment, along with various (non-Pashtun) radical groups, actively supported the Taliban, while Pakistan leaders shied from confronting the Taliban's local support base out of concern that the resulting instability would threaten the government and that fighting the Taliban would divert resources from the Indian front. Indeed, the Pakistan government resisted troop transfers from the Indian border. It also condoned US attacks on insurgent leaders and encampments only as long as Islamabad could deny its involvement,[27] withheld permission to US special forces teams to operate in Pakistan territory, resisted participation in intelligence gathering with US drone (Predator) aircraft,[28] and placated local demands by negotiating an agreement that permitted the institution of Islamic law in the Taliban-controlled Swat Valley to the east of the tribal lands and one hundred miles west of the capital.[29]

The Pakistan government went on the offensive when the Taliban reneged on the agreement by refusing to disarm and by seizing control of neighboring districts. With this new hard line, the government benefited from growing public opposition to the insurgents and their violent tactics, which included assassinations, mass kidnappings, assaults on government facilities and personnel, and deadly suicide bomb attacks, and from splits within the Taliban leadership that the government could exploit.[30] Yet the Pakistan military was severely tested. Its sweep into Swat and neighboring districts progressed slowly and raised doubts about whether the military could hold territory that was seized from the militants. The military had not initially established its control beyond roads and urban areas, killed or captured much of the Taliban leadership, and prevented militants from dispersing and hiding among the refugee population.[31] The offensive also raised doubts about whether Pakistan troops—absent forward bases and logistical support, possessing mixed loyalties, and beholden to fickle tribal leaders for support—could operate as successfully when they moved into the harsh mountainous terrain of South Waziristan, the tribal areas along the Afghanistan border, where these troops had failed to achieve their objectives in the past.[32] Furthermore, the offensive provoked skepticism over whether the Pakistan government could assuage the grievances of millions of people displaced in the fighting and obtain their support by providing essential services (judicial, police, health) when they returned home or the Pakistan military could resist the temptation to retaliate against those it believed had aided the insurgency.[33]

Ninth, the US effort was hampered by an absence of the manpower and resources needed to establish a Coalition presence across the vast rural expanse of the country. The United States had planned to deploy around 68,000 troops in Afghanistan by the end of 2009, to bring foreign troop contributions to around 100,000, counting allied contributions under the NATO command. Further augmentations would strain the US military and require contributions from US allies who strongly resisted US appeals for more troops. These levels would still leave the military mission severely understaffed by the standard of troop densities of prior successful counterinsurgencies and occupations as well as fractured among area-specific, national commands that controlled military and reconstruction operations in the country.[34]

Finally, the US effort was challenged by an Afghan population that had lost patience with Coalition forces. Afghanis were more accepting than Iraqis were of a lengthy foreign military presence; yet, seven years into the effort, Afghanis were severely disillusioned. In early 2009, a nationwide poll captured this sentiment. The Afghan public voiced its strong concerns about the absence of security in the country: only around 40 percent of the public believed that their country was moving in the right direction. Although 83 percent of the public held a favorable view of the United States in 2005, less than half of the public now viewed the United States in the same positive regard. Civilian casualties inflicted by the United States and its allies had shaped the perception that Coalition forces, more than the Taliban, were behind the death and destruction in the country. Whereas 41 percent of the public blamed the United States and Coalition forces for targeting innocent civilians, only 28 percent of the public blamed the Taliban for inviting the targeting of the civilian population (another 27 percent of the public blamed both sides). Therefore, a US troop surge into the country was not the solution preferred by most Afghanis. Only 18 percent of Afghanis wanted an increase, compared to 44 percent who wanted a *decrease,* in foreign troop levels within the country.[35] In their view, the US-proposed "solution"—more troops, conducting more operations—would only inflict more civilian casualties and provoke more Taliban attacks.[36]

The Obama administration sought to define goals and a role for the United States in Afghanistan that would take account of the challenges. Its preliminary response was to order an assessment of US policy toward Afghanistan and Pakistan (a meta-review in the form of a "review of the reviews" of prior assessments undertaken late in the Bush administration).[37] Over the succeeding months, the administration distanced the United States from Afghanistan's Karzai government, which the administration viewed as corrupt and ineffectual, ended Bush-administration practices (for example, weekly video conferencing) that had given Karzai political leverage,[38] ordered additional US troops and military advisors to Afghanistan, increased US military operations in southern and eastern Afghanistan where the insurgency was strongest (leading initially to the embedding of thousands of US Marines in Helmand Province in the south),[39] bolstered US civilian staff support for the US diplomatic and economic mission in the country, rallied additional support from NATO allies, replaced the US commander in Afghanistan with a military leadership that would give more attention to counterinsurgency, imposed stricter rules of engagement on US aircraft to reduce civilian casualties, and brought new emphasis to the deteriorating security conditions in Pakistan, which fed the conflict in Afghanistan and threatened broader US national security interests.[40] As important, however, as the rising level of US commitment were the limits to US actions and goals, as clear from the new US strategy (as outlined by President Obama in March 2009). The emphasis was placed on stabilizing Afghanistan and building its government capacities (not on establishing a "flourishing democracy"), reaching out to moderate Taliban leaders, targeting al-Qaeda and its support network to prevent attacks on the United States, obtaining broad international backing for the US approach, and looking to fellow NATO members to offer logistical and economic support in lieu of combat troops.[41] A half-year later, the president was highly reluctant to yield to military troop requests for tens of thousands of additional troops that, in his view, might increase US military involvement in Afghanistan without improving the final outcome.[42] For their part, US military commanders recognized that the counterinsurgency campaign must be conducted within clear limits: not only were resources unavailable to conduct such a campaign while fighting in the mountains of eastern Afghanistan, where the insurgents enjoyed an overwhelming home-field advantage, resources were unavailable to conduct a nationwide counterinsurgency campaign that focused on satisfying the needs of the Afghan people. As the new US military commander said of the situation, "We've got to ruthlessly prioritize, because we don't have enough forces to do everything, everywhere."[43] These limits were paramount, for example, when US officials revised US counternarcotics policies in Afghanistan to deemphasize the destruction of poppy crops so as not to alienate Afghan farmers and push them to support the Taliban.[44] They were obviously apparent when the US commander in Afghanistan ordered his commanders (over the objections of Afghan leaders) to pull US forces out of less populated areas, where they had long engaged in pitched battles with the Taliban, in order to concentrate US forces in more densely populated areas.[45]

Accordingly, the Obama administration generally sought to respond to various asymmetries that played to the US advantage and disadvantage. Yet the administration could not define US goals or a US role in the Afghanistan war to fit available US capabilities. In its first months in office, it acknowledged, explicitly and implicitly, that a strenuous effort was inevitable given the nature of the conflict.[46] With the new administration, the United States still had to (a) find ways to work with and around the weak and venal Afghan government and to build up its institutional capacities to realize long-term stability in the country; (b) look to private contractors (to unprecedented levels) to assume the traditional responsibilities of the uniformed military;[47] (c) separate useful from deceptive metrics for judging whether the United States was failing or succeeding (indeed, for judging eventually whether it *had* succeeded) at its mission;[48] (d) placate congressional demands that US economic and military support to Afghanistan be tied to its progress in meeting established criteria;[49] (e) develop, fund, and orchestrate a counter-narcotics program, as a complement to the US counterinsurgency effort, that would give farmers an incentive to turn away from the lucrative production of poppies for the Taliban-directed opium trade;[50] (f) scale the US force in Afghanistan to meet the enormous demands of the operation knowing that a large force would also increase the US investment in the conflict and potentially alienate the local population;[51] (g) choose between spreading US forces thin and concentrating them in areas (cities) where they might operate at a disadvantage, fail to engage or weaken the Taliban, drive it underground, or force insurgents to relocate to more hospitable parts of the country;[52] (h) convince local leaders and populations that their future lay in resisting the Taliban when insurgents forced US troops into battles that took priority over the planned stabilization effort and when the United States apparently lacked the troop strength to reduce the violence;[53] (i) recruit, train, and replenish an Afghan force that lacked essential requisites for success and would have to operate in a prohibitive security environment;[54] (j) cope with an adversary that was increasingly proficient militarily and could sabotage US counterinsurgency efforts by selecting targets that included roads, schools, and polling places; and (k) decide whether to endorse the results of a fraudulent presidential election at the price of alienating a substantial part of the population and reinforcing the unresponsive and corrupt Afghan leadership or to press for a recount or new election that would invite unrest, incur costs, and distract the Afghan government from the counterinsurgency effort. Perhaps, most important, the Obama administration had to extend the fight into Pakistan to control the violence in Afghanistan and to balance the demands of fighting on two sides of the border. Consequently, the United States had to decide how to choose appropriate targets (for instance, whether to target groups that primarily threatened the Pakistan government), how to limit cross-border effects (as militants fled from Afghanistan to Pakistan and vice versa), how to increase aid to Pakistan while holding it accountable for halting domestic militancy, how to get Pakistan forces to fight Taliban elements (for instance, in Baluchistan) that threatened the Afghan but not Pakistan government,[55] and how to manage lingering hostility between Pakistan and Afghan government forces.[56] Eventually, the administration might also have to decide how to craft a deal in Afghanistan that did not worsen military and political conditions in Pakistan and threaten its government.

In sum, most of the lessons drawn from Vietnam and Iraq listed above apply directly to the ongoing conflict in Afghanistan. The United States employed its conventional advantage—especially in air power—to rout the Taliban military (Lesson 1a) but struggled in the irregular warfare that followed the quick victory (1b). The United States was in an uphill battle trying to maintain and acquire indigenous public support for the war effort, win over tribal leaders, and convince neighboring states that the benefits of supporting the US fight in Afghanistan outweigh the costs (2). The United States also struggled to acquire the backing of an Afghan government that resisted political reforms, accommodated warlords and national power brokers, moved slowly to develop its institutional capacities, and compromised the standing of US and NATO forces by criticizing them publicly for inflicting civilian casualties (4a). The United States responded to the country's ineffective government by working around it, which furthered its inclination to pass the costs of securing and stabilizing the country to the United States and its Coalition partners (4b). US leaders worried, in fact, about losing leverage by pressing the Afghan government, should it react by digging in and becoming even *less* cooperative.[57]

The United States will likely continue to struggle given the limited resources that are available for counterinsurgency (1c) and the adversary's motivation and willingness, relative to the United States, to invest resources in the conflict (3a). Given the longevity of prior successful counterinsurgency efforts and the challenges peculiar to Afghanistan, even sympathetic US experts predicted that it would take many years of dedicated Coalition effort to reduce the threat of Taliban violence and many billion dollars in annual assistance—over a period of decades—to realize ongoing stability in the country. Indeed, by official military estimates, the cost of a single soldier in Afghanistan amounted (conservatively) to a quarter of a million dollars a year.[58] Six months into the administration, General Stanley McChrystal, the top commander in Afghanistan, in a stark, detailed assessment, made the case nevertheless for more troops and resources to conduct a counterinsurgency campaign—asserting bluntly that without these forces in the coming year, the US-led mission "will likely result in failure,"[59] a conclusion backed by the top military leadership.[60] The test here will come because "the Taliban appears to be applying an *exhaustion strategy* of sapping the energy, resources, and support of the Afghan government and its international partners, making the country ungovernable and hoping that the international community will eventually withdraw in exhaustion and leave the government to collapse under the weight of its own lack of effectiveness and legitimacy" (Kilcullen 2009, 52).

The US public already appears to have tired of the mission in Afghanistan—well before the US government views its work there as done (3b). The preliminary indicators for the Obama administration were not promising: only a narrow majority (51 percent) of Americans expressed the opinion in July 2009 that, given the costs, the war in Afghanistan was "worth fighting," and less than a majority (46 percent) expressed the view that the United States was making "significant progress toward achieving success" in that country.[61] By August, after weeks of deadly combat, a narrow majority (51 percent) now believed that the war was *not* worth fighting. Public support for prosecuting the war was dropping rapidly: the 45 percent of those polled in August advocating a *reduced* US troop presence in the country represented more than a 50 percent jump in this sentiment from the start of the year.[62] Whereas 50 percent of the US public claimed to favor the Afghan War in May 2009, only 39 percent (and less than a quarter of Democrats) expressed that view in September 2009, a ratio of support approximating Iraq War lows.[63] With mounting costs, Secretary of Defense Robert Gates was among those warning that the United States and its allies needed to show progress in Afghanistan soon or risk losing public support.[64] President Obama himself supposedly acknowledged the risk that he was following the path of Lyndon Johnson, that Afghanistan would become his Vietnam.[65] Obama had committed to a war that public opinion had moved against, manifest in growing domestic pressure on other NATO governments to bring their troops home and reticence in the US Congress to commit additional resources to the fight.[66] Indeed, congressional resistance to the US counterinsurgency approach rose as evidence mounted that it endangered US troops by treating air power as a weapon of last resort in order to limit civilian casualties.[67]

Even should progress occur, it appears likely that the Afghan government will seek to capitalize on any success by claiming a disproportionate share of the benefits (4c). In a troubling sign for the United States, the Karzai government revealed its willingness to grab benefits even when this imposed costs upon the United States and compromised its plans to stabilize the country. That was the effect when Karzai sought to boost his domestic political standing by negotiating deals with Afghan warlords and corrupting the electoral process, by holding Coalition forces accountable publicly for inflicting civilian casualties, and by standing up to US demands in "confrontations" (such as over the results of the August 2009 elections) that he apparently invented for that purpose.[68]

President Obama had no illusions about the challenge ahead and the hard decisions required.[69] Six months after adopting its highly touted strategy, the Obama administration was *again* engaged in a complete reassessment of the US approach in Afghanistan, well aware of the deteriorating military and political conditions in the country and the enormous human and material resources required to succeed along the current course. Whereas counterinsurgency had become the new conventional wisdom, many civilian officials now realized that they had not fully appreciated the doctrine's resource demands as foreseen by the US military.[70] Among the competing options the administration considered was jettisoning a counterinsurgency approach in favor of a counterterrorism approach that placed the focus on combating al-Qaeda (and only containing and weakening the Taliban).[71] It also considered putting greater relative weight on combating the Taliban in Pakistan where US interests were arguably more directly threatened and the host government was better prepared to combat an insurgency. But the administration still might not define a limited mission that offers a profitable return on any US investment, given the attending costs, challenges, and incompleteness of the mission. For instance, targeting terrorists is arguably impossible without also separating them from a supportive population, acquiring information from local sources, and strengthening local governing, policing, and welfare institutions via a counterinsurgency approach.[72] Likewise, a shift in focus to Pakistan would fail to deliver the desired result if Afghanistan continued to serve as an insurgent refuge or if the Pakistan government resisted US priorities and leverage attempts that included tying US aid to Pakistan's performance against the insurgency.[73] In deciding to commit another 30,000 US troops to the conflict with the intent of *weakening* the Taliban, shifting the combat burden eventually to Afghan forces, and starting a US pullback in July 2011, Obama might still not win the race against cumulating costs over time.

The possibility exists, then, that the United States and its allies will follow the negative example of the Soviet Union in Afghanistan. Soviet forces intervened (invaded) in 1979 to support Afghanistan's beleaguered Marxist government, with a relatively small force (roughly a hundred thousand strong) that was unable to control the vast expanses of the countryside, was unprepared for counterinsurgency, and received little relief from host-government forces. True, the Soviets tried—unlike the United States and its NATO allies—to compensate for their deficiencies with sheer brutality: the decade-long conflict would cost millions of lives and produce huge refugee flows in and out of the country. But even Soviet scorched-earth tactics were insufficient to overcome a loosely aligned and technologically inferior opponent (notwithstanding its clandestine US support) that relied on asymmetric guerrilla tactics, drew on nationalism and Islam for motivation, and could simply wait out the opponent. The resistance won in the end because it did not lose.

Beyond Afghanistan and into the Future

Despite the peculiarly tough US challenges in Afghanistan, it is appropriate to think of asymmetric conflict as present *whenever* the United States or some other intervening power cannot simply impose its will on an adversary. Asymmetric conflict, then, is always a matter of scope and degree.

At one extreme, the prohibitive environment might prevent intervening forces—at their level of commitment—from accomplishing all but the most immediate short-term goals. The US-led UN intervention in Somalia demonstrates this. The operation accomplished its noble objective of breaking the stranglehold of warlords who were impeding the flow of food and humanitarian supplies to the population and thereby averting a greater human catastrophe. Yet the operation will forever be associated with the image of US Army rangers being dragged through the streets of Mogadishu and the downing of two US Black Hawk helicopters in a notorious confrontation sparked by an unsuccessful US attempt to capture the Somali warlord, General Mohamed Farrah Aidid. In consequence, the Clinton administration was induced to pull US forces out of the country and to reconsider its general commitment to armed humanitarian intervention. Post-operation US public opinion polls indicated that Americans overwhelmingly believed that the Somali operation had failed: "Soldiers were seen as having died in a futile and losing exercise" (Johnson and Tierney 2006, 3, 225). The negative fallout from the US effort in Somalia was sufficient to prevent intervention shortly thereafter in Rwanda to stop a genocidal slaughter of monumental proportions.

At the other extreme, asymmetries challenged the United States when, by playing to its advantages, it appears to have accomplished its goals—in Kosovo, in 1999, when NATO relied principally on air power to press Serbian forces to loosen their grip on the province. In fact, the NATO victory was a tribute to favorable conditions. The United States and its NATO allies capitalized successfully on an indigenous Albanian population that welcomed foreign intervention, Serbian use of *conventional* tactics, Russia's withdrawal of support for Serbia, a credible threat of ground invasion that presented Serbian leaders with a realistic prospect of defeat, and a Serbian public that was quick to blame its leadership for the inflicted hardships (Byman and Waxman 2000; Daalder and O'Hanlon 2000; Lambeth 2001). Even then, the victory was limited, again, in critical respects. NATO's reliance on air power allowed Serbian security forces to evade destruction by hiding and dispersing and to intensify their war of terror on Kosovo's ethnic Albanian citizens, furthering their mass exodus from the country (Daalder and O'Hanlon 2000, 210–212). It also gave local allies a free hand to pursue their own agenda. By carrying the burden of the ground war, the Kosovo Liberation Army positioned its members to take charge in the province and chart their own course. A more tenuous situation existed in Bosnia-Herzegovina, where Bosniaks, Croats, and Serbs feuded violently in the early 1990s over control of Bosnia—horrifically manifest in the genocidal Serbian "ethnic cleansing" campaign. With the signing of the US-brokered Dayton Accords, which divided Bosnia between a Muslim-Croat Federation and a Serb Republic, the intervening parties still had to contend with the self-protective conflict that continued among the ethnic communities: "The accords established a cease-fire in which the war continued by other means, and none had renounced the resort to violence to achieve those goals" (Woodward 1999, 97). For that matter, almost fifteen years after the signing of the 1995 accords, thousands of European Union peacekeepers were required in the country to help maintain a fragile peace that was threatened by the accusations, suspicions, and political goals of the vying parties. Identities hardened, populations relocated to enforce a de facto partitioning of the country, and the Serb Republic stoked succession fears by trying to grab power at the expense of the national government.[74]

The challenges of asymmetric conflict arise, in fact, whenever a country seeks to impose its will on another that can capitalize on its favorable military capabilities and political or psychological position. This is illustrated by Israel's 2006 operation in Lebanon. The Israeli military sought a cheap and easy victory over Hezbollah forces by relying on air power to destroy Hezbollah's arms caches and rocket launchers and by destroying portions of the Lebanese roads and bridges that facilitated Hezbollah's military operations in southern Lebanon. Nonetheless, by relying on air power rather than risk Israeli troop casualties in a ground assault, Israel was never able to counter Hezbollah's tactics. These included hiding personnel and weapons within the civilian population, advertising the destruction of the civilian infrastructure and civilian casualties to bring pressure on Israel to halt the violence, using the violence to galvanize support at home, and playing for time to emerge "victorious" simply by surviving the assault. Testifying to asymmetric challenges, the Israeli government withdrew from Lebanon after failing to achieve even its stated military goals of clearing Hezbollah from southern Lebanon, destroying Hezbollah's rocketry, and halting the flow of illicit arms to the militants.

Certainly, the lessons learned in Lebanon helped the Israeli government in late 2008 when it invaded Gaza to stop the rocket fire, this time from Hamas militants. Whereas Israel had tried in Lebanon to defeat the insurgents from the air and to avoid a massive and costly ground invasion, the Israeli military moved en masse into Gaza, on the ground and in the air. It targeted the Hamas leadership and its governing and welfare infrastructure, engaged Hamas fighters, destroyed the tunnels that Hamas used to funnel military supplies into Gaza, and cleared border areas from which Hamas launched rockets. Yet, again, Israel's operation was—at best—a limited success. Damage to the local infrastructure and civilian casualties remained high, and Israel failed to achieve its maximum military goals, let alone its stated political goal of ending Hamas's leadership within Gaza. The disappointing results in Gaza and Lebanon were likely preordained inasmuch as Israel was on its own in hostile territory and could not look to the nominal host governments for support: neither the Palestinian Authority nor the fragile Lebanese government—despite their concerns about a militant challenge to the government—had the political resources and military power to confront the militias. Thus, Israel's efforts to pressure these governments to reign in the militants would likely fail and were potentially counterproductive—if provoking political or military confrontations that these governments would lose (Lebovic 2007, 121).

This is not to say that intervening powers are always defeated in asymmetric conflicts. Not every asymmetric conflict is a "battle with Hanoi"—a fight against an adversary that embraces millions of deaths and a multi-decade struggle to achieve nonnegotiable objectives. To the contrary, in the battle for Kosovo, Serbia's president capitulated relatively easily. In Afghanistan, the United States managed to drive the Taliban quickly from power and install a Western-leaning, secular government in its place, which held to power under challenging conditions. In Lebanon, Israel killed large numbers of Hezbollah fighters, cleared many others from the Israeli border, destroyed a large stock of Hezbollah rockets, and convinced Hezbollah's leader, perhaps, that the costs of provoking Israel outweigh the benefits (Kreps 2007, 75). In the aftermath of the conflict, the Lebanon front remained remarkably quiet despite Hezbollah's ample supply of rockets and temptation, in late 2008, to open up a second front to support Hamas in Gaza. In 2009, Hezbollah fared relatively poorly in national elections, partly in response to the Lebanese public's fear of the consequences, demonstrated in 2006, of allowing the group to operate outside the state. Likewise, the Israeli operation in Gaza was somewhat successful, measured by narrow military standards (for instance, Hamas rocket attacks declined significantly in number) and broader political criteria (a disillusioned Palestinian public increasingly blamed Hamas for losses and sacrifices endured).[75] Similarly, in Bosnia and Kosovo, intervention forces did stop the killing and brought some measure of political stability to these troubled vestiges of the former Yugoslavia.

But, success in *any* given asymmetric conflict is not best judged by asking, Who won and who lost? Instead, success must be assessed by asking, In what sense, and for how long? The harsh reality in these conflicts is that progress comes at an unexpectedly high price; inevitably falls short of the intervening power's initial goals; requires that the intervening power innovate, temporize, and accept tradeoffs across military, political, and economic goals (as solutions to problems create new problems); and carries a risk of trapping the intervening power in a lengthy conflict with no discernible exit. Although the United States has the resources, in principle, to accomplish its goals, it is inclined to under-invest in these conflicts given their relatively paltry stakes. One implication, then, is that the United States might well need to settle in Afghanistan for a "resolution" that leaves Taliban elements in control of parts of the country.

The intervening power can improve its performance with time: the US military did learn lessons in Iraq that were applicable to future engagements, including Afghanistan, as indicated by the new emphasis on stability operations in US war planning. In the closing months of the Bush administration, the US Army released *Stability Operations* (Field Manual 3-07), which situated military stability operations in the "broader context of United States Government reconstruction and stabilization efforts" and recognized that "military forces have to operate with the other instruments of national power to forge unity of effort through a whole government approach" (2008, vi, vii). The Defense Department also released a policy directive (the DOD Directive for Irregular Warfare) that placed "irregular war" on an equal standing with conventional combat in recognition that "more and more adversaries have realized it's better to take [the United States] in an asymmetric fashion."[76] Secretary of Defense Gates echoed the theme in warning that the greatest US threats now come not from states but from those who evade state control, that is, insurgents and extremists who will not play to traditional US advantages and strategies of war.[77]

By implication, the new awareness and progressive policy shifts tend, nevertheless, to understate the profound challenges to the US military as it struggles to find the optimal mix between the irregular and the conventional in preparing for future combat. It is wrong to suggest that the resulting bureaucratic struggles boil down to battles between forward thinkers and a crusty old guard. The fact is that innovators themselves rely on the past to predict the future, when the "next war" might assume any number of novel forms that could leave the United States struggling to achieve an appropriate balance in effort or struggling to employ military capabilities that are ill suited or undersupplied for the task at hand. A former Air Force Secretary has a point—albeit exaggerated for emphasis—when he insists that "our national interests are being reduced to becoming the armed custodians in two nations, Afghanistan and Iraq."[78] Much can be learned from the facts of internal policy debates—if not the fact of an internal debate—over how the military should organize and prepare itself to go forward. Illustrating this is the contentious Pentagon debate over the lessons to be learned from Israel's 2006 war in Lebanon between counterinsurgency advocates and those who highlighted Hezbollah's success employing rockets, antitank weapons, and antiship missiles against Israeli targets (which, in their view, begged for a US response that included deploying expensive, next-generation combat systems).[79] Obviously, these proponents have a bureaucratic agenda that might distort service priorities. They are correct, however, that a US military that is prepared for counterinsurgency might pay a price in other contingencies.[80]

The doctrinal changes also tend to understate the interrelated political, economic, and military challenges posed in asymmetric conflict. In these conflicts, the United States will find itself battling irregular forces in the streets or jungles of a besieged or failing state and expending great effort, perhaps, to drive a wedge between an insurgency and its supportive population. But this is only the beginning. In such conflicts, the United States will struggle, in all likelihood, to achieve or sustain progress in combat, to contain the spread of the conflict to adjacent states, to mediate disputes between various US "allies" (and move them to concede personal and political interests for broader national purposes), to acquire local support for (and fight rising local opposition toward) the US-led mission, to build national institutions, to pull a host government reluctantly into the war effort, and to do all of this while convincing a disbelieving US public and legislature that the gains to be had are worth the enormous costs. These challenges to the United States in asymmetric conflict cannot be overcome merely by modifying military doctrine, improving military training, or adopting more efficient procurement practices.

Thus, the big lesson of Vietnam and Iraq, insofar as there is one, is at once simple and complicated: policymakers and professionals who address the challenges of asymmetric or irregular warfare must not lose sight of the "asymmetries of conflict" that redefine the essential question in US military operations. The question is not whether the United States can defeat a given adversary; instead, it is whether the United States can accomplish its political, economic, and military goals by securing leverage over a changing variety of contending parties before US capabilities and resolve are exhausted. For this very reason, US leaders must assess carefully whether a particular military operation is necessary when considering US stakes, wide-ranging costs, unanticipated problems, and the US will to persevere through recurring disappointment. If choosing to employ force, US leaders must understand that "less is more." Ambitious goals bring higher costs, disabling problem interdependencies, unexpected results, and a greater risk of failure. Indeed, a liability of pursuing these goals is that they are difficult to narrow: a more modest mission is not necessarily viable or sustainable once the United States is heavily involved in a conflict that has increased the welfare and security needs of the local population, heightened host-government dependence on US resources and assistance, raised popular hopes for a better future, widened the fault lines of a society, and altered local power balances by empowering new leaders and groups. Then, the United States cannot easily withdraw from the conflict or reduce its commitment. Lower-cost options might promise little return on an investment or create bigger problems that will beg the United States to reengage, from a weaker military and political position, at some point in the future.

The solution is not for the United States to avoid military action entirely, nor for the United States always to start small. An inadequate commitment can set the stage for a mission to fail, and even seemingly modest operations invite unexpected setbacks and challenges. The fact is that the United States is likely poised initially for military action when relatively uninformed about the target country's governing institutions and unable to judge the full dimensions of the task at hand. US policymakers must try hard, then, to understand the potential pitfalls ahead, to consider fallback options, to plan operations with a realistic sense of what can (and cannot) be achieved, and to mobilize the military, economic, and political resources that are needed to ensure mission success. That US policymakers ignored these injunctions in the prelude to intervention is perhaps the most important lesson that emerges from the long and costly wars in Vietnam and Iraq.

Notes

CHAPTER 1: Introduction

1. Quoted in McCrisken 2007, 159.

2. Peter Baker, "Bush Prods Vietnamese President on Human Rights and Openness," *Washington Post*, June 23, 2007, A2.

3. Historical connections that are obvious to some policymakers fail to impress others, and a single analogy can provoke or reinforce any variety of conclusions and policy recommendations. Because the past is a deficient guide to the future, it is unsurprising that Santayana's precept is equally persuasive, in its opposite form: policymakers who remember history are prone to make the opposite mistakes (Jervis 1976).

4. Studies of *asymmetric warfare* focus on "avoiding the enemy's strength—his main fighting force—while striking at outposts and logistical support from unexpected directions" (Nagl 2005, 15). This understanding informs my thinking about *asymmetric conflict,* which I define differently than other scholars do. For instance, Paul (1994, 3) defines an asymmetric conflict as "a conflict in which two states with unequal power resources confront each other on the battlefield," and Arreguín-Toft (2005, xi) defines asymmetric conflicts as "those in which one side is possessed of overwhelming power with respect to its adversary." My definition builds on the idea that asymmetric conflicts are fought politically and psychologically as well as militarily—that parties win by playing to their nonmilitary strengths and by depleting the political will of militarily stronger opponents (Mack 1975). Hence, by my usage, asymmetric conflicts are those in which "a party offsets the military or economic strengths of another party by exploiting its military or economic vulnerabilities or by capitalizing on political, psychological, or sociological conditions." In this sense, asymmetric warfare is a type of asymmetric conflict.

5. In methodological terms, the analysis requires the use of a "most-similar case" design that assumes that the conflicts are quite similar but differ in their outcomes and a key independent variable. That design is useful for explaining changes over time in the success of the United States at influencing key parties. Conversely, a "most-different case" design that assumes that the conflicts—despite their prominent differences—produced the same outcomes is useful for understanding the limits of US capability in influencing adversary leaders or various third parties (including indigenous populations, societal groups, outside states, and the host government).

In applying these designs to the Vietnam and Iraq conflicts, this book recognizes that each conflict is composed of multiple cases to produce longitudinal and cross-sectional variation on key variables. On these designs, see George and Bennett 2004.

6. Baker, "Bush Prods Vietnamese President on Human Rights and Openness," A2.

7. Whereas journalists and cameramen traveled freely to the front lines of the Vietnam conflict—bringing war coverage, in its gory details, to the front pages of newspapers and broadcasts of the nightly news—journalists were restricted from distributing photographs of the dead and wounded in Iraq. Michael Kamber and Tim Arango, "4,000 US Combat Deaths, and Just a Handful of Images," *New York Times*, July 26, 2008, 1.

8. This is not to say that the administration was sanguine about the costs and prospects of victory. On this, see Downes 2009.

9. For an insightful comparison of the assorted claims in these works, see Jervis 2008–9.

10. Most of these differences draw from Record and Terrill 2004, which discusses them at length.

11. President Dwight Eisenhower was responsible for the domino metaphor.

12. As Record (2005, 6) puts it, "The problem with the invocation of Munich is its suggestion that aggressor states are inherently insatiable and that failure to act against them automatically endangers US security."

13. Sam Coates, "Weak Responses Led to 9/11, Cheney Asserts: Inadequate Retaliation Seen in 7 Cases," *Washington Post*, October 4, 2005, A18.

14. Just as easily, then, the seemingly effortless US success in driving Iraqi forces from Kuwait is taken as an expression of unlimited US military power—of sufficient magnitude that other countries would not dare challenge US power. On this message from Vietnam and vindication in Desert Storm, see Karnow 1997, 15–16.

15. Quoted in Massimo Calabresi, "Bush's Risky Vietnam Gambit," *Time*, August 23, 2007.

16. Michael Abramowitz, "Bush's Comments in Israel Fuel Anger: Linking Nazis, Iran Seen as Jab at Obama," *Washington Post*, May 16, 2008, A8.

17. Henry A. Kissinger, "Lessons for an Exit Strategy," *Washington Post*, August 12, 2005, A19.

18. Ann Scott Tyson and Ellen Knickmeyer, "US Signals Spring Start for Pullout," *Washington Post*, July 28, 2005, A18.

19. Robin Wright and Ellen Knickmeyer, "US Lowers Sights on What Can Be Achieved in Iraq," *Washington Post*, August 14, 2005, A1.

20. Ellen Knickmeyer, "Early Pullout Unlikely in Iraq," *Washington Post*, August 11, 2005, A1.

21. Quoted in Chris Baldwin, "Putin Says Russia Threatened by 'Unipolar World,'" *Reuters India*, November 5, 2007, available at http://in.reuters.com/article/worldNews/idINIndia-30329020071104, accessed September 15, 2009.

22. The practice can also ignore inequalities in capability of seemingly well-matched opponents. Despite apparent "bipolarity," a US-Soviet conventional war would have amounted to a battle of (rough) equals only in Europe. As Wagner (1993, 79) observes, "The distinctive feature of the postwar distribution of power . . . was not that two states were more powerful than the others . . . but that one state, the Soviet Union, occupied in peacetime a position of near-dominance on the Eurasian continent."

23. These debates have centered on a large variety of issues including whether long-range bombers substitute for aircraft carriers, light mobile forces substitute for boots on the ground, pre-positioned supplies substitute for forward bases in a combat zone, and attrition strategies meant to inflict heavy body counts substitute for a "hearts and minds" strategy of providing security and benefits to a population to undercut an insurgency. Some of these controversies have major ramifications for the kinds of weapons the US military will acquire. The Navy, for one, has considered the relative advantage of investing in large (though arguably vulnerable) aircraft carriers, smaller and faster vessels, amphibious capability, offshore pre-positioning of equipment for rapid and self-sustaining intervention, and quieter diesel submarines and littoral ships for operating in shallow waters (for instance, the Persian Gulf).

24. Bob Woodward, "Outmaneuvered and Outranked, Military Chiefs Became Outsiders," *Washington Post*, September 8, 2008, A1.

25. Even these numbers exaggerate available combat forces given their competing use in defensive operations.

26. This was due partly to logistical challenges in a dangerous security environment. Thom Shanker, "Pulling Out Combat Troops Would Still Leave Most Forces in Iraq," *New York Times*, December 10, 2006, 18. The five additional combat brigades that were introduced in Iraq as part of the 2007 surge also included support personnel.

27. These were in great demand in Afghanistan due to its poor infrastructure and harsh and inaccessible terrain. Ann Scott Tyson, "Support Sought in Afghan Mission: US Generals Want 20,000 New Troops," *Washington Post*, October 29, 2008, A1; Greg Jaffe, "In Remote Afghan Province, Mullen Finds Daunting Need," *Washington Post*, May 1, 2009, A1.

28. Ann Scott Tyson, "Experts Warn of Troops' Loss of Logistical Support," *Washington Post*, March 8, 2009, A14.

29. Lawrence J. Korb and Sean E. Duggan, "Out of Iraq in 10 Months or Less," *Washington Post*, November 22, 2008, A14.

30. These negotiations are complicated further because states have strong incentives to shift the burden (of enforcement or resource mobilization) to others or to "defect" from the coalition to capitalize on political and trade opportunities that are created with the target state by its isolation.

31. Craig Whitlock, "Germany Rebuffs US on Troops in Afghanistan," *Washington Post*, February 2, 2008, A10.

32. Peter Spiegel, "Gates Says NATO Force Unable to Fight Guerrillas," *Los Angeles Times*, January 16, 2008, A1. On the intra-NATO disputes, see also Karen DeYoung,

"Allies Feel Strain of Afghan War," *Washington Post*, January 15, 2008, A1. In one well-publicized incident, US and German military officials engaged in charges and countercharges when US aircraft killed large numbers of civilians in a strike that was called in by German ground units. US officials questioned both the necessity of the strikes, given the actual threat and evidence available to German troops, as well as their failure to travel to the scene of the attacks to handle the political fallout. The attack embroiled Germany in controversy at home and abroad and threatened alliance cohesion. Frank Jordans and Jason Straziuso, "Germany, U.S. Differ in Airstrike Assessment," *Washington Post*, September 7, 2009, A6; Craig Whitlock, "In Germany, Political Turmoil over Ordering of Airstrike," *Washington Post*, September 8, 2009, A1.

33. At the time, the rules of engagement for the US command were actually *more* permissive than the rules employed by the NATO command: whereas NATO allowed air strikes only with "overwhelming threat," the US command permitted attacks for "anticipatory self-defense." US forces were divided between the 14,000 under NATO and the 19,000 under US command. On rules of engagement and tension between the NATO and US Commands, see Candace Rondeaux and Karen DeYoung, "US Teams to Reinvestigate Deadly Strike in Afghanistan," *Washington Post*, September 9, 2008, A1.

34. Adam B. Ellick, 2009, "U.N. Official Calls for Review of American Raids," *New York Times*, June 13, 2008, 6.

35. Posen notes that "the Royal Navy could deliver an army many places around the globe, but the army's journey inland was usually difficult and slow" (2003, 9).

36. For an unusual, skeptical view of the contribution of air power to the 1991 Gulf War, see Press 2001.

37. Effective attacks on mobile, hidden, leadership, or infrastructure (for example, nuclear) targets depend on the quantity and quality of available intelligence, if only to verify and assure target destruction (Ellis and Kiefer 2004, 91–93).

38. In this sense, the deficiencies of US military capabilities draw from their "dispersal," that is, the relative priority given to various US global objectives and commitments.

39. Ann Scott Tyson, "Army's Next Crop of Generals Forged in Counterinsurgency," *Washington Post*, May 15, 2008, A4.

40. Ann Scott Tyson, "Standard Warfare May Be Eclipsed by Nation-Building," *Washington Post*, October 5, 2008, A16.

41. This speaks to a broad tendency of individuals to defer to analogies, past lessons and practices, and available reference points when planning for a future that might actually bring novelty and surprise (Jervis 1976).

42. Quoted in Josh White, "Defense Secretary Urges Military to Mold Itself to Fight Iraq-Style Wars," *Washington Post*, May 14, 2008, A4.

43. Josh White, "Gates Sees Terrorism Remaining Enemy No. 1," *Washington Post*, July 31, 2008, A1.

44. Greg Jaffe, "A Single-Minded Focus on Dual Wars," *Washington Post*, May 15, 2009, A1.

45. US preparedness suffers, in critical respects, when budgetary resources are used to fund short-term preparedness rather than to procure better or more numerous weapons; capabilities are acquired for immediate contingencies that have limited application in others; intense training takes a toll on military equipment, personnel, and stocks of spare parts, ammunition, and fuel; and inefficiencies are introduced by bottlenecks in procuring equipment, neglect of economies of scale, and claims on scarce resources.

46. Ann Scott Tyson, "Military Is Ill-Prepared for Other Conflicts," *Washington Post*, March 19, 2007, A1. A conscripted army brings additional problems in social upheaval, equity concerns (given the uneven demographics of draftees), and strife that ensues from involuntary service.

47. Quoted in Ann Scott Tyson and Josh White, "Strained Army Extends Tours to 15 Months," *Washington Post*, April 12, 2007, A1.

48. Quoted in Ann Scott Tyson, "Debate Grows on Pause in Troop Cuts," *Washington Post*, February 2, 2008, A11.

CHAPTER 2: Leveraging the Adversary's Forces

1. The lessons for devising US strategy were admittedly complicated, as reflected in post-mortem disputes on the actual effectiveness of bombing in World War II. Drawing from the conclusions of the postwar United States Strategic Bombing Survey, it is often surmised that bombing did not work, and was actually counterproductive socially and psychologically.

2. It stressed that communist encroachments anywhere in the world would be met by all-out retaliatory attacks against the Soviet Union.

3. Some Air Force officials concluded that aerial pounding pressed the North Koreans into accepting a negotiated armistice (Clodfelter 1989, 25).

4. Similarly, when the Nixon administration halted the bombing of Laos and North Vietnam with the Paris Peace Agreement of 1973, it shifted the focus to Cambodia. Whereas US aircraft (B-52s and fighter bombers) dropped over 50,000 tons of bombs on Cambodia in all of 1972, they dropped the same amount on Cambodia in *each* of various months that followed the agreement. By the end of US bombing in August 1973, the US had dropped tonnages on Cambodia, in the prior six months, over 60 percent higher than the 160,000 tons dropped on Japan during all of World War II (Shawcross 1987, 297).

5. North Vietnam itself depended heavily on inflows of Soviet and Chinese weapons and supplies (Record 2007, 50–53).

6. The terms of the agreement echoed the terms that North Vietnam appeared willing to accept as early as 1967. On this, see Herring 1986, 169.

7. This is not meant to imply that the principles of counterinsurgency theory reduce to a "hearts and minds" approach. Counterinsurgency theory has divided historically over whether theorists emphasize the manipulation of popular preferences (a "hearts and minds" approach) or the distribution of costs and benefits,

which assumes that rational peasants make self-interested decisions (Long 2006, 21–34).

8. Nor should the United States have expected to have reached the crossover point: "U.S. firepower, lavishly employed though it was, never came close to competing with either the communist birth rate or Hanoi's willingness to expend entire generations of young men on behalf of Vietnam's forcible reunification under communist auspices" (Record 1998, 80).

9. In 1967, the number of North Vietnamese regulars in the South was less than a quarter of the number of Viet Cong guerrillas (Pape 1996, 191).

10. McNamara's departure was announced prior to Tet.

11. It should be remembered that the disastrous French engagement a decade and a half earlier at Dien Bien Phu—forever associated with losing battles in lost causes—involved only a small fraction of French forces in Vietnam and produced French losses in numbers substantially below those incurred by the victorious Viet Minh.

12. The Vietcong would also heavily recruit—by one estimate at a rate of 85,000 guerrillas a year (Hennessy 1997, 136).

13. These included the declining number of US air strikes adjacent to South Vietnamese hamlets and confrontations between government and communist forces within populated rural areas, the increasing responsibility of South Vietnamese popular forces (mainly recruited locally) for security in the countryside, and the growing number of these forces involved in successful offensive operations (Thayer 1985, 132, 156–167).

14. The pacification effort brought with it an elaborate system of regularized data collection on demographics, economic conditions, popular attitudes, and communist political and military activity.

15. Henry Kissinger, "New Premises in Iraq: Prospects for Withdrawal Have to Be Viewed through the Lens of Progress," *Washington Post,* July 31, 2008, A19.

16. Henry Kissinger, "Lesson of Vietnam: Hope for A Successful Withdrawal from Iraq Could Succumb to Bitter Politics at Home," *Washington Post,* June 11, 2007, A17.

17. For a summary assessment and supporting documents, see US Congress 2007.

18. Quoted in Eric Schmitt, "Pentagon Contradicts General on Iraq Occupation Force's Size," *New York Times,* February 28, 2003, 1.

19. This is not to say that the Iraqi military could ably perform a task that had been the responsibility of Saddam Hussein's secret police.

20. The United States launched a major operation to clear Samarra in October 2004 (Wright et al. 2008, 44) because earlier attempts failed when insurgents regained control of the city once US forces departed.

21. John F. Burns, "Militants Said to Flee before U.S. Offensive," *New York Times,* June 23, 2007, 1.

22. Thomas E. Ricks, "Situation Called Dire in West Iraq," *Washington Post,* September 11, 2006, A1.

23. The Islamic State of Iraq was pronounced in October 2006 by Abu Ayyub al-Masri, who became the leader of al-Qaeda in Iraq with the death of Abu Musab al-Zarqawi.

24. Quoted in Karl Vick, "Insurgent Alliance is Fraying in Fallujah," *Washington Post*, October 13, 2004, A1.

25. Popular sentiment had turned against US forces for their heavy-handed military tactics in Anbar province (for instance, Fallujah) and mistreatment of the population. In one survey, most Iraqi respondents indicated their view of al-Sadr had improved; indeed, the percentage of people expressing at least some support for al-Sadr (77 percent) was greater than for any other prominent Iraqi figure including Ayatollah al-Sistani (at 70 percent, although al-Sistani received the most "strong support"). Al-Sadr was widely seen within Iraq as a national unifying force. Iraq Centre for Research and Strategic Studies, April 20–29, 2004, available at www.irqcrss.org.

26. Dexter Filkins, "Iraqi Cleric's Militia in Sadr City Promises to Hand Over Arms," *New York Times*, October 10, 2004, 1. See also Ricks 2006, 335–338; Wright et al. 2008, 39–41.

27. Joshua Partlow, "Mahdi Army, Not Al-Qaeda, is Enemy No. 1 in Western Baghdad," *Washington Post*, July 16, 2007, A1; Sabrina Tavernise, 2008, "Shiite Militia in Baghdad Sees its Power Ebb," *New York Times*, July 27, 2008, 1.

28. There, the British had achieved success with softer counterinsurgency methods (including foot patrols) tested previously in Northern Ireland.

29. Karen DeYoung and Thomas E. Ricks, "As British Leave, Basra Deteriorates," *Washington Post*, August 7, 2007, A1.

30. Sabrina Tavernise, "Relations Sour between Shiites and Iraq Militia," *New York Times*, October 12, 2007, 1.

31. On these contradictions, see, for example, Thomas E. Ricks and Sudarsan Raghavan, "Sadr Back in Iraq, U.S. Generals Say," *Washington Post*, May 25, 2007, A12; Sudarsan Raghavan, "Iraq's Sadr Overhauls His Tactics," *Washington Post*, May 20, 2007, A1.

32. For the Vietcong, violence served revenue raising and recruitment for the broader war effort; for elements of the Mahdi Army, expropriation and revenue raising appeared to have become an end in itself.

33. By comparison, 95 percent of Shiites held a favorable view of Sistani. Poll conducted September 1–4 on a nationwide sample. WorldPublicOpinion.org. Program on International Policy Attitudes. September 27, 2006.

34. Quoted in Ann Scott Tyson, "New Strategy for War Stresses Iraqi Politics: U.S. Aims to Oust Sectarians from Key Roles," *Washington Post*, May 23, 2007, A1. See Ricks 2006, 348.

35. Joshua Partlow, "Insurgents Hit Bridge North of Baghdad," *Washington Post*, June 3, 2007, A14.

36. For example, Iraqi forces "in training" were combined with trained forces in a subsequent report that listed both as "on duty" and later as "on hand." A later report

contained a figure that was 100,000 smaller for the number of Iraqi Security Forces "trained/on hand." Karen DeYoung, "Iraq War's Statistics Proving Fleeting," *Washington Post*, March 19, 2007, A1.

37. The points of contention include the dependence on estimates of the death rate prior to the US attack in 2003, the sample used to generate the estimates, and the veracity of the survey responses. See Lila Guterman, "Researchers Who Rushed into Print a Study of Iraqi Civilian Deaths Now Wonder Why It Was Ignored," *Chronicle of Higher Education*, January 27, 2005, available at http://iraqmortality.org/researchers-wonder-why-it-was-ignored, accessed September 15, 2009.

38. The study estimated with 95 percent certainty that the actual number fell between 104,000 and 223,000. David Brown and Joshua Partlow, "New Estimate of Violent Deaths among Iraqis is Lower," *Washington Post*, January 10, 2008, A18.

39. DeYoung, "Iraq War's Statistics Proving Fleeting," A1. The secretiveness and subterfuge in the disseminating of the data impugns or supports their veracity depending on one's inclination to believe the "official spokesperson" or the "anonymous source."

40. Lawrence K. Altman and Richard A. Oppel Jr., "W.H.O. Says Iraq Civilian Death Toll Higher than Cited," *New York Times*, January 10, 2008, 14.

41. DeYoung, "Iraq War's Statistics Proving Fleeting," A1.

42. Andrew Buncombe and Patrick Cockburn, "Iraq's Death Squads: On the Brink of Civil War," *The Independent*, February 26, 2006, available at www.independent.co.uk/news/world/middle-east/iraqs-death-squads-on-the-brink-of-civil-war-467784.html, accessed September 6, 2009.

43. Burns, "Militants Said to Flee before U.S. Offensive," 1.

44. According to a subsequent Army Inspector General's report. See Ricks 2006, 195.

45. These numbers are obtained from the Iraq Index. Tracking Variables of Reconstruction and Security in Post-Saddam Iraq, available at www.brookings.edu/saban/iraq-index.aspx, accessed September 6, 2009. US troop strength continued to increase into October 2007, when US forces reached 171,000.

46. On the Baghdad security plan, see Robinson 2008, 119–140.

47. Thom Shanker and Michael R. Gordon, "G.I.'s in Iraq Open Major Offensive against Al-Qaeda," *New York Times*, June 17, 2007, 1.

48. Ann Scott Tyson, "Military Reports Slow Progress in Securing Baghdad," *Washington Post*, June 5, 2007, A11.

49. David S. Cloud and Damien Cave, "Commanders Say Push in Baghdad Is Short of Goal," *New York Times*, June 4, 2007, 1.

50. Tyson, "Military Reports Slow Progress in Securing Baghdad," A11.

51. Ann Scott Tyson, "Iraqis Join U.S. in Fighting Al-Qaeda," *Washington Post*, June 30, 2007, A15.

52. John Ward Anderson, "Baghdad's Green Zone Is a Haven Under Siege," *Washington Post*, June 7, 2007, A21.

53. David Finkel, "Unit's Mission: Survive 4 Miles to Remember Fallen Comrade," *Washington Post,* July 9, 2007, A1.

54. "A Bloody Month," *Washington Post,* July 8, 2007, A9.

55. Ann Scott Tyson and John Ward Anderson, "Attacks on U.S. Troops in Iraq Grow in Lethality, Complexity," *Washington Post,* June 3, 2007, A1.

56. By June 2007, al-Qaeda–linked units that seemed unable to bring their suicide bomb vehicles into Baghdad—with roadblocks and checkpoints and a visible and active US military presence—appeared to have compensated by operating bomb factories within Baghdad. John Ward Anderson and Salih Dehima, "Offensive Targets Al-Qaeda in Iraq," *Washington Post,* June 19, 2007, A1.

57. Megan Greenwell, "Blast Kills at Least 25 in Long-Secure Baghdad Neighborhood," *Washington Post,* July 26, 2007, A15.

58. Richard A. Oppel and Ali Adeeb, "Attacker Kills 4 Sunni Sheiks who Aided U.S.," *New York Times,* June 26, 2007, 1.

59. In May and June, an average of 443 unidentified bodies were recovered in the capital; in July 2007, 407 unidentified corpses were found in Baghdad and taken to the morgue. In June, 90 unidentified bodies were found in provinces outside Baghdad, compared to 39 in January 2007. Although the June figures marked a reduction from the four prior months, a monthly average of 174 bodies was found in outlying provinces in the four months between January and June. "Ups and Downs in Iraq Violence," *Washington Post,* August 5, 2007, A18.

60. "Unabated Violence," *Washington Post,* June 14, 2007, A20.

61. Thomas E. Ricks, "Iraq Push Revives Criticism of Force Size," *Washington Post,* June 23, 2007, A1. Indeed, Al-Qaeda–linked groups had reinfiltrated Fallujah, where they were carrying out an assassination and bombing campaign. Burns, "Militants Said to Flee before U.S. Offensive," 1.

62. Megan Greenwell and Sudarsan Raghavan, "Attacks Across Baghdad Kill at Least 25," *Washington Post,* July 16, 2007, A11.

63. Joshua Partlow and John Ward Anderson, "Troops Pushing through Insurgent Area," *Washington Post,* June 22, 2007, A1.

64. Sudarsan Raghavan, "In the Land of the Blood Feuds," *Washington Post,* August 10, 2007, A1; Megan Greenwell, "Sporadic Raids South of Baghdad Yield Little," *Washington Post,* August 28, 2007, A7.

65. Anderson and Dehima, "Offensive Targets Al-Qaeda in Iraq," A1.

66. Alexandra Zavis, "Iraqi Valley Proves Fertile Haven for Brutal Militants," *Los Angeles Times,* February 5, 2008, A1.

67. Burns, "Militants Said to Flee before U.S. Offensive," 1; Michael R. Gordon, "U.S. Seeks to Block Exits for Iraq Insurgents," *New York Times,* June 20, 2007, 1; John Ward Anderson, "Dozens of Insurgents Killed in Iraq Offensive," *Washington Post,* June 21, 2007, A18.

68. Joshua Partlow, "Troops in Diyala Face a Skilled, Flexible Foe," *Washington Post,* April 22, 2007, A1.

69. Tyson and Anderson, "Attacks on U.S. Troops in Iraq Grow in Lethality, Complexity," A1.

70. Megan Greenwell, " 'House Bombs' a Growing Risk for U.S. Troops," *Washington Post*, August 16, 2007, A8.

71. Thom Shanker, "Iraqi Bombers Thwart Efforts to Shield G.I.'s," *New York Times*, June 2, 2007, 1.

72. Tyson and Anderson, "Attacks on U.S. Troops in Iraq Grow in Lethality, Complexity," A1.

73. "The Deadly Month of May," *Washington Post*, June 3, 2007, A20.

74. These figures are from the congressional testimony of General David Petraeus in September 2007. See "A Difficult Comparison," *Washington Post*, September 25, 2007, A15.

75. Megan Greenwell and Dlovan Brwari, "Toll in N. Iraq Passes 250; Attack Is Deadliest of War," *Washington Post*, August 16, 2007, A1. Despite a decrease, from 396 in February to 134 in June, in deaths nationwide in mass casualty attacks (defined as killing at least twenty people), deaths in such attacks rose again in July 2007, to 378 deaths.

76. On the reliability of civilian casualty data, see Stephen Biddle, "The Iraq Data Debate: Civilian Casualties from 2006 to 2007," *Council on Foreign Relations Backgrounder*, September 28, 2007, available at www.cfr.org/publication/14295/#4, accessed September 15, 2009.

77. Data from Megan Greenwell, "Iraqi Deaths in Major Blasts Rose in July," *Washington Post*, August 4, 2007, A18.

78. See "A Difficult Comparison," A15. For 2007, the US military claimed overall that al-Qaeda engaged in 4,500 attacks that killed 3,870 people and wounded nearly 18,000. Karen DeYoung, "Papers Paint New Portrait of Iraq's Foreign Insurgents," *Washington Post*, January 21, 2008, A1.

79. Tyson and Anderson, "Attacks on U.S. Troops in Iraq Grow in Lethality, Complexity," *Washington Post*, June 3, 2007, A1.

80. Joshua Partlow, "Iraq Safer but Still Perilous at Year-End, Petraeus Says," *Washington Post*, December 30, 2007, A23.

81. Ann Scott Tyson, "Violence Declines Further in Iraq," *Washington Post*, October 1, 2008, A14.

82. Amit R. Paley, "Al-Qaeda in Iraq Leader May Be in Afghanistan," *Washington Post*, July 31, 2008, A1.

83. Amit R. Paley and Joshua Partlow, "Blast Kills 6 as Troops Hunt Iraqi Insurgents," *Washington Post*, January 10, 2008, A1.

84. Amit R. Paley, "Major Offensive Targets Insurgents," *Washington Post*, January 9, 2008, A11.

85. Associated Press, "U.S. and Iraqi Forces Launch Offensive," *New York Times*, July 29, 2008.

86. Ernesto Londoño, "Suicide Blast in Iraq Kills Three, Injures 19," *Washington Post*, April 21, 2009, A12.

87. Roughly two dozen female suicide-bombing attacks had occurred earlier in the year.

88. On this series of bombings and the use of female suicide bombers in Iraq, see Sudarsan Raghavan, "Four Women Kill Dozens in Suicide Blasts in Iraq," *Washington Post*, July 29, 2008, A1.

89. "Deaths Worldwide Decreased in 2008," *Washington Post*, May 1, 2009, A4.

90. Ernesto Londoño and Qais Mizher, "Attacks Across Baghdad Leave at Least 48 Dead, Scores Injured," *Washington Post*, April 30, 2009, A12; Ernesto Londoño, "U.S. Says Iraq Is Withholding Key Detainee," *Washington Post*, May 2, 2009, A9.

91. The Iraqi civilian death toll reached 447 in June 2009, nearly twice the figure for May 2009. Greg Jaffe, "Link Between Iraq Violence, Troops Withdrawals Considered," *Washington Post*, July 5, A14.

92. Mary Beth Sheridan, "U.S. Cedes Control Over Iraq's Once-Bloody 'Triangle of Death,'" *Washington Post*, October 24, 2008, A15.

93. John F. Burns and Alissa J. Rubin, "U.S. Arming Sunnis in Iraq to Battle Old Qaeda Allies," *Washington Post*, June 11, 2007, 1.

94. Anderson, "Dozens of Insurgents Killed in Iraq Offensive," A18.

95. Michael Gordon, "G.I.'s Forge Sunni Tie in Bid to Squeeze Militants," *New York Times*, July 6, 2007, 1.

96. Joshua Partlow, "For U.S. Unit in Baghdad, An Alliance of Last Resort," *Washington Post*, June 9, 2007, A1.

97. In practice, the United States appears to have armed some groups, accepted or promoted arms transfers from Iraqi security forces, and allowed insurgents to keep munitions as prizes of war. In any case, as these groups were incorporated into a de facto Iraqi security force, the issue was largely moot.

98. Quoted in Partlow, "For U.S. Unit in Baghdad, An Alliance of Last Resort," A1.

99. Thomas E. Ricks, "Deals in Iraq Make Friends of Enemies," *Washington Post*, July 20, 2007, A1.

100. John Ward Anderson, "Fallujah Bombing Targets Mourners of Tribal Figure," *Washington Post*, May 24, 2007, A12.

101. Ann Scott Tyson, "A Deadly Clash at Donkey Island," *Washington Post*, August 19, 2007, A1.

102. Richard A. Oppel Jr., "Fallujah's Calm is Seen as Fragile if U.S. Leaves," *New York Times*, August 19, 2007, 1.

103. "The Deadly Month of May," A20.

104. Joshua Partlow, "In Mosul, A Hopeful Partnership," *Washington Post*, February 24, 2008, A1.

105. Anthony Shadid and Saad Sarhan, "Peacemaking Event Is Attacked in Iraq," *Washington Post*, January 3, 2009, A9.

106. In fact, the success of the Awakening in Anbar produced a surge of al-Qaeda fighters into Sunni parts of Baghdad. Partlow, "For U.S. Unit in Baghdad, An Alliance of Last Resort," A1.

107. Alissa J. Rubin and Damien Cave, "In a Force for Iraqi Calm, Seeds of Conflict," *New York Times,* December 23, 2007, 1.

108. Erica Goode and Mudhafer Al-Husaini, "U.S. and Iraqi Officials Try to Reassure Citizen Patrols about Transfer," *New York Times,* September 9, 2008, 8.

109. Ernesto Londoño, "For U.S. and Sunni Allies, a Turning Point," *Washington Post,* September 30, 2008, A12; see also Mary Beth Sheridan, "A Delicate Changing of the Guard," *Washington Post,* October 2, 2008, A17.

110. Jaffe, "Link between Iraq Violence, Troop Withdrawals Considered," A14.

111. Walter Pincus, "U.S. Unsure about the Future of Iraq's 'Sons,'" *Washington Post,* March 31, 2008, A17.

112. Erica Goode, "Friction Infiltrates Sunni Patrols on Safer Iraqi Streets," *New York Times,* September 23, 2008, 1.

113. Sudarsan Raghavan and Amit R. Paley, "Sunni Forces Losing Patience with U.S.," *Washington Post,* February 28, 2008, A1.

114. Erica Goode, "U.S. to Hand Over Security in Anbar to the Iraqis," *New York Times,* August 28, 2008, 14.

115. Sameer N. Yacoub, "Iraq: Government Takes Command of Sons of Iraq," *Time,* October 1, 2008.

116. Ernesto Londoño and Dlovan Brwari, "Iraqi Soldier Kills 2 U.S. Troops, Wounds 3," *Washington Post,* May 3, 2009, A14.

117. Mary Beth Sheridan, "U.S. Troops in Baghdad Take a Softer Approach," *Washington Post,* November 20, 2008, A1.

118. Quoted in Londoño, "For U.S. and Sunni Allies, a Turning Point," A12.

119. Megan Greenwell, "Fear Drives Baghdad's Housing Bust," *Washington Post,* September 21, 2008, A1.

120. Gian P. Gentile, "In the Middle of a Civil War," *Washington Post,* August 7, 2007, A13.

121. Damien Cave and Alissa J. Rubin, "Baghdad's Weary Start to Exhale as Security Improves," *New York Times,* November 20, 2007, 1.

122. Karen DeYoung, "Balkanized Homecoming," *Washington Post,* December 16, 2007, A1.

123. Partlow, "Troops in Diyala Face a Skilled, Flexible Foe," A1.

124. Kenneth H. Bacon and Kristele Younes, "Outside and Inside Iraq's Borders, a Forgotten Exodus," *Washington Post,* January 20, 2008, B2.

125. Alissa J. Rubin, "Shiite Refugees Feel Forsaken in Their Holy City," *New York Times,* October 19, 2007, 1.

126. Amit R. Paley and Walter Pincus, "U.S. Opens Site for Processing Iraqi Refugees," *Washington Post,* June 4, 2008, A12. Another international organization claimed that, as of March 2008, 2.4 million Iraqis had left the country and another 2.7 million remained internally displaced (Lischer 2008, 95).

127. Quoted in Partlow, "Mahdi Army, Not Al-Qaeda, Is Enemy No. 1 in Western Baghdad," A1.

128. Cloud and Cave, "Commanders Say Push in Baghdad Is Short of Goal," 1.

129. Iraqi Christians, numbering in the hundreds of thousands in the surrounding province, were caught in the middle. By October 2008, half the Christian population of Mosul had fled. Missy Ryan, "Iraq's Christians 'Sacrificial Lambs' as Attacks Mount," Reuters, October 19, 2008.

130. Sudarsan Raghavan, "Returnees Find a Capital Transformed," *Washington Post*, November 23, 2007, A1.

131. Cave and Rubin, "Baghdad's Weary Start to Exhale as Security Improves," 1.

132. Over 80 percent of the foreign refugees were former Baghdad residents, mostly Sunni (Lischer 2008, 102).

133. Sabrina Tavernise, "Fear Keeps Iraqis Out of Their Baghdad Homes," *New York Times*, August 24, 2008, 1.

134. On this score, the US military apparently warned the Iraqi government about using Iraqi troops for property evictions. Michael R. Gordon and Stephen Farrell, "Iraq Lacks Plan on the Return of Refugees, Military Says," *New York Times*, November 30, 2007, 1.

135. Raghavan, "Iraq's Sadr Overhauls His Tactics," A1.

136. Ricks and Raghavan, "Sadr Back in Iraq, U.S. Generals Say," A12.

137. John Ward Anderson and K. I. Ibrahim, "As Sunni Mosque Falls, Sadr Issues a Call," *Washington Post*, June 16, 2007, A17.

138. Raghavan, "Iraq's Sadr Overhauls His Tactics," A1.

139. Dan Murphy, "Samarra Shrine Attack: Less Incendiary Now?" *Christian Science Monitor*, June 14, 2007, 6.

140. See, for example, Alissa J. Rubin, "Shiite Rivalries Slash at Once Calm Iraqi City," *New York Times*, June 21, 2007, 1; Solomon Moore, "Ominous Signs Remain in City Run by Iraqis," *New York Times*, February 23, 2008, 1.

141. DeYoung and Ricks, "As British Leave, Basra Deteriorates," A1.

142. Quoted in Damien McElroy, "Moqtada al-Sadr Announces Ceasefire in Iraq," Telegraph.co.uk, August 30, 2007, available at www.telegraph.co.uk/news/worldnews/1561731/Moqtada-al-Sadr-announces-ceasefire-in-Iraq.html, accessed September 6, 2009.

143. Sudarsan Raghavan, "Shiite Contest Sharpens in Iraq," *Washington Post*, December 26, 2007, A1.

144. On the splits in the Sadrist movement and the composition of the "rogue" opposition, see Cochrane 2009, 23–31.

145. See Cochrane 2009, 34; Sudarsan Raghavan, "Sadr Extends Truce in Iraq," *Washington Post*, February 23, 2008, A1.

146. Sholnn Freeman and Sudarsan Raghavan, "Intense Fighting Erupts in Iraq," *Washington Post*, March 26, 2008, A1; James Glanz and Steven Lee Myers, "Assault by Iraq on Shiite Forces Stalls in Basra," *New York Times*, March 28, 2008, 1.

147. Sudarsan Raghavan and Sholnn Freeman, "U.S. Armor Forces Join Offensive in Baghdad against Sadr Militia," *Washington Post*, March 28, 2008, A1.

148. Sudarsan Raghavan and Ernesto Londoño, "Basra Assaults Exposed U.S., Iraqi Limits," *Washington Post*, April 4, 2008, A1. Other Iraqi sources place the

number of deserters at 1,300. See "Iraqi Troops Abandon Position," *New York Times*, April 18.

149. Karen DeYoung, "U.S. Has Little Influence, Few Options in Iraq's Volatile South," *Washington Post*, March 29, 2008, A11.

150. James Glanz and Stephen Farrell, "Crackdown on Militias Raises Stability Concerns," *New York Times*, April 8, 2008, 1.

151. James Glanz, "Iraqi Deaths Are on the Rise Again during Clashes with Militias," *New York Times*, April 2, 2008; see also Sudarsan Raghavan, "Attacks on U.S. Forces Soared at End of March," *Washington Post*, April 2, 2008, A12.

152. Charles Crain, "How Moqtada al-Sadr Won in Basra," *Time*, April 1, 2008.

153. "Spike in Attacks," *Washington Post*, April 2, 2008, A12.

154. Amit R. Paley and Ernesto Londoño, "Sadr Warns of 'Open War' if Crackdown Is Not Halted," *Washington Post*, April 20, 2008, A20; Amit R. Paley, "Sadr Extends Cease-Fire, Clarifies 'Open War' Threat," *Washington Post*, April 26, 2008, A10; Sudarsan Raghavan, "Delicate Deal Helps Decrease Violence in Baghdad's Sadr City Enclave," *Washington Post*, May 12, 2008, A14.

155. Reuters, "Iraqi Premier Threatens to Bar Sadr From Vote," *New York Times*, April 7, 2008.

156. Sudarsan Raghavan, "Shiites Across Iraq Protest U.S. Presence," *Washington Post*, May 31, 2008, A1.

157. Sudarsan Raghavan, "In Sadr City, a Repressed but Growing Rage," *Washington Post*, October 23, 2008, A12.

158. Mary Beth Sheridan, "Sadr Threatens Attacks on U.S. Troops if Accord Passes," *Washington Post*, November 15, 2008, A15.

159. The figure is from Jones 2007, 30.

160. Quoted in Raghavan, "In Sadr City, a Repressed but Growing Rage," A12.

161. Glanz, "Iraqi Deaths Are on the Rise Again during Clashes with Militias," 12.

162. DeYoung, "U.S. Has Little Influence, Few Options in Iraq's Volatile South," A11; Amit R. Paley, "Attacks on Green Zone Drop Sharply, U.S. Says," *Washington Post*, April 24, 2008, A10.

163. Tavernise, "Shiite Militia in Baghdad Sees Its Power Ebb," *New York Times*, 1.

164. These are the equivalent of US state elections.

165. These conflicts are zero-sum whether people target others out of hatred or whether people believe that others target them because of their transparent identities. If the latter, people must take sides in the conflict to avoid becoming its victims.

166. In point of fact, the counterinsurgency lessons that the US military took from Iraq (as recorded in the revised *US Army/Marine Corps Counterinsurgency Manual*) were not entirely germane in Iraq, let alone future US conflicts. On this, see Biddle 2008a.

167. This led to street confrontations between Shiite-dominated Iraqi army units and local police. Oppel, "Fallujah's Calm Is Seen as Fragile if U.S. Leaves," 1.

168. Quoted in Joshua Parlow, "U.S. Strategy on Sunnis Questioned," *Washington Post*, June 18, 2007, A11.

169. In the midst of the surge, the provincial police chief in Diyala Province refused to incorporate the local Sunnis into his police force; for its part, US forces in the area rejected Shiite recruits supplied from Baghdad. On these Sunni-Shiite tensions in Diyala, see Gordon, "G.I.'s Forge Sunni Tie in Bid to Squeeze Militants," 1.

170. Gentile, "In the Middle of a Civil War," A13.

171. Sudarsan Raghavan, "An Iraqi City Divided by Walls, by Sect, By Bitterness," *Washington Post*, April 13, 2009, A1.

172. Londoño and Mizher, "Attacks across Baghdad Leave at Least 48 Dead, Scores Injured," A12; Ernesto Londoño, "Separation Anxiety as U.S. Prepares to Leave Sadr City," *Washington Post*, May 17, 2009, A16.

173. Celeste Ward, "Countering the Military's Latest Mantra," *Washington Post*, May 17, 2009, B1.

CHAPTER 3: Leveraging the Adversary's Support Base

1. The US military did not read Chinese intervention to mean that the US military had to proceed with caution; instead, the military pushed for an expansion of the war to include Chinese airfields north of the Yalu River that were used to support Korean operations.

2. Jian 1995, 366, 376. See also Brigham 1999, 409–414; Prados 2004.

3. Admittedly, Johnson might have been exaggerating the dangers of Chinese intervention. China was not provoked to intervene when the Nixon administration dropped some Johnson-era prohibitions, including the mining of Haiphong Harbor, and had a problematic relationship with North Vietnam, which turned violent, of course, with the end of the Vietnam conflict. See Record 1998, 39–41.

4. US strategy in Laos "was determined not by what might be required to bring a conclusion to the conflict there, but by what might contribute to an American victory in Vietnam" (Stuart-Fox 1997, 139). The same can be said of US strategy in Cambodia.

5. Syria was the conduit for foreign fighters arriving from around the region, including roughly 80 percent of suicide bombers in the August 2006–7 period. Karen DeYoung, "Papers Paint New Portrait of Iraq's Foreign Insurgents," *Washington Post*, January 21, 2008, A1.

6. Hugh Naylor, "Syria Is Said to Be Strengthening Ties to Opponents of Iraq's Government," *New York Times*, October 7, 2007, 4.

7. By August 2007, US officials were claiming that as many as a third of US combat deaths in Iraq were attributable to weapons supplied by Iran. Robin Wright, "In the Debate over Iran, More Calls for a Tougher U.S. Stance," *Washington Post*, August 9, 2007, A12.

8. Michael R. Gordon, "Iran-Supplied Bomb Is Killing More Troops in Iraq, U.S. Says," *New York Times*, August 8, 2007, 1; Mark Mazzetti, "Documents Say Iran Aids Militias from Iraq," *New York Times*, October 19, 2008, 6. The implicating evidence grew substantially with the arrests of Shiite militia commanders and the confiscation of weapons stockpiles after the fighting in Basra and Sadr City.

9. On this, see Yacoubian, 2007; Naylor, "Syria Is Said to Be Strengthening Ties to Opponents of Iraq's Government," 4.

10. See Cochrane 2008, 9; Mohammed Tawfeeq and Jonathan Wald, "Sources: Iran Helped Prod al-Sadr Cease-Fire," CNN.com, March 31, 2008.

11. He was less charitable in describing US actions in Sadr City. See James Glanz and Alissa J. Rubin, "Iraqi Army Takes Last Basra Areas from Sadr Force," *New York Times,* April 20, 2008, 1.

12. Karen DeYoung, "Fewer Foreigners Crossing into Iraq from Syria to Fight: Drop Parallels Dip in Al-Qaeda Attacks," *Washington Post,* September 16, 2007, A19.

13. Ann Scott Tyson and Ellen Knickmeyer, "U.S. Calls Raid a Warning to Syria: Copter-Borne Troops Targeted Key Insurgent, Officials Say," *Washington Post,* October 28, 2008, A1.

14. Karen DeYoung, "Terrorist Traffic Via Syria Again Inching Up," *Washington Post,* May 11, 2009, A1.

15. Robin Wright, "Iranian Unit to Be Labeled 'Terrorist,'" *Washington Post,* August 15, 2007, A1; Robin Wright, "As U.S. Steps Up Pressure on Iran, Aftereffects Worry Allies," *Washington Post,* August 16, 2007, A9; Helene Cooper, "In Bush Speech, Signs of a Split on Iran Policy in the Administration," *New York Times,* September 16, 2007, 1.

16. Karen DeYoung, "Iran Cited in Iraq's Decline in Violence," *Washington Post,* December 23, 2007, A1; Mark Mazzetti, Steven Lee Myers, and Thom Shanker, "Questions Linger on Scope of Iran's Threat in Iraq," *New York Times,* April 26, 2008, 1.

17. Ann Scott Tyson, "U.S. Weighing Readiness for Military Action against Iran," *Washington Post,* April 26, 2008, A7.

18. In 2004, the Defense Department had authorized secret military operations worldwide against terrorist targets. That authority was the basis of the operation against al-Qaeda targets in Syria. Although the military apparently engaged in reconnaissance operations in Iran, it apparently did not engage in attacks in that country. Indeed, a large number of operations were apparently scrubbed worldwide over the years because of the apparent risks. See Eric Schmitt and Mark Mazzetti, "Secret Order Lets U.S. Raid Al Qaeda in Many Countries," *New York Times,* November 9, 2008, 1.

19. Mary Beth Sheridan, "Arab League Ambassador Arrives in Baghdad," *Washington Post,* October 7, 2008, A15.

20. The largest proportion, over 40 percent, of foreign fighters were from Saudi Arabia; another 40 percent were from North Africa (with roughly half arriving from Libya). DeYoung, "Papers Paint New Portrait of Iraq's Foreign Insurgents," 1.

21. Helene Cooper, "U.S. Officials Voice Frustrations with Saudis' Role in Iraq," *New York Times,* July 27, 2007, 1.

22. Karen DeYoung, "Iraq Finds Its Arab Neighbors are Reluctant to Offer Embrace," *Washington Post,* May 16, 2008, A9.

23. The 9th Infantry Division's activities in the Mekong Delta are described graphically, based on Army records and participant interviews, in Nick Turse, "A My

Lai a Month," *The Nation*, November 13, 2008, available at www.thenation.com/doc/
20081201/turse/single, accessed September 15, 2009.

24. Of those surveyed, 36 percent of the rural population believed that the country had "greatly" benefitted.

25. Interestingly, attitudes toward Americans and the US role in Vietnam were significantly more positive among the rural than the urban population, which presumably was relatively secure from the effects of war (including US-inflicted collateral damage) and benefiting economically from a US military presence. Although the urban population included war refugees from rural areas, its impressions were probably based on frequent nonmilitary interactions with US troops.

26. Telling is that few people thought, however, that withdrawal would actually reduce the violence within the country: by May 1972, only 4 percent of the public subscribed to this view (down from 14 percent in 1970). Most of the public recognized that a US withdrawal would be problematic—indeed, in the view of a quarter of the public in May 1972, "very dangerous." See Thayer 1985, 191–192.

27. A baseline of sorts is provided by the 1966 PROVN study, which polled hundreds of US advisors. They could report, with certainty, that only a small share of local populations provided at least moderate support to the South Vietnamese government (US Army 1966).

28. This finding was also reflected in the earlier PROVN study (US Army 1966).

29. On this, see Ricks 2006, 330–335, 343–346, 398–405.

30. Josh White, "Alleged Slayings in Fallujah Spur Military Inquiry," *Washington Post*, July 7, 2007, A11.

31. On this treatment, see, for example, Ricks 2006, 232–238. Three months into the surge, the US military claimed to be holding almost twenty thousand prisoners, a marked increase over those held when the new security plan was first implemented. These totals added to the numbers held by the Iraqi army and Interior Ministry in prisons where severe overcrowding was the norm, documented cases of torture and inhumane treatment abounded, and juveniles were held with adult prisoners. Joshua Partlow, "New Detainees Strain Iraq's Jails," *Washington Post*, May 15, 2007, A1.

32. The pressure for actionable intelligence in Iraq led, in fact, to mass arrests and a relaxing of the rules of conduct governing prisoners. The relaxing of standards resulted from the importing of practices from other US prisons (for instance, Guantanamo), the lack of clear prohibitions on certain conduct, the approval of coercive tactics by those high in the chain of command, the uncertainty about who had responsibility for the treatment of prisoners, and the devolution to front-line soldiers of responsibility for detaining and interrogating suspected insurgents (Wright et al. 2008, 242).

33. On the counterinsurgency approach as eventually applied to prisoners in Iraq, see Ricks 2009, 195.

34. Quoted in Thomas E. Ricks, "Iraq Push Revives Criticism of Force Size," *Washington Post*, June 23, 2007, A1.

35. Amit R. Paley, "U.S. Role Deepens in Sadr City," *Washington Post,* April 30, 2008, A1; Ernesto Londoño and Amit R. Paley, "In Iraq, a Surge in U.S. Airstrikes," *Washington Post,* May 23, 2008, A10.

36. These require proportionality in response to attacks and due caution to avoid civilian casualties.

37. States pursuing counterinsurgency strategies and wars of attrition sought traditionally to do whatever it took to starve insurgents of their human and material resources or to combat enemy forces by inflicting or ignoring the inflicting of great collateral damage (Valentino et al. 2004).

38. For a representative instance, see Sudarsan Raghavan and Qais Mizher, "U.S. Says 3 Iraqis Killed in June Were Law-Abiding," *Washington Post,* July 28, 2008, A10.

39. Quoted in Paley, "U.S. Role Deepens in Sadr City," A1.

40. Karin Brulliard, "Iraq Blast Kills 9 GIs, Injures 20 at Outpost," *Washington Post,* April 24, 2007, A1; Joshua Partlow, "Insurgents Hit Bridge North of Baghdad," *Washington Post,* June 2, 2007, A14.

41. Quoted in Sudarsan Raghavan, "In Iraqi Hamlet, 'A Funeral Service in Every House,'" *Washington Post,* July 9, 2007, A1.

42. Independent Institute for Administrative and Civil Society Studies (IACSS), May 14–23, 2004.

43. Private contractors constituted around half of the Pentagon's workforce in Iraq—roughly three times the levels obtained in the Vietnam War. James Glanz, "Contractors Outnumber U.S. Troops in Afghanistan," *New York Times,* September 2, 2009, 10.

44. See, for example, Steve Fainaru and Saad al-Izzi, "U.S. Security Contractors Open Fire in Baghdad," *Washington Post,* May 27, 2007, A1.

45. A civil affairs officer quoted in Henderson 2005, 7. These suspicions were only fueled by early US efforts to safeguard Iraqi oil facilities.

46. For instance, see "Iraqi Paper Conducts Opinion Poll on Coalition Forces, Services, Former Regime," BBC Monitoring International Reports, May 25, 2003; "Most Iraqis in Baghdad Welcome US: NDTV Poll," *Indian Express,* April 29, 2003, available at www.indianexpress.com/storyOld.php?storyId=22949, accessed September 15, 2009.

47. Douglas Jehl, "The Struggle for Iraq: Intelligence," *New York Times,* November 12, 2003, A17.

48. Independent Institute for Administrative and Civil Society Studies (IACSS), May 14–23, 2004.

49. WorldPublicOpinion.org, Program on International Policy Attitudes, January 31, 2006.

50. Poll conducted by D3 Systems for the BBC, ABC News, ARD (German TV), and *USA Today,* September 2007, available at http://news.bbc.co.uk/2/shared/bsp/hi/pdfs/19_03_07_iraqpollnew.pdf, accessed September 6, 2009.

51. Independent Institute for Administrative and Civil Society Studies (IACSS), May 14–23, 2004.

52. US troops were not held directly responsible for the violence and killings; relatively few Iraqis considered the direct threat of violence from Coalition forces as the predominant security threat. In point of fact, they regarded sectarian war and its lethal weapons (especially large vehicle bombs) as the greatest danger to Iraq. Independent Institute for Administrative and Civil Society Studies (IACSS), May 14–23, 2004.

53. Presuming a US withdrawal in six months. World Public Opinion.org, Program on International Policy Attitudes, January 31, 2006.

54. D3 Systems, September 2007.

55. World Public Opinion.org, Program on International Policy Attitudes, January 31, 2006.

56. Whereas 83 percent of Sunnis in January 2006 supported a withdrawal of US-led forces within six months, 57 percent of Sunnis held to that position by September 2006. Amit R. Paley, "Most Iraqis Favor Immediate US Pullout, Polls Show," *Washington Post*, September 27, 2006, A22.

57. World Public Opinion.org, Program on International Policy Attitudes, September 27, 2006.

58. D3 Systems, September 2007.

59. In fact, 77 percent of Sunnis voiced strong approval for these attacks. The poll was conducted January 2–5, 2006, by World Public Opinion.org, Program on International Policy Attitudes, January 31, 2006.

60. World Public Opinion.org, Program on International Policy Attitudes, September 27, 2006. A later poll conducted February 25–March 5, 2007 found that over half of Iraqis still viewed attacks on US forces as "acceptable." Poll conducted by D3 Systems for the BBC, ABC News, ARD (German TV), and *USA Today*, available at http://news.bbc.co.uk/2/shared/bsp/hi/pdfs/19_03_07_iraqpollnew.pdf, accessed September 6, 2009.

61. Poll conducted by D3 Systems for the BBC, ABC News, ARD (German TV), and *USA Today*, August 2007, available at http://news.bbc.co.uk/2/shared/bsp/hi/pdfs/10_09_07_iraqpollaug2007_full.pdf, accessed September 6, 2009.

62. Poll conducted by ABC News, *USA Today*, BBC, and ARD (German TV) February 25–March 5, 2007 as reported in "Fraying Nation, Dividing Opinions," *Washington Post*, May 13, 2007, B2.

63. The 87 percent of Iraqis expressing no confidence in Coalition forces in April 2004 closely matches the 85 percent of Iraqis who expressed the same attitude at the height of the surge in 2007. See the poll conducted by the Independent Institute for Administrative and Civil Society Studies (IACSS), May 14–23, 2004; and D3 Systems, September 2007.

64. Karen DeYoung, "All Iraqi Groups Blame U.S. Invasion for Discord, Study Shows," *Washington Post*, December 19, 2007, A14. The "good news" here was that Iraqis believe that reconciliation is possible with a US withdrawal.

65. International Republican Institute, "Attitudes towards Political Division and Security," March 23–31, 2006. By late 2007, 69 percent of Iraqis expressed considerable confidence in Iraqi security forces. D3 Systems, September 2007.

66. International Republican Institute, "Attitudes towards Political Division and Security," March 23–31, 2006.

67. Poll conducted on a nationwide sample for ABC News, the BBC, ARD, and NHK by D3 Systems of Vienna, Virginia, and KA Research Ltd. of Istanbul, Turkey, February 12–20, 2008, available at www.abcnews.go.com/images/PollingUnit/1060a1IraqWhereThingsStand.pdf, accessed September 6, 2009.

68. World Public Opinion.org, Program on International Policy Attitudes, September 27, 2006.

69. In taking this approach, the military failed to tap into a number of high-level government studies—most notably, by the US State Department (specifically the Future of Iraq Project)—that addressed possible US post-occupation challenges in Iraq (Bensahel et al. 2008, xix).

70. On the activities of these programs, see Tarnoff 2008.

71. CERP funds come largely from the Economic Support Fund (traditionally administered by the State Department) and from the Development Fund for Iraq (derived from monies obtained from Iraqi oil revenues and seized Iraqi assets).

72. Dana Hedgpeth and Sarah Cohen, "Money as a Weapon," *Washington Post*, August 11, 2008, A1.

73. This analysis of PRT performance is based on Perito 2007.

74. The State and Defense Departments were consistently at odds over whether the PRTs should be provided dedicated escorts or whether doing so would prevent troops from performing priority military operations. Rajiv Chandrasekaran, "Iraq Rebuilding Short on Qualified Civilians," *Washington Post*, February 24, 2007, A1. Security forces that were provided to PRTs would become caught in firefights or combine their security detail with insurgent scouting operations (Perito 2007, 8).

75. In March 2008, there were eleven PRTs and thirteen ePRTs operating in Iraq (Perito 2008a).

76. Chandrasekaran, "Iraq Rebuilding Short on Qualified Civilians," A1; Kiki Munshi, "Lessons Unlearned in Iraq," *Washington Post*, July 7, 2007, A15.

77. Hedgpeth and Cohen, "Money as a Weapon," A1.

78. Ernesto Londoño, "U.S. 'Money Weapon' Yields Mixed Results," *Washington Post*, July 27, 2009, A12.

79. Liz Sly, "A New Threat in Iraq: Recession," *Los Angeles Times*, May 11, 2009, A1.

80. The geographical and topographical distribution of the population militates against a definitive attributing of alignment to religion and ethnicity (Kalyvas and Kocher 2007a).

81. His theological commitment (quietism) required that he remain above political infighting and suspicion.

82. Al-Sistani was said to be sensitive to al-Sadr's nationalist claims but concerned about his tactics and motives (Rahimi 2007a, 2007b).

83. Indeed, "in Iraq, as elsewhere in the Arab World, tribes rarely provide the basis for sustained collective action"; a passing of a threat brings "a return to a state of competition and conflict" (Eisenstadt 2007, 19).

84. Anthony Shadid, "In Anbar, U.S.-Allied Tribal Chiefs Feel Deep Sense of Abandonment," *Washington Post,* October 3, 2009, A1.

85. See, e.g. Joshua Partlow, "Sunni Insurgent Leader Paints Iran as 'Real Enemy,'" *Washington Post,* July 14, 2007, A13; Ann Scott Tyson, "Sunni Fighters Find Strategic Benefits in Tentative Alliance with U.S.," *Washington Post,* August 9, 2007, A1.

86. Joshua Partlow, "Troops in Diyala Face a Skilled, Flexible Foe," *Washington Post,* April 22, 2007, A1.

87. Sudarsan Raghavan, "In Iraq, a Perilous Alliance with Former Enemies," *Washington Post,* August 4, 2007, A1.

88. Sudarsan Raghavan, "In the Land of the Blood Feuds," *Washington Post,* August 10, 2007, A1.

89. In the words of one US intelligence officer, "Some of them want to be reintegrated back in society, they want to push al-Qaeda out. Others want to be the next thug group that goes around and demands electricity payments." Quoted in Tyson, "Sunni Fighters Find Strategic Benefits in Tentative Alliance with U.S.," A1.

90. Joshua Parlow and John Ward Anderson, "Tribal Coalition in Anbar Said to Be Crumbling; U.S.-Backed Group Has Fought Al-Qaeda in Iraq," *Washington Post,* June 11, 2007, A11.

91. Sudarsan Raghavan, "A New Breed Grabs Reins in Anbar," *Washington Post,* October 21, 2008, A1.

92. On these tensions after the US early success in Anbar, see, for example, Partlow and Anderson, "Tribal Coalition in Anbar Said to Be Crumbling," A11.

93. The Awakening groups dismissed Party members' conservative Islamic views, life in exile under Saddam Hussein, and foreign residences, and they feared that the Party would use its power to orchestrate an electoral victory. Sudarsan Raghavan, "Rise of Awakening Groups Sets Off a Struggle for Power among Sunnis," *Washington Post,* July 4, 2008, A8.

94. Steven Lee Myers and Sam Dagher, "After Iraqi Elections, Next Big Test Is Acceptance," *New York Times,* February 10, 2009, 1.

95. Major General Rick Lynch quoted in John F. Burns and Alissa J. Rubin, "U.S. Arming Sunnis in Iraq to Battle Old Qaeda Allies," *New York Times,* June 11, 2007, 1.

96. Raghavan, "In Iraq, a Perilous Alliance with Former Enemies," A1.

97. Iraq's deputy national security adviser expressed a sentiment prevalent within the Shiite-led government when he observed that US support for former (Sunni) insurgents amounted to "preparation for civil war." James Glanz and Stephen Farrell, "A U.S.-Backed Plan for Sunni Neighborhood Guards Is Tested, *New York Times,* August 19, 2007, 8.

98. Sudarsan Raghavan and Anthony Shadid, "In Iraq, 2 Key U.S. Allies Face Off," *Washington Post,* March 30, 2009, A1.

CHAPTER 4: Leveraging the Adversary's Leaders

1. Resolve does not necessarily reduce to perceptions of benefits. It is also boosted by an unwillingness to accept defeat, a presumed absence of viable alternatives, a willingness to incur greater risks and accept higher costs to recover losses (Levy 1997), an indifference to cost, an irrational attachment to instrumental goals, and an inability to reverse policies once engaged.

2. As such, leverage increases with lower costs or a greater cost tolerance (which can be conceived as a cost weighting factor). Evaluating costs and cost tolerance is admittedly complex, in part, due to cost tradeoffs. For instance, the United States accepts considerable economic cost to avoid costs in the form of US troop casualties.

3. I use the phrase "small conflicts" to refer to the relative stakes for the United States in these conflicts and their relative demands on US military capability. Given US military preponderance, opponents, and objectives in these conflicts, they are also likely to be asymmetric.

4. Realist writings suggest as much in addressing the effects of bipolarity (Waltz 1979), nuclear deterrence (Waltz 1990), and patron-client relations (Efrat and Bercovitch 1991). The literature on collective goods (Olson and Zeckhauser 1966) also suggests that powerful states might tolerate conflict (defection). In fact, accommodation is arguably built into the definition of a "superpower," a nation that by merit of its capability can offset any combination of rival (nonsuper) powers and, consequently, need not worry about deflecting attacks from them. These arguments are developed in Lebovic 2003.

5. On this see Record 1998, 181–182. Such actions were proscribed by US international priorities (for instance, precedent setting) and the public (and moral) outcry that these actions would engender. By the same token, North Vietnam's non-urbanized (and progressively deconcentrated) population made it a poor candidate for saturated bombing, and its earthen dikes might not have been as vulnerable to attacks as was widely supposed (Pape 1996, 194–195).

6. For evidence that democracies have not historically shown restraint in inflicting civilian deaths, see Valentino et al. 2006.

7. One study concludes that major powers have had declining success in particular against insurgencies—defeating "their insurgent foes in nearly 81 percent of pre–World War I cases but in only 40 percent of the post–World War I cases" (Lyall and Wilson 2009, 69).

8. The result is a competition in which parties pursue security relentlessly but are perpetually insecure. This dilemma lacks the "tragic" proportions of its close relative, the "spiral" model (Jervis 1976). That model also depicts conflict as arising from an action-reaction process—a competition in which each party sees itself as the defender and blames the other for the conflict.

9. For that matter, given the relative value that individuals place on what they have lost (over what they might gain), a leader that is losing ground to an opponent might act rashly to avoid a further erosion in support or to *retrieve* what they once had.

10. As Wagner (2000, 469, 482) observes, "If fighting is expected to lead to agreement then fighting must be considered part of the bargaining process and not an alternative to it." Therefore, "if negotiated settlements of such a war are possible then any war that actually occurs will not necessarily be a contest in which states try to disarm each other, but may be instead a contest that is fought to influence expectations about the consequences of fighting such a war."

11. In the latter incident, insurgents were reported to have paraded through the streets after the blast in a symbolic show of force. Anthony Shadid, "Blast Kills Dozens in Iraqi Market," *Washington Post,* March 11, 2009, A8.

12. North Korea was placed in a no-loss position because (a) the United States (and the UN team) made a deliberate decision not to invite the costs of acquiring additional territory in the North (if only as a bargaining chip), once Chinese and North Korean forces had repelled the US-led invasion of North Korea (in the first year of the fighting), and (b) the United States had extended an offer that was now part of the negotiating record.

13. This does not necessarily mean that Kissinger himself conceded a North Vietnamese victory in the accords (after a "decent interval")—only that he accepted the risk of defeat over a stalemate that would leave US forces in Vietnam.

14. These ideas follow from Cold War–era writings on "escalation dominance."

15. Hostility within the communist camp was increasingly apparent through the 1970s, with military tension between China and Vietnam and between Vietnam and the newly installed Khmer Rouge government of Cambodia.

16. Interestingly, the credibility-based linkage argument was taken by some in the Johnson administration as arguing for US involvement in Vietnam, even if resulting in a US defeat (Downes 2009, 44).

17. According to many who chronicled the period, this led Kissinger to conclude that, short of victory, the United States required a "decent interval" between any US withdrawal and a South Vietnamese defeat. See, for instance, Kimball 2004.

18. It emphasized the role of al-Qaeda in Iraq and its ties to the global al-Qaeda organization. See Sudarsan Raghavan, "U.S. Military Calls Al-Qaeda in Iraq 'Principal Threat,'" *Washington Post,* July 11, 2007, A19; Michael R. Gordon and Jim Rutenberg, "Bush Distorts Qaeda Links, Critics Assert," *New York Times,* July 13, 2007, 1.

19. US officials argued, then, that combating the al-Qaeda enemy in Iraq was better than the inevitable alternative of fighting these same terrorists in the United States and that withdrawing from Iraq would strengthen the position of US adversaries who could use Iraq to launch operations against US interests.

20. These officials could try to boost the US position, through linkage, by alluding to Iran's support for Iraqi Shiite militia, relationship to Hezbollah in Lebanon, strong anti-Western rhetoric, and open defiance of the International Atomic Energy Association and UN Security Council in failing to allow international inspections of the country's suspect nuclear facilities.

21. For a quantitative study of this effect in Iraq, see Monten 2008.

22. Thus, it was expected that the Soviet Union would appreciate that the US aim was not to destroy Soviet cities per se and that the collateral damage incurred was limited *relative* to the damage that the US could have inflicted had it targeted the Soviet population directly. The question then, as always, is whether the initiator and target work with the same perceptual reference points. It is reasonable to suspect that the massive killing and enormous destruction inflicted by US nuclear weapons would overwhelm any consideration of US restraint—in fact, that restraint would have been read as but a brief respite before the next wave of US attacks.

23. It should be noted, too, that the signal was hardly cost-free. It increased the chances of an inadvertent nuclear war with the Soviet Union as well as a nuclear accident because standard safety precautions were relaxed.

24. Diplomatic tools are also blunt. To have the intended impact on the recipient, an act of US diplomacy must stand out when US leaders adopt qualified phraseology to allow themselves room for retreat and to appease hardline critics, when official statements issued by each and every US government agency on a given day create an overload of messages, when US leaders pair their statements with actions that implicitly undermine the verbal message, and when leaders in the recipient country must divert their attention to a host of competing issues and acquire additional information and advice from advisors.

25. Ironically, the US did not significantly increase its attacks on critical targets in North Vietnam until 1967, at which point key decision-makers had turned against the "graduated" approach and were pushing for restrictions on the US air war and the number of US land troops committed to the war (Thies 1980, 173).

26. That interpretation was only made more compelling, in 1968, when the United States paired its bombing halt over North Vietnam with a ferocious increase in bomb tonnages dropped on Laos.

27. The attack by the torpedo boats was apparently initiated at a low level of the North Vietnamese military command (McNamara et al. 1999).

28. Ken Adelman, "Cakewalk in Iraq," *Washington Post*, February 13, 2002, A27.

29. There is a high (.90) correlation between presidential approval, Bush's handling of the Iraq War, and whether the public believes the war was "worth it" (Gelpi and Reifler 2006, 195).

30. The Pew Research Center for the People and the Press. Awareness of Iraq War Fatalities Plummets. Political Knowledge Update. March 12, 2008.

31. Specifically, 28 and 66 percent supported withdrawal with and without these options, respectively; see Mueller 1971, 367.

32. This was based on public judgments about whether the United States "made a mistake sending troops to fight in Vietnam" (Mueller 1971, 363).

33. These data are from a nationwide Gallup poll on Iraq, available at www.gallup.com/poll/1633/Iraq.aspx, accessed September 8, 2009.

34. The Chicago Council on Global Affairs, *Global Views 2008*, 11, available at www.thechicagocouncil.org/curr_pos.php, accessed September 8, 2009.

35. I wish to thank my colleague, John Sides, for this information, presented at www.themonkeycage.org/2008/01/iraq_and_the_democratic_candid.html, accessed September 8, 2009.

36. Admittedly, unlike in 1968, the war was not the driving issue in the 2008 election, and Obama's candidacy was not taken as a referendum on the war or its strategy.

37. On this point, it is useful to note that public sentiment toward the war remained insensitive to a fairly dramatic rise—from 47 to 60 percent between January 2007 to July 2008—in the share of the public that did not believe an Iraq victory was required for success in the war on terrorism, though war supporters frequently linked the two wars in public discourse. ABC News/Washington Post poll conducted most recently, July 10–13, 2008, on a nationwide sample.

38. Jon Cohen and Jennifer Agiesta, "Poll Shows Obama Deflected Recent Attacks," *Washington Post*, November 3, 2008, A9.

39. "Awareness of Iraq War Fatalities Plummets: Political Knowledge Update," Pew Research Center for the People and the Press, March 12, 2008, available at http://people-press.org/report/401/awareness-of-iraq-war-fatalities-plummets, accessed September 8, 2009.

40. Ernesto Londoño and Amit R. Paley, "Western Journalists in Iraq Stage Pullback of Their Own," *Washington Post*, October 11, 2008, A1.

41. If casualties were not affecting perceptions of success (see Voeten and Brewer 2006), it is hard to explain the unwillingness of the public to bear minimal costs to achieve fairly noble objectives, for example, why the deaths of a small number of US soldiers in the early 1990s turned the US public against the humanitarian/nation-building effort in Somalia.

42. On this, see also Gartner and Segura 1998, 285–287.

43. Political Knowledge Update.

44. CBS News/New York Times Poll, most recently, September 12–16, 2008, based on a nationwide sample.

45. By mid-2008, 54 percent of the US public believed that victory was not still possible. NBC News/Wall Street Journal Poll, conducted June 6–9, 2008, on a nationwide sample. Moreover, by June 2008, 61 percent of the US public believed that Iraq would never become a stable democracy. CBS News Poll, conducted May 30–June 3, 2008, on a nationwide sample.

46. This is judged from responses, in nationwide Gallup polls, to the question of whether sending US troops to Iraq was a mistake. See www.gallup.com/poll/1633/Iraq.aspx. In contrast, presidential approval ratings appear to be a better fit with the logged casualty pattern: the share of the public voicing approval of the president plummeted from around three quarters at the commencement of major operations in April 2003, to less than half within a eighteen months, to around a third within another year (Gelpi et al. 2005, 8–9), to a quarter of respondents by late 2008.

47. Casualties rose dramatically in the last part of World War II, reached their high point in the early stages of the Korean War, and peaked (around the Tet Offensive) in the middle years of the Vietnam intervention. Yet the log of cumulative US

fatalities for all three wars produces a very rapid rise in casualties in the early part of each war followed by a gradual and declining rate of increase.

48. Consequently, cumulative casualties should be a statistically insignificant variable in the model when time effects are adequately accounted for. For this result, see, for instance, Voeten and Brewer 2006, 822. Moreover, the effect attributed to the log of cumulative casualties, which assumes that people differ in their propensities to accept casualties, might be explained, in part, by other model variables (such as party affiliation) that account for these propensities.

49. Evaluations of success are not necessarily exogenous sources of public support for a war: partisanship arguably determines whether citizens support a war *and* whether they believe a war is succeeding (see Berinksy and Druckman 2007).

50. The Iraq findings, from a nationwide Gallup poll, are available at www.gallup.com/poll/1633/Iraq.aspx.

51. Indeed, support for the war remained highest among those who, by merit of (high) income and education, were the least likely to be drafted (Karnow 1997, 502).

52. Birth dates were selected randomly from a container to determine the order in which men would be drafted such that a higher number would effectively select a person out of the conscription pool.

53. In fact, twice as many troops died in the first as in the second six months of their tour. On these statistics, see Thayer 1985, 112–114.

54. See Ann Scott Tyson, "Military Is Ill-Prepared for Other Conflicts," *Washington Post*, March 19, 2007, A1; Ann Scott Tyson, "Increase May Mean Longer Army Tours," *Washington Post*, March 29, 2007, A15; Josh White, "Army Recruiting Rebounds in July to Exceed Goals," *Washington Post*, August 11, 2007, A3; Josh White, "Army Off Target on Recruits," *Washington Post*, January 23, 2008, A2; Ann Scott Tyson, "Military Waivers for Ex-Convicts Increase," *Washington Post*, April 22, 2008, A1.

55. In 2008, the suicide rate among Army soldiers rose for the fourth consecutive year, to reach a thirty-year high. It also exceeded the civilian rate, a pattern not seen since the Vietnam War. Lizette Alvarez, "Suicides of Soldiers Reach High of Nearly 3 Decades, and Army Vows to Bolster Prevention," *New York Times*, January 30, 2009, 19. The number of US troops diagnosed with post-traumatic stress disorder in 2007 was up 50 percent from 2006 levels. Ann Scott Tyson, "Military Diagnosing More Post-Traumatic Stress," *Washington Post*, May 28, 2008, A2.

56. Ann Scott Tyson, "Army Offers Big Cash to Keep Key Officers," *Washington Post*, October 11, 2007, A1; Ann Scott Tyson, "Deployments Are a Factor in Army's Deficit of Majors," *Washington Post*, August 17, 2008, A4.

57. By 2009, the military benefitted from a growing applicant pool with the deteriorating US economy. See Ann Scott Tyson, "Army More Selective as Economy Lags," *Washington Post*, April 19, 2009, A6.

58. Indeed, shortly after the defeat of the McGovern-Hatfield Amendment, just over half of the American people supported the principles of the amendment: a few months later, three-quarters of the public held that view; see Manley 1971, 68.

59. For a detailed discussion of anti–Vietnam War protests and their impact on US policymakers, see Wells 1994.

60. Bob Woodward, "Outmaneuvered and Outranked, Military Chiefs Became Outsiders," *Washington Post,* September 8, 2008, A1.

61. For his part, General Petraeus described himself as a "minimalist" as he pushed the new US military plan to achieve "sustainable security" in the country, with the US troop surge of 2007 (Ricks 2009, 287–288).

62. Karen DeYoung, "Obama Sets Timetable for Iraq," *Washington Post,* February 28, 2009, A1.

63. Biden's comments were paraphrased, off the record, by the official in Nada Bakri, "Biden Warns of Ending Commitment," *Washington Post,* July 4, 2009, A8.

64. "US Warns Against Forgetting Iraq," BBC News, September 15, 2009, available at http://news.bbc.co.uk/2/hi/middle_east/8256134.stm, accessed September 15, 2009.

65. Schelling (1981, 17) echoes this in noting the "extraordinary difficulty of pulling out of a situation in which one has invested heavily"—that "no government ever surrenders the war that it fought. Some new government always has to come in to do the surrendering."

66. The head of the Coalition Provisional Authority in Iraq supposedly justified *expanding* the US mission to include the dismantling and rebuilding of Iraq's entire security infrastructure by arguing, "We didn't send our troops half-way around the world to overthrow Saddam to find another dictator taking his place" (quoted in Wright et al. 2008, 95).

CHAPTER 5: Leveraging Host Governments

1. In this chapter, the terms *leaders* and *host-government leaders* refer both to those in power and to those in the opposition; the term *host government* refers just to those leaders, such as the prime minister, who are in power.

2. For a similar argument, see Bueno de Mesquita and Downs 2006. For a related take on the problem of "moral hazard" in a deterrence context, see Crawford 2001–2.

3. Here, governing power is defined by the fragility of a leader's domestic and governmental base.

4. Contrary to the common conception, the Southern insurgency in these earlier years was galvanized by opposition to Diem and his American backers, though the National Liberation Front assumed control of opposition planning and coordination of political and military activities in the South and was itself, in the main, under the control of Hanoi (Hamilton 1998, 116; Lewy 1978, 15–18).

5. U. Alexis Johnson aptly summarized the US strategic problem dealing with countries with an insurgency: when "only radical reforms will obtain the necessary results, . . . the measures we advocate may strike at the very foundations of those aspects of a country's social structure and domestic economy on which rests the basis of a government's control" (quoted in Blaufarb 1977, 65).

6. As Spector (1985, 281) notes, "Many senior officers routinely supplemented their income by selling on the black market, embezzling official funds, exploiting prostitution, and dealing in drugs. The lower ranks committed extortion and sometimes even outright robbery against the local population, particularly in outlying districts. In those remoter areas, regional commanders occasionally attempted to establish themselves as local warlords."

7. Indeed, the Saigon government took measures—which included maintaining strict control over South Vietnamese military units (Hennessy 1997, 115)—that would prevent the United States from acquiring leverage by increasing Saigon's dependencies and decreasing Saigon's capability for independent action (and non-action).

8. This was hardly a revelation for many, if not most, US government officials. Johnson believed, for instance, that agreeing to General Westmoreland's request for a troop increase would prevent South Vietnamese troops from doing their part (Hunt 1995, 87).

9. On this, see Clarke 1988, 241–244, 324–331, 387–390, 506. The PROVN study noted that "on the American side, to report a deteriorating situation is all too frequently regarded as an admission of US, rather than Vietnamese, failure" (US Army 1966).

10. In consequence, it was easier to create new South Vietnamese military organizations than to reorganize existing ones for enhanced performance (Clarke 1988, 515–516).

11. The toll of the impasse was felt, then, in the death of over a thousand civilians on the ground and a hundred US pilots and their crew members and the loss of twenty-six US aircraft including fifteen US B-52 bombers (Karnow 1997, 664–669).

12. Melvin R. Laird, "A Model for Responsible Withdrawal: The Vietnam Plan Worked Until Aid Was Cut Off," *Washington Post,* June 29, 2007, A21.

13. Seats were similarly distributed in the election of the provincial assemblies for each of Iraq's eighteen provinces.

14. The United States exerted significant pressure to get Sunni representatives appointed to the drafting committee, but these Sunnis, whose legitimacy among the Sunni population was in doubt, had little influence on the resulting document.

15. Joshua Partlow and Robin Wright, "Top Iraqi Officials Growing Restless: Vice President Has Tried to Quit: Shiite Leaders in Disarray," *Washington Post,* June 21, 2007, A1; Joshua Partlow, "Six Members of Sunni Bloc Quit Iraqi Cabinet in Protest," *Washington Post,* June 30, 2007, A14; Megan Greenwell, "Sunni Group to End Five-Week Boycott of Iraqi Parliament," *Washington Post,* July 19, 2007, A15.

16. Joshua Partlow, "Missteps and Mistrust Mark the Push for Legislation," *Washington Post,* September 5, 2007, A12.

17. Their existing position in the provincial government allowed Kurds to maintain a security presence (in their Peshmerga militia) in the disputed city of Kirkuk (the provincial capital) and to push for its repopulation by Kurds, at the expense of Arabs, in advance of a constitutionally mandated referendum on the city's future. The conditions were ripe, then, for a military confrontation. In summer 2008, Pesh-

merga units were involved in tense confrontations with Iraqi security forces in Tamim and Diyala Provinces; in early 2009, the new Arab governor of Nineveh Province was also involved in a confrontation with Peshmerga units that refused to allow
him to pass to attend an annual kite flying festival. The immediate conflict was de-
fused because his order to mobilize supportive troops was refused. Nada Bakri, "Dispute over Land Simmering in Iraq," *Washington Post*, May 18, 2009, A10. Likewise, in
the summer of 2009, a military confrontation was averted between Peshmerga and
Iraqi Army units that the Kurds feared were planning to enter the predominantly
Kurdish town of Makhmur. Anthony Shadid, "Kurdish Leaders Warn of Strains with
Maliki," *Washington Post*, July 17, 2009, A1. Al-Maliki continued to send loyal troops
to areas bordering Kurdistan to contain its growth, while Kurdish Peshmerga units
continued to stake their claim in these regions. Ernesto Londoño, "Iraq May Hold
Vote on U.S. Withdrawal," *Washington Post*, August 18, 2009, A1.

18. Unintentional empowerment is an inevitable consequence of outside intervention. Studies show that even emergency relief efforts can increase the power of
local leaders who profit by selling humanitarian goods on the black market, distribute the goods to supporters to reward them for their support, or take credit for the
aid (see Byman and Seybolt 2003). For instance, the government of Myanmar took
advantage of international humanitarian aid after the 2008 monsoon devastated the
country by re-branding packages with the names of the country's generals so that
recipients would know to whom they owed their gratitude. "Myanmar Junta Hands
Out Aid Boxes with Generals' Names," *International Herald Tribune*, May 10, 2008.

19. Amit R. Paley and Joshua Partlow, "Iraq's New Law on Ex-Baathists Could
Bring Another Purge," *Washington Post*, January 23, 2007, A1.

20. The inadvertent empowerment problem exists down the chain of command:
the outside power can never appreciate the agendas, grievances, and personal and
familial relationships that bind or divide the various personnel through which the
power must work.

21. Alissa J. Rubin, "Maliki Gains Time, but Faces a Daunting Task," *New York
Times*, September 25, 2007, 13; David Ignatius, "A Surge against Maliki," *Washington
Post*, January 9, 2008, A15. At least, this is how Maliki viewed the US predicament—
which reduced US leverage. Amit R. Paley and Joshua Partlow, "Despite Problems,
Iraqi Leader Boasts of Success," *Washington Post*, February 29, 2008, A12.

22. This presumes the absence of a "hurting stalemate," but even efforts to create
a balance for such a stalemate can fail if the "leaders all prefer war to peace" (Byman
and Seybolt 2003, 62).

23. I wish to thank my colleague Nathan Brown for this observation.

24. Associated Press, "Iraq's PM May Be Weakened by Dealmaking over Pact,"
USA Today, November 29, 2008, available at www.usatoday.com/news/world/iraq/
2008-11-29-iraq-al-maliki_N.htm, accessed September 22, 2009.

25. On leveraging al-Maliki, see Robinson 2008, 11, 174–176, 280, 329.

26. Saddam Hussein had relied upon his paramilitary network to maintain order
in the country.

27. Although the United States originally sought decentralized controls over the Iraqi police force (and a military that was externally oriented) so that it could not threaten Iraq's emerging democracy (Rathmell et al. 2005, 36, 48), the United States moved in the opposite direction once focused on the insurgency.

28. As Kilcullen (2009, 67) observes, "Insurgent intimidation easily overcomes any residual gratitude effect."

29. Of course, de-Baathification also had a basis in security, that is, ending the Baathist threat.

30. Karen DeYoung, "Official Report Faults Iraq Reconstruction," *Washington Post,* December 15, 2008, A17. A substantial portion of the cost increase and time delay was caused when Iraqi officials forced a change in the plan to require a more modern treatment system. See SIGIR, 2008, 189–190.

31. Paley and Partlow, "Iraq's New Law on Ex-Baathists Could Bring Another Purge," A1.

32. The troop numbers themselves were suspect: they increased dramatically over fairly short time periods and then varied inexplicably by source and over time.

33. The attitudinal problems ensued in part from the military's unfavorable reward structure—barriers to promotion, poor financial rewards, paucity of medical care, and limited financial support for wounded or disabled soldiers and the families of those killed in action. For a graphic portrayal of the medical travails and financial burdens of wounded Iraqi soldiers, see Karin Brulliard, "For Iraqi Soldiers, a Medical Morass," *Washington Post,* May 6, 2007, A1.

34. On this point, a report by an oversight panel of the US House Armed Services Committee criticized the US military's progress reports on Iraqi forces by noting that they focus on force quantities and equipment, not on their ability to conduct operations. Ann Scott Tyson, "House Report Faults Pentagon Accounting of Iraqi Forces," *Washington Post,* June 27, 2007, A15.

35. For example, see Natalia Antelava, "Illusion of Security in Iraq," BBC News, August 11, 2009, available at http://news.bbc.co.uk/2/hi/middle_east/8194799.stm, accessed September 15, 2009; Andrew North, "Corruption Undermines Iraqi Security," BBC News, August 28, 2009, available at http://news.bbc.co.uk/2/hi/middle_east/8226076.stm, accessed September 15, 2009.

36. See Text of Memo from Colonel Timothy R. Reese, Chief, Baghdad Operations Command Advisory Team, MND-B, Baghdad, Iraq, available at www.nytimes.com/2009/07/31/world/middleeast/31advtext.html, accessed August 1, 2009.

37. Ernesto Londoño and Greg Jaffe, "Iraq Carnage Shows Sectarian War Goes On," *Washington Post,* August 20, 2009, A1.

38. Marc Santora and Abeer Mohammed, "After Blasts, Iraqi Officials Point Fingers," *New York Times,* August 22, 2009, 8.

39. These problems were identified in Jones 2007, 38, 69, 89.

40. See Ernesto Londoño, "Lower Oil Prices Put Iraq's Security Forces in Bind at Crucial Time," *Washington Post,* May 20, 2009, A8. With the US exodus from South

Vietnam, its military was hobbled by similar economic problems and deficiencies in conducting maintenance and managing spare parts.

41. For example, in promoting Iraqi self-reliance throughout the conflict, the unanswered question was how much corruption, sectarian bias, and nonperformance (neighborhoods that revert to militia control, border crossings that remain unsecured) is tolerable?

42. Iraqi budgetary resistance was felt even when Congress recognized the release of Iraqi funds for capital projects as a formal "benchmark" for assessing Iraqi governmental reform.

43. The Iraqi police force disintegrated largely on its own. See Perito 2008b.

44. As elsewhere, the burden was placed on US military troops, with limited resources and relevant experience, to train Iraqis to perform police functions.

45. These bipartisan studies were commissioned by the US Congress.

46. Ned Parker, "The Conflict in Iraq: A Ministry of Fiefdoms," *Los Angeles Times*, July 30, 2007, A1; Jones 2007, 44.

47. Michael R. Gordon and Alissa J. Rubin, "Shiite Ex-Officials Face Trial in Hundreds of Sunni Deaths," *New York Times*, November 5, 2007, 1.

48. Babak Dehghanpisheh, "When the Good Guys Are the Bad Guys," *Newsweek*, July 28, 2008.

49. Quoted in Ann Scott Tyson, "U.S. Commanders Say Iraqi Police Can Be Reformed," *Washington Post*, December 11, 2007, A14.

50. One assessment at the end of 2008 noted that, despite notable improvements, "political influence remains pervasive" within the Interior Ministry, which is itself "still personality driven" (Sherman and Carstens 2008, 3).

51. Karen DeYoung and Walter Pincus, "Corruption in Iraq 'Pernicious,' State Dept. Official Says," *Washington Post*, October 16, 2007, A13.

52. Alissa Rubin, "Iraqi Trade Officials Forced Out in Anticorruption Sweep," *New York Times*, September 24, 2008, 10.

53. The CPI is equivalent to the US Federal Bureau of Investigation. See Testimony of Stuart W. Bowen Jr., Special Inspector General for Iraq Reconstruction, "Assessing the State of Iraqi Corruption," House Committee on Oversight and Government Reform, October 4, 2007, available at http://oversight.house.gov/documents/20071004102651.pdf, accessed September 8, 2009.

54. Statement of Stuart W. Bowen Jr., Special Inspector General for Iraq Reconstruction, before the United States House of Representatives, Committee on the Judiciary Subcommittee on Crime, Terrorism, and Homeland Security, June 19, 2007, available at www.sigir.mil/reports/pdf/testimony/SIGIR_Testimony_07-012T.pdf, accessed September 22, 2009.

55. Dana Hedgpeth, "$13 Billion in Iraq Aid Wasted or Stolen, Ex-Investigator Says," *Washington Post*, September 23, 2008, A19.

56. A copy of the lengthy, untitled, uncredited report is available at www.fas.org/irp/eprint/anticorruption.pdf, accessed September 8, 2009.

262   *Notes to Pages 182–185*

57. The former chief investigator for the Commission on Public Integrity claimed that thirty-two of his staff had been murdered. Hedgpeth, "$13 Billion in Iraq Aid Wasted or Stolen, Ex-Investigator Says," A19. The report concluded that "several ministries are so controlled by criminal gangs or militias as to be impossible to operate without a tactical force protecting the investigator" (p. 640).

58. Bowen, "Assessing the State of Iraqi Corruption," October 4, 2007.

59. Sudarsan Raghavan, "Maliki's Impact Blunted by Own Party's Fears," *Washington Post*, August 3, 2007, A1; Damien Cave, "Iraqi Premier Stirs Discontent, Yet Hangs On," *New York Times*, August 19, 2007, 10. Al-Maliki had come to al-Sadr's aid (when al-Sadr was part of the governing coalition) by pressuring the United States to lift barriers around Shiite neighborhoods in Baghdad that were meant to curtail militia activities.

60. Joshua Partlow, "Maliki's Office Is Seen Behind Purge in Forces: Some Commanders had Pursued Militias," *Washington Post*, April 30, 2007, A1.

61. James Glanz and Riyadh Mohammed, "Premier of Iraq Is Quietly Firing Fraud Monitors," *New York Times*, November 18, 2008, 1.

62. Glanz and Mohammed, "Premier of Iraq Is Quietly Firing Fraud Monitors," 1.

63. "Government Vows to Cut Corruption," *Washington Post*, May 28, 2009, A10.

64. See, for example, Ned Parker, "Corruption Plays Central Role in Iraqi Justice," *Los Angeles Times*, June 29, 2009, A16.

65. Timothy Williams, "Bomb Kills G.I. in Baghdad as Attacks Continue to Rise," *New York Times*, May 28, 2009, 10.

66. Those charged with corruption have leveled charges of corruption against the investigators. Bowen, House Committee on Oversight and Government Reform, October 4, 2007.

67. Quoted on condition of anonymity in Ernesto Londoño, "U.S. Troops, Iraqi Civilians to Become Less Protected on July 1," *Washington Post*, June 26, 2009, A12.

68. At least partly for that reason, its security forces were still unprepared to take charge in parts of the country. With the US pullback from Iraqi cities on June 30, 2009, the Interior Ministry was supposedly fully responsible for security in only seven of Iraq's eighteen provinces, sharing responsibility with the Defense Ministry in eight other provinces (these included the cities of Baghdad, Basra, and Mosul). See Jawad al Bolani, "Iraq: Mission Not Yet Accomplished," *Washington Post*, June 30, 2009, A13.

69. The distinction and judgment, as it applies to Iraq, are drawn from remarks by Matt Sherman, former senior advisor to the minister of interior, Iraq (2003–2004), at "Iraq's Interior Ministry: The Key to Police Reform," June 18, 2009, United States Institute of Peace, Washington, D.C.

70. That the government will build a security force from one or more of the contending factions is always a danger in identity conflicts (Biddle 2006). Indeed, to create more efficient government institutions under these conditions "can simply be to create more proficient sectarians with a stronger technical capacity to direct ser-

vices to their followers and more systematically deny them to their rivals" (Biddle 2008b, 348–349).

71. Indeed, the decentralizing of power and creating of operational redundancies that hamper institutional performance and efficiency impede any single entity from usurping power.

72. With the US surge in 2007, the emphasis was now on quick progress on the ground, US military operations (over the transition to Iraqi security forces), negotiating agreements with hostile insurgent factions, offensive action on multiple geographical fronts, and security in Baghdad to facilitate reconciliation among rival government factions.

73. Indeed, the final plan apparently toned down the addressing of sectarian bias in government (that is, removing overtly sectarian officials) and reflected a recognition by these officials that they would have to work with Prime Minister al-Maliki. Michael R. Gordon, "U.S. Is Seen in Iraq until at Least '09," *New York Times*, July 24, 2007, 1; Ann Scott Tyson, "New Strategy for War Stresses Iraqi Politics," *Washington Post*, May 23, 2007, A1.

74. David E. Sanger and Thom Shanker, "Fending Off a Deadline: Bush Seeks Time on Iraq," *New York Times*, July 13, 2007, 8.

75. In its words, "It should be unambiguous that continued U.S. political, military, and economic support for Iraq depends on the Iraqi government's demonstrating political will and making substantial progress toward the achievement of milestones on national reconciliation, security, and governance" (p. 42).

76. Stephen Biddle, "Iraq: Go Deep or Get Out," *Washington Post*, July 11, 2007, A15. In this sense at least, an administration official was correct to argue that a US withdrawal of troops must await actual progress on the ground—that "the drawdown is an effect . . . not a cause." Quoted in Peter Baker and Karen DeYoung, "Bush Plans to Stress Next Phase in Iraq War," *Washington Post*, July 10, 2007, A1. The question took the form of a heated debate between US military commanders in Iraq and the regional command when it pressed for shifting US troops toward a support role in the country (Ricks 2009, 233).

77. This is the opinion of Lieutenant General James M. Dubik (2009, 2, 23), who headed the Multi-National Security Transition Command-Iraq, 2007–2008.

78. In fact, the Bush administration promoted the troop surge as an instrument for creating an environment conducive to meeting key benchmarks.

79. This is a negative consequence of a prominent argument for "conditional engagement" (Kahl et al. 2008), articulated by analysts who would later assume high-profile positions in the Defense Department of the Obama administration.

80. On this point, it should be noted that, in exchange for supporting the US-Iraq negotiated withdrawal agreement, the Sunni bloc in parliament pushed for the adoption of a list of reforms to address longstanding Sunni complaints against the Shiite-led, al-Maliki government. The complaints included the underrepresentation of Sunnis in Iraqi security forces, the slow release of prisoners under the country's amnesty law, and the continuing blockage of former Baathists from government

jobs. Alissa J. Rubin and Campbell Robertson, "Lawmakers in Baghdad Delay Vote on U.S. Pact," *New York Times,* November 27, 2008, 6; Sudarsan Raghavan, "Iraq's Parliament Delays Vote on Security Pact with U.S.," *Washington Post,* November 27, 2008, A19.

81. Karen DeYoung and Thomas E. Ricks, "Administration Shaving Yardstick for Iraq Gains," *Washington Post,* July 8, 2007, A1. That the administration struggled to justify its overall position in Iraq was clear from the administration's selective use of evidence. In point of fact, the numbers of deaths in June 2007 still exceeded those in March and April earlier in the year, and the numbers of unidentified bodies—a key indicator of sectarian violence—was around 50 percent higher (543 deaths) than in January (360 deaths), just before the start of the US troop surge. See Joshua Partlow, "Body Count in Baghdad Up in June," *Washington Post,* July 5, 2007, A1.

82. The study concluded that the Iraqi government had met three, partially met four, and did not meet eleven of the benchmarks (US GAO 2007a).

83. Michael Abramowitz, "As Iraq Situation Varies, Bush Sticks with Encouraging Words," *Washington Post,* August 28, 2007, A4.

84. As one administration official remarked, "The shelf life of a benchmark is pretty questionable." Quoted in Michael Abramowitz, "No Big Shifts Planned after Report on Iraq," *Washington Post,* August 25, 2007, A1.

85. There is considerable evidence that states try to use assistance, such as foreign aid, to shape the political practices of targeted countries—by rewarding states for their prior conduct (for instance, military support or UN voting) or punishing them for their rights abuses—but considerably less evidence that these efforts actually work, let alone work when the benefactor is highly committed to the target.

86. Thomas E. Ricks and Karen DeYoung, "For U.S., The Goal is Now 'Iraqi Solutions.'" *Washington Post,* January 10, 2008, A1.

87. Paley and Partlow, "Iraq's New Law on Ex-Baathists Could Bring Another Purge," A1; Glenn Kessler, "A New (Old) Law of the Land," *Washington Post,* January 23, 2008.

88. The assumption implicit in the policy, as before, was that the Party elite "could not have achieved their level without committing acts that seriously violated human rights standards or were deeply corrupt" (ICTJ 2008, 5–6).

89. Paley and Partlow, "Iraq's New Law on Ex-Baathists Could Bring Another Purge," A1. The implementing commission under the control of parliament appeared to amount to little more than giving the existing commission a new name.

90. Solomon Moore, "Ex-Baathists Get a Break. Or Do They?" *New York Times,* January 14, 2008, 6.

91. Quoted in Paley and Partlow, "Iraq's New Law on Ex-Baathists Could Bring Another Purge," A1.

92. Karen DeYoung, "U.S., Iraq Negotiating Security Agreements," *Washington Post,* April 11, 2008, A4; Karen DeYoung, "Iraqi Official: Security Pact Altered," *Washington Post,* June 18, 2008, A10.

93. On these agreements and the Iraqi SOFA in particular, see Mason 2008.

94. From the Iraqi government's perspective, in turn, the agreement would affect the ability of US forces to create threats inadvertently, for instance, by provoking attacks.

95. Karen DeYoung, "U.S., Iraq Remain Unresolved on Dates for U.S. Troop Pullout," *Washington Post,* August 10, 2008, A17.

96. Karen DeYoung, "In Pact, U.S. Won't Commit to Protecting Iraq," *Washington Post,* February 7, 2008, A17.

97. Ernesto Londoño, Mary Beth Sheridan, and Karen DeYoung, "Iraq Repeats Insistence on Fixed Withdrawal Date," *Washington Post,* November 7, 2008, A1.

98. Quoted in David Ignatius, "A Critical Stage in Iraq," *Washington Post,* October 22, 2008, A19.

99. The US position enjoyed support, however, from the Kurds and some Sunnis who considered US forces a counterweight to Shiite majority and Iranian influence. See Richard A. Oppel and Stephen Farrell, "Growing Opposition to Iraq Security Pact," *New York Times,* May 31, 2008, 6.

100. Karen DeYoung, "No Need for Lawmakers' Approval of Iraq Pact, U.S. Reasserts," *Washington Post,* March 6, 2008, A18.

101. DeYoung, "Iraqi Official: Security Pact Altered," A10. On this point, the secretaries of state and defense, in a joint statement, emphasized an "essential" US mission that involved "helping the Iraqi government fight al-Qaeda, develop its security forces, and stem the flow of lethal weapons and training from Iran." Condoleezza Rice and Robert Gates, "What We Need Next in Iraq," *Washington Post,* February 13, 2008, A19.

102. Michael Abramowitz, "Democrats Attack Iraq Security Proposal," *Washington Post,* January 24, 2008, A9.

103. Rice and Gates, "What We Need Next in Iraq," A19.

104. Karen DeYoung, "Lacking an Accord on Troops, U.S. and Iraq Seek a Plan B," *Washington Post,* October 14, 2008, A1.

105. The United States pressed to retain an even larger number of facilities in earlier negotiations.

106. Amit R. Paley and Karen DeYoung, "Iraqis Condemn American Demands," *Washington Post,* June 11, 2008, A1.

107. The impasse prompted efforts to negotiate a short-term agreement that would postpone longer-term issues to the next administration. Karen DeYoung, "U.S., Iraq Scale Down Negotiations Over Forces," *Washington Post,* July 13, 2008, A1.

108. Dan Eggen and Michael Abramowitz, "U.S., Iraq Agree to 'Time Horizon,'" *Washington Post,* July 19, 2008, A1.

109. Paul Richter and Ned Parker, "Accord Is Near on Iraq Pullout," *Los Angeles Times,* August 22, 2008, A1.

110. Karen DeYoung and Sudarsan Raghavan, "U.S., Iraqi Negotiators Agree on 2011 Withdrawal," *Washington Post,* August 22, 2008, A1.

111. Amit R. Paley, "Maliki Demands All U.S. Troops Pull Out by 2011," *Washington Post*, August 26, 2008, A6.

112. Ned Parker, "Iraq Shakes Up Talks on U.S. Troop Pullout," *Los Angeles Times*, August 31, 2008, A7.

113. Parker, "Iraq Shakes Up Talks on U.S. Troop Pullout," A7.

114. Qassim Abdul-Zahra, "Iraq Outlines Changes It Wants in Pact with U.S.," *USA Today*, October 29, 2008, available at www.usatoday.com/news/world/2008 -10-29-3418976217_x.htm, accessed September 1, 2009; Londoño, Sheridan, and DeYoung, "Iraq Repeats Insistence on Fixed Withdrawal Date," A1.

115. Ned Parker and Saif Hameed, "Iraq Security Pact Clears Major Hurdle," *Los Angeles Times*, November 15, A1.

116. Mary Beth Sheridan, "Iraqi Parliament Begins Debate," *Washington Post*, November 17, 2008, A12; Mary Beth Sheridan, "Iraqi Official Urges Pact Passage," *Washington Post*, November 23, 2008, A15; Campbell Robertson and Stephen Farrell, "Iraqi Cabinet Approves Security Pact with U.S.," *New York Times*, November 17, 2008, 1.

117. Raghavan, "Iraq's Parliament Delays Vote on Security Pact with U.S.," A19.

118. Al-Sistani announced through an official spokesman that he did not consider the slim majority vote in the legislature to have met his standard of widespread support. Although he did not call for a rejection of the agreement, he underscored inadequate protections in the document for Iraqi sovereignty and assets and suggested that the weakness of the Iraqi government would prevent it from standing up to the US in implementation. Sudarsan Raghavan and Saad Sarhan, "Top Shiite Cleric in Iraq Raises Concerns about Security Pact," *Washington Post*, November 30, 2008, A19.

119. Rania Abouzeid, "Iraq's Maliki Faces Challenge over Power Grab," *Time*, December 3, 2008, available at www.time.com/time/world/article/0,8599,1863762,00 .html, accessed September 8, 2009. Interestingly, al-Maliki's growing power coincided with a loss in support in the Iraqi legislature where the opposition was reputedly sufficient to win a "no-confidence" vote (though it chose not to press for a vote, lacking a viable replacement). Amit R. Paley, "In Iraq's Provincial Elections, Main Issue is Maliki Himself," *Washington Post*, January 17, 2009, A1.

120. Robinson 2008, 156–158; Partlow, "Maliki's Office Is Seen Behind Purge in Forces," 1.

121. Alissa J. Rubin, "Maliki Pushes for Election Gains, Despite Fears," *New York Times*, January 26, 2009, 1; Jim Michaels, "Chain of Command Concerns Raised in Iraq," *USA Today*, February 23, 2009, 2A.

122. Rubin, "Maliki Pushes for Election Gains, Despite Fears," 1.

123. Anthony Shadid, "In Iraq, a Different Struggle for Power," *Washington Post*, June 25, 2009, A9.

124. Quoted in Sudarsan Raghavan, "Arrests Based on a 'Lie,' Iraqi Interior Chief Says," *Washington Post*, December 20, 2008, A9.

125. Sudarsan Raghavan and Qais Mizher, "Arrests in Iraq Seen as Politically Motivated," *Washington Post*, December 19, 2008, A24; Campbell Robertson, "An Inquiry in Baghdad Is Clouded by Politics," *New York Times*, December 18, 2008, 11;

Campbell Robertson and Tareq Maher, "24 Officers to Be Freed, Iraqi Says," *New York Times,* December 20, 2008, 6.

126. Shadid, "In Iraq, a Different Struggle for Power," A9.

127. Anthony Shadid, "Worries about a Kurdish-Arab Conflict Move to Fore in Iraq," *Washington Post,* July 27, 2009, A1.

128. Greg Miller, "U.S. Spies on Iraqi Army, Officials Say," *Los Angeles Times,* July 2, 2008, A1.

129. Ernesto Londoño, "U.S. Troops Uneasy as Rules Shift in Iraq," *Washington Post,* January 12, 2009, A1.

130. Ernesto Londoño and Zaid Sabah, "Deaths in U.S. Raid Elicit Anger in Iraq," *Washington Post,* April 27, 2009, A6; Brian Murphy, "Iraq: US Raid 'Crime' that Breaks Security Pact," Associated Press, April 26, 2009, www.breitbart.com. The Iraqi government proved somewhat accommodating, however, when—in its view—the US military presence was necessary to maintaining stability in the country. It agreed to define US military bases located in the periphery of Baghdad as standing outside the city to permit a US presence there after the June 30 deadline. See Rod Nordland, "Exceptions to Iraq Deadline are Proposed," *New York Times,* April 27, 2009, 4.

131. Ernesto Londoño, "U.S. Says Iraq Is Withholding Key Detainee," *Washington Post,* May 2, 2009, A9.

132. Hamid Ahmed, "Iraq Committed to June 30 Withdrawal for American Troops," *Washington Post,* May 5, 2009, A7.

133. Ernesto Londoño, "Separation Anxiety as U.S. Prepares to Leave Sadr City," *Washington Post,* May 17, 2009, A16.

134. Quoted anonymously in Londoño, "Separation Anxiety as U.S. Prepares to Leave Sadr City," A16.

135. Steven Lee Myers and Marc Santora, "Premier Casting U.S. Withdrawal as Victory for Iraq," *New York Times,* June 26, 2009, 1.

136. Rod Nordland, "Iraqis Take the Lead, With U.S. Trailing Closely," *New York Times,* August 9, 2009, 6.

137. Ernesto Londoño and Karen DeYoung, "Iraq Restricts U.S. Forces," *Washington Post,* July 18, 2009, A1; Ernesto Londoño, "U.S. Troops in Iraq Find Little Leeway," *Washington Post,* July 20, 2009, A8; Ernesto Londoño, "After the Shooting, Another Showdown," *Washington Post,* July 25, 2009, A1.

138. Major General Daniel P. Bolger, quoted from an email, in Londoño and DeYoung, "Iraq Restricts U.S. Forces," A1. Whether or not his legal assertions were correct is less important for our purposes than that he felt compelled to make them. These sentiments were expressed graphically in a leaked memo written by a senior US military advisor in Baghdad. It articulated a litany of complaints against Iraqi Security Forces and questioned whether, under the circumstances, the United States could accomplish much by staying in Iraq in an advisory role. See Reese Memo, as described in Michael R. Gordon, "Declare Victory and Depart Iraq, U.S. Adviser Says," *New York Times,* July 31, 2009, 1.

139. The Iraqi government's move against the camp was made more disquieting by the presence in Iraq of the US Secretary of Defense. Rod Nordland, "Arrests of Sunni Leaders Rise in Baghdad," *New York Times,* July 30, 2009, 10; Ernesto Londoño, "Iraqi Raid Poses Problem for U.S.," *Washington Post,* July 30, 2009, A12.

140. Ernesto Londoño, "Iraqi Authorities to Remove Capital's Blast Walls," *Washington Post,* August 6, 2009, A8. A series of deadly vehicular bomb attacks in August 2009 led the Iraqi government to suspend the dismantling of blast wall in the capital. Rod Nordland, "Attacks Damage Maliki's Case that Iraq Can Safeguard Itself," *New York Times,* August 21, 2009, 1.

141. David Ignatius, "Security From Iraq's Neighbors," *Washington Post,* September 13, 2009, A25.

142. Londoño, "Iraq May Hold Vote on U.S. Withdrawal," A1.

143. Rod Nordland and Marc Santora, "Iraq Leader Omits a Bit in Lauding U.S. Pullout," *New York Times,* June 12, 2009, 6.

144. On the gathering, see Nordland and Santora, "Iraq Leader Omits a Bit in Lauding U.S. Pullout," 6; Myers and Santora, "Premier Casting U.S. Withdrawal as Victory for Iraq," 1.

145. Quoted in Fareed Zakaria, "No Velvet Revolution for Iran," *Washington Post,* June 29, 2009, A17.

146. Ernesto Londoño and Zaid Sarah, "Market Blast Kills More than 75 in Baghdad's Sadr City," *Washington Post,* June 25, 2009, A9.

147. Ernesto Londoño, "Jubilation in Iraq on Eve of U.S. Pullback," *Washington Post,* June 30, 2009, A1.

148. Alissa J. Rubin, "Iraq Celebrates U.S. Withdrawal from Its Cities," *New York Times,* July 1, 2009, 1.

149. Liz Sly, "Maliki Declines Biden's Help Offer," *Los Angeles Times,* July 4, 2009, A20.

150. See Domingue and Cochrane 2009; Anthony Shadid, "New Alliances in Iraq Cross Sectarian Lines," *Washington Post,* March 20, 2009, A1. Indeed, the al-Maliki government—unwilling to risk empowering adversaries—rebuffed US and British efforts to facilitate a reconciliation deal between the Iraqi government and former Baathists living in exile. Sam Dagher, "Iraq Resists Pleas by U.S. to Placate Baath Party," *New York Times,* April 26, 2009, 1.

151. Ernesto Londoño and K. I. Ibrahim, "Major Shiite Political Parties Exclude Maliki in Forming Coalition," *Washington Post,* August 25, 2009, A6.

CHAPTER 6: Conclusions

1. Kydd and Walter (2002) argue convincingly, for instance, that the Israeli perception that Yasser Arafat was weak and could not stop attacks by militants on Israeli military and civilian targets saved the peace process.

2. On the Afghan model of combined air-ground operations, see Andres et al. 2005–6; on its limitations, see Biddle 2005–6.

3. Despite strong US public backing for the Afghanistan war (in the aftermath of the September 11 attacks), US officials depended on indigenous fighters—of questionable motivation and loyalty—to seize territory and pursue militants rather than invite the investment and liabilities of a US occupation or US military casualties. For instance, the US military chose not to employ US troops to pursue fleeing al-Qaeda leaders and fighters into their elevated stronghold of caves in Tora Bora or to deploy US troops along the Pakistan border to cut off al-Qaeda exit routes. Instead, it contracted out these tasks to Afghan fighters and Pakistan troops that had little incentive to accept the attending risks and costs of preventing al-Qaeda units from escaping.

4. Helen Cooper and Eric Schmitt, "Afghan Plan Narrows U.S. War Goals," *New York Times*, March 28, 2009, 1.

5. Richard Holbrooke quoted in Craig Whitlock, "National Security Team Delivers Grim Appraisal of Afghanistan War," *Washington Post*, February 9, 2009, A13.

6. On conditions in Afghanistan, see Johnson and Mason 2008; Jones 2008.

7. A Pashtun identity limited the broad appeal of the Taliban but helped it embed within the Pashtun-populated areas.

8. Admittedly, factionalism and in-fighting also made it more difficult for the Taliban to present a united opposition. See Testimony of Stephen Biddle, "Assessing the Case for War in Afghanistan," Senate Committee on Foreign Relations, September 16, 2009, available at www.cfr.org/publication/20220/, accessed September 29, 2009.

9. Rajiv Chandrasekaran, "Troops Face New Tests in Afghanistan," *Washington Post*, March 15, 2009, A1.

10. Kilcullen 2009, 64; Dexter Filkins, "U.S. Sets Fight in the Poppies to Stop the Taliban," *New York Times*, April 28, 2009, 1; Craig Whitlock, "Diverse Sources Fund Insurgency in Afghanistan," *Washington Post*, September 27, 2009, A1.

11. Joshua Partlow, "Opium Cultivation in Afghanistan Down Sharply, Report Says," *Washington Post*, September 2, 2009, A10.

12. James Dao, "Afghan War's Buried Bombs Put Risk in Every Step," *New York Times*, July 15, 2009, 1; Karen DeYoung, "Taliban Surprising U.S. Forces with Improved Tactics," *Washington Post*, September 2, 2009, A1.

13. Ann Scott Tyson, "Dearth of Capable Afghan Forces Complicates U.S. Mission in South," *Washington Post*, July 25, 2009, A9.

14. See ICG 2008c; US GAO 2009a; Pamela Constable, "U.S. Troops Face a Tangle of Goals in Afghanistan," *Washington Post*, March 8, 2009, A1; Richard A. Oppel Jr., "Corruption Undercuts Hopes for Afghan Police," *New York Times*, April 9, 2009, 1; C. J. Chivers, "Erratic Afghan Forces Pose Challenge to U.S. Goals," *New York Times*, June 8, 2009, 1.

15. Mark Moyar, "Can the U.S. Lead Afghans?" *New York Times*, September 4, 2009, 21.

16. Available at www.brookings.edu/reports/2008/02_weak_states_index.aspx and www.foreignpolicy.com/images/fs2008/failed_states_ranking.jpg, accessed September 1, 2009.

17. Walter Pincus, "Analysts Expect Long-Term, Costly U.S. Campaign in Afghanistan," *Washington Post,* August 9, 2009, A8.

18. Rajiv Chandrasekaran, "Obama's War: A New Approach to Karzai," *Washington Post,* May 6, 2009, A1.

19. Chandrasekaran, "Obama's War: A New Approach to Karzai," A1.

20. Karen DeYoung, "Afghan Envoy Assails Western Allies as Halfhearted, Defeatist," *Washington Post,* March 12, 2009, A14.

21. See www.transparency.org.

22. Joshua Partlow, "Militia Commander Campaigns for Karzai," *Washington Post,* August 18, 2009, A6.

23. Pamela Constable, "A Tense Afghanistan Gears Up for National Elections," *Washington Post,* August 20, 2009, A9.

24. Joshua Partlow and Pamela Constable, "Accusations of Fraud Multiply in Afghanistan," *Washington Post,* August 28, 2009, A1; Pamela Constable and Karen DeYoung, "U.N.-Backed Panel Finds Fraud in Afghan Vote," *Washington Post,* September 9, 2009, A1.

25. Ann Scott Tyson, "Afghan Supply Chain a Weak Point," *Washington Post,* March 6, 2009, A10.

26. Pamela Constable, "Defiant Taliban Forces Advance to Within 60 Miles of Islamabad," *Washington Post,* April 24, 2009, A8.

27. Jane Perlez, "A Visit to a U.S. Ally, but an Increasingly Wary One," *New York Times,* February 9, 2009, 5.

28. Karen DeYoung, "Al-Qaeda Seen as Shaken in Pakistan," *Washington Post,* June 1, 2009, A1.

29. The purpose was ostensibly to undercut support for the Taliban; a consequence was potentially to legitimate its demands and strengthen the control of Taliban supporters.

30. Sabrina Tavernise and Pir Zubair Shah, "Tough Battle in Pakistan Insurgency Stronghold," *New York Times,* June 16, 2009, 6.

31. Jane Perlez and Pir Zubair Shah, "Taliban Losses Are No Sure Gain for Pakistanis," *New York Times,* June 28, 2009, 1.

32. Joshua Partlow, "Pakistani Pledge to Rout Taliban in Tribal Region is Put on Hold," *Washington Post,* July 27, 2009, A1.

33. Joby Warrick and R. Jeffrey Smith, "Gains in Pakistan Fuel Pentagon Optimism for Pursuing Al-Qaeda," *Washington Post,* June 13, 2009, A3; Pamela Constable, "Pakistan's Plans for New Fight Stir Concern," *Washington Post,* June 24, 2009, A12; Perlez and Shah, "Taliban Losses Are No Sure Gain for Pakistanis," 1. That the Pakistan military would embrace the counterinsurgency philosophy appeared doubtful in light of its apparent involvement in acts of "score settling" that included torture and retaliatory killings in areas that came under military control. Jane Perlez and Pir Zubair Shah, "Pakistan Army Is Said To Be Linked to Many Killings in Swat," *New York Times,* September 15, 2009, 1.

34. Chandrasekaran, "Troops Face New Tests in Afghanistan," A1.

35. Martha Raddatz, Richard Coolidge, Audrey Taylor, and Theresa Cook, "Where Things Stand: Afghanistan in Turmoil," ABC News, February 9, 2009; Jon Cohen and Jennifer Agiesta, "Poll of Afghans Shows Drop in Support for U.S. Mission," *Washington Post*, February 10, 2009, A11.

36. The United States faced a greater public opinion challenge in Pakistan, where a dramatic rise in opposition to the Taliban did not produce strong support for the United States or its military actions, such as missile strikes on Taliban targets. In a nationwide Pew Global Attitudes survey conducted in Pakistan between May 22 and June 9, 2009, only 16 percent of respondents claimed to have a favorable view of the United States, and 58 percent of respondents doubted the necessity of missile strikes. Available at http://pewresearch.org/pubs/1312/pakistani-public-opinion, accessed September 16, 2009.

37. David Ignatius, "A Three-Pronged Bet on 'AFPAK,'" *Washington Post*, February 29, 2009.

38. Pamela Constable, "Dispute over Timing of Afghan Vote Turns Messy," *Washington Post*, March 5, 2009, A10; Chandrasekaran, "Obama's War: A New Approach to Karzai," A1.

39. Rajiv Chandrasekaran, "Marines Deploy on Major Mission," *Washington Post*, July 2, 2009, A1.

40. Karen DeYoung, "Taliban Advance in Pakistan Prompts Shift by U.S.," *Washington Post*, April 29, 2009, A8.

41. Karen DeYoung, "Obama Outlines Afghan Strategy," *Washington Post*, March 28, 2009, A1.

42. Rajiv Chandrasekaran and Karen DeYoung, "Changes Have Obama Rethinking War Strategy," *Washington Post*, September 21, 2009, A1.

43. General Stanley A. McChrystal paraphrased and quoted in "New Afghanistan Commander Will Review Troop Placements," *Washington Post*, June 16, 2009, A10.

44. Thom Shanker and Elisabeth Bumiller, "In Afghanistan, U.S. Shifts Narcotics Strategy," *New York Times*, July 24, 2009, 8.

45. Greg Jaffe, "U.S. Commanders Told to Shift Focus to More Populated Areas," *Washington Post*, September 22, 2009.

46. Karen DeYoung, "For Obama, A Pivotal Moment in Afghanistan," *Washington Post*, September 8, 2009, A1.

47. Walter Pincus, "Military Weighs Private Security on Front Lines," *Washington Post*, July 26, 2009, A11.

48. David E. Sanger, Eric Schmitt, and Thom Shanker, "White House Struggles to Gauge Afghan Success," *New York Times*, August 7, 2009, 4. Richard Holbrooke, the US Special Representative to Afghanistan and Pakistan, obviously recognized the problems of devising useful metrics of success when he invoked Supreme Court Justice Potter Stewart's famous definition of pornography: "I know it when I see it." Quoted in Al Kamen, "In the Loop," *Washington Post*, August 14, 2009, A15.

49. Karen DeYoung, "U.S. Sets Metrics to Assess War Success," *Washington Post*, August 30, 2009, A1.

50. As the source of most of Afghanistan's poppies, Helmand province became the central testing ground, as well, for this feature of the US counterinsurgency campaign. See Karen DeYoung, "U.S. and Britain Again Target Afghan Poppies," *Washington Post*, August 8, 2009, A1.

51. Peter Baker and Elisabeth Bumiller, "Advisors to Obama Divided on Size of Afghan Force," *New York Times*, September 4, 2009, 1.

52. Rajiv Chandrasekaran, "In Kandahar, a Taliban on the Rise," *Washington Post*, September 14, 2009, A1.

53. Rajiv Chandrasekaran, "Insurgents Step Up Attacks on Marines," *Washington Post*, July 4, 2009, A8.

54. Ann Scott Tyson and Walter Pincus, "U.S., NATO to Revamp Afghan Training Mission," *Washington Post*, September 12, 2009, A3.

55. Pamela Constable, "U.S. Says Taliban Has a New Haven in Pakistan," *Washington Post*, September 29, 2009, A11.

56. See, for example, DeYoung, "Obama Outlines Afghan Strategy," A1.

57. Partlow and DeYoung, "With Karzai Favored to Win, U.S. Walks a Fine Line," A1.

58. Rajiv Chandrasekaran, "Civilian, Military Officials at Odds over Resources Needed for Afghan Mission," *Washington Post*, October 8, 2009, A1.

59. For example, see Pincus, "Analysts Expect Long-Term, Costly U.S. Campaign in Afghanistan," A8; Ann Scott Tyson, "General: Afghan Situation 'Serious,'" *Washington Post*, September 1, 2009, A1; Bob Woodward, "McChrystal: More Forces or 'Mission Failure,'" *Washington Post*, September 21, 2009, A1.

60. Karen DeYoung, "General's Review Creates Rupture," *Washington Post*, September 22, 2009, A1.

61. Based on the results of a Washington Post–ABC News Poll conducted July 15–18, 2009, on a randomly selected sample of 500 adults, as reported in "Assessing Obama's War," *Washington Post*, July 22, 2009, A7.

62. Sentiment had turned against the war, though only 36 percent of the public thought that the United States was losing, and most thought that the United States could ultimately achieve its economic, political, and military goals in the country. These data are from a *Washington Post*–ABC News Poll conducted August 13–17, 2009, on a randomly selected sample of 1,001 adults, as reported in Jennifer Agiesta and Jon Cohen, "Public Opinion in U.S. Turns against the War," *Washington Post*, August 20, 2009, A9.

63. "Support for Afghan War Drops, CNN Poll Finds," CNN Politics.com, August 6, 2009, available at http://edition.cnn.com/2009/POLITICS/08/06/poll.afghanistan, accessed September 15, 2009; "Poll: Support for Afghan War At All-Time Low," CNN Politics.com, September 15, 2009, available at http://edition.cnn.com/2009/POLITICS/09/15/afghan.war.poll, accessed September 15, 2009.

64. Ann Scott Tyson and Greg Jaffe, "U.S. Deaths Hit a Record High in Afghanistan," *Washington Post*, July 22, 2009, A7.

65. Peter Baker, "L.B.J. All the Way?" *New York Times*, August 23, 2009, 1.

66. Ann Scott Tyson, "Mullen: More Troops 'Probably' Needed," *Washington Post,* September 16, A1.

67. Ann Scott Tyson, "Less Peril for Civilians, but More for Troops," *Washington Post,* September 23, 2009, A1.

68. Helene Cooper, "Karzai Using Rift with U.S. to Gain Favor," *New York Times,* August 29, 2009, 1.

69. As his national security advisor, James Jones, described the situation in comparison to Iraq, "This is bigger than the surge." Bob Woodward, "No Deadline Set for Decision on Troops," *Washington Post,* September 27, 2009, A1.

70. Chandrasekaran, "Civilian, Military Officials at Odds over Resources Needed for Afghan Mission," A1.

71. Peter Baker and Elisabeth Bumiller, "Obama Considers Strategy Shift in Afghan War," *New York Times,* September 23, 2009, 1; Scott Wilson, "Emerging Goal for Afghanistan: Weaken, Not Vanquish, Taliban," *Washington Post,* October 9, 2009, A1.

72. Apart from its "military" effectiveness, targeting terrorists by air using drone aircraft risked doing more harm than good if it increased popular resentment toward US tactics.

73. Karen DeYoung and Scott Wilson, "Pakistanis Balk at U.S. Aid Package," *Washington Post,* October 8, 2009, A1.

74. Dan Bilefsky, "Tensions Rise in Fragile Bosnia as Country's Serbs Threaten to Seek Independence," *New York Times,* February 27, 2009, 11; Craig Whitlock, "Old Troubles Threaten Again in Bosnia," *Washington Post,* August 23, 2009, A10.

75. It remains an open question whether the local rallying effect that challenges the intervening force will endure as indigenous populations must cope with their losses in war, anticipate the next round of the conflict, and deal with the empowerment—from battle—of those with unappealing political views or agendas.

76. Assistant Secretary of Defense Michael G. Vickers quoted in Ann Scott Tyson, "U.S. Raise 'Irregular War' Capabilities," *Washington Post,* December 4, 2008, A4.

77. Tyson, "U.S. Raise 'Irregular War' Capabilities," A4.

78. Michael W. Wynne quoted in Greg Jaffe, "A Single-Minded Focus on Dual Wars," *Washington Post,* May 15, 2009, A1.

79. Greg Jaffe, "Short '06 Lebanon War Strokes Pentagon Debate," *Washington Post,* April 6, 2009, A1.

80. Some policy analysts suggest that the United States should focus on preparing to fight conventional wars (Mazarr 2008), while others argue for a more balanced approach (Nagl and Burton 2009).

References

Andres, Richard B., Craig Wills, and Thomas E. Griffith. 2005–6. Winning with Allies: The Strategic Value of the Afghan Model. *International Security* 30 (3): 124–160.

Arreguín-Toft, Ivan. 2005. *How the Weak Win Wars: A Theory of Asymmetric Conflict.* Cambridge, UK: Cambridge University Press.

Art, Robert J. 1980. To What Ends Military Power? *International Security* 4 (4): 3–35.

Avant, Deborah D. 1993. The Institutional Sources of Military Doctrine: Hegemons in Peripheral Wars. *International Studies Quarterly* 37 (4): 409–430.

Baram, Amatzia. 2005. Who Are the Insurgents? Sunni Arab Rebels in Iraq. *Special Report* 134. Washington, DC: United States Institute of Peace.

Bensahel, Nora. 2006. Mission Not Accomplished: What Went Wrong with Iraqi Reconstruction. *Journal of Strategic Studies* 29 (3): 453–473.

Bensahel, Nora, Olga Oliker, Keith Crane, Richard R. Brennan Jr., Heather S. Gregg, Thomas Sullivan, and Andrew Rathmell. 2008. *After Saddam: Prewar Planning and the Occupation of Iraq.* Santa Monica, CA: RAND Arroyo Center.

Berinsky, Adam J. 2007. Assuming the Costs of War: Events, Elites, and American Public Support for Military Conflict. *Journal of Politics* 69 (4): 975–997.

Berinsky, Adam J., and James N. Druckman. 2007. Public Opinion Research and Support for the Iraq War. *Journal of Politics* 71 (1): 126–141.

Betts, Richard K. 1995. *Military Readiness: Concepts, Choices, Consequences.* Washington, DC: Brookings Institution.

Biddle, Stephen. 2005–6. Allies, Airpower, and Modern Warfare: The Afghan Model in Afghanistan and Iraq. *International Security* 30 (3): 161–176.

———. 2006. Seeing Baghdad, Thinking Saigon. *Foreign Affairs* 85 (2): 2–14.

———. 2008a. The New U.S. Army/Marine Corps Counterinsurgency Field Manual as Political Science and Political Praxis. *Perspectives on Politics* 6 (2): 347–350.

———. 2008b. Patient Stabilized? *National Interest* 94 (March-April): 35–41.

Biddle, Stephen, Michael E. O'Hanlon, and Kenneth M. Pollack. 2008. How to Leave a Stable Iraq. *Foreign Affairs* 87 (5): 40–58.

Blaufarb, Douglas S. 1977. *The Counterinsurgency Era: U.S. Doctrine and Performance, 1950 to the Present.* New York: Free Press.

Bremer, L. Paul, III. 2006. *My Year in Iraq: The Struggle to Build a Future of Hope.* New York: Threshold Editions.

Brigham, Robert K. 1999. Three Alternative U.S. Strategies in Vietnam: A Reexamination Based on New Chinese and Vietnamese Sources. In *Argument without End: In Search of Answers to the Vietnam Tragedy*, ed. Robert S. McNamara, James Blight, Robert Brigham, Thomas Biersteker, and Col. Herbert Schandler. New York: Public Affairs.

Bueno de Mesquita, Bruce, and George W. Downs. 2006. Intervention and Democracy. *International Organization* 60 (3): 627–649.

Byman, Daniel L., and Taylor Seybolt. 2003. Humanitarian Intervention and Communal Civil Wars. *Security Studies* 13 (1): 33–78.

Byman, Daniel L., and Matthew C. Waxman. 2000. Kosovo and the Great Air Power Debate. *International Security* 24 (4): 5–38.

Clarke, Jeffrey J. 1988. *United States Army in Vietnam. Advice and Support: The Final Years, 1965–1973*. Washington, DC: Center of Military History, United States Army.

Clodfelter, Mark. 1989. *The Limits of Air Power: The American Bombing of North Vietnam*. New York: The Free Press.

Cohen, Eliot A. 1986. Distant Battles: Modern War in the Third World. *International Security* 10 (4): 143–171.

Cochrane, Marisa. 2008. The Battle for Basra. Iraq Report 9. Washington, DC: Institute for the Study of War. Available at www.understandingwar.org/report/battle-basra.

———. 2009. The Fragmentation of the Sadrist Movement. Iraq Report 12. Washington, DC: Institute for the Study of War. Available at www.understandingwar.org/report/fragmentation-sadrist-movement.

Converse, Philip E., Warren E. Miller, Jerrold G. Rusk, and Arthur C. Wolfe. 1969. Continuity and Change in American Politics: Parties and Issues in the 1969 Election. *American Political Science Review* 63 (4): 1083–1105.

Crawford, Timothy. 2001–2. Pivotal Deterrence and the Kosovo War: Why the Holbrooke Agreement Failed. *Political Science Quarterly* 116 (4): 499–525.

Currey, Cecil B. 1997. *Victory at Any Cost: The Genius of Viet Nam's Gen. Vo Nguyen Giap*. Washington, DC: Brassey's.

Daalder, Ivo H., and Michael E. O'Hanlon. 2000. *Winning Ugly: NATO's War to Save Kosovo*. Washington, DC: Brookings Institution.

Diamond, Larry. 2005. *Squandered Victory: The American Occupation and the Bungled Effort to Bring Democracy to Iraq*. New York: Henry Holt.

Domergue, Jeremy and Marisa Cochrane, 2009. Balancing Maliki: Shifting Coalitions in Iraqi Politics and the Rise of the Iraqi Parliament. Iraq Report 14. Washington, DC: Institute for the Study of War. Available at www.understandingwar.org/report/balancing-maliki.

Downes, Alexander B. 2009. How Smart and Tough are Democracies? Reassessing Theories of Democratic Victory in War. *International Security* 33 (4): 9–51.

Dubik, James M. 2009. Building Security Forces and Ministerial Capacity: Iraq as a Primer. Best Practices in Counterinsurgency, Report 1. Washington, DC: Institute for the Study of War. Available at www.understandingwar.org/report/building -security-forces-and-ministerial-capacity.

Duiker, William J. 1996. *The Communist Road to Power in Vietnam.* Boulder, CO: Westview Press.

Efrat, Moshe, and Jacob Bercovitch, eds. 1991. *Superpowers and Client States in the Middle East: The Imbalance of Influence.* London: Routledge.

Eisenstadt, Michael. 2007. Iraq: Tribal Engagement Lessons Learned. *Military Review* (September-October): 16–31.

Elkins, Zachary, and John Sides. 2007. Can Institutions Build Unity in Multiethnic States? *American Political Science Review* 101 (4): 693–708.

Elliott, David. 2003. *The Vietnamese War: Revolution and Social Change in the Mekong Delta, 1930–1975.* Volumes 1 and 2. Armonk, NY: M.E. Sharpe.

———. 2007. Parallel Wars? Can "Lessons of Vietnam" be Applied to Iraq? In *Iraq and the Lessons of Vietnam: Or, How Not to Learn from the Past,* ed. Lloyd C. Gardner and Marilyn B. Young. New York: New Press.

Ellis, J. D., and G. D. Kiefer. 2004. *Combating Proliferation: Strategic Intelligence and Security Policy.* Baltimore, MD: Johns Hopkins University Press.

Fearon, James D. 1994. Domestic Political Audiences and the Escalation of International Disputes. *American Political Science Review* 88 (3): 577–592.

———. 1995. Rationalist Explanations for War. *International Organization* 49 (3): 379–414.

Feith, Douglas, J. 2008. *War and Decision: Inside the Pentagon at the Dawn of the War on Terrorism.* New York: HarperCollins.

Fettweis, Christopher, J. 2007–8. Credibility and the War on Terror. *Political Science Quarterly* 122 (4): 607–633.

Freedman, Lawrence. 2004. *Deterrence.* Cambridge, UK: Polity Press.

Garthoff, Raymond L. 1978. On Estimating and Imputing Intentions. *International Security* 2 (3): 22–32.

Gartner, Scott S. 1998. Differing Evaluations of Vietnamization. *Journal of Interdisciplinary History* 29 (2): 243–262.

Gartner, Scott S., and Gary M. Segura. 1998. War, Casualties, and Public Opinion. *Journal of Conflict Resolution* 42 (3): 278–300.

Gelb, Leslie H., and Richard K. Betts. 1979. *The Irony of Vietnam: The System Worked.* Washington, DC: Brookings Institution.

Gelpi, Christopher. 2006. The Cost of War: How Many Casualties Will Americans Tolerate? *Foreign Affairs* 85 (1): 139–144.

Gelpi, Christopher, Peter D. Feaver, and Jason Reifler. 2005. Success Matters: Casualty Sensitivity and the War in Iraq. *International Security* 30 (3): 7–46.

Gelpi, Christopher, and Jason Reifler. 2006. Casualties, Polls, and the Iraq War. *International Security* 31 (2): 186–198.

George, Alexander L. 1971. Comparison and Lessons. In *The Limits of Coercive Diplomacy: Laos-Cuba-Vietnam,* ed. Alexander L. George, David K. Hall, and William R. Simon. Boston: Little, Brown.

George, Alexander L., and Andrew Bennett. 2004. *Case Studies and Theory Development in the Social Sciences.* Cambridge, MA: MIT Press.

Gluck, Jason. 2008. From Gridlock to Compromise: How Three Laws Could Begin to Transform Iraqi Politics. *USIPeace Briefing* (March). Available at www.usip.gov.

Gordon, M. R., and B. E. Trainor. 2006. *Cobra II: The Inside Story of the Invasion and Occupation of Iraq.* New York: Pantheon.

Grant, Zalin. 1991. *Facing the Phoenix.* New York: W.W. Norton.

Griffith, Thomas E. 1995. Strategic Air Attacks on Electric Power: Balancing Political Consequences and Military Action. *Strategic Review* 23 (4): 38–46.

Hamilton, Donald W. 1998. *The Art of Insurgency: American Military Policy and the Failure of Strategy in Southeast Asia.* Westport, CT: Praeger.

Hamilton, Eric. 2008. Expanding Security in Diyala. Iraq Report 10. Washington, DC: Institute for the Study of War. Available at www.understandingwar.org/report/expanding-security-diyala.

Henderson, Anne Ellen. 2005. The Coalition Provisional Authority's Experience with Economic Reconstruction in Iraq: Lessons Identified. *Special Report* 138. Washington, DC: United States Institute of Peace.

Hennessy, Michael A. 1997. *Strategy in Vietnam: The Marines and Revolutionary Warfare in I Corps, 1965–1972.* Westport, CT: Praeger.

Herring, George C. 1986. *America's Longest War: The United States and Vietnam, 1950–1975.* Philadelphia: Temple University Press.

Hopf, Ted. 1994. *Peripheral Visions: Deterrence Theory and American Foreign Policy in the Third World, 1965–1990.* Ann Arbor: University of Michigan Press.

Hunt, Richard A. 1995. *Pacification: The American Struggle for Vietnam's Hearts and Minds.* Boulder, CO: Westview Press.

Huntington, Samuel P. 1999. The Lonely Superpower. *Foreign Affairs* 78 (2): 35–49.

Ikenberry, G. John. 2003. "Strategic Reactions to American Preeminence: Great Power Politics in the Age of Unipolarity." National Intelligence Council 2020 Project. Unpublished paper.

Iklé, Fred Charles. 2005. *Every War Must End.* New York: Columbia University Press.

ICG (International Crisis Group). 2006. The Next Iraqi War? Sectarianism and Civil Conflict. *Middle East Report* No. 52. Available at www.crisisgroup.org.

———. 2008a. Iraq After the Surge I: The New Sunni Landscape. *Middle East Report* No. 74. Available at www.crisisgroup.org.

———. 2008b. Iraq's Civil War, the Sadrists and the Surge. *Middle East Report* No. 72. Available at www.crisisgroup.org.

———. 2008c. Policing in Afghanistan: Still Searching for a Strategy. *Asia Briefing* No. 85. Available at www.crisisgroup.org.

ICTJ (International Center for Transitional Justice). 2008. Iraq's New "Accountability and Justice" Law. *Briefing Paper.* Available at www.ictj.org/images/content/7/6/764.pdf.

Jentleson, Bruce W., and Rebecca L. Britton. 1998. Still Pretty Prudent: Post–Cold War American Public Opinion on the Use of Military Force. *Journal of Conflict Resolution* 42 (4): 395–417.

Jervis, Robert. 1976. *Perception and Misperception in World Politics*. Princeton, NJ: Princeton University Press.

———. 1978. Cooperation under the Security Dilemma. *World Politics* 30: 167–214.

———. 2008–9. War, Intelligence, and Honesty: A Review Essay. *Political Science Quarterly* 123 (4): 645–675.

Jian, Chen. 1995. China's Involvement in the Vietnam War, 1964–69. *China Quarterly* 142 (June): 356–387.

Johnson, Dominic D. P., and Dominic Tierney. 2006. *Failing to Win: Perceptions of Victory and Defeat in International Politics*. Cambridge, MA: Harvard University Press.

Johnson, Lyndon B. 1971. *The Vantage Point*. New York: Holt, Rinehart, and Winston.

Johnson, Thomas H., and M. Chris Mason. 2008. No Sign until the Burst of Fire: Understanding the Pakistan-Afghanistan Frontier. *International Security* 32 (4): 41–77.

Jones, James L. 2007. *The Report of the Independent Commission on the Security Forces of Iraq*. Available at http://csis.org/files/media/csis/pubs/isf.pdf.

Jones, Seth G. 2008. The Rise of Afghanistan's Insurgency: State Failure and Jihad. *International Security* 32 (4): 7–40.

Kagan, Kimberly. 2007. Securing Diyala. Iraq Report 7. Washington, DC: Institute for the Study of War. Available at www.understandingwar.org/report/securing -diyala.

Kahin, George McT. 1979–80. Political Participation in South Vietnam: U.S. Policy in the Post-Diem Period. *Pacific Affairs* 52 (4): 647–673.

Kahl, Colin. 2007a. COIN of the Realm: Is There a Future for Counterinsurgency? *Foreign Affairs* 86 (6): 169–176.

———. 2007b. In the Crossfire or the Crosshairs? Norms, Civilian Casualties, and U.S. Conduct in Iraq. *International Security* 32 (1): 7–46.

Kahl, Colin, Michèle A. Flournoy, and Shawn Brimley. 2008. *Shaping the Iraq Inheritance*. Washington, DC: Center for a New American Security.

Kalyvas, Stathis N. 2008. The New U.S. Army/Marine Corps Counterinsurgency Field Manual as Political Science and Political Praxis. *Perspectives on Politics* 6 (2): 351–353.

Kalyvas, Stathis N., and Matthew Adam Kocher. 2007a. Ethnic Cleavages and Irregular War: Iraq and Vietnam. *Politics and Society* 35 (2): 183–223.

———. 2007b. How "Free" is Free Riding in Civil Wars? Violence, Insurgency, and the Collective Action Problem. *World Politics* 59 (2): 177–216.

Karnow, Stanley. 1997. *Vietnam: A History*. New York: Penguin Books.

Katulis, Brian, Lawrence J. Korb, and Peter Juul. 2007. *Strategic Reset: Reclaiming Control of U.S. Security in the Middle East*. Washington, DC: Center for American Progress.

Katzman, Kenneth. 2008. Iraq: Reconciliation and Benchmarks. *CRS Report for Congress*. Congressional Research Service. The Library of Congress.

———. 2009. Iraq: Post-Saddam Governance and Security. *CRS Report for Congress*. Congressional Research Service. The Library of Congress.

Khong, Yuen Foong. 1992. *Analogies at War: Korea, Munich, Dien Bien Phu, and the Vietnam Decisions of 1965*. Princeton, NJ: Princeton University Press.

Kier, Elizabeth. 1997. *Imagining War: French and British Doctrine between the Wars*. Princeton, NJ: Princeton University Press.

Kilcullen, David. 2009. *The Accidental Guerrilla: Fighting Small Wars in the Midst of a Big One*. New York: Oxford University Press.

Kimball, Jeffrey. 2004. *The Vietnam War Files: Uncovering the Secret History of Nixon-Era Strategy*. Lawrence: University Press of Kansas.

King, Peter. 1971. The Political Balance in Saigon. *Pacific Affairs* 44 (3): 401–420.

Kissinger, Henry A. 1969. The Vietnam Negotiations. *Foreign Affairs* 47 (2): 211–234.

Klarevas, Louis J. 2006. Correspondence: Casualties, Polls, and the Iraq War. *International Security* 31 (2): 186–198.

Komer, Robert W. 1986: *Bureaucracy at War: U.S. Performance in the Vietnam Conflict*. Boulder, CO: Westview Press.

Korb, Lawrence. 2003. Rumsfeld's Folly. *The American Prospect* 14 (10). Available at www.newamericanstrategies.org.

Krepinevich, Andrew F. 1986. *The Army and Vietnam*. Baltimore, MD: Johns Hopkins University Press.

Kreps, Sarah E. 2007. The 2006 Lebanon War: Lessons Learned. *Parameters* 37 (1): 72–84.

Kydd, A., and B. F. Walter. 2002. Sabotaging the Peace: The Politics of Extremist Violence. *International Organization* 56: 263–296.

Lambeth, Benjamin S. 2001. *NATO's Air War for Kosovo: A Strategic and Operational Assessment*. Santa Monica, CA: RAND.

Lasensky, Scott. 2006. Jordan and Iraq: Between Cooperation and Crisis. *Special Report* 178. Washington, DC: United States Institute of Peace.

Layne, Christopher. 1993. The Unipolar Illusion: Why New Great Powers Will Rise. *International Security* 17 (4): 5–51.

———. 2006. *The Peace of Illusions: American Grand Strategy from 1940 to the Present*. Ithaca, NY: Cornell University Press.

Lebovic, James H. 1996. *Foregone Conclusions: U.S. Weapons Acquisition in the Post–Cold War Transition*. Boulder, CO: Westview Press.

———. 2003. The Limits of Reciprocity: Tolerance Thresholds in Superpower Conflict. *Journal of Peace Research* 40 (2): 139–158.

———. 2007. *Deterring International Terrorism and Rogue States: US National Security Policy after 9/11*. London: Routledge Press.

Levy, Jack S. 1997. Prospect Theory, Rational Choice, and International Relations. *International Studies Quarterly* 41 (1): 87–112.

Lewy, Guenter. 1978. *America in Vietnam*. New York: Oxford University Press.

Lischer, Sarah Kenyon. 2008. Security and Displacement in Iraq: Responding to the Forced Migration Crisis. *International Security* 95 (2): 95–119.

Lomperis, Timothy. 1996. *From People's War to People's Rule: Insurgency, Intervention, and the Lessons of Vietnam.* Chapel Hill: University of North Carolina Press.

Long, Austin, 2006. *On "Other War": Lessons from Five Decades of RAND Counterinsurgency Research.* Santa Monica, CA: RAND Corporation.

Lunch, William L., and Peter W. Sperlich. 1979. American Public Opinion and the War in Vietnam. *Western Political Quarterly* 32 (1): 21–44.

Lyall, Jason, and Isaiah Wilson III. 2009. Rage against the Machines: Explaining Outcomes in Counterinsurgency Wars. *International Organization* 63 (1): 67–106.

Lynch, Marc. 2008. Why Only U.S. Withdrawal Can Spur Iraqi Cooperation. *Foreign Affairs* 87 (6): 152–155.

Mack, Andrew. 1975. Why Big Nations Lose Small Wars: The Politics of Asymmetric Conflict. *World Politics* 27 (2): 175–200.

Malkasian, Carter. 2006. Signaling Resolve, Democratization, and the First Battle of Fallujah. *Journal of Strategic Studies* 29 (3): 423–452.

Manley, John F. 1971. The Rise of Congress in Foreign Policy-Making. *Annals of the American Academy of Political and Social Science* 397 (September): 60–70.

Mansoor, Peter R. 2008. *Baghdad at Sunrise: A Brigade Commander's War in Iraq.* New Haven, CT: Yale University Press.

Margesson, Rhoda, Jeremy M. Sharp, and Andorra Bruno. 2008. Iraqi Refugees and Internally Displaced Persons: A Deepening Humanitarian Crisis? *CRS Report for Congress* (RL33936). Washington, DC: Congressional Research Service.

Marr, Phebe. 2007. Iraq's New Political Map. Special Report 179. Washington, DC: United States Institute of Peace.

Mason, R. Chuck. 2008. Status of Forces Agreement (SOFA): What is It, and How Might One Be Utilized in Iraq? *CRS Report for Congress.* Congressional Research Service. The Library of Congress.

Mazarr, Michael J. 2008. The Folly of "Asymmetric War." *Washington Quarterly* 31 (3): 33–53.

McAllister, James. 2004. "A Fiasco of Noble Proportions": The Johnson Administration and the South Vietnamese Elections of 1967. *Pacific Historical Review* 73 (4): 619–651.

McClellan, Scott. 2008. *What Happened: Inside the Bush White House and Washington's Culture of Deception.* New York: Public Affairs.

McCrisken, Trevor B. 2007. No More Vietnams: Iraq and the Analogy Conundrum. In *Vietnam in Iraq: Tactics, Lessons, Legacies and Ghosts,* ed. John Dumbrell and David Ryan. London: Routledge Press.

McMaster, H. R. 1997. *Dereliction of Duty: Lyndon Johnson, Robert McNamara, the Joint Chiefs of Staff, and the Lies that Led to Vietnam.* New York: Harper Collins.

McNamara, Robert S., James Blight, Robert Brigham, Thomas Biersteker, and Col. Herbert Schandler. 1999. *Argument without End: In Search of Answers to the Vietnam Tragedy.* New York: Public Affairs.

McNerney, Michael J. 2005–6. Stabilization and Reconstruction in Afghanistan: Are PRTs a Model or a Muddle? *Parameters* 4 (Winter): 32–45.

Mercer, Jonathan. 1996. *Reputation and International Politics*. Ithaca, NY: Cornell University Press.

Merom, Gil. 2003. *How Democracies Lose Small Wars*. Cambridge, UK: Cambridge University Press.

Monten, Jonathan. 2008. Is There an "Emboldenment" Effect? Evidence from the Insurgency in Iraq. *National Bureau of Economic Research Working Paper* No. 13839. September.

Moon, Bruce E. 2009. Long Time Coming: Prospects for Democracy in Iraq. *International Security* 33 (4): 115–148.

Mueller, John. 1971. Trends in Popular Support for the Wars in Korea and Vietnam. *American Political Science Review* 65: 358–375.

———. 1980. The Search for the "Breaking Point" in Vietnam: The Statistics of a Deadly Quarrel. *International Studies Quarterly* 24 (4): 497–519.

———. 2005. The Iraq Syndrome. *Foreign Affairs* 84 (6): 44–54.

Nagl, John A. 2005. *Learning to Eat Soup with a Knife: Counterinsurgency Lessons from Malaya and Vietnam*. Chicago: University of Chicago Press.

Nagl, John A., and Brian M. Burton. 2009. Dirty Windows and Burning Houses: Setting the Record Straight on Irregular Warfare. *Washington Quarterly* 32 (2): 91–101.

Neustadt, Richard N. 1981. Vietnam Reappraised. *International Security* 6 (1): 3–26.

Newnham, Randall. 2008. "Coalition of the Bribed and Bullied?" U.S. Economic Linkage and the Iraq War Coalition. *International Studies Perspectives* 9 (2): 183–200.

O'Hanlon, Michael E. 2002. A Flawed Masterpiece. *Foreign Affairs* (May-June): 47–63.

Olson, Mancur Jr. 1965. *The Logic of Collective Action: Public Goods and the Theory of Groups*. Cambridge, MA: Harvard University Press.

Olson, Mancur Jr., and Richard Zeckhauser. 1966. An Economic Theory of Alliances. *Review of Economics and Statistics* 48 (3): 266–279.

Oneal, John R., and Anna L. Bryan. 1995. The Rally 'Round the Flag Effect in U.S. Foreign Policy Crises, 1950–1985. *Political Behavior* 17 (4): 379–401.

Pape, Robert A. 1996. *Bombing to Win: Air Power and Coercion in War*. Ithaca, NY: Cornell University Press.

Parker, Maynard. 1975. Vietnam: The War that Won't End. *Foreign Affairs* 53 (2): 352–374.

Paul, T. V., 1994. *Asymmetric Conflicts: War Initiation by Weaker Powers*. Cambridge, UK: Cambridge University Press.

Perito, Robert M. 2007. Provincial Reconstruction Teams in Iraq. *Special Report* 185. Washington, DC: United States Institute of Peace. Available at www.usip.gov.

———. 2008a. Embedded Provincial Reconstruction Teams. *USIPeace Briefing*. Available at www.usip.gov.

———. 2008b. Iraq's Interior Ministry: Frustrating Reform. *USIPeace Briefing*. Available at www.usip.gov.

———. 2009. The Interior Ministry's Role in Security Sector Reform. *Special Report* 223. Washington, DC: United States Institute of Peace. Available at www.usip.gov.

Pillar, Paul R. 1983. *Negotiating Peace: War Termination as a Bargaining Process*. Princeton, NJ: Princeton University Press.

Pollack, Kenneth M. 2009. The Battle for Baghdad. *The National Interest* 103 (September/October): 8–17.

Popkin, Samuel L. 1970. Pacification: Politics and the Village. *Asian Survey* 10 (8): 662–671.

Posen, Barry R. 2003. Command of the Commons: The Military Foundation of U.S. Hegemony. *International Security* 28 (1): 5–46.

Prados, John. 2004. The Mouse that Roared: State Department Intelligence in the Vietnam War. Contextual Introduction. *National Security Archive Electronic Briefing Book* No. 121. Available at www.gwu.edu/~nsarchiv/NSAEBB/NSAEBB121/prados.htm.

Press, Daryl G. 2001. The Myth of Air Power in the Persian Gulf War and the Future of Warfare. *International Security* 26 (2): 5–44.

———. 2005. *Calculating Credibility: How Leaders Assess Military Threats*. Ithaca, NY: Cornell University Press.

Putnam, Robert D. 1988. Diplomacy and Domestic Politics: The Logic of Two-Level Games. *International Organization* 42 (3): 427–460.

Rahimi, Babak. 2007a. Ayatollah Sistani and the Democratization of Post-Ba'athist Iraq. Special Report 187. Washington, DC: United States Institute of Peace.

———. 2007b. A Shiite Storm Looms on the Horizon: Sadr and SIIC Relations. *Terrorism Monitor* 5, 10 (May 24), 1–4.

Randolph, Stephen P. 2007. *Powerful and Brutal Weapons: Nixon, Kissinger, and the Easter Offensive*. Cambridge, MA: Harvard University Press.

Rathmell, Andrew, Olga Oliker, Terrence K. Kelly, David Brannan, and Keith Crane. 2005. *Developing Iraq's Security Sector: The Coalition Provisional Authority's Experience*. Santa Monica, CA: RAND National Defense Research Institute.

Record, Jeffrey. 1998. *The Wrong War: Why We Lost in Vietnam*. Annapolis, MD: Naval Institute Press.

———. 2005. *Appeasement Reconsidered: Investigating the Mythology of the 1930s*. Monograph, Strategic Studies Institute, United States Army War College. Available at www.strategicstudiesinstitute.army.mil.

———. 2007. *Beating Goliath: Why Insurgencies Win*. Washington, DC: Potomac Books.

Record, Jeffrey, and W. Andrew Terrill. 2004. *Iraq and Vietnam: Differences, Similarities, and Insights*. Monograph, Strategic Studies Institute, United States Army War College. Available at www.strategicstudiesinstitute.army.mil.

Reiter, Dan, and Allan C. Stam. 2002. *Democracies at War*. Princeton, NJ: Princeton University Press.

Ricks, Thomas E. 2006. *Fiasco: The American Military Adventure in Iraq.* New York: Penguin.

———. 2009. *The Gamble: General Petraeus and the American Military Adventure in Iraq, 2006–2008.* New York: Penguin.

Ripsman, Norrin M., and Jack Levy. 2008. Wishful Thinking or Buying Time? The Logic of British Appeasement in the 1930s. *International Security* 33 (2): 148–181.

Robinson, Linda. 2008. *Tell Me How This Ends: General David Petraeus and the Search for a Way Out of Iraq.* New York: Public Affairs.

Rosen, Stephen, P. 1982. Vietnam and the American Theory of Limited War. *International Security* 7 (2): 83–113.

Sagan, Scott D., and Jeremi Suri. 2003. The Madman Nuclear Alert: Secrecy, Signaling, and Safety in October 1969. *International Security* 27 (4): 150–183.

Sambanis, Nicholas. 2004. What is Civil War? Conceptual and Empirical Complexities of an Operational Definition. *Journal of Conflict Resolution* 48 (6): 814–858.

Schaub, Gary, Jr. 1998. Compellence: Resuscitating the Concept. In *Strategic Coercion: Concepts and Cases,* ed. Lawrence Freedman. New York: Oxford University Press.

Schelling, Thomas C. 1960. *The Strategy of Conflict.* London: Oxford University Press.

———. 1966. *Arms and Influence.* New Haven, CT: Yale University Press.

———. 1981. Vietnam Reappraised. *International Security* 6 (1): 3–26.

Serwer, Daniel, and Sam Parker. 2009. Maliki's Iraq between Two Elections. *USIPeace Briefing* Washington, DC: United States Institute of Peace. Available at http://library.usip.org/articles/1012229.1108/1.PDF.

Shannon, Vaughn P., and Michael Dennis. 2007. Militant Islam and the Futile Fight for Reputation. *Security Studies* 16 (2): 287–317.

Shawcross, William. 1987. *Sideshow: Kissinger, Nixon, and the Destruction of Cambodia.* New York: Simon and Schuster.

Sherman, Matt, and Roger D. Carstens. 2008. "Independent Task Force on Progress and Reform." Unpublished Manuscript. Institute for the Theory and Practice of International Relations. The College of William and Mary.

SIGIR (Special Inspector General for Iraq Reconstruction). 2008. *Hard Lessons: The Iraq Reconstruction Experience.* Available at www.sigir.mil/hardlessons/pdfs/Hard_Lessons_Report.pdf.

Smith, Hedrick. 1971. The Kennedy Years: 1961–1963. In *The Pentagon Papers,* ed. Neil Sheehan, Hedrick Smith, E. W. Kenworthy and Fox Butterfield. New York: Bantam Books.

Snepp, Frank. 1977. *Decent Interval: An Insider's Account of Saigon's Indecent End Told by the CIA's Chief Strategy Analyst in Vietnam.* New York: Random House.

Snyder, Jack, and Robert Jervis. 1999. Civil War and the Security Dilemma. In *Civil Wars, Insecurity, and Intervention,* ed. Barbara F. Walter and Jack Snyder. New York: Columbia University Press.

Sorley, Lewis. 1998. To Change a War: General Harold K. Johnson and the PROVN Study. *Parameters* 28 (1): 93–109.

Spector, Ronald H. 1985. *Advice and Support: The Early Years of the United States Army in Vietnam, 1941–1960.* New York: Free Press.

———. 1993. *After Tet: The Bloodiest Year in Vietnam.* New York: Vintage Books.

Steinberg, Guido. 2006. The Iraqi Insurgency: Actors, Strategies, and Structures. *SWP Research Paper.* Berlin: German Institute for International and Security Affairs.

Stuart-Fox, Martin. 1997. *A History of Laos.* Cambridge, UK: Cambridge University Press.

Sullivan, Patricia L. 2007. War Aims and War Outcomes: Why Powerful States Lose Limited Wars. *Journal of Conflict Resolution* 51 (3): 496–524.

Summers, Harry G. Jr. 1982. *On Strategy: A Critical Analysis of the Vietnam War.* Novato, CA: Presidio Press.

Suri, Jeremi. 2008. The Nukes of October: Richard Nixon's Secret Plan to Bring Peace to Vietnam. *Wired Magazine* (February 25).

Tarnoff, Curt. 2008. *Iraq: Reconstruction Assistance.* CRS Report For Congress. Washington, DC: Congressional Research Service.

Tenet, George. 2007. *At the Center of the Storm: My Years at the CIA.* New York: Harper Collins.

Thayer, Thomas C. 1985. *War without Fronts: The American Experience in Vietnam.* Boulder, CO: Westview Press.

Thies, Wallace J. 1980. *When Governments Collide: Coercion and Diplomacy in the Vietnam Conflict, 1964–1968.* Berkeley: University of California Press.

Thompson, Robert. 1966. *Defeating Communist Insurgency: The Lessons of Malaya and Vietnam.* New York: Praeger.

Thompson, William R. 2006. Systemic Leadership, Evolutionary Processes, and International Relations Theory: The Unipolarity Question. *International Studies Review* 8 (1): 1–22.

Trager, Robert F., and Dessislava P. Zagorcheva. 2005. Deterring Terrorism: It Can Be Done. *International Security* 30: 87–123.

US Congress, Senate Select Committee on Intelligence. 2007. *Report on Prewar Intelligence Assessments about Postwar Iraq.* Available at http://intelligence.senate.gov/prewar.pdf.

US Department of the Army, Office of the Deputy Chief of Staff for Military Operations. 1966. *A Program for the Pacification and Long-Term Development of South Vietnam* (PROVN), Vol. 1. Washington, DC. Declassified.

US Department of the Army. 2007. *The U.S. Army/Marine Corps Counterinsurgency Field Manual.* Chicago: University of Chicago Press.

US Department of the Army. 2008. *Stability Operations (Field Manual 3–07).* Washington, DC: Available at http://usacac.army.mil/cac2/repository/FM307/FM3-07.pdf.

US Department of State, Bureau of Political-Military Affairs. 2009. *U.S. Government Counterinsurgency Guide.* Available at www.state.gov/documents/organization/119629.pdf.

US GAO (U.S. General Accounting Office). 2007a. Securing, Stabilizing, and Re-building Iraq: Iraqi Government Has Not Met Most Legislative, Security, and Eco-nomic Benchmarks. GAO-07-1195. September 4.

———. 2007b. Securing, Stabilizing, and Rebuilding Iraq: Iraqi Government Has Not Met Most Legislative, Security, and Economic Benchmarks. Testimony before the Committee on Foreign Affairs, House of Representatives. GAO-1222T, September 5.

———.2008. Securing, Stabilizing, and Rebuilding Iraq. Progress Report: Some Gains Made, Updated Strategy Needed. GAO-08-837. June.

———. 2009a. Afghanistan Security: U.S. Programs to Further Reform Ministry of Interior and National Police Challenged by Lack of Military Personnel and Af-ghan Cooperation. Report to the Committee on Foreign Affairs, House of Repre-sentatives. GAO-09-280.

———. 2009b. Iraq and Afghanistan: Availability of Forces, Equipment, and Infra-structure Should Be Considered in Developing U.S. Strategy and Plans. Testimony before the Committee on Armed Services, House of Representatives. GAO-09-380T. February.

———. 2009c. Iraq: Key Issues for Congressional Oversight. Report to the Congres-sional Committees. GAO-09-294SP. March.

Valentino, B., P. Huth, and D. Balch-Lindsay. 2004. Draining the Sea: Mass Killing and Guerilla Warfare. International Organization 58 (2): 375–407.

Valentino, Benjamin A, Paul K. Huth, and Sarah Croco. 2006. Covenants without the Sword: International Law and the Protection of Civilians in Times of War. World Politics 58 (3): 339–377.

Voeten, Erik, and Paul R. Brewer. 2006. Public Opinion, the War in Iraq, and Presi-dential Accountability. Journal of Conflict Resolution 50 (6): 809–830.

Wagner, R. Harrison. 1993. What was Bipolarity? International Organization 47 (1): 77–106.

———. 2000. Bargaining and War. American Journal of Political Science 44 (3): 469–484.

Wahab, Bilal A. 2006. How Iraqi Oil Smuggling Greases Violence. Middle East Quar-terly (Fall): 53–59.

Waltz, Kenneth N. 1979. Theory of International Politics. Reading, MA: Addison-Wesley.

———. 1990. Nuclear Myths and Political Realities. American Political Science Review 84 (3): 731–745.

———. 1993. The Emerging Structure of International Politics. International Security 18 (2): 44–79.

Weed, Matthew C. 2008. U.S.-Iraq Strategic Framework and Status of Forces Agree-ment: Congressional Response. July 11. Washington, DC: Congressional Research Service. Available at http://fas.org/sgp/crs/natsec/RL34568.pdf.

Wells, Tom. 1994. The War Within: America's Battle over Vietnam. Berkeley: University of California Press.

Werner, Suzanne. 1998. Negotiating the Terms of Settlement: War Aims and Bar-gaining Leverage. Journal of Conflict Resolution 42 (3): 321–343.

Woodward, Susan L. 1999. Bosnia and Herzegovina: How Not to End Civil War. In *Civil Wars, Insecurity, and Intervention*, ed. Barbara F. Walter and Jack Snyder. New York: Columbia University Press.

Wohlforth, William C. 1999. The Stability of a Unipolar World. *International Security* 24 (1): 5–41.

Wohlstetter, Albert. 1968. *On Vietnam and Bureaucracy*. D-17276-1-ISA/ARPA. Santa Monica, CA: RAND Corporation.

Wolfers, Arnold. 1962. *Discord and Collaboration: Essays on International Politics*. Baltimore, MD: Johns Hopkins University Press.

Wright, Donald P., Timothy R. Reese, and the Contemporary Operations Study Team. 2008. *On Point II: Transition to the New Campaign: The United States Army in Operation IRAQI FREEDOM May 2003–January 2005*. US Army Combined Arms Center. Fort Leavenworth, KS: Combat Studies Institute Press.

Yacoubian, Mona. 2007. Syria's Relations with Iraq. *USIPeace Briefing*. April. United States Institute of Peace.

Index